Mission SSC

Tips, Techniques & Strategies

to Crack CGL/ CHSL/ Multi Tasking/ Jr. Engg. Exams

- **Corporate Office :** 45, 2nd Floor, Maharishi Dayanand Marg, Corner Market, Malviya Nagar, New Delhi-110017
  Tel. : 011-49842349 / 49842350

Mentor & Advisor: Deepak Agarwal

Chief Editor: Dr. Md. Usmangani Ansari

Project Incharge : Nimisha Aggarwal

Contributors: Sonu Gupta, Khurshid Ali, J. kumar

Typeset by Disha DTP Team

Printed at Repro Knowledgecast Limited, Thane

For further information about books from DISHA,

Log on to **www.dishapublication.com** or email to **info@dishapublication.com**

Index

CHAPTER 1

What is Staff Selection Commission (SSC) Services?

INTRODUCTION

Background of SSC

The Government of India, in the Department of Personnel and Administrative Reforms vide its Resolution No. 46/1(S)/74-Estt.(B) dated the **4th November, 1975** constituted a Commission called the **Subordinate Services Commission** that was subsequently re-designated as **Staff Selection Commission**, effective from the **26th September, 1977** to make recruitment to various Class III (now Group "C") (non-technical) posts in the various ministries/departments of the Govt. of India and in Subordinate Offices. The functions of the Staff Selection Commission have been expanded from time to time and now it carries out the recruitment for all Group "B" posts in the pay scale of ₹ 9300 to 34800 with a grade pay of ₹ 42000. The functions of the Staff Selection Commission were redefined by the Government of India, Ministry of Personnel, Public Grievances and Pensions vide its Resolution No.39018/1/98-Estt.(B) dated 21st May, 1999 (may be seen under the heading Resolution). **The new constitution and functions of the Staff Selection Commission came into effect from 1st June 1999.**

The Staff Selection Commission is an attached office of the **Department of Personnel and Training** and comprises of a Chairman, two Members and a Secretary-cum-Controller of Examinations who are appointed on such terms and conditions as may be prescribed by the Central Government from time to time. The Commission is provided with a supporting staff as considered necessary by the Central Government.

Headquarter of SSC

The Staff Selection Commission has its headquarter at **New Delhi**. All Examinations, as well as administrative matters, are submitted to the Chairman through two members. The Secretary functions under both the members. Besides, there are posts of one Director, one Deputy Secretary, two Joint Directors, nine Under Secretaries, four Deputy Directors, one Finance & Budget Officer, one Assistant Director (OL), 24 Section Officers and more than 183 supporting officers / staff working at the Headquarters for discharging the duties and responsibilities of the Commission.

Regional/Sub-Regional Offices of SSC

For smooth conduct of examinations through a large network of examination centres/sub-centres, situated in different parts of the country for the convenience of the candidates, the Commission has been provided with a regional set-up. At present, there are seven regional offices at Allahabad, Mumbai, Delhi, Kolkata, Guwahati, Chennai and Bangalore and two Sub-Regional Offices at Raipur and Chandigarh. Each regional office is headed by a Regional Director and each Sub-Regional office is headed by a Deputy Director.

Regional/Sub Regional offices and their Operative Jurisdiction

Region & H.Q.	States/UTs	Address	Helpline	Fax No.	E-mail ID	Website
Northern @ New Delhi	Delhi, Rajasthan & Uttarakhand	SSC(NR), Block No.12, 5th Floor, CGO Complex, Lodhi Road, New Delhi -110 003	011-69999845 011-69999846	011-24360944	1.enquirysscnr@gmail.com 2. rdsscnr@gmail.com	www.sscnr.net.in
Central @ Allahabad	Uttar Pradesh & Bihar	SSC(CR),21-23 Lowther Road, George Town, Allahabad-211002 (U.P.)	0532-2460511 9452424060	0532-2460514	rdcrssc@gmail.com	www.ssc-cr.org
Eastern @ Kolkata	West Bengal, Sikkim, Odisha, Jharkhand & Andaman and Nicobar	SSC (ER), Nizam Palace, 1st M.S.O. Building, (8th Floor) 234/4, A.J.C. Bose Road, Kolkatta(West Bengal)	9477461228 9477461229	033-22904424	contact@sscer.org	www.sscer.org
Western @ Mumbai	Maharashtra, Gujarat, Goa, Daman and Diu & Dadra and Nagar Haveli	SSC (WR), 1st Floor, SouthWing, PratishthaBhawan (Old CGO Building) 101 M.K. Road, Near Churchgate, Mumbai (Maharashtra)	7738422705 9869730700	022 22018527	sscwr@yahoo.com, examsscwr@gmail.com	www.sscwr.net
Southern @ Chennai	Andhra Pradesh, Telangana, Tamil Nadu & Puducherry (UT)	SSC (SR), 2nd Floor, EVK Sampath Building, DPI Campus, College Road, Chennai-600 006 (TN)	044-28251139 9445195946	044-28270561	sscsr.tn@nic.in	www.sscsr.gov.in

Region	Jurisdiction	Address	Phone	Phone	Email	Website
North West @ Chandigarh	Jammu and Kashmir, Punjab, Haryana, Himachal Pradesh & Chandigarh (UT)	Staff Selection Commission (NWR), Block No.3, Ground Floor, Kendriya Sadan, Sector-9, Chandigarh-160009	0172-2744366	0172-2742144	sscnwrgoi@gmail.com	www.sscnwr.org
Karnataka Kerala Region @ Bengaluru	Karnataka, Kerala & Lakshadweep (UT)	SSC (KKR), Kendriya Sadan, 1st Floor, 'E' Wing, 2nd Block, Koramangala, Bengaluru-560034	080-25502520 9483862020	080-25520653	rdssckkr@nic.in	www.ssckkr.kar.nic.in
North East Region @ Guwahati	Arunachal Pradesh, Assam, Manipur, Meghalaya, Nagaland, Tripura & Mizoram	Staff Selection Commission, (NER), Housefed Complex, West End Block, Beltola-Basistha Road, Dispur, Guwahati-781006	9085015252 9085073593	0361-2224779	rdner.ssc@gmail.com	www.sscner.org.in
MPR Region @ Raipur	Madhya Pradesh, Chattisgarh	SSC (MPR), J-5 Anupam Nagar, Raipur-492001 (Chattisgarh)	0771-2423678 0771-2422507	0771-2423678	sscraipur@gmail.com	www.sscmpr.org
Headquarters @ New Delhi	India	Staff Selection Commission, Block No-12 , 4th Floor, CGO Complex, Lodhi Road, New Delhi-110 003	011-24368090			

FUNCTIONS OF SSC

1. **To make recruitment to**

   (i) All Group "B" posts in the various ministries/departments of the Govt. of India and their attached and subordinate offices, which are in the pay scales, wherein the maximum amount is ₹10,500 or below

   (ii) All non-technical Group "C" posts in the various ministries/departments of the Govt. of India and their attached and subordinate offices, except those posts which are specifically exempted from the purview of the Staff Selection Commission.

2. **To conduct examinations and/or interviews,** whenever required for recruitment to the posts within its purview. The examinations would be held as far as possible, at different centres and successful candidates posted, to the extent possible, to their home State/Region.

3. **In particular, to hold Open Competitive Examinations for recruitment to the posts of:**

   (i) **Lower Division Clerks (LDC)** in

       (A) various ministries/departments, attached and subordinate Offices of the Government of India, including those participating in the Central Secretariat Clerical Service /Indian Foreign Service (IFS)

       (B) Railway Board Secretariat Clerical Service and the Armed Forces Headquarters Clerical Service

   (ii) **Grade "C" and Grade 'D" Stenographers** of

       (A) the Central Secretariat Stenographers Service and equivalent Grades of Indian Foreign Service

       (B) Railway Board Secretariat Stenographers Service/Armed Forces Headquarters Stenographers Service and to the posts of Stenographers in other Departments, including attached and subordinate offices of the Government of India not participating in the aforesaid Services

   (iii) **Assistants** in

       (A) various ministries/departments including attached and subordinate offices of the Government of India, including the ones participating in the Central Secretariat Service/ IFS

       (B) Railway Board Secretariat Service/Armed Forces Headquarters Civil Service

   (iv) **Inspectors of Central Excise** in different Collectorates of Central Excise; Inspectors of Income-Tax in different charges of the Commissioners of Income-Tax; Preventive Officers and Examiners in different Custom Houses; Assistant Enforcement Officers in Directorate of Enforcement

   (v) **Sub-Inspectors** in Central Bureau of Investigation(CBI) and Central Police Organisations (CPO)

(vi) **Divisional Accountants, Auditors and Accountants** under the Office of Comptroller and Auditor General of India and other Accounts Departments and Upper Division Clerks in Attached and Subordinate Offices of the Government of India

(vii) **Junior Engineer** (Civil & Electrical) in CPWD, a Group 'C' non-gazetted, non-ministerial, General Central Services (Technical) post

(viii) **Statistical Investigators**, Grade IV of Subordinate Statistical Service (SSC), a Group 'C' non-gazetted, non-ministerial post in the Ministry of Statistics and Programme Implementation

(ix) **Tax Assistant**, a Group C non – gazetted Ministerial post in various Commissionerates of Central Board of Direct Taxes (CBDT) and Central Board of Excise and Customs(CBEC);

(x) **Section Officer (Commercial Audit)**, a Group "B" non-gazetted post in the Indian Audit and Accounts Department

(xi) **Section Officer (Audit)** , a Group B non-gazetted post in the Office of the Comptroller and Auditor General

4. **The Commission also holds Departmental Examination for the promotion** from:

(i) **Group "D" to Lower Division Clerk Grade** of the Central Secretariat Clerical Service and equivalent grades in Indian Foreign Service (B)/ Railway Board Secretariat Clerical Service/Armed Force Hqrs. Clerical Service

(ii) **Lower Divisional Clerks to Upper Divisional Clerks Grade** of the Central Secretariat Clerical Service and equivalent Indian Foreign Service (B)/Railway Board Secretariat Clerical Service/Armed Forces Hqrs. Clerical Service

(iii) **Stenographers Grade "D" to Stenographers Grade "C"** of the Central Secretariat Stenographers Service and equivalent grades in Indian Foreign Service (B)/Railway Board Secretariat Stenographers Service/Armed Forces Hqrs. Stenographers Service.

5. **The Commission conducts periodical Typewriting Tests in English and Hindi**.

6. **The Commission prepares schemes for recruitment to all Group "B" posts** which are in the payscale of ₹ 9300 to 34800 with a grade pay of ₹ 42000 or below and Group "C" non-technical posts in the ministries/ departments of the Govt. of India, including its attached and subordinate offices in consultation with the Departments concerned.

7. **The Commission conducts examinations/selections for recruitment to all Group "B" posts** which are in the payscales, wherein the maximum of which is ₹10, 500 or below and all Group "C" non-technical posts in the ministries/departments of the Govt. from time to time.

8. **The Commission performs such other functions as may be entrusted to it by the Central Government from time to time.**

A.Why Aspirants Prefer SSC Services?

What are the career options that the candidates are looking for these days, after graduation or the 12th standard? They are looking for careers that offer job security with fixed salary, fixed working hours and guaranteed time-bound promotions. SSC is the gateway to these types of jobs. Let's see how.

1. **SSC isn't a hard nut to crack:** SSC is easier to crack, when an aspirant compares it with IAS, PCS, CAT and Banking.

2. **Better job security in Central government jobs:** Job security is the main and most important point in taking up a career option. Central Government jobs are stable, unlike many private sectors, where hire and fire work culture is seen. Thus, these jobs are secured and recession proof.

3. **Opportunity to maintain an equal balance in work and life:** SSC offers a wonderful opportunity of work-life balance. Unlike the private sector, wherein job performance is of utmost importance, a Central Government job gives an ample time for personal enrichment. For example, today you are young and can work very hard. But with time, as you grow older and have a family to take care of, job security is must that offers you mental peace to spend time and hard earned money with your family.

4. **Lucrative salary structure:** Pay Commissions regularly review the salary structure that is offered to the Central Government workforce. Salaries in public sector go up, whenever the recommendations of a Pay Commission are implemented. These recommendations are employee-friendly, thereby making the Central Government jobs even more lucrative.

5. **Opportunity without discrimination:** Central Government offers an equal opportunity to all without discrimination on the basis of caste, creed, religion, ethnicity or any other parameter except given in the rule. The recruitments made are seen to be, by and large, transparent. One has to prove one's merit in a competitive exam, in order to get selected.

6. **Distinguished Social Stature:** A Central Government employee enjoys a dignified standing and respect in the society. Many candidates take up SSC as the first step towards their dream of becoming a gazetted officer some day in future.

7. **Felicitous promotions in SSC jobs**: SSC jobs provide time bound promotion and at the same time, give yearly incentive and lucrative salary right from the beginning. Seniority is a crucial factor in Central Government promotion policy. Due importance is given to the time that one has spent in the job. Employees get fairly rewarded on the basis of how experienced they are.

8. **Career development**: SSC keeps conducting grade-wise departmental competitive exams for existing Central Government staff members. This provides them with ample growth prospects. Exemplary performance in these exams can set a person on the path of accelerated career progression.

9. **Beneficial Schemes for Financial Security: Numerous schemes are especially crafted with government employees in mind. For instance, Gratuity** is a provision for Central Government employees who work for five years without any break; **Central Government Pension Scheme** is a scheme for retired personnel for their financial security.

10. **Attractive Loan options:** Public and Private Banks prefer Central Government employees for loan as they have a continuous and stable job, unlike their counterparts in private job who not only have an uncertain job but also are dependent on the wavy salary structure offered to them.

Here is striking evidence from the print media that shows why are government jobs a hot favourite.

Why Indian PhD and BTech holders love lowly government jobs

ANALYSIS

Narayanan Madhavan
Hindustan Times

> For most Indians with graduate degrees, government jobs offer three benefits: long-term job security, comfortable working hours, a recurring income with little link to performance or productivity and a chance to make that extra buck from bribes – though few would admit it.(Vipin Kumar/HT File Photo)
>
> Last December, the **Uttar Pradesh government** issued orders to appoint some 35,700 employees on contract for cleaning jobs in municipalities, with an aim to finish hiring in 50 days. Among those who applied were MBAs, BTechs and PhDs.
>
> In January, the **Punjab government** held examinations to appoint **"patwaris"** (a clerical job in which land records are maintained in villages). Those who sought this job included LLBs, PhDs, MBAs and BTechs.
>
> Source: https://www.hindustantimes.com/analysis/why-indian-phds-and-btechs-love-lowly-government-jobs/story-n7aGMi5UGeisaWQKvPR9uI.html

B. SSC as Career Backup Plan for IAS/ PCS Aspirants

Why Backup Plan?

- For the reason of uncertainty involved in UPSC adventures, it is **not a good idea to put all eggs in one basket**.
- Aspirants are suggested that there are no cut and dry methods of "backup plans for UPSC", so evaluate all the pros and cons, based on your personality and alternative-career ambitions.
- Those who are MBBS, CA, IITs etc. need not worry much about "backup". But for the others who don't have any career back-up plans, they are advised to think for those government jobs that can be easier to crack than IAS. For example, SSC, Railway, Banking, CDS etc.

Aforesaid are the reasons why majority of aspirants for government jobs take up Central Government jobs offered through the annual SSC-CGL/CHSL/MTS/SA/SI/LDC/JE/Stenographers, etc. exams. However, some of them who have secured a stable and lucrative career with Central Government Jobs aspire to reach the higher level of the Indian governmental machinery, i.e. the Civil Services. Preparing for IAS exams is a very rigorous task, involving not a few months but years of preparation along with complete dedication and commitment from the aspirants. With such a challenging task ahead, many of these IAS aspirants start asking themselves if it is possible to continue their SSC Jobs in continuum with the preparation for the IAS Exam.

Is it possible to prepare for IAS exam along with SSC Jobs?

If the IAS aspirants, who have become the Central Government employees, after clearing their SSC exams, are confused whether they will get time, atmosphere and cooperation for the preparation of IAS Exam, while still in service, there is a good news. Every year, many Central Government employees who have joined their SSC jobs, are not only attempting but also clearing the IAS examinations. It may seem unlikely, but that is the thing with IAS aspirants, they always find innovative ways of dealing with challenges and competition. In fact, many such SSC job holders have also pointed out that, although they picked up the **job as a backup**, the SSC CGL jobs helped them crack the Civil Services exam. This was possible because of the cooperative and encouraging attitude of seniors, who inspired them to go for the big exam. The second and probably the most important advantage that SSC CGL employees have, is of being close to the government officers and civil servants, who have already cleared the big exam. Along with the guidance and tips for the exam, watching the daily working keeps the spark alive and fire burning to achieve their dream of becoming an IAS officer.

What others say about Career Back-up Plan

1. <u>R.A. Israel Jebasingh</u>, worked at Indian Administrative Service

He says,

"There is nothing wrong in having a backup plan."

"In fact, I would say a matured individual will always have an alternative plan of sustaining himself if plan 1 doesn't work."

2. <u>Preeti Maithil</u>, **IAS Officer 2009 Batch, Collector Rewa (ex Collector Mandla)**

She says,

"Having a backup plan is important because

i. It gives you confidence

ii. keeps you away from stress during preparations

iii. Helps you moving on after you exhaust your attempts at UPSC.

I went for UPSC preparations after graduation but I gave JRF exam too and was selected.

If I would not have cleared UPSC, I would have done my masters and then gone for a career in research."

3. <u>Ayesha Siddique</u> **(an IAS Aspirant)**

She says,

"UPSC is one of the most difficult competitive exam where the results are highly unpredictable. In this scenario, I think that having a backup plan is not only good but also necessary and it should mainly depend on your reason ...

If you want to clear UPSC to obtain a stable government job with a decent salary and government amenities, you can write any one of the below exams depending on your field of interest. As the level of any other government exam is well below UPSC, you can clear these exams easily. These are SSC, CDS, Railway, Banking/IBPS, etc."

Chapter 3

Who can Succeed in SSC Exams

Those who are willing to work harder than anyone else can succeed in SSC exams. They should also have the following:

- An inquisitive mind
- Sharp analytical ability to quickly weigh the pros and cons of an issue
- Ability to sift through data to focus on the essentials
- Clarity of approach, coupled with the talent of planning by balancing present and future needs
- Dedication and ability to work hard
- Being a people's person is an added advantage

  If you are serious about being successful in your career and life, then you can do nothing better than reading the inspirational stories of successful candidates. Here are various motivating success stories of SSC recruits that will help you to achieve your goals!

> *"Dear aspirants! If you are born to the parent facing poverty it is not your mistake but if you die before your children facing poverty, it is definitely your mistake. To achieve your goals and reach to the destination always compete with yourself each day to be better than yesterday with the help of determination, hard work and analytical approach."*
>
> **Dr. Md. Usmangani Ansari**

MYTH BREAKING SUCCESS STORIES

1. Can a non-math background, Hindi medium aspirant, preparing from village, compete in SSC Exam?

Let's know how Sagar Gupta broke above myths!

Success Story of Mr. Sagar Gupta (selected as DA in CGL 13).

Here are the preparation tips and strategy shared by Sagar Gupta (selected as DA in CGL 13 and in CGL 2014 getting 460 marks in written).Accolades for his efforts to break the myths regarding SSC preparation. It is advised to read his success story to get constructive information for cracking SSC examination.

First of all, I want to introduce myself so that I can break some myths related to SSC CGL

Exam. I am Sagar Gupta, from a small village of Jharkhand (a naxal belt area). I am a B.COM. graduate. I completed my studies viz. Matriculation, Intermediate, Graduation from my village only. There is no English medium school here. So, I have completed all my studies from Hindi medium school. I am saying this all to break **myths like**

(i) A student from Hindi medium can't compete with students from English medium.

When I was a **novice** at the beginning of the preparation of SSC CGL, I used to consult "Bhaiyas" who were preparing for SSC/Bank. They used to say, *"Are yaar, Hum log Hindi medium se hain, English medium wale log se kaha compete kar payenge. SSC/Bank unke liye hi bana hai"*. In short, the so called **"Elder Bhaiyas",** preparing for SSC/Bank will just demotivate you. Being a student from Hindi medium, I was always apprehensive that SSC will be a tough nut to crack.One day I asked one of those Bhaiyas, what did they do to improve your English. One said *"Kuch nahi"* (nothing). Another said *"Newspaper kabhi kabhi padh leta hu. But sudharta nahi hai"*. Here, I want to tell you that *"kuch nahi karne ya kabhi kabhi newspaper padhne se kam nahi chalega"*. You will have to work hard with sheer perseverance to achieve anything in life. I am not saying that you will have to read 10-12 hours a day. I am just saying that in a day, give 4 to 5 hours, maximum and that is enough. In these 4 to 5 hours, just study. I have seen people who waste their time using Whatsapp, talking with … friend etc. in their study time. *Wo sab karo but padhte time nahi karo.*

(ii) A person who is living in a village and preparing from there only, can't crack SSC/Bank.

I am born and brought up in my village and still cracked SSC CGL EXAM in my first attempt, with good marks and without any coaching and also got a respectable post. After completing my Matriculation, people started telling me "Go to town for further studies. Why are you wasting your time living here in village? *Yaha se kuch nahi kar paoge, kewal awaragiri karoge. Aishe aishe word sab log mujhe bolte the ki kya batau."* I have heard sarcastic words and became sad sometimes. But I never said anything to them because somewhere in my mind and heart, I was determined to show them what I could do; . and see, in my first attempt, I cleared SSC- CGL! Now, those people appreciate me and say, *"Beta, tumne to Kamal kar diya."* In a nutshell, I want to say that hard work will surely bear fruit.

(iii) Third myth: SSC mai sab setting se hota hai.

This myth is almost stated by failures or the person who want to hide their insincerity towards studies. The failures always used to say,*"Bhai, hamara selection nahi hoga. SSC mai sab setting se hota hai...aj tak 350 se jyada cut off kabhi gaya nahi...aur 2013 mai cut off 420 ho gaya aur 2014 mai cut off 426 ho gaya hai. Itna cut off hike ho jayega kya ..sab SSC* wale corrupt ho *gaye hai...jinka selection ho raha hai, wo log paise se selection pa rahe hai, wo log cheaters hai..."* and all that. I want to tell you that all this doesn't make sense.

Do you know why the cut off has increased drastically? This is due to the rising demand for the government job among students. People want respect, job security and handsome salary and perks. A government job offers each of these things. So, be it a B.Tech., MBA or a Bank PO, everyone opts for SSC. Due to these things, the cut off has increased. So don't be a slacker. Don't think that students selected in SSC are cheaters. It is their hard labour which has earned them this position. Stop listening to those guys who say **all the meaningless things. Believe in yourself and give your best!**

(iv) Fourth myth: How can a student with non-Maths background compete with the student from Maths background?

This myth is natural. Even when I started preparing for SSC, I used to think the same. But in due time, I realised that this is also a myth. As I have told earlier, I am from a non-math background and a simple graduate in Commerce. So, I also used to think in the earlier stage of my SSC preparation that B.Tech. (Engineering students) and M.B.A. students are also preparing for SSC and they have a good command over English and Mathematics as these subjects have been major fields of study for them. But during the preparation, I realized that in SSC, questions are not asked of engineering level and that SSC Mathematics is all about practice and accuracy. SSC English too might look hard at the inception, but it is not so when you start studying and grasping the concepts. A student from Hindi medium, like me, may think that I can't get even 15 marks out of 50. But after adoption of the focused strategies and right books, you will see the changes in yourself. If you don't believe me then I want to tell you that even I have completed my graduation from Hindi medium of study. But now after directed and attentive study, my English is "thik thak (so so)" to crack the English section of SSC.

IN A NUTSHELL- These are the myths and should not be trusted. Remember:

i.   Studying with sheer perseverance will aid even a student from Hindi medium to compete with students from English medium.

ii.   If you are working hard towards achieving your goal, then you will definitely crack the SSC/Bank exams. Hailing from village or city is never a criteria.

iii. Government jobs being lucrative have rapidly become the most preferred career choice amongst aspirants. This is the sole reason for the hike in cut off marks of SSC exams.

iv.   When you prepare in the right direction, then there remains no difference between B. Tech. and M.B.A. students and students from non-Maths background.

PREPARATION STRATEGIES AND BOOKS

There are lots of books in the market for SSC. They all claim that after reading these books, you will clear the exam easily. I don't know the veracity of their claim. But I want to tell that when I started my preparation, I had no one to guide me about books and strategies. So, I bought almost every book. I had 4 to 5 Maths books of different publications. But after reading those books partly,

I realised which book was the right one to prepare for SSC. And then I started my preparation from the best book. Books may differ from person to person. May be, *"Jo book maine padha hai, dusra banda jiska selection hua hai, ho sakta hai ki wo ye book na padha hoga"*. But I started my preparation from zero level. I am sharing few books for different sections, which I used during my SSC preparation.

1. FOR MATHEMATICS

    i.   **Objective Mathematics**

    ii.   **Advanced Mathematics**

    [Try to learn every concept and theorem first and then start solving questions.] You might not be able to solve all the questions; skip them. Solve every previous year question given at the end of chapter.

There are … lot of good books for Advanced mathematics too.

2. FOR ENGLISH

"…common error … answer and explanation ki help se dekho ki kaun sa part mein error tha …reason kya tha uska.." Learn every synonym and antonym asked in the sets. Also, learn the word-meaning given at the end of each set to improve your vocabulary for SSC exam. Try to use these words in your daily life so that the words will be in your mind forever.

The most important thing to improve your English is **to read an English newspaper daily for 1 hour**. If you are a student from Hindi medium initially you won't be able to understand the newspaper. But don't lose heart. Within 2-3 months of continuous study of newspaper, your English will improve a lot. Reading newspaper will help you in **COMPREHENSION, CLOSE TEST, PARA JUMBLE, SENTENCE IMPROVEMENT,** etc. So, **read newspaper daily.**

3. FOR REASONING

This is the easiest section of SSC CGL. No need to buy book. Just practice the sets. After practicing 20 to 30 sets, You can easily score 45 to 48 out of 50 in exam.

4. FOR GENERAL AWARENESS

I was very dull in the General Awareness Section. When I had given SSC CGL 2013 exam, that was cancelled, I got 1 marks in the GA section. So, you can imagine how prepared I was for the GA section at that time. Then one of my friends suggested to read. He said ,"Don't try to learn it by rote method. Just read the book again and again. For example, if you are reading page no. 1 to 4 today, revise them again the next day, after that, next day, read page no.5 to 8 and then again revise it next day and so on. After one or two week, I revised from page no.1. Actually, whatever he said is on the basis of the research done by scientist which says that if one studies like this, then whatever he read, will be in mind for a long time. Then I did the same and saw the improvement in me. This method worked very well and "mujhe sara history, civics, etc. … pura yaad ho gaya tha". I scored 28 marks out of 50 in CGL in 2014. You will have to study the GA section every day.

5.   FOR PRACTICE SETS

At the beginning of the preparation, I used to think, *"Practice sets se kya hoga"*. But gradually, After this revised method of study, I realised that this is one thing, which will ultimately take you near to your success in SSC. When you start solving questions sets, then your **speed & accuracy** will improve. It will also help you in preparing each section of the exam. But the method to solve sets is:

I.   First, complete the chapters of Mathematics and make your concept clear.

II.   Also, do a complete self study of the sections(given at the beginning) of SSC.

III.   Then start solving 1 practice set every day.

IV.   After completing each practice set, analyse it completely, i.e. see those questions in all the sections, which you were not able to solve or found difficult; write them down in a separate note book. Also, see the general awareness section and see the explanation and remember them. Also, see common error, antonym, synonym, Idioms and phrases, close test, etc. in English section. In short, to get the benefit of solving practice sets, it is mandatory to analyse the set completely.

V.   If you have one or two friend who are sincere in studies then you can solve model sets with them. It will make solving practice set enjoyable. Because solving model questions alone sometimes might be boring.

DO'S AND DON'TS

BELOW MENTIONED THINGS SHOULD BE TAKEN IN CONSIDERATION, IF YOU WANT TO CLEAR SSC IN FIRST ATTEMPT WITH VERY GOOD MARKS-

I.   I have seen people making WhatsApp Study group. First, I want to tell straight forward that *"WhatsApp se padhai nahi ho sakti…"* But according to me, *"WhatsApp se padhai nahi hogi ya agar hui bhi to bahut kam, time jyada waste hoga"*.

II.   I am not saying that don't make …friend or if you have … friend, then break your relation. I am just saying that see If having … friends, is hampering your preparation for the exam. You have heard a idiom," ***KUCH PANE KE LIYE, KUCH KHONA HOTA HAI"***. I am not saying that … "chhor do". I am saying that give less time to your friends and more time to your studies. Because after getting job, you can enjoy your life with your friends. But if you fail to secure a job then everything will be destroyed. I have lots of friends in towns preparing for SSC/Bank. They used to talk to their friends for 3 to 4 hours and thus wasted their time. Sometimes, due to a small dispute between him and other friends, he couldn't concentrate in his studies. He is still struggling for the job. So, it's better to decide first, what you want in your life?

Do you want happiness of your family or loved ones who are spending thousands of rupees for your study? Or, Do you want to betray them? In my opinion, if have one friend, then he/she should be supportive. He or she should say, "first make your life, take a government job and I am always with you." Because in today's era, some people make friends just for fun. They don't think about their happiness. They just want to have fun. Take a wise decision.

III. Don't be alcoholic. According to the research done by various scientists,"… alcohol reduces concentration." It will also hamper your study.

IV. **Don't** make lots of friends. I am not saying that don't make friends. Make friends, but don't indulge with them every time. Make limited friends who will help you in your studies. When aspirants study in hostels or take room on rent, they make lots of friends. The problem is that when you study, they come to your room and you start talking to them. Some times, they will say *"chalo yaar ghum ke ate hai"*, and you go with them. It can be an obstacle in your way to your dream job. If you have friends, tell them straightly that this time is for your studies and you can go with them in evening to make mind fresh.

V. **Do excerise** on regular basis. I am not saying to go to gym. A simple walk in the morning or evening, alone or with friends, is enough to make your mind healthy. You can spend one to two hours in the evening with your friends but only one to two hours.

VI. **People** think that those who are selected in SSC/Bank, study 24×7 or for 10 to 12 hours a day. This is completely a myth. Selected students say, so just to impress others. Some students might study for 10 hours. But in my opinion, if you study for 3 to 4 hours a day with full concentration, then this time is enough to clear SSC/Bank within 6 months. But the time in which you study, should be only for study. Don't use WhatsApp or Facebook while studying. It reduces concentration. In short, if you study 3 to 4 hours daily, with solving practice sets for 2 hours and giving 1 hour to analyse the set, then this $(3+2+1=6$ hours) is enough to clear the exam within less than 6 months.

VII. **Many people** think to commit suicide when they don't clear the exam. I am requesting you all that please never do this. I know you might be listening harsh words from others when you are not clearing the exam. But never think to commit suicide. Life is precious. If a person doesn't clear the exams, then it does not mean that he can't do anything in life. Government job is not everything. Give your best to get a government job. But if you don't get a government job, then you can do private jobs as well. I have seen people starting from very low position in private jobs and going to very high post with experience and hard work. So, never be sad. Just be positive and give your best.

VIII.   **When** I started my preparation for SSC, I met some students who were extremely brilliant in some sections. For instance, I have met a student who remembered more than 10,000 words. I also met a person who has completed General Awareness only by rote method. That time I used to think that if these brilliant students are not able to clear SSC then how will I clear SSC? But in due course, I realised that if one is brilliant in one section (say in ENGLISH) and he is weak in other sections, then he will not clear the exam. For clearing SSC, one should have command over each section viz. Reasoning, Mathematics, English. I will not say about General Awareness section because "ye almost sabki weakness hoti hai…" I am not trying to say that one should be brilliant in each section. I am just saying that one should have command over each section.

IX.   **AT LAST, I** want to tell you all that just keep believing in yourself. Don't listen to failure people who say that you can't clear SSC. Just keep believing in yourself and I assure you that you will definitely clear the exam. And that will be the slap on the face of those failure people. I also want to make clear that *"Kewal suggestion lene se kuch na hoga. Un suggestions ko adopt karna hoga aur apna best dena hoga."* I also used to give suggestions to my friends, they listen to me and they do whatever I say to them for one or two week and again they stop implementing those suggestions in their studies. Give your best and see the results yourself.

2. Can a slum born, whose father and mother working as labourer, compete in SSC Exam?

Let's know how Ghan Shyam Verma broke all odds!

On the demand of some of my friends, I am writing about my small success story so that some of my friends get motivated. Well, I am born in a slum of East Delhi, RAMANAND CAMP, West Vinod Nagar, Delhi-110092.

My father was a labourer and mother was also working with him. Daily income of my family was not more than 80-100 rupees. When I became 5 year old, my father put me in a local M.C.D. school. The environment was worst in my dwelling locality for any study purpose. People from criminal background like, murderer, rapist, thief, drunkards, etc. were living there, i.e. a typical slum area. Daily fighting of the people was very common in that time. Due to death of my Tauji(father's elder brother), my family had to shift to Rajasthan and my father left me in slum for my study purpose. It was 2001 and I was in class 8. But due to lack of money, I had to do many kind of works. I had to go in parties as a **waiter to clean plates** or sometime as a English waiter (those who wear dress in parties).

I usually came at home **from school at 6:30 pm** and at the same time I had to **go in parties** and had to **come at home in early morning usually at 6 am or 7 am** (I can't forget these days). I earned 70-80 rupees per day. Well, above all, this I was a top ranker till class 10. I decided to take Science (PCMB) and took admission in a reputed school of DARYA GANJ (ASVJ Sr. Sec. school) and at the same time my **father was suffering from CANCER**. But still he came to Delhi so that he can earn some money for me to buy books. Many refreshers were so costly. But by luck, one day when I went to take water in a park I met a lady, I don't KNOW how she knew about me and she offered me her child's books for class 11. This is a clear example of **"where there is a will, there is a way"**. Suddenly in Sept-2004, I got a sad news about the death of my papa. Now there was no one to look after my family. I have 3 younger brothers, one younger sister and mom. People of my village advised me to quit my studies and look after my family. But **I remembered my father's hard work**. I decided to continue my studies. I passed class 11 with poor marks. Suddenly, in Class 12th one great person came to my slum and offered me to teach her daughter who was in class 10th. He paid 600 rupees per month to me. It was enough for my expenditure on education. Remaining I managed with my work as a waiter in parties. After some time, in class 12th my slum was demolished and again I was on road. I slept more than 12-15 days on road with my books and went school from there. I took a room on rent in West Vinod Nagar only. I passed my 12th with satisfactory marks. I got admission in **Delhi University** in Mathematics honours and studied one year there. Parallely, I continued giving tuitions. Now I was earning about 3000/- p.m. **I topped Delhi University** in 2006 in first year (got **100% marks** in vector algebra). But I was not satisfied with this course so I took admission in B.Tech.(IPU, Delhi) and continued my tuition. Now I was becoming stronger financially and left my job of waiter and gave my extra time in tuition. I completed my engineering with my own money earned by tuition and at just after completion of B.Tech., I took admission in M.B.A (Noida). In 2012, I was selected as an auditor in Hyderabad, FCI and in 2015 I was again selected as assistant in AFHQ Delhi through CGL-2013. Now, my whole family is on a happy note. I have purchased my own home in Delhi (which I used to dream only by the money earned through tuition) and have all those things which I wanted from my life. My brothers are studying in a reputed schools and sister got married.

P.S: *Never give up and always be positive in your life. Do hard work and it will always work.*

3. Success Story of Ravi Kumar

Hello Friends,

Today I want to share my story. I am from a simple family. I was good at study but after 6th standard I did not focus on my study and just somehow passed 10th standard with 67%. After tenth, I chose Science because most of my friends chose this. But in few months, I realised that without proper guidance, I can't handle this and everybody knows that the education in Bihar is not in very good condition. Lack of resources, shortage of good teachers in colleges, no classes and only exam is the reality. So, how can an average students do well in studies without coaching. I have passed these 2 years of my life and passed 12th with 63.8%. At that time, I was thinking about IIT but it was not possible without proper guidance and hard work.

After 12th, I enrolled myself in BA-History(Honours). Because there was no study in college, so I decided to prepare for competitive exam like Railways, SSC and Bank (2011). At that time, I didn't know anything about SSC, so I started preparation for Railway. But after some time, I realised that there is no certainty of vacancy in Railways and I did not want to work in bank. So, I shifted to SSC.

I was not very confident that time but in few months I realised that I was much better than most of my friends because my score was more than them in practice sets.

My first exam was **CGL 2012** but without graduation. I was scared at exam centre because I mentioned wrong information for this. I had given the paper and scored 90 marks but did not give mains because of fear.

My first official exam was SSC (CHSL) 10+2 (2012). I scored 123 marks but was not prepared well for typing and was disqualified by .5% mistake margin in typing. I was very disappointed after that. So I decided to work hard both on study and typing. I had given another exam of Railway (technical) in Dec. 2012 but not qualified.

So I decided to focus only on SSC. I started teaching Maths for competition and gave **SSC- MTS and SSC (CHSL)**10+2 (2013). I cleared both exams. I was the topper of Bihar region in MTS but did not go for document verification because I did not want to do this job. In **SSC (CHSL)**10+2, I scored 133 marks and my typing was in good condition so I cleared typing easily.

At that time, I had given another exam DRDO (clerk) and also cleared it. Now, my confidence was very high. I completed my graduation in 2013 and submitted 2014 CGL application form in January 2014.

I was working hard for CGL but it was delayed in 2013. I was again disappointed. But two good news were waiting for me. Final result of **SSC (CHSL)** 10+2. (2013) and DRDO were announced and I was qualified in both exams.

Now, I was distracted from studies because I was over confident. In November 2014, I had given 2014 CGL pre and was waiting for result.

I was also waiting for my joining in either DRDO or in DEO but due to red-tapism, my police verification took very long time.

Finally I got my first government job joining in Feb. 2015 and joined on 12th Feb. 2015 in **Visakhapatnam.**

After few weeks, I had to give CGL mains, but I didn't have much resources. I started preparation with the help of a few books. I had given mains in April, 15. The paper was easy so I was confident about my result. After few weeks, result was announced and I was selected for IP post and scored overall 453 marks (123.75+173.5+156).

I gave interview without much preparation and scored 50 marks in it. When final result came I was selected for income tax inspector with total 503.25 marks.

After that, my joining of DEO also came and I joined Bhubaneswar on 4th August 2015.

Now, I am waiting for my joining of income tax. In last few years, I have changed from a shy personality to a confident personality.

I want to say a lot of things about myself but I have narrated my story in short.

Just one thing, I want to say keep faith in your ability and be confident. God makes everybody with a special talent, if you are determined, you can do anything. I was not regular with my study but I have got a good job because I have confidence in myself and work really hard.

4. How do I prepare for SSC Exams while doing a full time job?

This is a question which generally confuses or creates a tension in the mind of the students who wants to be a bureaucrat. In this article, we will discuss this question and give you some tips so that you can do better with your life.

No one can answer this question better than you. You just have to prepare your mind and maintain your confidence level. It all depends on how much time you can give to your study consistently. Initially, with this idea in mind, you must have a proper planning to execute your plan. Try to manage your time and give at least four hours daily to your study. Now, the question comes–how will you manage to get four hours from your busy job schedule?

Here is the schedule of your life during preparation time

- Manage to wake up at 5.30 in the morning and study for **2 hours.** Initially, it will be hard to wake up but think of your aim and goal. Make a habit of waking up at time. You have to choose between your pleasure of sleeping or your commitment that you make with your life.

- Generally, the people come from office at 8.00pm. So, you have **2 hours from 9.30 to 11.30 pm** for study. Just make a rule in your life or let's say, a habit that you will not sleep without studying 2 hours and you will wake up early in the morning so that you can give 2 hours easily, to your study.

- You can easily utilise travelling time for **English portion**. In this time, you can learn **one word substitution, idiom, phrase.** Make it your habit.
- Now, on weekend, try to study **9 hours per** day.
- Never fall prey to the temporary pleasure. Make a commitment with yourself that you will use this precious time to make your life dynamic, vibrant and a life of permanent pleasure. Never think negatively and always be optimistic. Whenever you feel tired or burdened, just focus your mind on your aim. You can relax once you achieve your goal.

So, aspirants, start your preparation with full energy and confidence. You must definitely crack the SSC. Do not waste even a single second. Use this time to achieve your goal. This time will make your future and you will relax in your whole life.

Topper's Interview

5.   Mani Bharti: CAPF-2012/AIR-5 (SSC-CGL 2012) Tamil Nadu

Introduction

Q. Tell us something about yourself. When and why did you enter in the competitive exam field?

I am from Neyveli in Cuddalore district of Tamil Nadu, did my graduation from College of Engineering Guindy, Anna University,Chennai. Uniformed services had always been my passion right from the school days. After getting into the college I came to know about the UPSC examinations for Civil Services and Central Police forces. I started preparing for the examinations after completing my graduation in 2011.

Essay/ Descriptive

Q. How did you prepare the Essay, grammar, précis and report writing?

I didn't prepare specifically for essay paper since I prepared for civil services main exam in October 2012. Other than that reading editorials and articles in magazines improve our essay writing skills a lot.

Q. In CAPF-2012 Exam, Which essay did you write and what keypoints did you include in it?

I chose to write the essay on regional parties affecting federal structure of India. Incidentally I am from Tamil Nadu which is ruled by regional parties for the last 40 years. So I had more ideas regarding the effect on federal structure. Key points include hung parliament, impasse in legislation, instability of the government and consequent effects such as inconsistent public policies, incoherent cabinet etc.., state governments which have regional parties in power raise issues in NDC and other councils and complain of unequal treatment by Centre, misuse of federal provisions in Constitution.

Interview

Q. What specific preparation did you do for the interview? Who was the chairman? Provide the list of questions asked in CAPF Interview. How was the overall interview experience? And any tips for future aspirants.

A. I prepared about my home town (Neyveli Thermal Power Station), hobbies, graduation, Tamil Nadu affairs such as Cauvery river dispute and SC rulings, Caste violence , Kudankulam Nuclear plant issue, about the 5 CAPFs, etc.. The chairman of my interview panel was Smt.Alka Sirohi. Here is the list of questions asked in my interview which I could remember:

Q. What is different about Pondicherry?

A. Actually I didn't expect this question as my home town is Neyveli, but in the summary sheet only our birthplace will be there. I managed it by saying that it is a Union Territory, was under the control of French, administrative divisions (Mahe Yanam,Karaikal) etc..

Q. What is fuzzy logic?

A. I don't know. She told that it is used in washing machines.

Q. What do you mean by an agent of change? Give me examples.

A. Something which must improve or transform the society. For example, education, inspirational leader.

Q. Difference between inspiration and motivation.

A. Inspiration is getting attracted towards one's way of living or achievement, motivation is improving the morale of someone who is feeling low. Inspiration doesn't require communication but motivation does.

Q. Difference between rogue state and failed state. Examples for both.

A. Rogue state is one which acts against the interests of world peace. For example, North Korea. Failed state is one in which the government is not able to discharge it's duties. For example, Afghanistan, Somalia

Q. Is it ethical to demand back the Bharat Ratna Award? Your opinion? (Amartya Sen issue)

A. No. Only based on solid evidence of incompetence in the relevant field of achievement it can be demanded back.

Q. What is Pendleton Act?

A. Don't know.

Q. What is the difference between LCD and LED TVs?

I told about the viewing angle, brightness etc. He expected something else.

Q. What are the chemical compounds used for producing different colour LEDs?

A. Don't know.

Q. Nearest star to our Sun?

A. Proxima Centauri.

Q. Concept of time travel.

A. Don't know.

Questions based on my leadership positions: How many persons can be served with 1 kg of rice?

A. (I was mess secretary in my college hostel) How do you ensure the right amount of nutrients in food for vegetarian and non- vegetarian students?

Approximately 5 to 6 can be served. By including pulses in a higher proportion to vegetarian students.

Q. What are highest peacetime military awards and other military awards?
A. Ashok Chakra, PVC, VSM, PVSM, SM, AVSM etc..

Q. What are the measures of dispersion(Statistics)?

A. Don't know.

They asked many other questions based on my answers. Summary Sheet in DAF is very important. Around 60% of the questions are based on it.

Q. How was interview: normal, stress, mixed? Did they ask any uncomfortable questions, if yes how did you answer it?

A. My interview was mixed. They asked some uncomfortable questions, many questions were psychological questions, and some were easier ones. One thing I came to know is that you must honestly admit if you don't know. Taking more time, beating around the bush, etc. won't help.

Marksheet: CAPF-2012

Paper I (MCQ): 157

Paper II (Descriptive): 96

Interview: 97

Q. On an average, how many hours do you study?

A. On an average I study 4 hours a day and the time gets longer when the exams get nearer. 8 hours a day is more than enough for this exam.

Civil Service

Q. Did you appear in Civil Service (Mains) 2012? If yes, share the experience, marks, what Essay did you write?

A. Yes I appeared in Civil Services Main exam 2012. I wrote the essay on working Indian women. As this is my first attempt, I gained a lot of experience. My marks were GS(192), Public Administration(179),Geography(195),Essay(94). Total marks 650.

Q. Are you appearing in Civil Service (Mains) 2013? If yes, how are you approaching/preparing the ethics, and other new topics of GS?

A. Yes I am appearing in 2013 Main exam. As ethics is a new topic I am trying to collect materials from various sources and coaching institutes.

Career Backup Plan

Q. If you were not selected, what was your career backup plan?

A. I would have joined in Central Excise department and tried for Civil Services exam.

Wisdom

Q. Through this journey and success, what wisdom did you gain about competition and life? What is your message to the aspirants?

A. Working hard is the only way to success. The hard work I had done for the 2012 prelims, for Physical Test and Medical Examination brought me this success…

6.   SSC CGL Success Story of Kamalika Das

"Believe in yourself and all that you are. Know that there is something inside you that's greater than any obstacle."

Q1. What was your educational background?

My education background is Engineering and I have completed my M. Tech.

Q2. What made you want to try for this exam? Did you take any other exam before this? What were your results?

I wanted a job which provides good work-life balanced with a good social status. I took SSC CGL in 2014. I could not clear Tier II cutoff that year. I appeared for SSC CGL in 2016 again.

Q3. How did you plan your preparation for your exam? How many months ago did you start preparation?

I couldn't prepare for the SSC Exam as I was pursuing my M. Tech. However, I used to take 10-20 days off from my academic work before exam date and took online Mock Tests. I did not refer any book and focused more on solving the previous year question papers and mock papers.

Q4. What was the strategy you adopted in preparing for the exam? What was your study schedule? What were the major hurdles you overcame?

My strategy was simple. I studied 7-8 hours a day during those 10-20 days I took off from my M. Tech study. I mostly used this time in solving test papers. My speed of solving test papers was good but accuracy was a problem. My accuracy was about 80% initially. I improved that area through rigorous practice.

Q5. What strategies did you apply specifically for different sections?

I solved easy questions first and left the difficult ones for later on. For me, mathematics took most of the time. So I attempted mathematics in the end during Tier I. In Tier II, I practiced 20 question papers to improve my speed. I learned to write structured essays on any topic and practiced about 30 essays for Tier III.

Q6. Most of the students prefer to go to Coaching Centers rather than prepare on their own. Which one do you prefer and why?

I have understood that self-study with online resources is enough to crack exams like SSC CGL. I can say this from my personal experience. Therefore, I did self-study for 2 weeks prior to the scheduled examination.

Q7. How important was Test Series in your success and how did it help you improve?

I took test series for Tier I and Tier II. I got similar questions in the actual exam.

Q8. How many tests did you take overall?

To be honest, I took about 20 tests for Tier I, 40 tests for Tier 2. Basically, I took 20 tests each for Math and English, 30 tests for Tier III.

Q9. Comment on the difficulty level of the exam paper. How did you tackle it? What were the challenges faced during the actual exam?

According to me. Tier I paper was very easy in which I scored 156. But the difficulty level of Tier II was higher than what I was expecting. I was puzzled after I saw the question paper. Initially, I panicked for a good 30 minutes. Then I concentrated and gave the exam. However, I got only 143 in mathematics while I was expecting to score at least 175. For English, I expected it to be tough like mathematics. Moreover, I was not prepared at that level either. Therefore, I could secure only 300 overall. My aim was to score 340. As my marks were not so good in Tier II, I worked harder for Tier III and Tier IV. Fortunately, I cleared Auditor in CGDA cut off. Therefore, according to me, I scored above 65 in Tier III.

Q10. Any words of wisdom for future Aspirants?

In my opinion, one should find out his/her weak points and improve them through constant practice. Moreover, do not lose hope even if you score less in any Tier because you can recover your position by working hard. Hence, according to me, practice is the key to clear SSC CGL.

Different SSC Services

Staff Selection Commission (SSC) conducts exams for different government services/posts. They get a good salary and enjoy a good reputation too in the society. These services and posts are discussed in detail below.

Exams conducted by SSC are:

- Combined Graduate Level (CGL) Examination
- Combined Higher Secondary Level (CHSL) 10+2 Examination
- Multitasking (Non-Technical) Staff/MTS Examination
- Scientific Assistant Examination
- Stenographers Grade 'C' and 'D' Examination
- SSC Constables (GD) in CAPFs, NIA & SSF Examination
- Sub Inspector in CPOs Examination
- Junior Engineer (Civil & Elect) Examination
- Lower Division Clerk (LDC) Grade Limited Departmental Competitive Examination
- Junior Translators (CSOLS) /Junior Hindi Translators Examination

SERVICE PROFILE

More and more people have started appearing in SSC exams as it is conducted yearly, has a large number of attractive posts, is entirely objective type and the results are declared in just a year span. It offers a large number of options in the same way as UPSC Civil Services Exam. Officer positions in Customs, Central Excise, Income Tax, Comptroller and Auditor General (CAG), etc. are offered through this exam. However, it is not as vast as IAS Exam. For those who see IAS as a distant dream or want a decent paying job, SSC jobs are very important. For example:

1. SSC-COMBINED GRADUATE LEVEL (CGL) EXAMINATION

SSC has been conducting the Combined Graduate Level (CGL) Exam, yearly for the past couple of years. Prior to 2010, it used to be irregular and with very few vacancies.

Before applying for the selection in the CGL, an applicant must know about the various posts for which SSC-CGL exams are conducted. It is important for an applicant to know,exactly *which post he/she will apply* to, if selected in the exam.

The Commission has introduced some new posts under SSC CGL Recruitment 2017. The newly introduced posts are:

Post	Ministries/Dept./ Offices/ Cadre	Post Code
Assistant Accounts Officer	Indian Audit & Accounts Department under CAG	$
Assistant	Other Ministries/ Departments/Organisations	>, <, &
Assistant in Serious Fraud Investigation Officer (SFIO)	Ministry of Corporate Affairs	-

Analysis of SSC CGL Posts based on Salary, Group, Pay Scale, Age Limit

1. Group "A" Posts: Pay Scale – ₹ 9300-34800 (pre-revised)

Post Code	Post Name	Ministries/ Dept./ Offices/ Cadre	Offices/ Cadre Classification	Grade Pay	Age Limit
F	Assistant Audit Officer	Indian Audit & Accounts Department under CAG	Group 'B' Gazetted (Non-Ministerial)	4800	Not exceeding 30 years
$	Assistant Accounts Officer	Indian Audit & Accounts Department under CAG	Group 'B' Gazetted (Non-Ministerial)	4800	Not exceeding 30 years

2. Group "B" Posts:| Pay Scale – ₹9300-34800 (pre-revised)

Post Code	Post Name	Ministries/ Dept./ Offices/ Cadre	Offices/ Cadre Classification	Grade Pay	Age Limit
A	Assistant Section Officer	Central Secretariat Service	Group "B"	4600	20-30 years
C	Assistant Section Officer	Intelligence Bureau	Group "B"	4600	Not exceeding 30 years

D	Assistant Section Officer	Ministry of Railway	Group "B"	4600	20-30 years
E	Assistant Section Officer	Ministry of External Affairs	Group "B"	4600	20-30 years
G	Assistant Section Officer	Armed Forces Headquarters (AFHQ)	Group "B"	4600	20-30 years
H	Assistant	Other Ministries/ Departments/ Organisations	Group "B"	4600	18-30 years
>	Assistant	Other Ministries/ Departments/ Organisations	Group "B"	4600	20-30 years
<	Assistant Section Officer	Other Ministries/ Departments/ Organisations	Group "B"	4600	Not exceeding 30 years
I	Assistant	Other Ministries/ Departments/ Organisations	Group "B"	4600	Not exceeding 30 years
&	Assistant/ Superintendent	Other Ministries/ Departments/ Organisations	Group "B"	4600	Not exceeding 30 years
J	Inspector of Income Tax	Central Board of Direct Taxes (CBDT)	Group "C"	4600	Not exceeding 30 years
K	Inspector (Central Excise)	Central Board of Excise and Customs (CBEC)	Group "B"	4600	Not exceeding 30 years
L	Inspector (Preventive Officer)	CBEC	Group "B"	4600	Not exceeding 30 years
M	Inspector (Examiner)	CBEC	Group "B"	4600	Not exceeding 30 years
N	Assistant Enforcement Officer	Directorate of Enforcement, Department of Revenue	Group "B"	4600	Up to 30 years
O	Sub Inspector	Central Bureau of Investigation	Group "B"	4600	20-30 years

P	Inspector Posts	Department of Posts	Group "B"	4600	18-30 years
Q	Divisional Accountant	Offices under CAG	Group "B"	4200	Not exceeding 30 years
S	Inspector	Central Bureau of Narcotics	Group "B"	4600	18-27 years
%	Sub Inspector	National Investigation Agency (NIA)	Group "B"	4200	Up to 30 years
R	Junior Statistical Office	Ministry of Statistics and Programme Implementation	Group "B"	4200	Up to 32 years

3. Group "C & D" Posts: Pay Scale –₹9300-34800 (pre-revised)

Post Code	Post Name	Ministries/Dept./ Offices/ Cadre	Offices/ Cadre Classification	Grade Pay	Age Limit
T	Auditor	Offices under CAG	Group "C"	2800	18-27 years
U	Auditor	Offices under Controller General of Defence Accounts (CGDA)	Group "C"	2800	18-27 years
V	Auditor	Other Ministry/ Departments	Group "C"	2800	18-27 years
W	Accountant	Offices under CAG	Group "C"	2800	18-27 years
X	Accountant/ Junior Accountant	Other Ministry/ Departments	Group "C"	2800	18-27 years
Y	Senior Secretariat Assistant/ Upper Division Clerks	Central Govt. Offices/Ministries other than Central Secretariat Clerical Services (CSCS) cadres	Group "C"	2400	18-27 years
Z	Tax Assistant	CBDT	Group "C"	2400	18-27 years
@	Tax Assistant	CBEC	Group "C"	2400	20-27 years
#	Sub Inspector	Central Bureau of Narcotics	Group "C"	2400	18-27 years

Description of Posts/ Job Profile & Promotion

To decide the top prioritised SSC CGL post preferences, an aspirant should be aware of the following aspects:

- Pay Scale & Benefits(given in the table above)
- Nature of Work
- Posting / Vacancies
- Promotion/ Career Development

1. **Assistant Audit Officer/ Post Code – F**

   Nature of Work: Conduct audits of govt./public sector organisations Travelling during the inspection.

   Posting / Vacancies: Limited Vacancies

   Promotion/ Career Development: The post is recently added.

2. **Inspector (Examiner) (CBEC)/ Post Code – M**

   Nature of Work: Clerical or file related work (If posted in headquarters) Verifying taxations on goods, passing through ports (if posted in the field)

   Posting / Vacancies: Limited vacancies/ posting in coastal areas

   Promotion/ Career Development: Employees will be promoted as: Appraiser => Assistant Commissioner   => Deputy Commissioner => Commissioner. 1st promotion will be availed after completing 3 years of service.

3. **Income Tax Inspector (CBDT) | SSC CGL Post Code – J**

   Nature of Work: Assessing, verifying and processing IT records of individuals and businesses, conducting raids, local travelling, etc

   Posting / Vacancies: All India posting/ Many vacancies

   Promotion/ Career Development: Employees will be promoted as: Income Tax Officer => Assistant

   Commissioner => Deputy Commissioner => Commissioner.

   1st promotion will be availed after completing 8 years of service.

4. **Assistant in Ministry of External Affairs (MEA) | SSC CGL Post Code – E**

   Nature of Work: Clerical/ Administration work like typing, compiling reports, emailing, calling, updating about, Events, maintaining the files etc.

   Posting / Vacancies: Posting in Delhi. Foreign posting for few years is also possible.

   Promotion/ Career Development: 1st promotion in 15-17 years (without clearing departmental exam).

   1st promotion in 8 years (if departmental exam is cleared).

5. **Inspector (Central Excise) (CBEC) | SSC CGL Post Code – K**

   Nature of Work: Executive work (augmentation of Central Excise & Service tax) Clerical or file work (if posted in headquarter),

   Detection of evasion of taxes, etc. if posted in the field.

Posting / Vacancies: All India posting/ A lot of vacancies.

Promotion/ Career Development: Employees will be promoted as: Superintendent => Assistant,   Commissioner => Deputy Commissioner => Commissioner.

1st promotion after completing 8 years of service and clearing departmental exam.

6. **Inspector (Preventive Officer) (CBEC) | SSC CGL Post Code – L**

    Nature of Work: Executive work (prevention of smuggling).

    Clerical or file work (If posted in headquarter).

    Assessment of customs duty on goods, arrest, seize, search, detain etc. (if posted in the field-airport/coast), Round-the-clock duty

    Posting / Vacancies: Posting in cities with ports/airports.

    Promotion/ Career Development: Employees will be promoted as: Superintendent => Assistant,   Commissioner => Deputy Commissioner => Commissioner.

    1st promotion after completing 8 years of service and clearing departmental exam.

7. **Assistant Enforcement Officer (AEO) | SSC CGL Post Code – N**

    Nature of Work: Preventing money laundering/forgery etc.

    Posting / Vacancies: Posting in enforcement directorate offices in 21 cities.

    Promotion/Career Development: Employees will be promoted as: Enforcement Officer => Assistant, Director => Deputy Director => Director. There is no fixed promotion period for this post.

8. **Assistant (Central Vigilance Commission) | SSC CGL Post Code – B**

    Nature of Work: Update case files, contact respective department to collect required information, record keeping etc.

    Monitor vigilance activities carried out by various Central Government organisations.

    Posting / Vacancies: All India Posting

    Promotion/ Career Development: Employees will be promoted as: Sectional Officer => Under Secretary => Deputy Secretary => Director. 1st promotion after completing about 7-8 years of service.

9. **Assistant in AFHQ | SSC CGL Post Code – G**

    Nature of Work: Clerical work like compiling files, reports and many kinds of paperwork.

    Keeping track of ongoing cases and subsequent follow-up.

    Posting / Vacancies: Posting in Delhi or other metro cities.

    Promotion/ Career Development: Employees will be promoted as: Section Officer => Deputy Director => Joint Director => Director => Principal Director. 1st promotion after 4 years; 2nd promotion after 6 years; 3rd promotion after 5 years; 4th promotion after 5 years.

10. Assistant in Ministry of Railway | SSC CGL Post Code – D

Nature of Work: Clerical work (above upper division clerk). Free and discounted railway passes for travelling anywhere in India.
Posting / Vacancies: Posting in cities/regional headquarters.
Promotion/ Career Development: Employees will be promoted as: Section Officer => Under Secretary => Deputy Secretary => Director.
1st promotion is after about 7-8 years, if the candidate doesn't appear for the departmental exam. But this time is reduced to 5-6 years, if the candidate takes the departmental exam.

11. Assistant in Intelligence Bureau | SSC CGL Post Code – C

Nature of Work: Work as an Investigative Officer.
Computer/ data oriented work in the Intelligence Bureau.
Posting / Vacancies: Posting at state headquarters in IB cell or in Delhi
Promotion/ Career Development: Employees will be promoted as: Section Officer => Under Secretary => Deputy Secretary.

12. Assistant Section Officer (CSS) | SSC CGL Post Code – A

Nature of Work: Preparing notes and reports and sending them to their superiors.
Posting / Vacancies: Posting in various ministries in Delhi.
Promotion/ Career Development: Employees will be promoted as: Section Officer => Under Secretary => Deputy Secretary => Director. 1st promotion is after 10 years, if the candidate doesn't appear for the departmental exam. But this time is reduced to 5 years, if the candidate takes the departmental exam. 2nd promotion is after 4 years.

13. Sub Inspectors (CBI) | SSC CGL Post Code – O

Nature of Work: Work as a state police with more powers.
Job is very challenging. Training duration – 32 weeks.
Posting / Vacancies: Maximum chances of posting in Delhi zone.
Promotion/ Career Development: Employees will be promoted as: Inspector => Deputy Superintendent => Superintendent => Senior Superintendent. 1st promotion is after minimum 5 years, 2nd promotion after 10-12 years and 3rd promotion after 5-7 years.

14. Assistant (Other Ministries) | SSC CGL Post Code – H

Nature of Work: Work under government organisations like Department of Personnel & Training, Parliamentary Affairs and Election Commission etc.
Posting / Vacancies: Posting in Delhi.
Promotion/ Career Development: Employees will be promoted as: Section Officer => Under Secretary => Deputy Secretary.

15. Divisional Accountant (CAG) | SSC CGL Post Code – Q

Nature of Work: Auditing of works carried out by the state government. It requires less travelling and has minimum probability of transfer.

Posting / Vacancies: Posted in the cities having offices coming under CAG
Promotion/ Career Development: Employees will be promoted as: Divisional Account Officer II => Divisional Account Officer I => Sr. Divisional Account Officer.

16. Inspector (Narcotics) | SSC CGL Post Code – S

Nature of Work: Checking on the cultivation of opium poppy. Conducting periodic checks in companies. Monitoring smuggling of banned drugs. It requires local travel.
Posting / Vacancies: Posting in North India.
Promotion/ Career Development: Employees will be promoted as: Superintendent of Narcotics => Assistant Narcotics Commissioner => Deputy Narcotics Commissioner => Narcotics Commissioner.

17. Assistant (Other Ministries) | SSC CGL Post Code – I

Nature of Work: Work under government organisations like Department of Personnel & Training, Parliamentary Affairs and Election Commission etc.
Posting / Vacancies: Posting in Delhi.
Promotion/ Career Development: Depends upon the department organisation.

18. Sub Inspector in National investigation Agency (NIA) | SSC CGL Post Code – %

Nature of Work: Investigate terrorism and other national security issues. A lot of travel is required to collect evidence from sites and gather intelligence inputs regarding terrorists etc. Work pressure will be more during the terrorist attacks.
Posting / Vacancies: Posting will be mostly in Delhi.
Promotion/ Career Development: Employees will be promoted as: Inspector => Deputy Superintendent => Superintendent. 1st promotion will be after 5 years.

19. Statistical Investigator | SSC CGL Post Code – R

Nature of Work: Data collection and processing to gather useful information for the government to implement schemes, both in office and field job.
Posting / Vacancies: 100 – 300 vacancies every year.
Promotion/ Career Development: Employees will be promoted as: Senior Statistical Officer => Assistant Director => Deputy Director => Joint Director. Promotions are very slow.

20. Inspector (Department of Post) | SSC CGL Post Code – P

Nature of Work: Promote business of post offices. It requires a lot of travel and performance pressure to meet numbers.
Take charge of 60-70 post offices, assisted by two Mail overseers.

Posting / Vacancies: Posting at any Postal Division, i.e. All India posting.

Promotion/ Career Development: Employees will be promoted as: Assistant Superintendent of Post => Postal Superintendent => Senior Superintendent of Post (GP: 5400) => Senior Superintendent of Post (GP: 6600). **1st** promotion is after 5 years after taking the departmental exam.

21. Sub-Inspector (Central Bureau of Narcotics) | SSC CGL Post Code –

Nature of Work: Work as an inspector, but more field work. It requires a lot of traveling to prevent entry of narcotic drugs into the state.

Posting / Vacancies: All India Posting.

Promotion/ Career Development: Employees will be promoted as: Inspector => Superintendent of Narcotics => Assistant Narcotics Commissioner => Deputy Narcotics Commissioner => Narcotics Commissioner.

22. Auditor (C&AG) | SSC CGL Post Code – T

Nature of Work: Audit expense reports of State Department (C&AG), Accounts of defense forces (CGDA) and general accounts of the country (CGA).

Posting / Vacancies: Posting in Accountant General Office located in State Capital (Delhi).

Promotion/ Career Development: Employees will be promoted as: Senior Auditor => Assistant Audit Officer.

1st promotion will be after 3 years and 2nd promotion after 2 years after clearing departmental exam.

23. Auditor (CGDA) | SSC CGL Post Code – U

Same as *"Auditor (C&AG) | Post Code – T"*

24. Auditor (CGA) | SSC CGL Post Code – V

Same as *"Auditor (C&AG) | Post Code – T"*

25. Tax Assistant (CBEC) | SSC CGL Post Code – @

Nature of Work: Working as a desk officer, assessing, verifying and modifying tax data of an individual or business (CBDT) and goods and services. It also requires periodic administration work & assisting higher officers (CBEC).

Posting / Vacancies: Posting in metro cities/a lot of vacancies.

Promotion/ Career Development: Employees will be promoted as: Senior Tax Assistant => Excise Inspector => Superintendent/Appraiser => Assistant Commissioner => Deputy Commissioner => Joint Commissioner => Additional Commissioner of Income Tax. 1st promotion is after 3 years and 2nd promotion after 3-4 years.

26. Tax Assistant (CBDT) | SSC CGL Post Code – Z

Same as *"Tax Assistant (CBEC) | Post Code – @"*

27. Accountant/ Junior Accountant (Offices under C&AG) | SSC CGL Post Code – W

Nature of Work: It is a clerical work which involves passing various bills, salary allowances and office expenses. It also requires working on pensions, GPF and Receipts and Payments accounting of Civil Ministries.

Posting / Vacancies: Fewer vacancies/ posting in Delhi.

Promotion/ Career Development: Employees will be promoted as: Senior Accountant => Assistant Accounts Officer => Principal Accounts Officer => Senior Accounts Officer. 1st promotion is after 3 years, 2nd promotion after AAO exam and 3rd promotion after 15 years after AAO.

28. Accountant/ Junior Accountant (CGA & others) | SSC CGL Post Code – X
Same as *"Accountant/ Junior Accountant (CGA & others) | Post Code – W"*

29. Senior Secretariat Assistant | SSC CGL Post Code – Y

Nature of Work: Maintain files in the concerned department. Reply mails received in department. Drafting RTI replies and sending them for approval and Data entry.

Posting / Vacancies: Postings in various ministries in Delhi/ Fewer vacancies.

Promotion/ Career Development: Employees will be promoted as: Assistant => Section Officer. 1st promotion is after 5 years and 2nd promotion after 6-7 years.

30. Compiler (Registrar General of India) | SSC CGL Post Code – $
Nature of Work: Clerical work. Drafting and compiling report and conducting census.

Posting / Vacancies: Posting in Statistical Division.

Promotion/ Career Development: Less chances of promotion. 1st promotion is after 7-8 years, if there are some vacancies left and will be promoted to the post of Director of the department.

Eligibility

Education Qualification:

Posts-wise CGL Qualification detail

Posts Name	Education Qualification
Officer	Bachelor Degree
	Desirable Qualification: Chartered Accountant or cost & Management Accountant or Company Secretary or Masters in Commerce or Masters in Business Studies or Masters in Business Administration (Finance) or Masters in Business Economics.

Statistical Investigator Grade- 2	Bachelor degree with having 60% marks in Mathematics in 12th class OR Bachelor degree with Statistics at degree level
Compiler	Bachelor degree with Statistics or Mathematics or economics subject at degree level
Other Posts- Assistant Audit Officer / Assistant Accounts	Any bachelor degree

2018 Age Limit:

SSC had made changes in the minimum and maximum age limit as compared to the past years. SSC has notified that upper age limit will be 30 years and minimum age limit will be 20 years.

Old age limit: 18-27 years

New age limit: 20-30 years

SSC Relaxation in Upper Age limit

Category	Age-Relaxation beyond 30 years
SC/ ST	5 years
OBC	3 years
PH	10 years
PH + OBC	13 years
PH + SC/ST	15 years
Ex-Servicemen (Unreserved / General)	03 years
Ex-Servicemen (OBC)	06 years
Ex-Servicemen (SC/ST)	08 years
Central Govt. Civilian Employees (General/ Unreserved) who have rendered not less than 3 years regular and continuous service as on crucial date.	Up to 40 years of age

Central Govt. Civilian Employees (OBC) who have rendered not less than 3 years regular and continuous service as on crucial date.	Up to 43 years
Central Govt. Civilian Employees (SC/ST) who have rendered not less than 3 years regular and continuous service as on crucial date.	Up to 45 years of age
Candidates who had ordinarily been domiciled in the State of Jammu & Kashmir(Unreserved/General)	5 years
Candidates who had ordinarily been domiciled in the State of Jammu & Kashmir(OBC)	8 years
Candidates who had ordinarily been domiciled in the State of Jammu & Kashmir(SC/ST)	10 years
Widows / Divorced Women / Women judicially separated and who are not remarried (Unreserved/ General)	Up to 35 years of age
Widows / Divorced Women / Women judicially separated and who are not remarried(OBC)	Up to 38 years of age
Widows / Divorced Women / Women judicially separated and who are not remarried(SC/ST)	Up to 40 years of age
Defence Personnel disabled in operation during hostilities with any foreign country or in a disturbed area and released as a consequence thereof (Unreserved/General)	3 years
Defence Personnel disabled in operation during hostilities with any foreign country or in a disturbed area and released as a consequence thereof (OBC)	6 (3 + 3) years
Defence Personnel disabled in operation during hostilities with any foreign country or in a disturbed area and released as a consequence thereof (SC/ST)	8 (3 + 5) years
Service Clerks in the last year of their colour service in the Armed Forces (Unreserved/General)	Up to 45 years of age
Service Clerks in the last year of their colour service in the Armed Forces (OBC)	Up to 48 years of age
Service Clerks in the last year of their colour service in the Armed Forces (SC/ST)	Up to 50 years of age

	3 years plus length of service rendered by them in connection with census, before retrenchment and Weightage of past service.
Retrenched census employees of Office of Registrar General of India (RGI) (Unreserved/General) (They will be considered only for offices under RGI in their order of merit and subject to the availability of vacancies)	
Retrenched census employees of Office of Registrar General of India(RGI) (OBC) (They will be considered only for offices under RGI in their order of merit and subject to the availability of vacancies)	-do- + 3 years
Retrenched census employees of Office of Registrar General of India (SC/ST) (They will be considered only for offices under RGI in their order of merit and subject to the availability of vacancies)	-do- + 5 years

Nationality: Interested candidate must be an Indian citizen. There are candidates from some other countries who too can apply through an online application form. Here are some of these countries.

1. Nepal and Bhutan

2. A person of Indian origin who has migrated from Myanmar, Pakistan, Sri Lanka, Uganda, East African Countries of Kenya, The United Republic of Tanzania, Zambia, Malawi, Zaire, Ethiopia and Vietnam with the intention of permanently settling in India.

Number of Attempts: The Department of Personnel & Training (DoPT), Ministry of Personnel, Public Grievances & Pensions, Government of India on 20th May has issued a notification regarding amendments to Central Secretariat Service Assistants' Grade (Direct Recruitment Competitive Examination) Regulations, 2010.

As per the Regulations 2010, it was considered to remove the restrictions on the number of attempts in the competitive examination for the direct recruitment of candidates to this Grade.

Reservation Criteria: SSC CGL Reservation will be as decided by the organising body. Here are some key points.

- There will be no state-wise reservation.
- Aspirants belonging to the SC/ ST/ OBC or PH category are eligible for reservation.
- Ex-Serviceman candidates will also have reservation of seats.

- Reservation, wherever applicable and admissible, would be as determined by the indenting Ministries/ Departments/ Offices or Cadres, as per extant Government orders.

- There is no separate reservation for female candidates. However, they are exempted from paying any application fee.

- The candidates from reserved category and female candidates will be given relaxation in age for appearing for the test.

2. SSC-COMBINED HIGHER SECONDARY LEVEL (CHSL) 10+2 EXAMINATION

To provide the benefits of lucrative jobs to the 10+2 qualified candidates, SSC has come up with enormous job opportunities for the candidates who want to start their career with the government jobs, just after qualifying their 10+2 exams.

SSC CHSL Exam is conducted every year for the recruitment of 4 dedicated positions:

- **Lower Division Clerk (LDC)**
- **Data Entry Operators (DEO)**
- **Postal/Sorting Assistants**
- **Court Clerk**

SSC CHSL Post-wise Grade Pay Scale

Post Name	Pay Band	Grade Pay	Gross Salary
LDC (Lower Division Clerk)	PB -1 (5200-20200)	1900	22,392 – 26,026
DEO (Data Entry Operator)	PB -1 (5200-20200)	2400	29,340 – 35,220
Court Clerk	PB -1 (5200-20200)	1900	22,392 – 26,026
Postal Assistant/Sorting Assistant	PB -1 (5200-20200)	2400	29,340 – 35,220

SSC CHSL Allowances & Perks

Type of City	Basic Pay	HRA	TA
X- Category	19900	4776	1350
Y- Category	19900	3184	900
Z- Category	19900	1592	900
X- Category	25500	6120	3600
Y- Category	25500	4080	1800
Z- Category	25500	2040	1800

[**Note:** In 2016, the Government of India announced to implement 7th **Pay Commission** on Central Government jobs from 2017 till 2024. It is proposed to raise the grade pay of SSC CHSL employees from ₹1900 to 2400 (Post wise).]

Classification of City for HRA & TA

X-Category City: Mumbai, Kolkata, Hyderabad, Delhi, Chennai, Bengaluru, Ahmedabad

Y-Category City: Bhopal, Kanpur, Jaipur, Nagpur, Lucknow, Patna, Pune, Surat, Visakhapatnam, Vijayawada, Kochi, Madurai, Coimbatore, Warangal, Trivandrum, Rajkot, Vadodara, Ludhiana, Agra, Meerut, Nashik, Faridabad, Varanasi, Jabalpur, Jamshedpur, Allahabad, Amritsar, Indore, Gorakhpur, Hubli – Dharwad, Bhavnagar, Raipur, Mysore, Mangalore, Belgaum, Guntur, Bhubaneshwar, Cuttack, Amravati, Aurangabad, Srinagar, Bhilai, Rajahmundry, Kakinada, Nellore, Solapur, Ranchi, Guwahati, Gwalior, Chandigarh, Patiala, Jodhpur, Tiruchirappalli, Pondicherry, Salem, Asansol

Z-Category City : All other cities

1. Lower Division Clerk (LDC)

They are associated with daily office tasks and required to take responsibility to maintain the data, files and documents of the office in a systematic manner.

Job Profile & Nature of Work: Lower Division Clerk is generally the first level of clerks in any government organization. His nature of work or job profile includes:

- Dealing with the entire clerical work, maintaining the work flow in office, registration of mails.
- Entering data on computer.
- Indexing, registering and maintaining file registers in an efficient manner.
- Receiving documents and maintaining their record.
- Organising important files and documents for their seniors.
- Typing official letters, notices, notifications and other official documents.
- Preparation of simple drafts and statements.
- Making salary slips of the staff.
- Fetching important data from the library and bringing them for the seniors.
- Supervision of correction of reference books.

Promotion/ Career Development

Beginning your career journey with the first level of clerk i.e. LDC will take you to the promotion on the following positions –

LDC > Assistant / Upper Division Clerk (UDC) > Division Clerk > Assistant Section Officer.

With the rise in designation, the salary packages are also incremented.

Note: However, this will require 5 years of experience at each level of the cadre. This means after having worked for 5 years as an LDC, you will be promoted to UDC and after another 5 years, you will get division clerk post and so on, until you are at the position of assistant section officer.

2.SSC CHSL Data Entry Operator (DEO)

Data Entry Operators are hired for entering, maintaining and updating data on a routine basis. Government organisations have huge amounts of user and therefore, client data needs to be filtered and managed accordingly.

Job Profile & Nature of Work: Handling Computers. So, candidates are required to have a sufficient knowledge of computers, good typing speed and should be well versed with MS Excel, Word and Power Point.

- Preparation of notes and reports.

- Entering and managing the data.

- Inserting customer and account data by inputting text based and numerical information from source documents within specified time limits.

- Collecting all the important information, tables and structure of the company to prepare a proper database for the company.

- Inputting the data and fetching the outputs.

- Scanning and printing the important documents.

- Research and obtain further information for incomplete documents.

- Make it easy for others to access the files and provide them with relevant information about the data entered in the file.

- Apply data program techniques and procedures.

- Writing letters and handling the work in the absence of SSC CHSL LDC.

- Right from the details of the company to its products, clients and sales reports, SSC CHSL DEO maintains all the necessary records.

Note: A DEO will be responsible for maintaining accurate, up-to-date and useable information in the Company's systems.

Promotion/ Career Development

Like LDC Position, Data Entry Operators are also first level position in any government organisation. Based on their performances, such candidates are promoted to the positions given below –

DEO > DEO Grade B > DEO Grade F > DEO Grade C

Note: The ideal candidate has essential data entry skills, like fast typing, with a familiarity with spreadsheets and online forms.

3. SSC CHSL Postal/Sorting Assistant

Postal Assistant (PA) is a clerical cadre post that has the same rank as Sorting Assistant. These posts are usually offered in the Postal Department of the Indian Government. If a candidate is posted as Postal Assistant, he has an advantage that he/she can get the job in home town because language proficiency is the essential criteria for the candidates who are seeking to get recruited as PA in any Govt. organisation.

Job Profile & Nature of Work: Though the duties may vary from department to department, main roles are

- Attending to mails and maintaining the data.
- Customer support, i.e. handling customer queries and providing them a feasible solution.
- Monitoring all the tasks that are related to his/her work.
- Locating the correct address of the addressee, if not located, by locating the address of sender.
- Returning the mail to the sender, in case of not being able to locate the address of the receiver.
- Intra-city transmission of mail between mail offices and post offices.
- Transmission of foreign articles through post office networking.

Department Allocation for Postal Assistants

The Postal Assistant can be recruited in any of the following departments –

i.   Army Postal Service

ii.   Circle Office & Regional Office

iii.   Foreign Post Offices

iv.   Mail Motor Services

v.   Post Offices

vi.   Postal Stores Depots

vii.   Railway Mail Service

viii. Saving Bank Control Organisation

Promotion/ Career Development

The candidates aspiring for the post of Postal Assistant will have the career path as follows –

1.   Postal Assistant to

2.   Lower Selection Grade (LSG) i.e. Supervisor to

3.   Higher Selection Grade (HSG) II i.e. Senior Supervisor to

4.   Higher Selection Grade (HSG) II i.e. Chief Supervisor.

4. SSC CHSL Court Clerk

Court Clerk is the newly introduced position in SSC CHSL Exam. The candidates who are recruited as Court Clerks perform administrative duties in the criminal and civil justice systems, assisting other officers of the court as well as judges and lawyers.

They are either appointed for each court by the dedicated judge to that court or selected by the state level or country level exams. They perform the tasks like Administrative Assistants.

Job Profile & Nature of Work: A Court Clerk performs following tasks –

- Maintaining the court records.
- Administering oaths during court hearings.
- Documenting the receipts of legal documents.
- Sealing up the copies of the courts' orders and judgements.
- Performing accounting and bookkeeping duties.
- Preparing meeting agendas.
- Issuing licenses or permits.
- Preparing draft agendas or bylaws for town or city councils.
- Answering official correspondences.
- Researching and documenting information for judges.

Promotion/ Career Development

These people are promoted to High Courts or Central Administrative Tribunal, National Green Tribunal, Debt Recovery Tribunal or Supreme Court.

The promotions associated are dependent on the person's experience at the same post. They may be promoted to Personal Assistant, Sr. Court Clerk and Sr. Personal Assistant posts.

The career path for a Court Clerk will proceed as follows –

Court Clerk > Assistant Clerk > Bench Clerk > Head Clerk

Eligibility Conditions

1. **Nationality/ Citizenship:** A candidate must be either:

   (a) a citizen of India, or

   (b) a subject of Nepal, or

   (c) a subject of Bhutan, or

   (d) a Tibetan refugee who came to India, before 1ˢᵗ January,1962, with the intention of permanently settling in India, or

   (e) a person of Indian origin who has migrated from Pakistan, Burma, Sri Lanka, East African countries of Kenya, Uganda, the United Republic of Tanzania (Formerly Tanganyika and Zanzibar), Zambia, Malawi, Zaire, Ethiopia and Vietnam with the intention of permanently settling in India.

   Provided that a candidate belonging to categories (b), (c), (d) and (e) above shall be a person in whose favour, a certificate of eligibility has been issued by the Government of India.

2. **Age Limit:** Candidate's age should be 18-27 years as on 01.08.2018 (Candidates born not before 02-08-1991 and not later than 01-08-2000).

Permissible relaxation in upper age limit for different categories is as under:

Code No.	Category	Permissible age relaxation
01	SC/ ST	5 years
02	OBC	3 years
03	Persons with Disabilities (PwD)	10 years
04	PwD + OBC	13 years
05	PwD + SC/ ST	15 years
09	Ex-Servicemen	3 years after deduction of the military service rendered from the actual age as on the closing date
15	Central Govt. Civilian Employees who have rendered not less than 3 years regular and continuous service as on closing date	Up to 40 years of age
19	Central Govt. Civilian Employees (SC/ ST) who have rendered not less than 3 years regular and continuous service as on Closing date.	Up to 45 years of age
21	Candidates who have ordinarily been domiciled in the state of Jammu & Kashmir, during the period from 1st January 1980 to 31st December 1989	5 years
24	Widows/ Divorced Women/ Women judicially separated and who are not remarried	Up to 35 years of age
26	Widows/ Divorced Women/ Women judicially separated and who are not remarried (SC/ ST)	Up to 40 years of age
27	Defence Personnel disabled in operation during hostilities with any foreign country or in a disturbed area and released as a consequence thereof	3 years
29	Defence Personnel disabled in operation during hostilities with any foreign country or in a disturbed area and released as a consequence thereof (SC/ ST)	8 (3+5) years
33	Service Clerks in the last year of their colour service in the Armed Forces	Up to 45 years of age
35	Service Clerks in the last year of their colour service in the Armed Forces (SC/ ST)	Up to 50 years of age

36	Retrenched census employees of Office of Registrar General of India (They will be considered only for offices under RGI in their order of merit and subject to the availability of vacancies)	3 years plus length of service rendered by them in connection with census, before retrenchment, and weightage of past service.

3. Educational Qualification

i. Must have passed 12th Standard or equivalent examination from a recognised Board or University.

ii. For Data Entry Operator in the Office of Comptroller and Auditor General of India (C&AG): 12th Standard pass in Science stream with Mathematics as a subject from a recognised Board or equivalent.

3. SSC-MULTITASKING (NON-TECHNICAL) EXAMINATION

Job Profile: Multi Tasking Staff (MTS) is a group 'C' cadre position that was created as per the 6th CPC recommendation.

Group 'D' posts such as peon, daftary, jamadar, junior gestetner operator, farash, chowkidar, safaiwala etc. were clubbed together recently and henceforth, will be called as MTS.

While the minimum education to become a MTS is to pass Class 10th.Candidates with BE/ B.tech/ MBA degree may find it awkward to work as MTS, considering the type of duties they need to do every day, such as carrying files, taking photocopies, cleaning furniture etc. .But if an aspirant feels comfortable in a Central Govermment job and can handle or perform the above mentioned activities, then he/she may very well apply.

Nature of Work: The roles and responsibilities of the **Multi-Tasking Staff (Non-Technical)** would broadly include:

- Physical maintenance of records of the Section.
- General cleanliness and upkeep of the Section/Unit.
- Carrying of files and papers within the building.
- Photocopying, sending of fax, etc.
- Other non-clerical work in the Section/Unit.
- Assisting in routine office work like maintaining entry register, dispatch, etc.
- Assisting on computer.
- Delivering of posts (outside the building).
- Watch and ward duties.
- Opening and closing of rooms.
- Cleaning of rooms and dusting of furniture etc.
- Cleaning of building, fixtures, etc.
- Work related to his/her ITI qualifications, if it exists.
- Driving of vehicles, if in possession of valid driving license.
- Upkeep of lawns, parks, potted plants, etc.
- Any other work assigned by the superior authority.

Note: Ministries or Departments may add to the above list of duties.

Salary Structure: The salary structure of Multi-Tasking Staff (Non-Technical) in Pay Band- 1 (₹ 5200- ₹20200/-) + Grade Pay ₹1800/- according to three groups of cities, i.e. X, Y, Z, is as follows:

Particulars	City X	City Y	City Z
Grade Pay	1800	1800	1800
Total Pay	7000	7000	7000
Dearness Allowance (DA) @ 113%	7910	7910	7910
House Rent Allowance (HRA)	2100	1400	700
Transport Allowance (TA)	600	400	400
DA of TA	678	452	452
Gross Salary	18288	17162	16462
Central Provident Fund (CPF)	1491	1491	1491
Central Government Health Scheme (CGHS)	125	125	125
Central Government Employees Group Insurance Scheme (CGEGIS)	30	30	30
Deductions	1646	1646	1646
Salary in Hand	16642	15516	14816

Increments: There are two types of increments provided under Pay Band-I scheme, i.e. Annual increments and Promotional increments.

Annual Increments

- Annual increments are to be paid at the rate of 3% of the total pay in the Pay Band and the corresponding Grade Pay.
- The date of annual increments, in all cases, is 1st of July.
- Employees completing six months and above in the scale, as on 1st of July are eligible.

Promotional Increments

Departmental exams are conducted in order to promote employees in the government offices of various ministries. At the time of promotion from one post to another, the grade pay attached to the posts in different levels within the same running pay band, changes.

The Grade Pay increases with every promotion:

- First Promotion: ₹ 1900/- after 3 years of service.
- Second Promotion: ₹ 2000/- after 3 years of service.
- Third Promotion: ₹ 2400/- after 5 years of service.
- And so on up to ₹ 5400/-

Career Progression

According to the Rule 5(2) of Central Civil Accounts Service (Lower Division Clerk, Group 'C' post) Recruitment Rules 2010, 5 % of the vacancies in the grade of LDCs are to be filled by promotion on seniority basis through common "Range of Seniority" from amongst Group 'C' staff (Multi-Tasking Staff) who have three year regular service in post with the Grade Pay of ₹ 1800.

Eligibility Criteria

Nationality / Citizenship: Same as in Combined Higher Secondary Level (CHSL) 10+2 Examination

Educational Qualification: Candidates must have passed Matriculation Examination OR equivalent with good academic records from a recognised Board / Institute.

Candidates who have not acquired but will acquire the educational qualification and acquire documentary evidence from the Board/University are also eligible.

Age Limit: Age of candidates should not be less than 18 years and not more than 25 years.

Candidate should note that Date of Birth as recorded in the Matriculation / Secondary Examination Certificate or an equivalent certificate, available on the date of submission of application, will only be accepted by the Commission for determining the age eligibility.

Relaxation in Age: Same as in Combined Higher Secondary Level (CHSL) 10+2 Examination.

4. SSC-SCIENTIFIC ASSISTANT EXAM

Job Profile & Nature of Work: Broadly, the SSC Scientific Assistant work profile consists of the following duties:

- The first and foremost duty of SSC Scientific Assistant is to offer support to the scientist in research and educational subject matter pertaining to the research in which Indian Meteorological Department (IMD) is engaged.
- They have to assist the scientist in carrying out various researches of IMD.
- They are responsible for performing administrative tasks.
- They need to coordinate different studies for the successful completion of the research project.
- They need to carry out researches related to weather forecasting, flood forecasting and planning.

Salary & Allowances

Here is the salary structure of an SSC Scientific Assistant.

- The Final Salary or pay Band of ₹ 9300-34800 is now ₹ 35400/- (Basic Salary) after the approval of 7th Pay Commission. It will increase along the career path.

- Apart from the salary, there are a number of allowances that he/she gets. This will cover Travel Allowance, HRA & DA making total salary of ₹ 48912.

- However, the SSC Scientific Assistant Salary and other allowances are also determined by the cities in which an employee is employed in. This is as given in the table below,

Salary & Allowances	City-X	City-Y	City-Z
Basic Salary	35400	35400	35400
Travel Allowance	3600	3600	1800
HRA (24%)	8496	5664	2832
DA (4%)	1416	1416	1416
Total	**48912**	**46082**	**41448**

Promotion/ Career Development

There is a tremendous scope for progress in this job and it gives bright future prospects. SSC Scientific Assistant also has the chances of being promoted to Higher Scale level. This is a government job which ensures job security and has several other benefits. Aspirants should consider this as an entry position to make a career in this sector.

Eligibility Criteria

Nationality / Citizenship: Same as in Combined Higher Secondary Level (CHSL) 10+2 Examination.

Educational Qualification: The candidates should have their Graduation passing certificate, with Science subjects and Physics as a compulsory subject.

Candidates can also have the diploma certificate in electronics & telecommunication engineering.

Age Limitation: The minimum age limit to apply for this exam is 18 years, whereas the maximum age limit to apply for this exam is 30 years.

The candidates will also get the relaxation in age criteria as per the table which is given below,

S. No.	Categories	Relaxation criteria for age
1	Scheduled Caste & Tribe	5 years
2	Other Backward class	3 years
3	Handicapped	10 years
4	Handicapped + OBC	13 years
5	Handicapped + SC/ST	15 years
6	Ex-Servicemen (General)	3 years after deduction of the military service rendered from the actual age as on the closing date for receipt of application

		6 years(3 years + 3 years) after deduction of the military service rendered from the actual age as on the closing date for receipt of application
7	Ex-Servicemen (OBC)	

5. SSC-STENOGRAPHERS GRADE 'C' AND 'D' EXAMINTION

Job Profile

Staff Selection Commission is authorised to enroll eligible aspirants for Stenographers in various Department/ Ministries. Moreover, these posts are under two Grades – C and D. The specific nature of a Stenographer's work varies because it depends on where you are posted.

Candidates who will be selected for Stenographer Grade 'C' posts will be posted in Delhi at Ministries/Departments of the Central Government.

Applicants who will be appointed for Stenographer Grade 'D', have to work under Group X and Group Y.

- In Group X, Stenographers work in Departments of Central Government located primarily in Delhi.

- In Group Y, Stenographers work in Departments of Central Government located throughout India.

Nature of Work: SSC Stenographer's roles and responsibilities are:

Speech Writing

- The main role of Stenographers is to work with assigned senior officers and note down any speech given by the officer.

- Their job includes doing the above task efficiently as these speech details can be important governmental records.

Press Conference Briefing

- Stenographers also have to attend the press conferences along with the assigned officer or minister.

- They have to note down the details and speeches of the conference.

- They need to help the assigned officer or minister people in making press releases of these press conferences.

Minister/Officer Assisting

- Another work for stenographers is to assist the assigned officers and ministers in preparing speech.

- Stenographers are involved in different governmental proceedings; they know important information about it that is useful for the officer/minister.

Public Relations Helping

- Stenographers make notes daily.

- These notes are about different governmental departments and their stands on issues.
- This information needs to reach public and so stenographers share these details with the Public Relations Officers, who in turn pass them on to the public.

Salary & Allowances

As SSC Stenographer will be appointed in Grades i.e. C & D, thus the pay scale for each grade will differ as given below:

Category of Salary	Grade-C	Grade-D
Pay Scale	9300 – 34800	5200 – 20200
Grade Pay	4200 (Pay Band 2)	2400 (Pay Band 1)
Initial Pay	5200	5200
Total Pay (1) + (2)	14500	7600

Other Allowances

Along with the salary, the Staff Selection Commission will also offer some other benefits to the candidates who will be appointed for Stenographer posts. These allowances will be paid as per the directive of the Government of India. These allowances are:

- Dearness Allowance

- House Rent Allowance

- Transport Allowance

- Mediclaim

Promotion/ Career Development

While the eligibility criteria for SSC Stenographer are not many, there is a tremendous scope for progress within this job as well. On the basis of experience, the selected candidates will be promoted from one post to another post.

- Promotions are time-bound. Hence, with proper work, Stenographers will easily get promotion.
- These people will be promoted according to their seniority level or working years.
- The people working in this capacity can increase their Grade after clearing the departmental exams conducted by the UPSC.
- The pay scale can also increase as much as ₹ 23,000 per month.
- The promotions are as follows:
- Stenographer Grade C(PA) → Private Secretary(PS) → Principal Private Secretary(PPS) → Senior Principal Private Secretary(Sr. PPS) → Principal Staff Officer(PSO).

Eligibility Criteria

Nationality / Citizenship: Same as in Combined Higher Secondary Level (CHSL) 10+2 Examination.

Educational Qualification: Candidate must have passed the 12th examination or its equivalent from any board. The candidate has to produce his/her marksheet or proof of passing the examination by 1st August 2018.

Age Limitation: Candidate must have attained the age of 18 years and must be below 27 years of age as measured on 01.08.2018.

Category	Age Relaxation
SC/ST	5 years
OBC	3 years
PH (GEN)	10 years
PH (SC/ST)	15 years
PH(OBC)	13 years
Ex-Servicemen (GEN)	3 years
Ex-Servicemen (SC/ST)	8 years
Ex-Servicemen (OBC)	6 years

6. SSC- CONSTABLES (GD) IN CAPFS, NIA & SSF EXAMINATION

Job Profile & Nature of Work

1. The candidate will be appointed as a guard or an escort.
2. Selected candidates are liable to obey all orders and duties given by the Station House Officer (SHO).
3. GD Constables are responsible for all activities in the absence of Assistant Sub-inspector and sub-inspectors.
4. GD Constable has the right to investigate any case when the Sub-inspector asks him to do so.
5. He/She may also be asked to perform duties of a station writer in rural and urban areas.
6. If he/she is promoted to the post of a head constable, then he/she will be employed to be in charge of police stations.

Salary & Allowances

Basic Salary of SSC GD Constable is ₹ 5,200-20,000 with a grade pay of ₹ 2000. He/she will also be entitled to other benefits like medical facilities, pension, gratuity and annual leaves.

Promotion/ Career Development

GD Constables will be promoted to higher ranks, starting from Senior constable to Inspector based on their performance. Their career path is as follows:

- Senior Constables
- Head Constables

- Assistant Sub-Inspector
- Sub-Inspector
- Inspector

Eligibility Criteria

Physical Standards for GD Constable Exam 2018

Height

For Males: 170 cms

For Females: 157 cms

Chest

For Male: Expanded 80 cms

Minimum expansion 5 cms

Weight: Proportionate as per the height and medical standard for male and female

SSC GD Physical Eligibility (Male Candidates)			
Category of Candidates	Height (in cms)	Chest (in cms)	
		Unexpanded	Expanded (Min. of 4 cms)
Only GENERAL/ OBC	170	81	85
Scheduled Castes (SC)	170	81	85
Scheduled Tribes (ST)	165	76	80
Residents of hill areas i.e. Garhwalis, Kumaonis, Gorkhas, Dogras, Marathas and candidates belonging to states of Sikkim, Nagaland, Arunachal Pradesh, Manipur, Tripura, Mizoram, Meghalaya, Assam, Himachal Pradesh, Kashmir and Leh & Ladakh regions of J&K.	165	76	80
Sons of serving, deceased, retired police personnel/ Multi-Tasking Staff (Formerly group 'D' employees) of Delhi Police.	165	76	80
SSC GD Physical Eligibility (Female Candidates)			
Only GENERAL/ OBC	157	-	-
Scheduled Castes (SC) and Scheduled Tribes (ST)	155	-	-
Residents of hill areas i.e. Garhwalis, Kumaonis, Gorkhas, Dogras, Marathas and candidates belonging to the states of Sikkim, Nagaland, Arunachal Pradesh, Manipur, Tripura, Mizoram, Meghalaya, Assam, Himachal Pradesh, Kashmir and Leh & Ladakh regions of J&K.	155	-	-

Daughters of serving, deceased, retired police personnel/ Multi-Tasking Staff (Formerly group 'D' employees) of Delhi Police.	152	-	-

Educational Qualifications: Candidates who want to apply for GD Constable (BSF, CRPF, CISF, ITBP, SSF, SSB, NIA and riflemen) must have a 12th passed Certificate from any recognised Board/ University.

If a candidate has not acquired the educational qualification at the time of filling of application form, the Delhi Police will cancel the candidature of such candidate.

Age Limit: Candidate's age should be between 18 to 23 years. Age relaxation will be applicable as per the government rules for the candidates from the reserved category.. The age relaxation will be applicable according to the table mentioned below.

S. No.	Category	Age Limit
1	OBC	26 years
2	ST/SC	28 years
3	Ex-Servicemen (GEN)	26 years
4	Ex-Servicemen (OBC)	29 years
5	Ex-Servicemen (SC/ST)	31 years
6	Domiciled in the State of Jammu & Kashmir during the period from 1st Jan 1980 to 31st Dec 1989 (GEN)	28 Years
7	Domiciled in the State of Jammu & Kashmir during the period from 1st Jan 1980 to 31st Dec 1989 (OBC)	31 Years
8	Domiciled in the State of Jammu & Kashmir during the period from 1st Jan 1980 to 31st Dec 1989 (SC/ST)	33 Years
9	Children and dependent of victims KILLED in the 1984 riots OR communal riots of 2002 in Gujarat (GEN)	28 years
10	Children and dependent of victims KILLED in the 1984 riots OR communal riots of 2002 in Gujarat (OBC)	31 years
11	Children and dependent of victims KILLED in the 1984 riots OR communal riots of 2002 in Gujarat (SC/ST)	33 years

Nationality:

- A citizen of India or
- A subject of Nepal or a subject of Bhutan or Tibetan Refugee who came to India before 1st January 1962, to be settled permanently in India.

A person of Indian origin migrated from Pakistan, Burma, Sri Lanka, East African countries of Kenya, the United Republic of Tanzania (formerly Tanganyika and Zanzibar), Uganda, Zambia, Malawi, Zaire, Ethiopia, and Vietnam with the intention of permanently settling in India

7. SSC- SUB INSPECTOR IN CPOS EXAM

SSC has recently announced a notification for the recruitment in various forces i.e. Central Industrial Security Force (CISF), Central Reserve Police Force (CRPF), Indo-Tibetan Border Police Force (ITBPF), Sashastra Seema Bal (SSB), Delhi Police(DP), Border Security Force (BSF) and Central Industrial Security Force (CISF).

The different posts and postcodes are given below:

S. No.	Post Code	Name of the Posts
1.	A	Sub – Inspector in Delhi Police
2.	B	Sub – Inspector of Border Security Force
3.	C	Sub – Inspector of Industrial Security Force
4.	D	Sub – Inspector in Central Reserve Police Force
5.	E	Sub – Inspector in Indo-Tibetan Border Police Force
6.	F	Sub – Inspector in Sashastra Seema Bal
7.	G	Assistant Sub – Inspector in Central Industrial Security Force

Salary Structure

Sub – Inspector (SI) in Central Armed Police Forces (CAPFs)

- Grade Pay: 4200
- Pay Scale: 35,400 – 1,12,400
- Group "B" (Non – Gazetted) Non – Ministerial

Sub – Inspector (Executive: Male & Female)- in Delhi Police

- Grade Pay: 4200
- Pay Scale: 35,400 – 1,12,400
- Group "C" (Non – Gazetted)

Assistant Sub – Inspector (ASI) (Executive) in Central Industrial Security Forces (CISF)

- Grade Pay: 2800
- Pay Scale: 29,200 – 92,300
- Group"C" (Non – Gazetted)

Job Profile & Nature of Work

1.Delhi Police: Sub – Inspector of Delhi Police is responsible for maintaining the Law & Order.

2. Assistant Sub – Inspector in CISF

They are responsible for the following duties.

- Airport security
- Industrial security
- Search operation
- Power of seizure
- Clerical duties

3. CAPFs

These are Paramilitary Forces. Five forces come under CAPFs. The candidates who are selected for CAPFs can be posted anywhere in India.

4. BSF

This force is responsible for the following duties.

- Prevent trans-border crimes
- Promote the sense of security
- Protect the border between India and Pakistan
- Assist the refugees.

5. CISF

This force is responsible for the following duties.

- Protect the industrial units
- Protect the government infrastructure projects all over India
- Provide consultancy services to various private and Government-owned organisations.

6. ITBPF

They are responsible for the following duties.

- Promote sense of security among local people living near borders
- Prevent border violation
- Provide security at northern borders and restore and maintain peace
- Prevent trans-border smuggling and illegal immigration.

7. SSB

This force is responsible for the following duties.

- Prevent anti-national activities
- Prevent cross-border crimes and smuggling.

Promotion & Career Development

The candidates are selected for ASI in CISF then they can get promoted to the post of SI but after 5 years of regular service. For the promotion, candidates are chosen from the Zonal Security. Candidates can also get the promotion with the help of department examination.

Eligibility Criteria

Educational Qualifications

1. A candidate must have a Bachelor's Degree in any discipline from a recognised University.

2. For the post of SI in Delhi Police (only) – Male candidates must possess a valid Driving License for LMV (Motorcycle and Car) as on the date fixed for Physical Endurance and Standard Tests. Otherwise, they will not be allowed to undergo Physical Endurance and Standard Tests.

Age Limit

Category	Minimum age limit	Maximum age limit
General Candidates	20 Years	25 Years
OBC Candidates	20 Years	28 Years
SC/ST Candidates	20 Years	30 Years
General Candidates (Jammu & Kashmir domiciled during 1st January 1980 – 31st December 1989)	20 Years	30 Years
OBC Candidates (Jammu & Kashmir domiciled during 1st January 1980 – 31st December 1989)	20 Years	33 Years
SC/ST Candidates (Jammu & Kashmir domiciled during 1st January 1980 – 31st December 1989)	20 Years	35 Years
For Group 'B' and 'C' Posts:(i) General Candidates (Ex-Servicemen)	20 Years	28 Years
(ii) OBC Candidates (Ex-Servicemen)	20 Years	31 Years
(iii) SC/ST Candidates (Ex-Servicemen)	20 Years	33 Years
For Group 'C' Posts Only:(i) General Candidates (Widows/Divorced Women/ Women judicially separated and who are not remarried)	20 Years	35 Years
(ii) OBC Candidates (Widows/Divorced Women/ Women judicially separated and who are not remarried)	20 Years	38 Years
(iii) SC/ST Candidates (Widows/Divorced Women/ Women judicially separated and who are not remarried)	20 Years	40 Years

Physical Standard Test (PST Criteria)

Category	Height	Chest (Normal in cms)	Chest (Expanded in (cms)
Male (General)	170 cms (5'7")	80 cms	85 cms
Male (Hill area)	165 cms (5'5")	80 cms	85 cms
Male (ST)	162.5 cms (5'4")	77 cms	82 cms

Female (General)	157 cms (5'2")	-	-
Female (Hill Area)	155 cms (5'1")	-	-
Female (ST)	154 cms (5'0")	-	-

Physical Efficiency (Endurance) Test (PET) (For all Posts)

Activity	PET Criteria (Male)	PET Criteria (Female)
100 Metre Race	Completed in 16 Seconds	Completed in 18 Seconds
1600/800 Metre Race	1600 Metre Race Completed in 6.5 Minutes	800 Metre Race Completed in 4 Minutes
Long Jump	3.65 Metres in 3 Chances	2.7 Metres in 3 Chances
High Jump	1.2 Metres in 3 Chances	0.9 Metres in 3 Chances
Shot Put	4.5 Metres in 3 chances	-

8. SSC- JUNIOR ENGINEER (CIVIL, MECHANICAL & ELECTRICAL) EXAMINATION

Various departments come under SSC Junior Engineer (JE) Exam

Given below is the list of department to which a successful candidate may get into if he/she is selected in SSC- JE Exam.

- CWC (Central Water Commission)- Junior Engineer (**Civil**)

- CWC (Central Water Commission) – Junior Engineer (**Mechanical**)

- CPWD (Central Public Works Department) – Junior Engineer (**Civil**)

- CPWD (Central Public Works Department) – Junior Engineer (**Electrical**)

- DP (Department of Post) – Junior Engineer (**Civil**)

- DP (Department of Post) – Junior Engineer (**Electrical**)

- MES (Military Engineering Service) – (**Civil**) Junior Engineer

- MES (Military Engineering Service) – **Electrical and Mechanical** Junior Engineer

- MES (Military Engineering Service) – **Quantity Surveying and Contract** Junior Engineer

Salary Structure 2018

Given below is a chart for the post wise/department wise grade pay, gross salary and inhand salary for the posts offered to a candidate successful in the JE exam.

Department name	Post Name	Grade Pay	Gross Salary	Inhand Salary
CWC (Central Water Commission)	Junior Engineer (Civil)	4200	32,667 to 37,119	29,455 to 33,907
CWC (Central Water Commission)	Junior Engineer (Mechanical)	4200	32,667 to 37,119	29,455 to 33,907
CPWD (Central Public Works Department)	Junior Engineer (Civil)	4200	32,667 to 37,119	29,455 to 33,907
CPWD (Central Public Works Department)	Jr Engineer (Electrical)	4200	32,667 to 37,119	29,455 to 33,907
DP (Department of Post)	Junior Engineer (Civil)	4200	32,667 to 37,119	29,455 to 33,907
DP (Department of Post)	Junior Engineer (Electrical)	4200	32,667 to 37,119	29,455 to 33,907
MES (Military Engineering Service)	Civil Junior Engineer	4200	32,667 to 37,119	29,455 to 33,907
MES (Military Engineering Service)	Electrical and Mechanical Junior Engineer	4200	32,667 to 37,119	29,455 to 33,907
MES (Military Engineering Service)	JE Quantity Surveying and Contract	4200	32,667 to 37,119	29,455 to 33,907

Allowances for Junior Engineer

All the JE, irrespective of post, will get various allowances, in addition to the in hand salary. Following are the few allowances that the JEs will get.

- Dearness Allowances (DA)
- Medical Allowances
- Special Allowances.

SSC JE Salary after 7th Pay Commission

The salary of a SSC JE is revised after the 7th Pay Commission and now they will get around 44,000 in hand.

Job Profile & Nature of Work

A newly recruited JE will be given the charge of a section in one of the departments mentioned above. He or she will be responsible for the various functions carried out by the section. It starts from taking stock of daily work done by the labourers to making plans for the next day regarding allotment of work, supervising the work etc. The various functions under SSC JE job profile are:

Supervision of Work: In the initial days, JE will have to ensure supervision of work. This is the main function of an engineer as this provides the best opportunity to understand the functions of an organisation.

Planning: JEs will start from a small level by making plans and estimates from a repair or renovation work. Then, he/ she will need to make an exhaustive plan for flagship activities carried out by his or her section.

Accounts: A JE is responsible for maintaining the stock of his or her section efficiently. Along with this, they have to pass bills for the work done by the contractor or for any expenditure incurred by the section.

Scheme Execution: In the organisations, there are various government schemes which require execution. Junior Engineers need to ensure smooth flow of work related to these schemes.

Assisting Seniors: A JE is the boss of his or her section and therefore, he/ she will have the ultimate opportunity of briefing up about their sections. If his or her section is dealing with an important project, he or she has to report to the higher authority on a daily basis.

Promotion & Career Development

Junior Engineer will get promotions as follows:

1. Senior Section Engineer

2. Executive Engineer

The JEs can also write departmental exams and get the higher ranks within the organisation/department from time to time.

Eligibility Criteria

Educational Qualification

Posts	Educational Qualification
Junior Engineer (Civil)	CPWD – B.E. / B.Tech. / Diploma in Civil Engineering from a recognised University/Institute
Junior Engineer (Civil & Mechanical)	Central Water Commission – B.E. / B.Tech. / Diploma in Civil/Mechanical Engineering from a recognised University/Institute
Junior Engineer (Electrical)	CPWD – B.E./B.Tech /Diploma in Electrical Engineering from a recognised University/Institute

Junior Engineer (Civil)	Department of Posts – B.E. / B.Tech. / 3 years Diploma in Civil Engineering from a recognised University/Institute
Junior Engineer (Electrical)	Department of Posts- B.E. / B.Tech. / 3 years Diploma in Electrical Engineering from a recognised University/ Institute
Junior Engineer (Electrical & Mechanical)	MES – B.E./B.Tech. in Electrical/Mechanical Engineering OR 3 years Diploma in Electrical/Mechanical Engineering from a recognised University/Institute and with 2 years work experience in Electrical/Mechanical Engineering works
Junior Engineer (Civil)	MES – B.E./B.Tech. in Civil Engineering OR 3 years Diploma in Civil Engineering from a recognised University/Institute and with 2 years work experience in Civil Engineering works
Junior Engineer (QS&C)	MES – B.E./B.Tech. / 3 years Diploma in Civil engineering from a recognised University/Institute OR Passed Intermediate examination in Building and Quantity Surveying (Sub Divisional-II) from the Institute of Surveyors (India)

Age Limit

Candidates can check the table given below to have an idea about the minimum and maximum age for all the posts as on January 1, 2018.

Post name	Age	Organisation
Junior Engineer (Civil)	18- 32 years	Central Water Commission
Junior Engineer (Mech)	18-32 years	Central Water Commission
Junior Engineer (Civil)	18-32 years	CPWD
Junior Engineer (Elect)	18-32 years	CPWD
Junior Engineer (Civil)	18- 30 years	Department of Post
Junior Engineer (Electrical and Mechanical)	18- 30 years	MES
Junior Engineer (Surveying and Contract)	18-27 years	MES
Junior Engineer (Civil)	18- 30 years	MES
Junior Engineer (Electrical / Mechanical)	18- 30 years	Farrakka Barrage (Project)
Junior Engineer (Civil)	18- 30 years	Farrakka Barrage (Project)

Junior Engineer (Civil)	18- 30 years	Central Water Power Research Station
Junior Engineer (Electrical)	18- 30 years	Central Water Power Research Station
Junior Engineer (Naval Quality Assurance)- Mechanical)	18- 30 years	Date of Quality Assurance (Naval)
Junior Engineer (Naval Quality Assurance)- (Electrical)	18-30 years	Date of Quality Assurance (Naval)

Relaxations in Age Limit

Codes	Category	Age-Relaxation
1	SC/ST	5 Years
2	OBC	3 Years
3	PH (OH/HH)	10 Years
4	PH (OH/HH) + OBC	13 Years
5	PH (OH/HH) + SC/ST	15 Years
6	Ex-Servicemen (Unreserved / General)	03 years after deduction of the military service rendered from the actual age as on the closing date
7	Ex-Servicemen (OBC)	06 years (3 years + 3 years) after deduction of the military service rendered from the actual age as on the closing date
8	Ex-Servicemen (SC/ ST)	08 years (3 years + 5 years) after deduction of the military service rendered from the actual age as on the closing date
12	Central Govt. Civilian Employees (General/Unreserved) who have rendered not less than 3 years regular and continuous service as on Closing date	05 Years
13	Central Govt. Civilian Employees (OBC) who have rendered not less than 3 years regular and continuous service as on Closing date	08 (5+3) years

14	Central Govt. Civilian Employees (SC/ST) who have rendered not less than 3 years regular and continuous service as on Closing date	10 (5+5) years
21	Candidates who had ordinarily been domiciled in the State of Jammu & Kashmir (Unreserved/ General)	5 years
22	Candidates who had ordinarily been domiciled in the State of Jammu & Kashmir (OBC)	8 years
23	Candidates who had ordinarily been domiciled in the State of Jammu & Kashmir (SC/ST)	10 years
27	Defence Personnel disabled in operation during hostilities with any foreign country or in a disturbed area and released as a consequence thereof (Unreserved/ General)	5 years
28	Defence Personnel disabled in operation during hostilities with any foreign country or in a disturbed area and released as a consequence thereof (OBC)	8 (5+3) years
29	Defence Personnel disabled in operation during hostilities with any foreign country or in a disturbed area and released as a consequence thereof (SC/ST)	10 (5+5) years

Nationality

A candidate must be either:

- ❖ a citizen of India, or
- ❖ a subject of Nepal, or
- ❖ a subject of Bhutan, or
- ❖ a Tibetan refugee who came over to India before 1st January, 1962 with the intention of permanently settling in India, or
- ❖ a person of Indian origin who has migrated from Pakistan, Myanmar, Sri Lanka, East African countries of Kenya, Uganda, the United Republic of Tanzania (Formerly Tanganyika and Zanzibar), Zambia, Malawi, Zaire, Ethiopia and Vietnam with the intention of permanently settling in India.
- ❖ Any applicant who belongs to the categories (b), (c) and (d) should have a certificate of eligibility issued in his or her favour by the Government of India.

9. SSC- LDC GRADE LIMITED DEPARTMENTAL COMPETITIVE EXAMINATION

Staff Selection Commission will hold a Limited Departmental Competitive Examination for the recruitment to vacancies in Lower Division Clerk (LDC) Grade reserved for regularly appointed Group 'C' Staff in the Grade Pay of ₹ 1800 in

(i) Central Secretariat Clerical Service

(ii) Armed Forces Headquarters Clerical Service

(iii) Indian Foreign Service (IFS) (B)

(iv) Central Passport Organisation under Ministry of External Affairs

(v) Ministry of Railways (Railway Board)

(vi) Department of Legal Affairs (DoLA) and

(vii) O/o Registrar General of India under the Ministry of Home Affairs

Only eligible employees for each of the above cadres will be considered for appointment in respective vacancies in the cadres.

The examination will be held at New Delhi, Kolkata, Mumbai, Allahabad, Chennai, Bengaluru, Guwahati, Chandigarh and Raipur.

In case, the Commission receives less than ten (10) applications from eligible candidates for appearing in the examination at a particular centre, such candidates may be directed by the Commission to appear from the Delhi Centre at their own expense and risk.

There will be no Centre at any Indian Mission abroad. A candidate serving at an Indian Mission abroad will have to appear in this examination from any of the Examination Centres mentioned above on his/her own.

SSC LDC Departmental Exam 2018

Post Name: Lower Division Clerk

Eligibility Criteria (as on 01.01.2018)

- Applicants must have passed 12th Standard examination from a recognised Board or equivalent for SSC LDC Recruitment.

- Applicants who do not possess the minimum education qualification as on 01.01.2018 are not eligible to apply for SSC LDC Departmental Competitive Exam.

Length of Service

As on 01.08.2018, the candidates must have rendered not less than three years' regular service as a Group-C employee with Grade Pay of ₹1800.

Note-I: A Group 'C' employee with Grade Pay of ₹1800, who is on deputation to ex-Cadre post, with the approval of the Competent authority, shall be eligible to be admitted to the examination, if otherwise eligible.

Note-II: A Group 'C' employee with Grade Pay of ₹1800, who has been appointed to an Ex-Cadre post or to another service on transfer, and continues to have a lien in the said Group 'C' post for the time being, shall also be eligible to be admitted to the examination, if otherwise eligible.

Limitation on Age

Age of candidates should not be more than 45 years as on 01.01.2018. This age limit is relaxable up to a maximum of 5 years for SC/ST applicants.

Salary Offered

Selected applicants will get an impressive amount of ₹5200-20200 as salary with Grade Pay of ₹1900.

Method of Selection

- After screening of applications, shortlisted candidates will be called for Written Examination / Typewriting Test / Personal Interview.

- The allocation will be made service-wise, as per the vacancies. The final merit position will be determined by adding marks of Paper-I and Paper-II.

Scheme of Examination

Paper No	Subject	Maximum Marks	Duration and Timing for General Candidates	Duration and Timings for VH/OH
I	Short Essay (Hindi or English)	100	1 hour 30 minutes 10.00 AM to 11.30 AM	2 Hours 10.00 AM to 12.00 Noon
II Objective Type in Computer Based Mode	Language (General English or Samanya Hindi) (50 questions) – 50 marks General Knowledge (50 questions) – 50 marks	100	2 Hours 02.00 PM to 04.00 PM	2 Hours 40 minutes 02.00 PM to 04.40 PM

10. SSC- JUNIOR HINDI TRANSLATORS (JHT) EXAMINATION

Staff Selection Commission conducts the recruitment exam for the candidates for the post of the Junior Hindi Translator. The candidates, who will be selected for the post of the JHT, will have to do the job of the translator at junior level in various departments and the agencies of the Central Government.

Some of the places of postings are as follows:

- JHT in Central Secretariat Official Language Service (CSOLS)
- JHT in Ministry of Railways (Railway Board)
- JHT in Armed Forces Headquarters (AFHQ)
- JHT in subordinate offices
- Hindi Pradhyapak in Central Hindi Training Institute (CHTI)

Job Profile & Nature of Work

The Junior Hindi Translators have to perform different works allotted by the departments.

Nature of work is different in different agencies/departments, as given below:

1. **Junior Hindi Translator in Central Secretariat Official Language Service (CSOLS)**

- Translation/Typing of the documents from English to Hindi.
- Ensuring the use/promotion of Hindi.
- Any other work assigned by the superior authority.

2. **JHT in Ministry of Railways (Railway Board)**

- Translation of various documents from Hindi to English and vice-versa.
- Assisting Hindi Officer in organising Hindi Meeting and Hindi Workshop.
- Maintaining files and records relating to Hindi.

3. **JHT in Armed Forces Headquarters (AFHQ)**

- Translation of various documents from Hindi to English and vice-versa.
- Maintaining files and records relating to office work.

4. **Junior Hindi Translator in Subordinate Offices**

- Translating various official journals, books, forms, circulars, manuals, articles etc. in Hindi.
- Translating of day to day official letters, office orders, departmental orders etc. from English to Hindi and vice versa.
- Assisting Hindi Officer in the implementation of work of official language policy and in various official matters.

5. **Hindi Pradhyapak in Central Hindi Training Institute (CHTI)**

- Assisting Hindi Officer in organising Hindi Meeting and Hindi Workshop.
- Acting as a Teaching Officer for Hindi Teaching Scheme.

Salary Structure

S.No.	Post	Post Code	Pay Scale	Pay Band
1	Junior Hindi Translator in CSOLS	A	Level 6 (Group B)	35400-112400
2	JHT in Railway Board	B	Level 6 (Group B)	35400-112400
3	Junior Hindi Translator in AFHQ	C	Level 6 (Group B)	35400-112400
4	Junior Hindi Translator in Subordinate Offices	D	Level 6 (Group B)	35400-112400
5	Hindi Translator in various Central Government Ministries/ Departments	E	Level 7 (Group B)	44900-142400
6	JTL in Subordinate Offices	F	Level 6 (Group B)	35400-112400
7	Hindi Pradhyapak in Central Hindi Training Institute (CHTI)	G	Level 8 (Group B)	47600-151100

The structure given above is the official structure for the salary of JHT in different departments. The allowances will be according to the pattern or budget of the respective department.

JHT Promotion Chances

The promotion of the candidates working at the post of JHT will be according to the department in which they are working. Thus, the candidates will get the promotion to the upper class of the post, according to the department. Further, the promotion will be based on the performance of the employee in the office works. The candidates can also get the promotion by appearing for the exams of the respective department.

Eligibility Criteria

Education

Education Qualification for the Post Code "A" to "E"

- Candidates must have passed Master's degree from the recognised university in Hindi with English as an elective or compulsory subject or as the medium of examination at the degree level. **OR**
- Candidates must have passed Master's degree from the recognised university in any subject other than Hindi or English, with Hindi medium and English as an elective or compulsory subject or as the medium of examination at the degree level. **OR**

- Candidates must have done recognised diploma or certificate course in translation from Hindi to English & vice versa or two years' experience of translation work from Hindi to English and vice versa in Central or State Government Office, including Government of India Undertaking.

Education Qualification for the Post Code "F"

- Candidates must have passed Master's degree from the recognised university in Hindi or English with English or Hindi as an elective or compulsory subject at degree level. **OR**
- Candidates must have passed Bachelor's degree with Hindi and English as main subjects (which includes the term compulsory and elective).

Education Qualification for the Post Code "G"

Candidates must have passed Bachelor's degree in Hindi with English as one of the subjects at degree level, either as compulsory or optional from the recognised university or institute plus Master's degree in any subject from the recognised university or institute plus Bachelor of Education from the recognised university/ institute.

Age Limit

Candidates who want to apply for SSC Junior Hindi Translator 2018 examination, age should not be more than 30 years as on 1st January, 2018.

Age Relaxation

S.No	Category	Age-Relaxation beyond 30 Years
1	SC/ ST	5 years
2	OBC	3 years
3	PH	10 years
4	PH + OBC	13 years
5	PH + SC/ST	15 years
6	Ex-Servicemen (Unreserved / General)	03 years
7	Ex-Servicemen (OBC)	06 years
8	Ex-Servicemen (SC/ST)	08 years
9	Central Govt. Civilian Employees (General/ Unreserved) who have rendered not less than 3 years regular and continuous service as on crucial date.	5 years
10	Central Govt. Civilian Employees (OBC) who have rendered not less than 3 years regular and continuous service as on closing date.	8 (5 +3) years

11	Central Govt. Civilian Employees (SC/ST) who have rendered not less than 3 years regular and continuous service as on closing date.	10(5+5) years
12	Candidates who have ordinarily been domiciled in the State of Jammu & Kashmir(Unreserved/General)	05 years
13	Candidates who have ordinarily been domiciled in the State of Jammu & Kashmir(OBC)	08 years
14	Candidates who have ordinarily been domiciled in the State of Jammu & Kashmir(SC/ST)	10 years
15	Defence Personnel disabled in operation during hostilities with any foreign country or in a disturbed area and released as a consequence thereof (Unreserved/General)	5 years
16	Defence Personnel disabled in operation during hostilities with any foreign country or in a disturbed area and released as a consequence thereof (OBC)	8 (5+3) years
17	Defence Personnel disabled in operation during hostilities with any foreign country or in a disturbed area and released as a consequence thereof (SC/ST)	10 (5+5) years

Nationality / Citizenship

A candidate must be either:

(a)   a citizen of India, or

(b)   a subject of Nepal, or

(c)   a subject of Bhutan, or

(d)   a Tibetan refugee who came over to India, before the 1st January 1962, with the intention of permanently settling in India, or

(e)   a person of Indian origin who has migrated from Pakistan, Myanmar, Sri Lanka, East African countries of Kenya, Uganda, the United Republic of Tanzania(Formerly Tanganyika and Zanzibar), Zambia, Malawi, Zaire, Ethiopia and Vietnam with the intention of permanently settling in India.

SSC Exam Pattern & Trend Analysis

A. EXAM PATTERN OF QUESTION PAPERS

1. COMBINED GRADUATE LEVEL (CGL) EXAM

Exam Pattern

Tier	Mode of examination	Scheme of Examination	Marks	Time
I	Computer based	**A.** General Intelligence & Reasoning 25 Questions **B.** General Awareness 25 Questions **C.** Quantitative Aptitude 25 Questions **D.** English Comprehension 25 Questions	50 Marks 50 Marks 50 Marks 50 Marks = 200	**75 Minutes** (General) For VH and candidates suffering from Cerebral Palsy: **100 Minutes**
II	Computer based	**A.** Quantitative Abilities (Paper 1) **B.** English Language & Comprehension (Paper 2) **C.** Statistics (Paper 3) **D.** General Studies (Finance and Economics) (Paper 4)	A. 200 B. 200 C. 200 D. 200	**2 Hours**: 10.00 AM to 12.00 Noon **2 Hours**: 2.00 PM to 4.00 PM **2 Hours**: 10.00 AM to 12.00 Noon **2 Hours**: 2.00 PM to 4.00 PM

In addition to above, the Commission has introduced a Descriptive Paper of English/Hindi as Tier-III. The Question Paper will be bilingual. The candidates will have the option to choose any one medium. The details are as under:

Tier	Mode of Examination	Scheme of Examination	Marks	Time
III	Pen and Paper mode	Descriptive Paper in English/Hindi (writing of Essay/ Precis/Letter / Application Writing etc	Total marks 100	60 minutes For VH and candidates suffering from Cerebral Palsy: 80 Minutes
IV	Data Entry Skill Test (DEST) / Computer Proficiency Test (CPT) (wherever applicable)	Same as published in the Notice of Examination	Qualifying	Same as published in the Notice of Examination

The final merit will be prepared on overall performance in Tier-I, Tier-II and Tier-III. However, the candidate will need to qualify all the tiers i.e. Tier-I, Tier-II and Tier-III separately. There will be no sectional cut-off.

Document Verification will also be conducted as per the provisions of the notice of examination.

SYLLABUS: TIER-I

A. General Intelligence & Reasoning

It would include questions of both verbal and non-verbal types. This component may include questions on analogies, similarities and differences, space visualization, spatial orientation, problem solving, analysis, judgement, decision making, visual memory, discrimination, observation, relationship concepts arithmetical reasoning and figural classification, arithmetic number series, non-verbal series, coding and decoding, statement conclusion, syllogistic reasoning etc. The topics are, Semantic Analogy, Symbolic/Number Analogy, Figural Analogy, Semantic Classification, Symbolic/Number Classification, Figural Classification, Semantic Series, Number Series, Figural Series, Problem Solving, Word Building, Coding & de-coding, Numerical Operations, symbolic Operations, Trends, Space Orientation, Space Visualization, Venn Diagrams, Drawing inferences, Punched hole/pattern – folding & unfolding, Figural Pattern – folding and completion, Indexing, Address matching, Date & city matching, Classification of centre codes/roll numbers,

Small & Capital letters/numbers coding, decoding and classification, Embedded Figures, Critical thinking, Emotional Intelligence, Social Intelligence, Other sub-topics, if any.

B. General Awareness

Questions in this component will be aimed at testing the candidate's general awareness of the environment around him and its application to society. Questions will also be designed to test knowledge of current events and of such matters of every day observations and experience in their scientific aspect as may be expected of any educated person. The test will also include questions relating to India and its neighbouring countries especially pertaining to History, Culture, Geography, Economic Scene, General Policy & Scientific Research.

C. Quantitative Aptitude

The questions will be designed to test the ability of appropriate use of numbers and number sense of the candidate. The scope of the test will be computation of whole numbers, decimals, fractions and relationships between numbers, Percentage. Ratio & Proportion, Square roots, Averages, Interest, Profit and Loss, Discount, Partnership Business, Mixture and Alligation, Time and distance, Time & Work, Basic algebraic identities of School Algebra & Elementary surds, Graphs of Linear Equations, Triangle and its various kinds of centres, Congruence and similarity of triangles, Circle and its chords, tangents, angles subtended by chords of a circle, common tangents to two or more circles, Triangle, Quadrilaterals, Regular Polygons , Circle, Right Prism, Right Circular Cone, Right Circular Cylinder, Sphere, Hemispheres, Rectangular Parallelepiped, Regular Right Pyramid with triangular or square base, Trigonometric ratio, Degree and Radian Measures, Standard Identities, Complementary angles, Heights and Distances, Histogram, Frequency polygon, Bar diagram & Pie chart.

D. English Comprehension

Candidates' ability to understand correct English, their basic comprehension and writing ability, etc. would be tested.

The questions in Posts A,B & D will be of a level commensurate with the Essential Qualification prescribed for the post viz. graduation and questions in Part C will be of 10+2 level.

Tier-II

Tier-II of the Combined Graduate Level Examination is of Objective Type Multiple Choice.

Exam Mode	Paper	Subject	Max. Marks	Number of Questions	Duration & Timings for General candidates	Duration & Timings for VH and Cerebral Palsy candidates
Computer based	IV	General Studies (Finance and Economics)	200	200	2 Hours 10.00 AM to 12.00 Noon	2 Hours. and 40 Min. 10.00 AM to 12.40 PM
	III	Statistics	200	100	2 Hours 2.00 PM to 4.00 PM	2 Hours and 40 Min. 2.00 PM to 4.40 PM
	I	Quantitative Abilities	200	100	2 Hours 10.00 AM to 12.00 Noon	2 Hours. and 40 Min. 10.00 AM to 12.40 PM
	II	English Language & Comprehension	200	200	2 Hours 2.00 PM to 4.00 PM	2 Hours. and 40 Min. 2.00 PM to 4.40 PM

Scheme of Written Examination (Tier-II):

(i) Paper-I & II are compulsory for all the categories of posts.

(ii) Paper-III is only for those candidates who apply for the post of Statistical Investigator Gr.II & Compiler.

(iii) Paper IV is only for those candidates who apply for the post of Assistant Audit Officer.

(iv) Candidates opting for the post of Compiler and/or Statistical Investigator Gr. II and Assistant Audit Officer must ensure that they possess the requisite qualifications. Commission reserves the right to take appropriate action against applicants who do not possess the requisite eligibility while opting for the post of Compiler and/or Statistical Investigator Gr. II and Assistant Audit Officer.

SYLLABUS: TIER-II

Paper-I: Quantitative Ability: The questions will be designed to test the ability of appropriate use of numbers and number sense of the candidate. The scope of the test will be the computation of whole numbers, decimals, fractions and relationships between numbers, Percentage. Ratio & Proportion, Square roots, Averages, Interest, Profit and Loss, Discount, Partnership Business, Mixture and Alligation, Time and distance, Time & Work, Basic algebraic identities of School Algebra & Elementary surds, Graphs of Linear Equations, Triangle and its various kinds of centres, Congruence and similarity of triangles, Circle and its chords, tangents, angles subtended by chords of a circle, common tangents to two or more circles, Triangle, Quadrilaterals, Regular Polygons , Circle, Right Prism, Right Circular Cone, Right Circular Cylinder, Sphere, Hemispheres, Rectangular Parallelepiped, Regular Right Pyramid with triangular or square base, Trigonometric ratio, Degree and Radian Measures, Standard Identities, Complementary angles, Heights and Distances, Histogram, Frequency polygon, Bar diagram & Pie chart.

Paper-II : English Language & Comprehension: Questions in this component will be designed to test the candidate's understanding and knowledge of English Language and will be based on spot the error, fill in the blanks, synonyms, antonyms, spelling/detecting misspelt words, idioms & phrases, one word substitution, improvement of sentences, active/passive voice of verbs, conversion into direct/indirect narration, shuffling of sentence parts, shuffling of sentences in a passage, cloze passage & comprehension passage.

Paper-III: Statistics for Investigator Grade-II, Ministry of Statistics & Programme Implementation & Compiler in RGI. Collection, Classification and Presentation of Statistical Data – Primary and Secondary data, Methods of data collection; Tabulation of data; Graphs and charts; Frequency distributions; Diagrammatic presentation of frequency distributions.

- **Measures of Central Tendency-** Common measures of central tendency – mean median and mode; Partition values- quartiles, deciles, percentiles.

- **Measures of Dispersion-** Common measures dispersion – range, quartile deviations, mean deviation and standard deviation; Measures of relative dispersion.

- **Moments, Skewness and Kurtosis** – Different types of moments and their relationship; meaning of skewness and kurtosis; different measures of skewness and kurtosis.

- **Correlation and Regression** – Scatter diagram; simple correlation coefficient; simple regression lines; Spearman's rank correlation; Measures of association of attributes; Multiple regression; Multiple and partial correlation (For three variables only).

- **Probability Theory** – Meaning of probability; Different definitions of probability; Conditional probability; Compound probability; Independent events; Bayes' theorem.

- **Random Variable and Probability Distributions** – Random variable; Probability functions; Expectation and Variance of a random variable; Higher moments of a random variable; Binomial , Poisson, Normal and Exponential distributions; Joint distribution of two random variable (discrete).

- **Sampling Theory** – Concept of population and sample; Parameter and statistic, Sampling and non-sampling errors; Probability and non-probability sampling techniques (simple random sampling, stratified sampling, multistage sampling, multiphase sampling, cluster sampling, systematic sampling, purposive sampling, convenience sampling and quota sampling); Sampling distribution (statement only); Sample size decisions.

Paper –IV: General Studies (Finance and Economics)

Part A: Finance and Accounts-(80 marks)

Financial Accounting:

1. Nature and scope
2. Limitations of Financial Accounting
3. Basic concepts and Conventions
4. Generally Accepted Accounting Principles

Basic concepts of accounting:

1. Single and double entry
2. Books of journal Entry
3. Bank Reconciliation
4. Journal
5. Ledgers
6. Trial Balance
7. Rectification of Errors
8. Manufacturing, Trading, Profit & loss, Appropriation Accounts
9. Balance Sheet
10. Distinction between Capital and Revenue Expenditure
11. Depreciation Accounting
12. Valuation of Inventories
13. Non-profit organisations Accounts
14. Receipts and Payments and Income & Expenditure Accounts
15. Bills of Exchange
16. Self Balancing Ledgers

Part B: Economics and Governance-(120 marks)

- **Comptroller & Auditor General of India**
  1. Constitutional provisions
  2. Role and responsibility

- **Finance Commission**
  Role and functions
- **Basic Concept of Economics and introduction to Micro Economics**
  1. Definition
  2. Scope and nature of Economics
  3. Methods of economic study
  4. Central problems of an economy
  5. Production possibilities curve
- **Theory of Demand and Supply**
  1. Meaning and determinants of demand,
  2. Law of demand and Elasticity of demand,
  3. Price, income and cross elasticity,
  4. Theory of consumer's behaviour- Marshallian approach and Indifference curve approach,
  5. Meaning and determinants of supply,
  6. Law of supply and Elasticity of Supply
- **Theory of Production and cost**
  1. Meaning and Factors of production;
  2. Laws of production- Law of variable proportions and Laws of returns to scale.
- **Forms of Market and price determination in different markets**
  1. Various forms of markets - Perfect Competition, Monopoly,
  2. Monopolistic Competition and Oligopoly and Price determination in these markets.
- **Indian Economy**
  1. Nature of the Indian Economy.
  2. Role of different sectors - Role of Agriculture, Industry and Services- their problems and growth.
  3. National Income of India-Concepts of national income, Different methods of measuring national income.
  4. Population-Its size, rate of growth and its implication on economic growth.
  5. Poverty and unemployment- Absolute and relative poverty, types, causes and incidence of unemployment.
  6. Infrastructure-Energy, Transportation, Communication.
- **Economic Reforms in India**
  1. Economic reforms since 1991
  2. Liberalisation
  3. Privatisation
  4. Globalisation
  5. Disinvestment

- **Money and Banking**

  Monetary/Fiscal policy- Role and functions of Reserve Bank of India; Functions of commercial Banks/RRB/Payment Banks, Budget and Fiscal deficits and Balance of payments, Fiscal Responsibility and Budget Management Act, 2003.

NOTEI: (i) The Commission will have full discretion to fix separate minimum qualifying marks in each of the papers in Tier II and in the aggregate of all the papers separately for each category of candidates (viz. SC/ST/OBC/ including minority sub-quota /PH/Ex-Servicemen/General (UR)). Only those candidates who qualify in all the papers as well as in the aggregate would be eligible to be considered for being called for Interview and/or Skill Test.

(ii) There will be different set of Questions for Visually Handicapped (VH) candidates in Paper-I-Quantitative Ability, which shall not have any component of Map/Graphs/Statistical Data/ Diagrams/Figures/Geometrical problems/Pie-chart etc. However, components of other papers will be the same as that for general candidates.

2. COMBINED HIGHER SECONDARY LEVEL (CHSL) EXAMINATION

The SSC-CHSL exam is conducted by the Staff Selection Commission (SSC) to recruit candidates for various posts such as Lower Divisional Clerk (LDC)/ Junior Secretariat Assistant (JSA), Postal Assistant (PA)/ Sorting Assistant (SA) and Data Entry Operator (DEO).

SSC CHSL Exam Pattern

Tier I- Computer Based Examination (Objective type)

Part	Subject	Max Marks	Total Timing
I	General Intelligence (25 Qs)	50	60 minutes
II	English (25 Qs.)	50	(For VH/OH afflicted by Cerebral Palsy
III	Quantitative Aptitude (25 Qs.)	50	OH with deformity in writing hand
IV	General Awareness (25 Qs.)	50	– 80 minutes)

- The written examination consists of Objective Type – Multiple choice questions only.
- The questions will be set both in English & Hindi for Part-I, III & IV.
- There will be negative marking of 0.50 marks for each wrong answer.

Tier II – Descriptive Paper (Tier II)

The SSC CHSL Tier II takes place in Pen and Paper Mode.

Topics	Word Count	Marks	Time
Essay	200-250	100	1 hour
Letter/ Application	150-200		

The minimum qualifying marks in Tier-II is 33 per cent.

- You can write the paper either in Hindi or in English.

Tier III– Skill Test

- Tier-III of the Examination will be the Skill Test / Typing Test which would be of a qualifying nature.

- **Note**: Your final result would be determined on the basis of total score obtained by you in Tier-I and Tier-II.

SSC-CHSL Syllabus

SSC-CHSL Syllabus for Tier I – Objective Paper

I. General Intelligence: It includes questions of both verbal and non-verbal type. The test will include questions on Semantic Analogy, Symbolic operations, Symbolic/Number Analogy, Trends, Figural Analogy, Space Orientation ,Semantic Classification, Venn Diagrams, Symbolic/Number Classification, Drawing inferences, Figural Classification, Punched hole/pattern-folding & unfolding , Semantic Series, Figural Pattern – folding and completion, Number Series, Embedded figures, Figural Series, Critical Thinking, Problem Solving, Emotional Intelligence, Word Building, Social Intelligence, Coding and de-coding, other sub-topics, if any Numerical operations.

II. English Language: Spot the Error, Fill in the Blanks, Synonyms/Homonyms, Antonyms, Spellings/ Detecting, Misspelt words, Idioms & Phrases, One word substitution, Improvement of Sentences, Active/ Passive Voice of Verbs, Conversion into Direct/Indirect narration, Shuffling of Sentence parts, Shuffling of Sentences in a passage, Cloze Passage, Comprehension Passage.

III. Quantitative Aptitude

Computation of Whole Numbers, Decimal and Fractions, Relationship between numbers, Percentages, Ratio and Proportion, Square roots, Averages, Interest (Simple and Compound), Profit and Loss, Discount, Partnership Business, Mixture and Allegation, Time and distance, Time and work. Basic algebraic identities of School Algebra and Elementary surds (simple problems) and Graphs of Linear Equations, Triangle and its various kinds of centres, Congruence and similarity of triangles, Circle and its chords, tangents, angles subtended by chords of a circle, common tangents to two or more circles. Mensuration: Triangle, Quadrilaterals, Regular Polygons, Circle, Right Prism, Right Circular Cone, Right Circular Cylinder, Sphere, Hemispheres, Rectangular Parallelepiped, Regular Right Pyramid with triangular or square Base. Trigonometry, Trigonometric ratios, Complementary angles, Height and distances (simple problems only) Standard Identities like $\sin20 + \cos20 = 1$ etc.

Statistical Charts: Use of Tables and Graphs: Histogram, Frequency polygon, Bar-diagram, Pie-chart.

IV. General Awareness: Questions are designed to test the candidates' general awareness of the environment around them and its application to society. Questions are also designed to test knowledge of current events and of such matters of everyday observation and experience in their scientific aspect as may be expected of an educated person. The test will also include questions relating to India and its neighbouring countries especially pertaining to History, Culture, Geography, Economic Scene, General policy and scientific research.

Note: For VH candidates of 40% and above visual disability and opting for SCRIBES there will be no component of Maps/Graphs/Diagrams/Statistical Data in the General Intelligence & Reasoning / Quantitative Aptitude.

Skill Test

A skill test is a test in which a candidate's data entry speed of minimum 8,000 (eight thousand) key depressions per hour on a computer is tested. The duration of the test is 15 minutes and printed matter in English containing about 2000-2200 strokes/key-depressions is given to enter into the computer. The 'Speed of 8000 key depressions per hour on Computer' is adjudged on the basis of the correct entry of words/key depressions as per the given passage.

3. SUB INSPECTOR (SI) IN CPO EXAM

Staff Selection Commission organizes exam for Sub-Inspectors in Delhi Police, CAPFs and Assistant Sub-Inspector.

SI- CPO Exam Pattern

SSC CPO SI written Exam is conducted in two phases or parts which are given below:

1. Tier – I
2. Tier – II

SI- CPO: Tier – I

Section	Subjects	No. of Questions	Marks
I	General Intelligence and Reasoning	50	50
II	General Knowledge and General Awareness	50	50
III	Quantitative Aptitude	50	50
IV	English Comprehension	50	50

SI- CPO: Tier – II

Subjects	No. of Questions	Maximum Marks	Time Duration
English Languages and Comprehension	200	200	2 Hours

NOTE: Only those candidates declared qualified in PET/ PST will be called for Tier – II and that the Medical Examination would be conducted subsequently.

Exam Syllabus

Tier – I

General Intelligence and Reasoning: It includes the questions of both verbal and non-verbal type. Questions will be asked from analogies, similarities and differences, space visualization, spatial orientation, problem solving, analysis, judgment, decision making, visual memory, discrimination, observation, relationship concepts, arithmetical reasoning and figural classification, arithmetic number series, non-verbal series, coding and decoding, statement conclusion, syllogistic reasoning etc. The topics are, Semantic Analogy, Symbolic/Number Analogy, Figural Analogy, Semantic Classification, Symbolic/Number, Classification, Figural Classification, Semantic Series, Number Series, Figural Series, Problem Solving, Word Building, Coding & de-coding, Numerical Operations, symbolic Operations, Trends, Space Orientation, Space Visualization, Venn Diagrams, Drawing inferences, Punched hole/pattern-folding & unfolding, Figural Pattern- folding and completion, Indexing Address matching, Date & city matching, Classification of centre codes/roll numbers, Small & Capital letters/ numbers coding, decoding and classification, Embedded Figures, Critical thinking, Emotional Intelligence, Social Intelligence, Other subtopics if any.

General Awareness: Questions in this component are aimed at testing the candidates' general awareness of the environment around him and its application to society. Questions will also be designed to test knowledge of current events and of such matters of every day observations and experience in their scientific aspect as may be expected of any educated person. The test also includes questions relating to India and its neighbouring countries especially pertaining to History, Culture, Geography, Economic Scene, General Polity, Indian Constitution, scientific Research etc.

Numerical Aptitude: The questions will be designed to test the ability of appropriate use of numbers and number sense of the candidate. The scope of the test will be computation of whole numbers, decimals, fractions and relationships between numbers, Percentage, Ratio and Proportion, Square roots, Averages, Interest, Profit & Loss, Discount, Partnership Business, Mixture and Allegation, Time and distance, Time & work, Basic algebraic identities of School Algebra and Elementary surds, Graphs of Linear Equations, Triangle and its various kinds of centres, Congruence and similarity of triangles, Circle and its chords, tangents, angles subtended by chords of a circle, common tangents to two or more circles, Triangle, Quadrilaterals, Regular Polygons, Circle, Right Prism, Right Circular Cone, Right Circular Cylinder, Sphere, Hemispheres, Rectangular Parallelepiped, Regular Right Pyramid with triangular or square base, Trigonometric ratio, Degree and Radian Measures, Standard Identities, Complementary angles, Heights and Distances, Histogram, Frequency polygon, Bar diagram & Pie chart.

English Comprehension: In this, candidates' ability to understand correct English, their basic comprehension and writing ability, etc. is tested.

Tier – II

English Language & Comprehension: Questions in this components will be designed to test the candidate's understanding and knowledge of English Language and will be based on error recognition, filling in the blanks (using verbs, preposition, articles etc), Vocabulary, Spellings, Grammar, Sentence Structure, Synonyms, Antonyms, Sentence Completion, Phrases and Idiomatic use of Words, comprehension etc.

SI- CPO : Physical Pattern

For Male Candidates

- 100 meters race in 16 seconds
- 1600 meters race in 6.5 minutes
- Long jump: 3.65 meters in 3 chances
- High jump: 1.2 meters in 3 chances
- Shot up (16 laps): 4.5 meters in 3 chances

For Female Candidates

- 100 meters race in 18 seconds
- 800 meters race in 4 minutes
- Long jump: 2.7 meters in 3 chances
- High jump: 0.9 meters in 3 chances

4. JUNIOR ENGINEER EXAMINATION

Number of papers: Two

Total marks of exam:

- Paper 1: 200 marks
- Paper 2: 300 marks

Nature of questions:

- Paper 1: Objective type
- Paper 2: Conventional type

SSC JE Exam Pattern

Paper 1 will be divided into three sections namely, General Intelligence and Reasoning, General Awareness and Part A (Civil), Part B (Electrical) and Part C (Mechanical). There is a negative 0.25 marks for each wrong answer in Paper 1.

Paper 1

Papers	Mode of Examination	Subjects	Maximum Marks	Duration & Timings
Paper-I Objective type	Computer Based Test	General Intelligence & Reasoning	50	2 Hours Morning shift [10.00 AM to 12.00 Noon] Afternoon Shift [2.00 PM to 4.00 PM]
		General Awareness	50	
		Part – A General Engineering (Civil & Structural) Or Part-B General Engineering (Electrical) Or Part-C General Engineering (Mechanical)	100	

SSC JE Paper 2 Exam Pattern: The paper 2 is a conventional type paper which is held in offline mode. It comprises of Part-A General Engineering (Civil & Structural) or Part- B General Engineering (Electrical) or Part-C General Engineering (Mechanical).

Paper 2

Paper	Mode of exam	Subjects	Total Marks	Time Duration
Paper-II Conventional Type	Written	**Part-A** General Engineering (Civil & Structural) Or **Part- B** General Engineering (Electrical) Or **Part-C** General Engineering (Mechanical)	300	3 hours

SSC JE Syllabus

Subjects	Syllabus
General Intelligence & Reasoning	- Questions on analogies, similarities, differences, space visualization, problem solving, analysis, judgment, - decision making, visual memory, discrimination, observation, relationship concepts, arithmetical reasoning, - Verbal and figure classification, arithmetical number series etc. - Questions designed to test the candidate's abilities to deal with abstract ideas and symbols and their relationships, - Arithmetical computations and other analytical functions.
General Awareness	Questions relating to India and its neighbouring countries especially pertaining to History, Culture, Geography, Economic Scene, General Polity and Scientific Research, etc.
General Engineering (Civil)	**Part-A: Civil Engineering** - Building Materials, Estimating, - Costing and Valuation, - Surveying, Soil Mechanics, - Hydraulics, - Irrigation Engineering, - Transportation Engineering, - Environmental Engineering. - Structural Engineering: Theory of Structures, - Concrete Technology, - RCC Design, Steel Design.
General Engineering (Electrical)	**Part-B: Electrical Engineering** - Basic concepts, - Circuit law, - Magnetic Circuit, - AC Fundamentals, - Measurement and Measuring instruments, - Electrical Machines, - Fractional Kilowatt Motors and single phase induction Motors, - Synchronous Machines, - Generation, Transmission and Distribution, - Estimation and Costing, Utilization and Electrical Energy, - Basic Electronics.

General Engineering (Mechanical)	**Part C: Mechanical Engineering** ▪ Theory of Machines and Machine Design, ▪ Engineering Mechanics and Strength of Materials, ▪ Properties of Pure Substances, ▪ 1st Law of Thermodynamics, ▪ 2nd Law of Thermodynamics, ▪ Air standard Cycles for IC Engines, ▪ IC Engine Performance, ▪ IC Engines Combustion, ▪ IC Engine Cooling & Lubrication, ▪ Ranking cycle of System, ▪ Boilers, ▪ Classification, ▪ Specification, ▪ Fitting & Accessories, ▪ Air Compressors & their cycles, ▪ Refrigeration cycles, ▪ Principle of Refrigeration Plant, ▪ Nozzles & Steam Turbines. ▪ Properties & Classification of Fluids, ▪ Fluid Statics, ▪ Measurement of Fluid Pressure, ▪ Fluid kinematics, ▪ Dynamics of Ideal fluids, ▪ Measurement of Flow rate, ▪ Basic principles, ▪ Hydraulic Turbines, ▪ Centrifugal Pumps, ▪ Classification of steels.

SSC JE Syllabus Paper 2

Part A – Civil & Structural Engineering

Subjects	Syllabus
Building Materials	▪ Physical and Chemical properties, ▪ classification, standard tests, ▪ uses and manufacture/quarrying of materials e.g. building stones, silicate based materials, cement (Portland), ▪ asbestos products, timber and wood based products, ▪ laminates, bituminous materials, paints, varnishes.
Estimating, Costing and Valuation	▪ estimate, glossary of technical terms, ▪ analysis of rates, methods and unit of measurement, ▪ Items of work – earthwork, Brick work (Modular &Traditional bricks), ▪ RCC work, Shuttering, Timber work, Painting, Flooring, Plastering.

	<ul><li>Boundary wall, Brick building, Water Tank, Septic tank, Bar bending schedule,</li><li>Centre line method, Mid-section formula, Trapezodial formula,</li><li>Simpson's rule.</li><li>Cost estimate of Septic tank, flexible pavements, Tube well, isolates and combined footings, Steel Truss, Piles and pile-caps.</li><li>Valuation – Value and cost, scrap value, salvage value, assessed value, sinking fund, depreciation and obsolescence, methods of valuation.</li></ul>
Surveying	<ul><li>Principles of surveying, measurement of distance, chain surveying, working of prismatic compass,</li><li>compass traversing, bearings, local attraction,</li><li>plane table surveying, theodolite traversing, adjustment of theodolite, Levelling,</li><li>Definition of terms used in levelling, contouring, curvature and refraction corrections,</li><li>temporary and permanent adjustments of dumpy level,</li><li>methods of contouring, uses of contour map,</li><li>tachometric survey, curve setting, earth work calculation, advanced surveying equipment.</li></ul>
Soil Mechanics	<ul><li>Origin of soil,</li><li>phase diagram,</li><li>Definitions-void ratio,</li><li>porosity, degree of saturation,</li><li>water content, specific gravity of soil grains, unit weights,</li><li>density index and interrelationship of different parameters,</li><li>Grain size distribution curves and their uses.</li><li>Index properties of soils, Atterberg's limits, ISI soil classification and plasticity chart. Permeability of soil,</li><li>coefficient of permeability, determination of coefficient of 12 permeability,</li><li>Unconfined and confined aquifers, effective stress, quick sand, consolidation of soils,</li><li>Principles of consolidation, degree of consolidation, pre-consolidation pressure, normally consolidated soil,</li></ul>

	<ul><li>E-log p curve, computation of ultimate settlement.</li><li>Shear strength of soils, direct shear test, Vane shear test, Triaxial test.</li><li>Soil compaction, Laboratory compaction test, Maximum dry density and optimum moisture content, earth pressure theories, active and passive earth pressures,</li><li>Bearing capacity of soils, plate load test, and standard penetration test.</li></ul>
Hydraulics	<ul><li>Fluid properties,</li><li>hydrostatics,</li><li>measurements of flow,</li><li>Bernoulli's theorem and its application, flow through pipes,</li><li>flow in open channels,</li><li>weirs, flumes, spillways, pumps and turbines</li></ul>
Irrigation Engineering	<ul><li>Definition, necessity, benefits, effects of irrigation, types and methods of irrigation,</li><li>Hydrology – Measurement of rainfall, run off coefficient, rain gauge, losses from precipitation – evaporation, infiltration, etc.</li><li>Water requirement of crops, duty, delta and base period, Kharif and Rabi Crops, Command area, Time factor, Crop ratio, Overlap allowance, Irrigation efficiencies.</li><li>Different type of canals, types of canal irrigation, loss of water in canals.</li><li>Canal lining – types and advantages.</li><li>Shallow and deep to wells, yield from a well.</li><li>Weir and barrage, Failure of weirs and permeable foundation, Slit and Scour, Kennedy's theory of critical velocity.</li><li>Lacey's theory of uniform flow. Definition of flood, causes and effects, methods of flood control, water logging, preventive measure.</li><li>Land reclamation, Characteristics of affecting fertility of soils, purposes, methods, description of land and reclamation processes.</li><li>Major irrigation projects in India</li></ul>

Transportation Engineering	<ul><li>Highway Engineering – cross sectional elements, geometric design, types of pavements, pavement materials – aggregates and bitumen, different tests,</li><li>Design of flexible and rigid pavements – Water Bound Macadam (WBM) and Wet Mix Macadam (WMM), Gravel Road, Bituminous construction,</li><li>Rigid pavement joint, pavement maintenance, Highway drainage, Railway Engineering- Components of permanent way – sleepers, ballast,</li><li>Fixtures and fastening, track geometry, points and crossings, track junction, stations and yards.</li><li>Traffic Engineering – Different traffic survey, speed-flow-density and their interrelationships, intersections and interchanges, traffic signals, traffic operation, traffic signs and markings, road safety</li></ul>
Environmental Engineering	<ul><li>Quality of water,</li><li>Source of water supply, purification of water,</li><li>Distribution of water, need of sanitation, sewerage systems,</li><li>Circular sewer, oval sewer, sewer appurtenances,</li><li>Sewage treatments. Surface water drainage.</li><li>Solid waste management – types, effects, engineered management system.</li><li>Air pollution – pollutants, causes, effects, control. Noise pollution – cause, health effects, control.</li></ul>

Structural Engineering

Subject	Syllabus
Theory of Structures	<ul><li>Elasticity constants,</li><li>Types of beams – determinate and indeterminate,</li><li>Bending moment and shear force diagrams of simply supported,</li><li>Cantilever and over hanging beams.</li><li>Moment of area and moment of inertia for rectangular & circular sections,</li><li>Bending moment and shear stress for tee,</li><li>Channel and compound sections,</li><li>Chimneys, dams and retaining walls</li></ul>

Concrete Technology	• Properties, Advantages and uses of concrete, • Cement aggregates, importance of water quality, • Water cement ratio, workability, mix design, • Storage, batching, mixing, placement, • Compaction, finishing and curing of concrete, • Quality control of concrete, hot weather and cold weather concreting, • Repair and maintenance of concrete structures
RCC Design	• RCC beams-flexural strength, • Shear strength, bond strength, • Design of singly reinforced and double reinforced beams, • Cantilever beams. T-beams, lintels. • One way and two way 12 slabs, isolated footings. • Reinforced brick works, columns, staircases, retaining wall, • Water tanks (RCC design questions may be based on both Limit State and Working Stress methods)
Steel Design	• Steel design and construction of steel columns, • Beams roof trusses plate girders

Part B – Electrical Engineering

Subjects	Syllabus
Basic Concepts	• Concepts of resistance, • inductance, • Capacitance and various factors affecting them. • Concepts of current, voltage, power, energy and their units
Circuit Law	• Kirchhoff's law, • Simple Circuit solution using network theorems
Magnetic Circuit	• Concepts of flux, mmf, reluctance, • Different kinds of magnetic materials, • Magnetic calculations for conductors of different configuration e.g. straight, circular, solenoid, etc. • Electromagnetic induction, self and mutual induction
AC Fundamentals	• Instantaneous, peak, R.M.S. and average values of alternating waves, • Representation of sinusoidal wave form, simple series and parallel AC Circuits consisting of R.L. and C, Resonance, Tank Circuit. • Poly Phase system – star and delta connection, • 3 phase power, • DC and sinusoidal response of R-Land R-C circuit

Measurement & Measuring Instruments	<ul><li>Measurement of power (1 phase and 3 phase, both active and re-active) and energy,</li><li>2 wattmeter method of 3 phase power measurement.</li><li>Measurement of frequency and phase angle.</li><li>Ammeter and voltmeter (both moving oil and moving iron type), extension of range wattmeter, Multimeters, Megger, Energy meter AC Bridges.</li><li>Use of CRO, Signal Generator, CT, PT and their uses. Earth Fault detection.</li></ul>

Electrical Machines

Subjects	Syllabus
D.C. Machine	<ul><li>Construction,</li><li>Basic Principles of D.C. motors and generators, their characteristics, speed control and starting of D.C. Motors.</li><li>Method of braking motor,</li><li>Losses and efficiency of D.C. Machines</li></ul>
1 phase and 3 phase transformers	<ul><li>Construction and Principles of operation,</li><li>Equivalent circuit,</li><li>Voltage regulation,</li><li>O.C. and S.C. Tests,</li><li>Losses and efficiency.</li><li>Effect of voltage,</li><li>Frequency and wave form on losses.</li><li>Parallel operation of 1 phase /3 phase transformers.</li><li>Auto transformers3 phase induction motors,</li><li>Rotating magnetic field,</li><li>Principle of operation,</li><li>Equivalent circuit,</li><li>Torque-speed characteristics,</li><li>Starting and speed control of 3 phase induction motors.</li><li>Methods of braking,</li><li>Effect of voltage and frequency variation on torque speed characteristics</li></ul>
Synchronous Machines	<ul><li>Generation of 3-phase e.m.f. armature reaction,</li><li>Voltage regulation,</li><li>Parallel operation of two alternators,</li><li>Synchronizing,</li><li>Control of active and reactive power.</li><li>Starting and applications of synchronous motors</li></ul>

Generation, Transmission and Distribution	<ul><li>Different types of power stations,</li><li>Load factor,</li><li>Diversity factor,</li><li>Demand factor,</li><li>Cost of generation,</li><li>Inter-connection of power stations.</li><li>Power factor improvement,</li><li>Various types of tariffs,</li><li>Types of faults,</li><li>Short circuit current for symmetrical faults.</li><li>Switchgears – rating of circuit breakers,</li><li>Principles of arc extinction by oil and air,</li><li>H.R.C. Fuses,</li><li>Protection against earth leakage / over current, etc</li></ul>
Estimation and Costing	<ul><li>Estimation of lighting scheme,</li><li>Electric installation of machines and relevant IE rules.</li><li>Earthing practices and IE Rules.</li></ul>
Utilization of Electrical Energy	<ul><li>Illumination,</li><li>Electric heating,</li><li>Electric welding,</li><li>Electroplating,</li><li>Electric drives and motors</li></ul>
Basic Electronics	<ul><li>Working of various electronic devices e.g. P N Junction diodes, Transistors (NPN and PNP type),</li><li>BJT and JFET</li></ul>

Part C – Mechanical Engineering

Subjects	Syllabus
Theory of Machines and Machine Design	<ul><li>Concept of simple machine,</li><li>Four bar linkage and link motion,</li><li>Flywheels and fluctuation of energy,</li><li>Power transmission by belts – V-belts and Flat belts,</li><li>Clutches – Plate and Conical clutch,</li><li>Gears – Type of gears, gear profile and gear ratio calculation,</li><li>Governors – Principles and classification,</li><li>Riveted joint,</li><li>Cams,</li><li>Bearings,</li><li>Friction in collars and pivots</li></ul>

Engineering Mechanics & Strength of Materials	▪ Equilibrium of Forces, ▪ Law of motion, ▪ Friction, ▪ Concepts of stress and strain, ▪ Elastic limit and elastic constants, ▪ Bending moments and shear force diagram, ▪ Stress in composite bars, ▪ Torsion of circular shafts, ▪ Bucking of columns – Euler's and Rankin's theories, ▪ Thin walled pressure vessels
Thermal Engineering	▪ Properties of Pure Substances P-V & P-T diagrams of pure substance like H_2O, ▪ Introduction of steam table with respect to steam generation process; ▪ Definition of saturation wet & superheated status. ▪ Definition of dryness fraction of steam, degree of superheat of steam. ▪ H-S chart of steam (Mollier Chart)
Properties & Classification of Fluid	▪ Ideal & real fluids, ▪ Newton's law of viscosity, ▪ Newtonian and Non-Newtonian fluids, ▪ Compressible and incompressible fluids
Fluid Statics	▪ Pressure at a point. ▪ Measurement of Fluid
Pressure	▪ Manometers, ▪ U-tube, ▪ Inclined tube
Fluid Kinematics	▪ Stream line, laminar & turbulent flow, ▪ External & internal flow, ▪ Continuity equation
Dynamics of Ideal Fluids	▪ Bernoulli's equation, ▪ Total head; ▪ Velocity head; ▪ Pressure head; ▪ Application of Bernoulli's equitation
Centrifugal Pumps	▪ Classifications, ▪ Principles, ▪ Performance

Production Engineering Classification of Steels	▪ Mild steal & alloy steel, ▪ Heat treatment of steel, ▪ Welding – Arc Welding, ▪ Gas Welding, ▪ Resistance Welding, ▪ Special Welding Techniques i.e. TIG, MIG, etc. (Brazing & Soldering), ▪ Welding Defects & Testing; ▪ NDT, Foundry & Casting – methods, defects, different casting processes

5. STENOGRAPHERS GRADE 'C' & 'D' EXAMINATION

Exam Pattern

1. **Computer Based Test (CBT):** The CBT will consist of Objective Type Multiple Choice Questions.

- There will be three parts in the test. Part-I and Part-II will consist of 50 questions each. Both the part will be for 50 marks each.

- The maximum marks allotted to Part-III of SSC Stenographer 2017 examination is 100 marks.

- The questions except Part III will be set both in English and Hindi.

- The time duration for general candidates will be 2 hrs. and 2 hrs. 40 minutes for visually handicapped candidates.

- There will be negative marking of 0.25 marks for each wrong answer.

Part	Subjects	Maximum Marks	Total Duration / Timing for General candidates	Total Duration/ Timing for Visually Handicapped/ cerebral palsy candidates
I	General Intelligence & Reasoning (50 questions)	50	2 Hours 10.00 A.M. to 12.00 Noon OR 2.00 PM to 4.00 PM	2 Hours 40 minutes 10.00 A.M. to 12.40 PM OR 2.00 PM to 4.40 PM
II	General Awareness (50 questions)	50		
III	English Language and Comprehension (100 questions)	100		

2. **Skill Test in Stenography**

- Candidates who obtain the qualifying marks in the CBT as may be prescribed by the Commission will only be called for the Skill Test.

- Commission may also prescribe qualifying marks in each part of the Written Examination.

- The skill Test will be qualifying in nature and the Commission will fix the qualifying standards in the skill test for different categories of candidates.

- It is mandatory for the candidates to appear in Skill Test.

- The candidates will be given one dictation for 10 minutes in English / Hindi at the speed of 100 w.p.m. for the post of Stenographer Grade C and 80 w.p.m. for the post of Stenographer Grade D.

- The matter will have to be transcribed on computer only.

- VH candidates will be required to transcribe the matter in 75 minutes for English Shorthand or in 100 minutes for Hindi Shorthand for the post of Stenographer Grade D and in 70 minutes for English Shorthand test and in 95 minutes for Hindi Shorthand test for the post of Stenographer Grade C.

- The skill test will be held at the Commission's Regional/Sub Regional Offices or at other Centre(s) as may be decided by the Commission.

Transcription time

SSC Stenography		
Post Name	**Speed**	**Transcription Time**
Stenographer Grade 'D'	80 w.p.m.	50 minutes (English) 65 minutes (Hindi)
Stenographer Grade 'C'	100 w.p.m.	40 minutes (English) 55 Minutes (Hindi)

SSC Stenographer Syllabus

General Intelligence & Reasoning: It includes questions of both verbal and non-verbal type. The test will include questions on the following topics. The test will also include questions designed to test the candidate's abilities to deal with abstract ideas and symbols and their relationship, arithmetical computation, and other analytical functions.

- Analogies, similarities, and differences
- Space Visualization
- Problem-solving
- Analysis
- Judgement
- Decision Making

- Visual Memory
- Discriminating Observation
- Relationship Concepts
- Arithmetical Reasoning
- Verbal and Figure Classification
- Arithmetical Number Series, Non-Verbal Series etc.

General Awareness: Questions are designed to test the ability of the candidate's general awareness of the environment around him/ her and its application to society. Questions will also be designed to test knowledge of current events and of such matters of everyday observation and experience in their scientific aspects as may be expected of an educated person. The test will also include questions relating to the following topics. These questions will be such that they do not require a special study of any discipline.

- India and its Neighbouring countries especially pertaining to Sports
- History, Culture, Geography, Economic scene
- General Polity including Indian Constitution, and Scientific Research etc.

Note: For VH candidates of 40% and above visual disability /cerebral palsy affected candidates and opting for scribe there will be no component of Maps/ Graphs/Diagrams/Statistical Data in the General Intelligence & Reasoning / General Awareness Paper.

English Language & Comprehension: In addition to the testing of candidates' understanding of the English Language, its vocabulary, grammar, sentence structure, synonyms, antonyms and its correct usage, etc. his/her writing ability, would also be tested.

- Active and passive voice.
- Synonyms and antonyms.
- Homonyms.
- Fill in the blanks.
- Direct and Indirect Conversion.
- Comprehension passage.
- Spellings.
- Misspelt words detection.
- Cloze passage.

6. SCIENTIFIC ASSISTANT EXAM

Exam Pattern

- The Exam is computer based.
- The Exam is of 200 marks with 200 questions.
- The Time duration for the Examination is of 02 hours (120 minutes).
- The Exam is divided into 2 Parts.
- There will be a negative marking of 0.25 marks for each wrong answer.

Sl. No.	Type	Papers	Subjects	No. of Questions	Total No. of Marks	Total Time
1.	Objective Type	Part I	General Intelligence & Reasoning	25	200	120 Mins
2.			Quantitative Aptitude	25		
3.			English Language & Comprehension	25		
4.			General Awareness	25		
5.		Part II	Physics, Computer Science and Information Technology, Electronics & Telecommunication Engineering	100		

Syllabus

Part-I

(i) General Intelligence & Reasoning: The Syllabus for General Intelligence would include questions of both verbal and non-verbal type. The test may include questions on analogies, similarities, differences, space visualization, problem solving, analysis, judgement, decision making, visual memory, discrimination, observation, relationship concepts, arithmetical reasoning, verbal and figure classification, arithmetical number series etc. The test will also include questions designed to test the candidate's abilities to deal with abstract ideas and symbols and their relationships, arithmetical computations and other analytical functions.

(ii) Quantitative Aptitude: The questions will be designed to test the ability of appropriate use of numbers and number sense of the candidate. The scope of the test will be computation of whole numbers, decimals, fractions and relationships between numbers, Percentage, Ratio & Proportion, Square roots, Averages, interest, Profit and Loss, Discount, Partnership Business, Mixture and Alligation, Time and Distance, Time & Work, Basic algebraic identities of School Algebra & Elementary Surds, Graphs of Linear Equations, Triangle and its various Kinds of centers, Congruence and similarity of triangles, Circle and its chords, tangents, angles subtended by chords of a circle, common tangents to two or more circles, Triangle, Quadrilaterals, Regular Polygons, Circle, Right Prism, Right Circular Cone, Right Circular Cylinder, Sphere, Hemispheres, Rectangular Parallelepiped, Regular Right Pyramid with triangular or square base, Trigonometric ratio, Degree and Radian Measures, Standard Identities, Complementary angle, Heights and Distances, Histogram, Frequency polygon, Bar diagram & Pie chart.

(iii) English Language & Comprehension: English grammar, Vocabulary, Spellings, Synonyms and Antonyms, Comprehension, Correct and incorrect usages, etc.

(iv) General Awareness: General, physical, geographical, topographical, economic and climatic features of India, Current events, Matters of everyday observation and experience on scientific aspects and reasoning, Basic topics of mathematics, Chemistry and Physics, History of India, its cultural heritage, freedom movement, salient feature of the Constitution of India, Economic and social aspect of the country and its people.

Part-II

(a) Physics

Mechanics: Units and dimensions, SI Units, Newton's Laws of Motion, conservation of linear and angular momentum, projectiles, rotational motion, moment of inertia, rolling motion, Newton's Law of gravitation, Planetary motion, Kepler's Laws of Planetary motion, artificial satellites, Fluid motion, Bernoulli's theorem, Surface tension, Viscosity, Elastic Constants, bending of beams, torsion of cylindrical bodies, elementary ideas of special theory of relativity.

Thermal Physics, Radiation & Sound: Thermometry, Zeroth, first and second laws of thermodynamics, reversible and irreversible processes, Internal energy, Heat engines, Maxwell's relation, ideal and real gases, equations of state, Heat Capacities, Adiabatic and Isothermal processes, Clausius-Clapeyron relation, Thermal Conductivity, Entropy, Enthalpy, Dalton's law of partial pressure, Vapour pressure, Kinetic theory of gases, Brownian motion, Maxwell's velocity distribution, Equipartition of energy, mean free path Vander walls' equation of State, Liquefaction of gases, Blackbody radiation, Kirchhoff's law, Stephen's law, Planck's law, Conduction in solids.

Wave and Oscillations: Simple harmonic motion, wave motion, superposition principle, Damped oscillations; forced oscillations and resonance; simple oscillatory systems; vibrations of rods, strings and air columns. Doppler Effect; Ultrasonic; Sabine's law of reverberation; Recording and reproduction of sound.

Optics: Nature and propagation of light; Reflection & Refraction, Interference; diffraction; polarization of light; simple interferometers, Determination of wavelength of spectral lines, Electromagnetic spectrum, Rayleigh scattering, Raman effect, Lenses and mirrors, combination of coaxial thin lenses, spherical and chromatic aberrations, and their corrections, Microscope, Telescope, Eyepieces and Photometry.

Electricity and Magnetism: Electric charges, fields and potentials, Gauss's theorem, Electrometers, Dielectrics, Magnetic properties of matter and their measurement, Elementary theory of Dia, Para and Ferro-magnetism, Hysteresis, Electric current and their properties, Ohm's law, Galvanometers, Whetstone's bridge and applications, Potentiometers, Faraday's law of E.M. induction, self and mutual inductance and their applications, alternating currents, impedance and resonance, LCR circuit, Dynamos, motors, transformers, Peltier-Seebeck and Thomson effects and applications, electrolysis, Hall effect, Hertz experiment and electro-magnetic waves, Particle accelerators and cyclotron.

Atomic Structure: Electron, measurement of "e" and "e/m", measurement of Planck Constant, Rutherford-Bohr Atom, X-rays, Bragg's law, Moseley's law, Radioactivity, Alpha-Beta-Gamma emission, Elementary ideas of nuclear structures, Fission, Fusion and Reactors, Louis de Broglie waves and Electron Microscope.

Electronics: Thermo-ionic emission, diodes and triodes, p-n diodes and transistors, simple rectifier, amplifier and oscillator circuits.

(b) Computer Science and Information Technology

Computer: History of Computer and their classification, Basic Organization, Memory – RAM, ROM, EPROM, etc. Magnetic-Floppy, Hard disks, CDROM, WORM etc. Concept of Virtual Memory and Cache Memory, Number systems, binary octal, Hexadecimal, Binary Addition, Subtraction and Multiplication, Flotation, point representation and arithmetic, Arithmetic through stacks.

Operating systems: assemblers, elements of Assembly, language programming, Overview of the Assembly process, assembler for the IBM PC, Process synchronization, Memory Management – address Binding – dynamic Loading and linking – overlays – logical and Physical address space – Contiguous Allocation –Internal & External Fragmentation. Non-Contiguous Allocation: Paging and Segmentation Schemes – Implementation – Hardware Protection – Protection – sharing – Fragmentation.

Virtual Memory: Demand Paging – Page Replacement – Page Replacement algorithms – Thrashing.

File System: File Concepts, Assess Methods, Directory Structures, Protection Consistency Semantics, File system Structures, Allocation Methods, Free Space Management.

I/O System: Overview, I/O hardware, Application I/O Interface, Kernel I/O subsystem, Performance, Secondary Storage Structures, Protection, Goals, Domain , Access matrix.

Assemblers: Elements of assembly language programming, Overview of the Assembly process, Design of a low-pass Assembler, a single pass Assembler for the IBM PC, The security Problem, Authentication, Threats, Threat Monitoring, Encryption.

Fundamentals of programming: Unix Programming, Programming in FORTRAN, C, Object Oriented Programming in C++, programming in Java, Basics of compilers.

Database Management Systems: Advantages and components of a Database Management Systems, Data Types, Data Dictionary, Query Basics, Forms and Reports, Graphical objects, Error Handing, Distributing Application, Data Storage Methods, Data Clustering and Partitioning, Database Administration, Backup and Recovery, Security and Privacy, Distributed Databases, Client/Server Databases, Object Oriented Databases, Integrated Applications, SQL, RDBMS.

Internet Technology: Basics, topologies, layers, switching in the networks, bridges, routers and gateways, types of networks, WWW. Client/Server Applications, Internet Standards and specifications, ISP, Broad Band Technologies, Protocols, web-servers, browsers, and security, fire walls, date security, HTML, dHTML, XML, Web designing.

Fundamentals of Geographical Information System (GIS): GIS Data and Spatial Models, Topology ad Spatial Operations, Projections, Scale and Coordinate Systems, Mapping, GIS Analysis, Cartography, Basics of GIS application development.

(c) Electronics & Telecommunication

(i) Electronics: Conductors, Semi-conductors, Insulators, Magnetic, Passive components, characteristics of Resistors, Capacitors and inductors.PN Junction diode, forward and reverse bias characteristics and equivalent circuits of diode, Zener diode and applications, clipping, clamping and rectifier circuits using diodes. Bipolar Junction Transistors (BJT) Field Effect Transistor (FET) and MOSFET; Biasing and stability, Emitter follower and its applications – Negatives feed back Transistor as a switch, Multistage Amplifiers, Feedback, Oscillators, Multivibrators, Voltage regulation, Power amplifiers. Introduction to Network Theorems: Kirchoff's laws, superposition, Thevenin's Norton's and Maximum power theorems. Voltage and Current relationship in the resistance, inductance and capacitance, Concept of reactance, susceptance, conductance, impedance and admittance in series and parallel RL, RC and RLC circuits, Three phase supply-star and delta connection diagrams, Relation between line and phase & voltages and currents, series and parallel resonance circuits, condition of resonance, resonant frequency, Q factor and bandwidth.

Digital electronics: Logic gates, Demorgan's theorem, Boolean algebra, frequency counters, flip-flops, shift resistors, Basic concepts of Digital to Analog and Analog to Digital Converters, Timing circuits, Digital logic circuits, systems & codes, Combinational logic design.

(ii) Telecommunication: Basic antenna principle directive gain, directivity, radiation pattern, broad-side and end-fire array, Yagi antenna, Parabolic antenna, Ground wave propagation, space waves, ionosphere propagation and electromagnetic frequency spectrum, Modulation, types of modulation, Amplitude Modulation (AM), Modulation index, Power relation in AM, Generation and Demodulation of AM.

Single Side Band (SSB): Power requirement in comparison with AM, Advantages of SSB over AM, Concept of Balanced Modulator, Generation of SSB, Pilot Carrier System. Independent Side System, Vestigial Sideband Transmission.

Frequency Modulation (FM): Definition of FM, Bandwidth, Noise triangle, Preemphasis and De-emphasis.

Pulse Modulation (PM): Definition of PM, Difference between AM and FM, Radio receivers, Sampling Theorem, PAM, PTM, PWM, PPM, pulse code modulation, Quantization noise, commanding, PCM system, differential PCM, Delta modulation.

Multiplexing: FDM/TDM

Introduction of digital Communication: PSK, ASK, FSK, introduction to fiber optics system, Propagation of light in optical fiber and ray model, Propagation of signals at HF, VHF, UHF and microwave frequency and satellite communications.

7. JUNIOR HINDI TRANSLATOR EXAM

SSC JHT Exam Pattern

Paper	Subject	No. of Questions/ Marks	Total Time Duration for Normal candidates	Total Time Duration for Visually handicapped Candidates
Paper-1 (Objective)	(I) General Hindi (II) General English	100/100 marks 100/100 marks	2 Hours	2 Hours 40 minutes
Paper-2 (Conventional)	Translation & Essay	200	2 Hours	2 Hours 40 minutes

SSC Hindi translator syllabus

Syllabus – General Hindi

- Antonyms.
- Vocabulary.
- Synonyms.
- Fill in the Blanks.
- Error Detection.
- Translation of Sentences.
- Comprehension.
- Phrases/ Muhavare.
- Grammar.
- Plural Forms etc.

Syllabus – General English

- Grammar.
- Sentence Rearrangement.
- Comprehension.
- Fill in the Blanks.
- Idioms & Phrases.
- Vocabulary.
- Articles.
- Tenses.
- Unseen Passages.
- Synonyms.
- Verb.
- Cloze Test.
- Error Correction.
- Antonyms etc.

NOTE: There will be negative marking of **0.25 marks.** Paper-I will consist of Objective Type- Multiple choice questions only. Paper-II shall be evaluated in respect of only those candidates, who attain the minimum qualifying standard in Paper-I or part thereof as may be fixed at the discretion of the Commission.

8. CONSTABLES (GD) IN CAPFS, NIA & SSF EXAM

Exam Pattern

The selection process comprises following three rounds-

- Physical Standard Test/Physical Efficiency Test
- Written Exam
- Medical Examination

1. Physical Standard Test (PST)

Test	Male	Female
Height	170 cms	157 cms
Chest: For Males only	80 cms & Expanded- Min. 5 cms	-
Weight	Proportionate to height and age as per medical standards	Proportionate to height and age as per medical standards

Physical Efficiency Test (PET)

Test	Male	Female
Race	5 Kms in 24 Minutes	1.6 Kms in 8½ Minutes
For Ladakh Region		
Race	1 Mile in 6½ Minutes	800 Meters in 4 Minutes

2. Written Exam

Exam Pattern

Part	Subjects	No. of Questions	Marks	Time Duration
Part A	General Intelligence & Reasoning	25	25	
Part B	General Knowledge and Awareness	25	25	2 Hours
Part C	Elementary Mathematics	25	25	
Part D	English/Hindi	25	25	
Total Marks			100	

Syllabus

A. General Intelligence & Reasoning

Analytical aptitude and ability to observe and distinguish patterns will be tested through questions principally of non-verbal type. This component may include questions on analogies, similarities and differences, spatial visualization, spatial orientation, visual memory, discrimination, observation, relationship concepts, arithmetical reasoning and figural classification, arithmetic number series, non-verbal series, coding and decoding, etc.

B. General Knowledge and General Awareness

Questions in this component are aimed at testing the candidate's general awareness of the environment around him/her. Questions will also be designed to test knowledge of current events and of such matters of every day observations and experience in their scientific aspect as may be expected of any educated person. The test will also include questions relating to India and its neighbouring countries especially pertaining to sports, History, Culture, Geography, Economic Scene, General Polity, Indian Constitution, Scientific Research, etc. These Questions will be such that they do not require a special study of any discipline.

C. Elementary Mathematics

This paper includes questions on problems relating to Number Systems, Computation of Whole Numbers, Decimals and Fractions and relationship between Numbers, Fundamental arithmetical operations, Percentages, Ratio and Proportion, Averages, Interest, Profit and Loss, Discount, Mensuration, Time and Distance, Ratio and Time, Time and Work, etc.

D. English/Hindi: Candidates' ability to understand basic English/ Hindi, their basic comprehension and writing ability, etc. would be tested.

Note: The questions in all the above components will be of Matriculation level.

3. Medical Examination

SSC has decides GD Constable Medical fit candidate list and set the medical fitness criteria accordingly. Candidates need to bring the testimonials while going for appearing in the medical exam. The main focus of the Commission is on eye sight and you can look the criteria at the beneath section.

Eye Sight

Visual Acuity Unaided (NEAR VISION)		Uncorrected Visual Acuity (DISTANT VISION)		Refraction	Colour Vision	Remarks
Better Eye	**Worse Eye**	**Better Eye**	**Worse Eye**			
N6	N9	6/6	6/9	Visual Correction of any kind is not permitted even by glasses.	CP-III BY ISIHARA	In right handed person, the right eye is better eye and vice-versa. Binocular vision is required.

Mentally Fit

They must be in good mental and physical health for duties in all places including in high altitude and be fit to serve in border areas with extreme climatic conditions and must be free from any defect likely to interfere with efficient performance of the duties.

Note: Candidates declared unfit may file an appeal/representation to the designated authority in the CAPFs within 15 days of declaring him/her unfit by the medical board.

B. PREVIOUS YEARS QUESTIONS TREND ANALYSIS

1. COMBINED GRADUATE LEVEL (CGL) EXAM TREND ANALYSIS
CGL- TIER I TREND ANALYSIS

1. General Awareness

Subject (Topics/subtopics)	2010	2011	2012	2013	2014	2015	2016	2017
Biology Plant parts (Stem, root, Flower, embryo, etc.), Photosynthesis; Nitrogen metabolism, Plant products, Soils, Classification of living organisms, Physiology(Circulatory system, Digestive system, Excretory system) ; Blood (Groups, Cells, Haemoglobin); Enzymes, Hormones,Cells, Nucleic acids, Diseases (Bacterial,fungal,Viral,Pr otozoan),Wild life,forests,Conservation,Pollution,Vitamins (Types & Deficiency diseases),Vaccines	06	04	08	06	08	9-13	12-16	14-17
Chemistry Chemical reactions and Bonds, Common Chemicals, Gas (Properties & laws) ,Periodic table (Atomic number); Smog, Radioactivity, Metals/Ores	04	04	03	09	03	5-10	4-6	07-10
Physics Light (wave-particle nature ,Properties of Light, Reflection, Refraction, Diffraction, Phenomenon and laws related with light; Current, Sound, Energy spectrum), Vector-Scalar; Conductor, Insulator , Gravitation, Laws of motion, Forces, SI Units	07	06	04	03	04	4-5	06-10	03-05
Computer Science Computer (Programming/ Languages/generation), OS, Hardware/ Software); Data & database, Terminologies	01	02	02	02	02	2-4	3-4	2-4

Subject								
Economics Price, Revenue, Taxes, National Income , Banking & Finance, Budget, Profits, Policies, Market (Supply-Demand),Economic theories	11	07	04	06	05	07-11	08-11	08-10
GK Authors & Books, Sports, Awards, Important days & Events, current affairs, Arts & Culture (Architecture, Dance, Music, Artists), Scheme & Plans. Organisations, Inventions & Discovery, Current Affairs	03	05	10	08	10	10-13	08-10	15-24
Geography Universe & Solar system (Planets, Rules governing movement of celestial system) Indian Geo.,Climate, Ecology (Wild life, Sanctuary, Park, Biosphere reserve, forests, Global warming) Human Geo; Census data, Economic Geo. (Minerals, Oil & natural resources, Types of Rocks) Different landscapes (due to erosion, deposition); Drainage (Oceans, Ponds & Lakes, Rivers, canals) Means of Transport; Agriculture ,World /Political Geography), Physical Geo./Geomorphology	06	11	06	06	07	02-04	12-16	4-5
Indian History and Culture Mauryan and Post-Mauryan Era, Delhi Sultanate , Mughal period, Regional powers, Sangam Era, Social & Religious movements, Indian Independence Movement, World History	05	06	05	06	05	06-12	05-08	06-09

Polity	2010	2011	2012	2013	2014	2015	2016	2017
Legislature (Parliament - Rajya Sabha & Lok Sabha) & State Assemblies (Vidhan Sabha/ Parishad), Speaker, Members, Finance & Other Bills, Election, Voting ; Head of State/Government (Executive)- President, VP, PM, Governor, CM (Eligibility, Election, Impeachment, Resignation, Power); Constitution (Parts, Preamble, Articles, Fundamental Duties & Rights, Committees, Writs); Commissions (Planning, Finance, NITI Aayog)	07	05	08	04	06	5-7	6-9	5-6

2. Quantitative Aptitude

Topics	2010	2011	2012	2013	2014	2015	2016	2017
Algebra	06	00	05	05	05	06-13	07-17	09-16
Average	03	03	02	02	02	3-4	2-4	3-4
Percentage, Profit & Loss, Interest (SI/CI)	06	14	05	06	07	10-11	12-16	12-16
Trigonometry	00	00	09	08	07	10-13	08-11	08-14
Mensuration/ Basic Maths	11	11	05	01	03	5-6	4-6	2-4
Geometry	03	05	12	09	14	10-15	12-16	09-16
Ratio & Proportion	03	03	01	03	01	2-4	1-3	2-4
Number System, HCF,LCM	06	05	02	02	03	2	1	4
Data Interpretation	03	04	05	07	05	4-5	4	4
Time & Work	02	02	01	02	00	6	4	4
Time, Speed & Distance	04	03	02	03	03	5	3	4
Simplification, Roots (Square/Cube), Misc.	03	00	02	02	00	2-3	2	0

3. General Intelligence & Reasoning Analysis

Topics	2010	2011	2012	2013	2014	2015	2016	2017
Analogy	08	09	09	08	04	4-6	3-6	3-6
Series	08	05	05	05	04	2-4	6	4-6
Blood Relations	01	02	00	01	00	01	03	04
Direction & distance	02	04	02	04	02		2-4	
Mathematical operation & Arithmetical Reasoning						5-6	6-9	9-11
Coding-decoding test	02	02	04	03	03	10	07	08
Sitting arrangements/ Cubes & Dices	01-02	02	02	01-02	00	01	01	00
Venn diagram	02	01	01	02	03	2-3	4	4
Statement & Arguments and Statement & conclusions	02	01	02	02	05	2-4	4	4
Figures (counting, formation, analysis, grouping)	0-2	0-2	0-2	0-2	0-2	2	2	2-4
Alphabetical Test	02	02	01	01	03	3-4	3-4	7-8
Images (Water /Mirror)	01	01	01	01	01	2	4	
Paper (folding/cutting)	01	01	01	01	01	01	4	4

Number Puzzle/Trends etc.	02	06	05	06	05	5-6	4	4
Completion of figures & Embedded figures	01	02	02	03	07	6	7-8	8
Classification	06	06	07	06	06	0	3-6	4-6
Word formation+ Visual reasoning	01	02	03	02	02	2	2	0

4. English Comprehension

Topics	2010	2011	2012	2013	2014	2015	2016	2017
Spotting Errors	05	05	05	05	05	0-5	0-5	0-5
Synonyms	05	05	05	03	03	2-3	2-3	2-4
Antonyms	05	05	05	03	03	3-5	3-4	2-4
Fill in the blanks & Cloze test	05	15	05	05	05	5-10	5-10	5-10
Spelling test	05	05	05	02	02	2-5	3-4	2-5
One word substitution	05	05	05	07	07	5-8	5-7	5-10
Idioms & phrases	00	05	05	05	05	5-10	5-10	5-10
Parajumble	05	00	05	00	00	0	0	05
Sentence Improvement	05	05	05	10	10	5-10	5-10	5-10
Reading comprehension/Voices/ speeches	05	00	05	10	10	5-10	5-10	5-10

CGL- TIER II TREND ANALYSIS

1.   English Language & Comprehension

Topics	2015	2016	2017
Spot the error	15-20	15-20	18-20
Fill In the Blanks	5	5	5
Synonyms	3	2-3	2-3
Antonyms	3	3-4	2-3
Wrong-Spelt words	3	3-5	5-6
Idioms & Phrases	10	5-10	10
Single word substitution	12	12-14	10-12
Sentence Improvement	20-22	18- 22	15-20
Sentence Arrangement/completion	18-22	18-20	18-25
Active/Passive voice of verbs	15-20	15-20	15-20
Narration (Direct/Indirect)	20-25	20-25	20-25
Parajumbles	15- 20	20	20-25
cloze passage	20-25	20-25	20-25
Comprehension Passage	30	30	30

2.   Quantitative Abilities

Topics	2017	2016	2015
Geometry	14	13	12-18
Mensuration	11	11	12-13
Trigonometry	10	12	8-10
Data Interpretation	05	5	4-5
Algebra	9-11	16	6-7
Number System/HCF/LCM	4-8	8	4-7
Simplification	00	2	5-6
Average	3-5	5	5-6
Ratio & Proportion	4-5	2-3	5
Mixture & Allegations	4-7	2-3	2-4
Time & Work	6	5-8	6-7
Time, Speed & Distance	4	4-5	4-5
Profit & Loss, Discount	7-10	8-12	10-13
Interest (Simple & Compound)	4-5	4-5	4-5
Percentage	04	2-5	2-4

2. COMBINED HIGHER SECONDARY LEVEL (CHSL) EXAMINATION TREND ANALYSIS

TIER-I TREND ANALYSIS

1. English Language

Topics	2017	2016	2015
Reading comprehension	0-5	-	5-10
Fill in the blanks/Cloze text	0-5	2-7	5-10
Sentence correction	3-4	2	1-3
Sentence Improvement	2	2	4-7
Synonym	2-4	2	4-6
Antonym	4-6	2	2
One Word Substitution	4	1-2	4-5
Spelling test	2	2	4-6
Spotting Errors	2	2	4-6
Idiom/Phrases	2	2	4-6
Parajumble	0	-	4-6
Voice/ Narration	-	2	-

2. Quantitative Aptitude

Topics	2017	2016	2015
Algebra	3	3	7
Average	1	-	1
Percentage, Profit & Loss, Interest (SI/CI)	3	4	9
Trigonometry	1	3	5
Mensuration/ Basic Maths	1	1	6
Geometry	1	3	4
Ratio & Proportion	1		2
Number System, HCF,LCM	2	3	2
Data Interpretation	2-4	4	3-4
Time & Work	1	1	2
Time, Speed & Distance	1	-	2

3. Reasoning Ability

Topics	2017	2016	2015
Series	10-15	2-5	5-10
Direction & distance		2	1	4

Analogy	4	4	8-10
Blood Relations	1	1	0
Coding-decoding test	2	1	5
Time sequence, Ranking & Number test	0	1	3
Sitting arrangements	1	0	0
Venn diagram	0	1	1-2
Statement & Arguments and Statement & conclusions	1	1	2-3
Figures (counting, formation, analysis, grouping)	0	1	2
Alphabet Test	1	1-2	7-9
Images (Water /Mirror)	0	1	1
Paper (folding/cutting)	0	1	0
Number Puzzle	1	-	2-4
Completion of figures & Embedded figures	5	-	3
Classification	4	-	7-9

4.   General Awareness

Subject (Topics/subtopics)	2017	2016	2015
GK Authors & Books, Sports, Awards, Important days & Events, Arts & Culture (Architecture, Dance, Music, Artists), Scheme & Plans. Organisations, Inventions & Discovery, Current Affairs	8-10	3-5	15-25
History Mauryan and Post-Mauryan Era, Medieval history, Delhi Sultanate , Mughal period, Regional powers, Sangam Era	4	3	4-6
Geography Physical, Geomorphology, Universe & Space (Planets, Rules governing movement of celestial system) Indian Geo., Climate, Ecology (Wild life, Sanctuary, Park, Biosphere reserve, forests, Global warming) Human Geo; Census data, Economic Geo. (Minerals, Oil & natural resources, Types of Rocks) Different landscapes (due to erosion, deposition); Drainage (Oceans, Ponds & Lakes, Rivers, canals) Means of Transport Agriculture, World (Political Geography)	4-5	3	12-18
Polity Legislature (Parliament- Rajya Sabha & Lok Sabha) & State Assemblies (Vidhan Sabha/Parishad), Speaker, Members, Seats, Numbers, Finance & Other Bills, Election, Voting	2	3	5

Subject			
Physics Light (Properties & Phenomenon); Current, Sound, Energy spectrum), Vector-Scalar; Conductor, Insulator , Gravitation, Laws of motion, Forces, SI Units	2	2	8
Chemistry Chemical reactions and Bonds, Common Chemicals, Gas (Properties & laws) ,Periodic table (Atomic number); Smogs, Ores of metals	2	3	6
Biology Plant parts (Stem, root, Flower, Fruit etc.); Classification of living organisms ; Blood (Groups, Cells, Haemoglobin); Enzymes, Hormones,, Diseases (Bacterial, fungal, Viral, Protozoan); Vitamins (Types & Deficiency diseases),Drugs & Vaccines	4	3	10
Economics Price, Revenue, Taxes, National Income , Banking & Finance, Budget, Profits, Policies, Market (Supply-Demand),Economic theories	2	2	7
Computer Science Computer Programming, Languages, OS, Generation, Hardware/Software, Networking, Data & database, Terminologies	01	1	04

3. MULTI-TASKING (NON-TECHNICAL) STAFF EXAMINATION TREND ANALYSIS

TIER-I

MTS: QUESTIONS ANALYSIS

General English

Topics	2017
Idioms & phrases	2-3
Synonyms	3
Antonyms	3
Spotting Errors	3-4
Fill in the blanks/Cloze test	5
Single word substitution	1-2
Sentence improvement	2
Reading comprehension	5
Spelling test	1-2

General Awareness

Subject (Topics/Subtopics)	2017
General Knowledge Authors & Books, Sports, Awards, Important days & Events, Current Affairs, Arts & Culture	
Physics Light (Properties, Phenomenon & equipments) ;Mechanics, Thermodynamics, Laws of motion, Forces, SI Units	1-2
Chemistry Chemical reactions and Bonds, Common usage chemicals, Gas (Properties & laws), Periodic table , Metallurgy	2-3
Biology Plant and animal Physiology and morphology Blood (Groups, Cells, Haemoglobin); Diseases ; Vitamins, Vaccines, Pollution	2-3
Computer Science Computer Programming, Languages, OS, Generation, Hardware/ Software, Networking, Data & database, Terminology	1-2
History Mauryan and Post-Mauryan Era, Delhi Sultanate , Mughal period, Regional powers, Sangam Era, Social & Religious movements, Indian Independence Movement	3-4
Polity Legislature , Finance & Other Bills, Head of State/Government Constitution & Constitution amendments, (Parts, Preamble, Articles, Fundamental Duties & Rights, NITI Aayog)	3-4
Geography Ecology (Wild life); Physical Landforms); (Oceans, Rivers) ,World Geography),	2-3
Economics Price, Banking & Finance, Budget, Profits, Policies, Market (Supply-Demand),Economic theories, Import-Export	2-3

General Intelligence & Reasoning

Topics	2017
Analogy	4
Venn diagram	1
Number Puzzle	1
Figures (counting, formation, analysis, grouping)	1
Alphabetical Test	2

Time sequence, Number & ranking test	0
Number Puzzle/ Trends Etc.	1
Coding-decoding test	2
Images (Water /Mirror)	0
Series	2
Paper folding	0
Figure problems (Completion, embedded)	2
Mathematical operation & Arithmetical Reasoning	3
Classification	3
Statement & Arguments and Statement & Conclusions	1
Direction & distance	1

Numerical Aptitude

Topics	2017
Algebra	3
Average	1
Percentage, Profit Loss, Discount. Interest	9
Mensuration /Basic Maths	1
Geometry	0
Data Interpretation	2
Number System, HCF,LCM	2
Ratio & Proportion	4
Time & Work	2
Time, Speed & Distance	1

4. SUB INSPECTOR (SI) IN CPOs EXAM TREND ANALYSIS

TIER-I

SUB INSPECTOR (SI) QUESTION ANALYSIS

General Awareness

Subjects (sub-topics)	2017	2016	2015
History Vedic Period, Indus Valley Civilization, Mauryan and Post-Mauryan Era, Mughal period, Indian Independence Movement, Sangam Era	5	6	10
Geography Physical; Planetary System, (Indian Geo., Climate, Ecology, Human Geo; Census data, Economic Geo. Different landscapes, Oceans, Rivers, canals); Agriculture, World Geography	4	4	7
Polity Legislature , Finance & Other Bills, Head of State/ Government ,Election & Voting, Constitution & Constitution amendments, (Parts, Preamble, Articles, Fundamental Duties & Rights, Reorganisation of states, Power distribution	6	4	8
Economics Price, Banking & Finance, Budget, Profits, Policies, Market (Supply-Demand),Economic theories, Import-Export	5	3	5
General Knowledge Authors & Books, Sports, Awards, Important days & Events, current affairs, Arts & Culture, Inventions & Discovery	14	2	4

Subject	2017	2016	2015
Chemistry Chemical reactions and Bonds, Common Chemicals, Gas (Properties & laws), Periodic table (Atomic number); Smog, Ores of metals	5	3	5
Physics Light (Properties & Phenomenon) ;Current, Sound, Energy spectrum), Vector-Scalar; Conductor ,Insulator , Gravitation, Laws of motion, Forces, Different Units	5	2	2
Biology Plant and animal Physiology and morphology, Blood (Groups, Cells, Haemoglobin); Diseases ; Vitamins, Vaccines, Pollution	5	6	7
Computer Science Computer Programming, Languages, OS, Generation, Hardware/Software, Networking, Data & database, Terminology	2	2	2

General Intelligence and Reasoning

Topics	2017	2016	2015
Analogy	6	0	6
Venn diagram	3	3	3
Number Puzzle	2	4	3
Figures (counting, formation, analysis, grouping)	2	0	0
Alphabetical Test	3	4	4
Time sequence, Number & ranking test	2	1	0
Number Puzzle/ Trends etc.	2	4	3
Coding-decoding test	4	2	3
Images (Water /Mirror)	0	1	2
Series	4	3	4
Paper folding	0	1	2
Figure problems (Completion, embedded)	4	3	3

	2017	2016	2015
Mathematical operation & Arithmetical Reasoning	0	3	6
Classification	6	5	6
Statement & Arguments and Statement & conclusions	0	4	2
Direction & distance	1	2	2
Blood relations / Virtual reasoning	0	2	1

Quantitative Aptitude

Topics	2017	2016	2015
Algebra	2	6	5
Average	2	1	1
Percentage, Profit Loss, Discount. Interest	8	7	7
Mensuration /Basic Maths	5	0	6
Geometry	5	5	5
Data Interpretation	9	0	4
Number System, HCF,LCM	3	0	0
Ratio & Proportion	2	2	1
Time & Work	2	2	2
Time, Speed & Distance	2	2	2
Trigonometry	5	5	4
Simplification, Roots (Square/Cube), Misc.	2	2	4

English Comprehension

Topics	2017	2016	2015
Idioms & phrases	5	5	5
Synonyms	5	0	5
Antonyms	5	5	5
Spotting Errors	5	5	5
Fill in the blanks/Cloze test	10	5	5
Single word substitution	5	5	5
Sentence improvement	5	5	5
Reading comprehension	5	10	5
Spelling test	5	5	5

TIER-II

English Language & Comprehension

Topics	2017
Spotting Errors	20
Synonyms	03
Antonyms	03
Fill in the blanks & Cloze test	28-30
Spelling test	3-4
Single word substitution	10
Idioms & phrases	10-12
Sentence Improvement	22-24
Parajumble	05
Sentence Rearrangement	24-25
Reading Comprehension	30
Direct/Indirect Conversion	20
Conversion(Voice of verbs)	20

Quantitative Abilities

Topics	2017
Algebra	10-12
Average	3-4
Percentage, Profit and Loss, Interest	15-20
Trigonometry	6-10
Mensuration/Basic Maths	10-12
Geometry	6-8
Ratio & Proportion/Mixture& Alligation,Misc.	8-10
Number System, HCF,LCM	4-5
Data Interpretation	5
Time & Work	5
Time, Speed & Distance	4-5

5. STENOGRAPHER GRADE 'C' & 'D' EXAM TREND ANALYSIS

General Awareness Section Analysis

Subject (Topic/Subtopic)	2016	2017
Biology Vitamins , Hormones, Diseases, Virus/ Bacteria, Vaccines, Organisms (Morphology & Physiology)	2	7
Chemistry Chemical reactions and Bonds, Common Chemicals, Gas (Properties & laws) ,Periodic table (Atomic number); Smogs, Ores, Alloys	1	3
Computer Science Computer Programming, Languages, OS, Generation, Hardware/Software, Networking, Data & database, Terminology	2	1-2
Economics Price, Revenue, Taxes, National Income, Banking & Finance, Budget, Profits, Policies, Market (Supply-Demand),Economic theories	6	3
Geography Physical Geo, Indian Geo., Climate, Ecology (Wild life, forests, Global warming) Economic Geo. (Minerals, Oil & natural resources, Rocks) Landscapes, Lakes & Rivers etc. Agriculture geo., Government Schemes/projects	8	5
History and Culture Indus Valley Civilization, Vedic Period, Delhi Sultanate , Mughal period, Regional powers, Sangam Era, Indian Independence Movement, World History	7	4
General Knowledge Authors & Books, Sports, Awards, Important days & Events, Govt. Schemes, current affairs, Arts & Culture	19	17
Physics Properties of (Light, Current, Sound, fluids (surface tension), Vector-Scalar; Laws of motion, Forces, SI units	0	1-2
Polity Legislature, Finance & Other Bills, Head of State/Government Constitution & Constitution amendments, (Parts, Preamble, Articles, Fundamental Duties & Rights, NITI Aayog)	5	9

English Trend Analysis

Topics	2016	2017
Spotting Errors	10	10
Synonyms	5	5
Antonyms	5	5
Fill in the blanks & Cloze test	25	20-25
Speech/ voices	20	20
Idioms & phrases	5	5
Reading comprehension	15	15
Parajumble	5	5
Sentence Improvement	10	10

Reasoning Ability Trend Analysis

Topics	2016	2017
Series	6	7-8
Direction & distance	2	2
Analogy	10	4-5
Blood Relations	1	2
Coding-decoding test	4	3
Time sequence, Ranking & Number test	2	1
Sitting arrangements	1	1
Venn diagram	1	1
Statement & Arguments and Statement & conclusions	2-4	2
Figures (counting, formation, analysis, grouping)/ Miscellaneous	1-2	5-7
Alphabet Test	5	6
Images (Water /Mirror)	1	-
Paper (folding/cutting)	1	-
Number Puzzle	4	4
Completion of figures & Embedded figures	2	-
Classification	7	7
Mathematical Operations/Arithmetical Reasoning	1-2	3

6. JUNIOR ENGINEER EXAM TREND ANALYSIS

General Awareness

Topics	2015	2017	2018
Economy (Market structure, Cooperative society, Unemployment)	2	3-4	2-3
Miscellaneous (Railways, Ideologies, Important days, Currency)	14	13	11-12
Polity (President, Election Commission, articles)	4	4-5	3-4
History (Sultanate, Marathas, Guptas)	4	3-5	2-3
Geography (Agriculture, Dams, Ozone	7	3	5-6
Science (Plants,human body, light, Physics, Chemistry)	13	16-17	15-16
Computers	2	1-2	1-2
Current Affairs (Sports, National, International)	4	5-6	8-9

General Intelligence and Reasoning

Topics	2015	2017	2018
Analogy	4	3	3
Syllogism	4	3	3
Odd One Out	8-9	5-6	2
Arrangement	3	2-3	2
Series	6	3-4	5-6
Problem Solving	3	2-3	4-5
Mirror Image & Water Image	1	4	2
Word Formation	1	1	2
Matrix	1	1	1
Coding-Decoding	2	4-5	2-3
Patterns & Figures	2	2-3	2-3
Equations	2	2-3	1
Paper Cutting and Folding	1	2	1
Missing Number	2	1-2	1-2
Directions	2	2-3	2-3

Counting of figures	2	2-3	2-3
Venn Diagram	2	2-3	2-3
Statement and Conclusions	2	2-3	2-3

Quantitative Aptitude

Topics	2017
Number System	7
Time and Work	1
Mensuration	2
Profit and loss	2
Miscellaneous	2
Average	1
Time and Distance	1
S.I. and C.I.	1
Coordinate Geometry	3
Trigonometry	3
Pie Chart	4

Civil Structural, Electrical and Mechanical Engineering

Topics	2015	2017	2018
Building Materials (Timber & Paints)	17-18	18-20	20-22
Surveying (Principles, Linear and Angular measurement, Levelling, Contouring, Tachometric Survey)	7-8	6-8	8-10
Hydraulics	11-12	13-14	10-12
Strength of materials (Numericals based on columns, SFD, Principle Stress, Spring)	9-10	8-10	10-12
RCC Design	4-5	5-6	10-12
Steel Design (Pre Stress Concrete)	6-7	6-7	8-9
Estimating, Costing and Valuation)	5-6	7-8	5-6
Soil Mechanics	4-5	4-5	2-3
Irrigation Engineering	4-5	6-7	3-5
Transportation Engineering (Highway and Railway based questions)	3-4	3-4	3-4

7. SCIENTIFIC ASSISTANT EXAM 2017 ANALYSIS

Quantitative Aptitude

Topics	2017
Profit and loss	2
Miscellaneous	2
Average	1
Time and Distance	1
S.I. and C.I.	1
Coordinate Geometry	3
Trigonometry	3
Pie Chart	4

General Intelligence/ Reasoning

Topics	2017
Ordering/Ranking	1-2
Analogy	2-3
Classification	2-3
Mirror Image	1
Paper Cutting/Folding	1-2
Series	1-2
Coding/Decoding	3-4
Embedded Figure	1
Matrix(Cube)	1
Odd One Out	1
Distance/Direction	1
Pattern Completion	1
Syllogism	2-3

English

Topic	2017
Common Errors	2
Fill in the blanks	2
Synonym/Antonym	4

Idioms/Phrases	2
Sentence Improvement	2
One word substitution	2
Spelling test	2
Parajumbles	1
Active/Passive	1
Direct/Indirect	1
Close Test	5

General Awareness

Topics	2017
Polity (articles, age-limit)	2
Miscellaneous (Revolution, Movements, Distance, Govt. Schemes, International issues)	5
History (Invasions, modern history)	2
Geography	5
Current Affairs	7

Computers

Topics	2017
Computer Organisations + Operating system	15-20
SQL	8-10
Computer Network	8-10
Programming	2
Theoretical Programming	8-10
DBMS	20-25
Miscellaneous	20-25

Electronics/Communication

Topics	2017
Communication(Antenna/Satellite)	35-40
Analog/Basics	25-30
Circuit	12-15
Digital Electronics	15-20
Miscellaneous	12-13

Topics	2017
AMU	1-2
ESU	1-2
Thermodynamics rules	5-6
Refraction	3-4
Simple Harmonic Motion	2-3
Rainbow	1-2
Bohr radius relation	3-4
Elastic constant dimensional	8-9
Energy of state hydrogen atom	3-4
Focal length related	12-13
Magnetic force	4-5
Electrostatic force	6-7
Transistor related common emitter	3-4
Resistance calculation	4-5
Capacitive energy	2-3
Venchuri meter and Bernoulli's	2-3
Nodes – antinodes	3-4
Doppler effect	4-5

Your Success – Disha's Goal

If you have a drive to succeed and really want to crack the SSC Exams, nothing is going to stop you. With the mix of our study material and your efforts, you can be on the right path of fulfilling your dream **and serving the nation.**

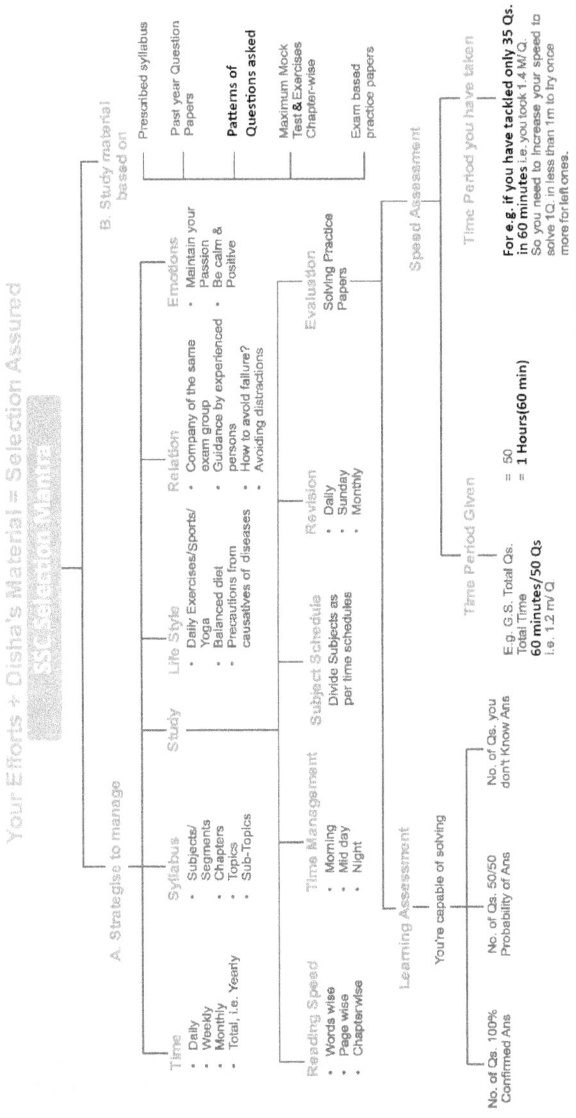

Your Efforts + Disha's Material = Selection Assured

SSC Selection Mantra

A. Strategise to manage

Time
- Daily
- Weekly
- Monthly
- Total, i.e. Yearly

Syllabus
- Subjects/ Segments
- Chapters
- Topics
- Sub-Topics

Study

Life Style
- Daily Exercises/Sports/ Yoga
- Balanced diet
- Precautions from causatives of diseases

Relation
- Company of the same exam group
- Guidance by experienced persons
- How to avoid failure?
- Avoiding distractions

Emotions
- Maintain your Passion
- Be calm & Positive

Reading Speed
- Words wise
- Page wise
- Chapterwise

Time Management
- Morning
- Mid day
- Night

Subject Schedule
Divide Subjects as per time schedules

Revision
- Daily
- Sunday
- Monthly

Evaluation
Solving Practice Papers

Learning Assessment

You're capable of solving

No. of Qs. 100% Confirmed Ans

No. of Qs. 50/50 Probability of Ans

No. of Qs. you don't Know Ans

Speed Assessment

Time Period Given

E.g. G.S. Total Qs. = 50
Total Time = 1 Hours(60 min)
60 minutes/50 Qs
i.e. 1.2 m/ Q

Time Period you have taken

For e.g. if you have tackled only 35 Qs. in 60 minutes i.e. you took 1.4 M/ Q. So you need to increase your speed to solve 1Q. in less than 1m to try once more for left ones.

B. Study material based on

- Prescribed syllabus
- Past year Question Papers
- **Patterns of Questions asked**
- Maximum Mock Test & Exercises Chapter-wise
- Exam based practice papers

दूर दृष्टि और ऊँची उड़ान सफलता की यही पहचान

A. GENERAL STRATEGY TO SUCCEED

Well formulated strategy along with optimum time management are the only two ladders for the aspirants dream goal. It is very important for the aspirants to formulate their own strategy as it pays in ssc examination more, if it is theirs. However, here are some of the general guidelines which will help the aspirants to achieve success.

Do's & Don'ts While Preparing for the Exam

Do's

The aspirants should do the following:

- Follow a healthy schedule while preparing for the exam, i.e. a good balanced diet, including fresh vegetables and fruits.
- Drink a lot of water to keep the body hydrated. A healthy body does possess a healthy mind.
- Plan every day according to the need and try to achieve the targets daily.
- Have sufficient sleep; a tired brain cannot work productively. Try to have a sound 6-8 hours sleep.
- Read out some jokes, poems or short stories in between studies to give yourself a break from the monotonous study routine.
- Play some games with friends sometimes to feel refreshed.
- Watch a movie that once motivated you to do good in life.
- Indulge into some light Yoga or Breathing Exercise. This is the best ways to one way stay fit and not feel lethargic.
- Be confident always. This is the best way to motivate self.
- Revise more than once to gain confidence and this will surely serve as constant motivator.
- Try to surround self with all the positive energy. This will give a good feeling all the time for a better and easier preparation.
- After the tier-I exam, take a short break, refresh self and then start studies immediately.
- Always keep some time for any emergency situation. Flexibility must be a part of plan.

Don'ts

- Do not panic if the target cannot be fulfilled, we all are human beings, we have limitations. Instead of panicking or feeling bad, give it a second chance and try to fulfil them one at that time.
- Wasting time after tier-I by waiting for the results is a grave mistake which many aspirants commit. This may cost a lot.

- Do not cut completely from the social life, just because it is exam time. As breaks between studies, go out for some time and talk to people who are close to you.

- Do not indulge too much into tea and coffee; maximum 2 cups a day. As tea and coffee contain caffeine, so consuming them in huge quantities will create health problems.

- Don't indulge into eating too much junk food, to take proper care of health.

- Do not exhaust with longer study hours. Take breaks in between for better retention and productivity.

- *Do not plan any new topic for study when only a few days are left for exam. This may, lead to confusion and bring lower confidence level.*

- Do not get involved into any negative emotions before exam. Avoid any kind of emotional stuff that gives a bad feeling during exam preparation.

- Avoid studying late into the night as researches have shown that things learned in the morning can be easily retained. Also, waking up early maintains body's biological rhythm and keeps one healthy. It also leads to better time management as it gives you extra hours.

HOW TO MANAGE EXAM STRESS

Stress is a feeling of an aspirant or a person when he has to perform more than he is used to perform. **Suppose you are stressed, your body responds accordingly as you are in danger. It makes hormones to speedup your heart beat, breathe faster and release energy.**

Some stress is normal and useful for you that helps to work hard and react quickly. But, if it happens too often and lasts for too long, it can cause health problems and hindrance in work and performance.

SSC aspirants often become stressful due to syllabus of exam, complex questions asked in exam, tough competition and long duration of preparation. These stress causing factors often make them vulnerable to problems such as headaches, anxiety and depression.

SSC aspirants can manage and avoid stress during exam preparation by adopting the following effective steps in their daily routine.

1. **Physical Activities**

   It may be sports, exercise, walking, jogging in the morning, yoga or meditation. Exercises keep the body active and stimulated throughout the day. Meditation and yoga help the body relax, de-stress fight anxiety, depression, and get ready for the tough schedule.

2. **Balanced Diet**

   There is proverb, **"There is a sound mind in a sound body"**. It is more relevant to SSC aspirants as they have to deal with many challenges at a time. A balanced diet is most important for SSC aspirants which keeps them healthy and physically fit to cope with the pressure and stress of exam preparation.

In addition, there are some healthy and unhealthy ways to cope with exam stress.

Healthy ways to cope with stress

(i)   Take out some time for entertainment and relaxation.

(ii) Develop a hobby and keep it.

(iii) Rest and sleep well.

(iv) Be positive and confident.

(v)   Engage socially: reach out and build relationship by:

* Reaching out to a colleague who is an SSC aspirant.

* Helping someone in need.

* Having lunch or tea with a friend.

* Calling an old friend.

* Going for a walk with like minded people.

(vi) **Avoid unnecessary stress**

There are a number of stressors in life and during exam preparation that can be eliminated.

Simply follow the tips given below.

* Avoid people who stress you out.

* Take control of your environment. Eg. you can turn off the T.V., can study in library, etc.

(vii) **Alter the situation.**

It can be done in the following ways:

* Express your feelings, instead of bottling them up.

* Be willing to compromise.

* Manage your time better.

(viii) **Accept the things you can't change**

Many sources of stress are unavoidable. You can't prevent or change them, like death of loved one; a serious illness, etc. Here, the best way to cope up with them, is to accept them as they are. These ways are:

* Don't try to control the uncontrollable.

* Look for the upside, i.e. taking challenges as opportunities for future betterment.

* Learn to forgive.

Unhealthy ways to cope with stress

Unhealthy coping strategies may temporarily reduce stress, but they cause more damage in the long run.

These are:

(i) Smoking

(ii) Drinking alcohol

(iii) Taking junk food

(iv) Sitting for hours infront of T.V. or computer

(v) Withdrawing from family, friends and activities

(vi) Using pills or drugs to relax

(vii) Sleeping too much

(viii) Procrastinating.

(ix) Utilising every minute of the day to avoid facing work delay.

(x) Taking out self stress on others, i.e. lashing out, being angry, outburst, physical violence.

HOW TO STAY MOTIVATED

Cracking SSC exam is not a short term game like '**One Day**' cricket match. It is a long term game plan of preparation, which needs passion to keep the aspirants motivated throughout their preparation. Few qualifiers crack finally in first term of appearance. Majority of aspirants take more terms. So, motivation is the only tonic that keeps an aspirant stay ready for longer duration of preparation to win the war of MISSION SSC.

What is Motivation?

The term '**motivation**' means the **reason** and the feelling to do something, especially that involves hard work and effort for longer duration in achieving the goal set before. The reward of clearing SSC and being a government employee can be an ultimate motivational reason for the aspirants, but it rarely inspires the kind of commitment and hardwork that is necessary to take on the daily challenges faced during the preparation phase. Therefore, aspirants must look at other factors and motivational reasons that can help them focus and **stay motivated till they get the ticket from SSC to join training.** These factors and motivational reasons are classified below.

Stay Motivated

	Keep off De-motivators		**Keep on Motivators**
1.	Eliminate your distractions.	1.	(a) Discover the ultimate purpose of being a Central Government employee (b) Make sure that your goal is within your reach.
2.	Don't lie to yourself.	2.	**See the invisible**, i.e- remind yourself of your goal 24/7.

3.	Stay away from strong stimulants, eg. alcoholic drink.	3.	Split the final goal into sub-goals, i.e. goal of day, week, month and year.
4.	Overcome your weaknesses	4.	**Set reward** for each goal.
5.	Don't set multi-tasks at a time.	5.	Target first the goal of the day to achieve the goal of week, month and the year.
6.	Don't let the past dictate your future.	6.	**Reward** yourself on achieving goal in order.
7.	Don't hang around negative people, i.e. de-motivators.	7.	**Make check points** for day, week and months to check the progress of your preparation.
8.	Let go off things which demotivate you.	8.	**Give break** in study to stay energised.
9.	Refuse to be a victim of life's hurdles and failures.	9.	**Break** long and complex task into manageable pieces.
10.	Don't involve in complain or conflict/ enmity with others.	10.	**Surprise** yourself by outdoor lunch, game with friend, home-cooking, etc.
11.	Stop worrying about what is beyond control.	11.	Be practical and make actionable strategy.
12.	Don't repeat mistake.	12.	**Discover** strength.
		13.	**Keep calm** and be pressure free.
		14.	**Learn** from mistake.
		15.	**Make a plan** to target goal. Because "If you fail to plan, you plan to fail".
		16.	**Build a team** that target the same goal.
		17.	**Build a support team** of winners to guide, support and motivate at the need of hour.
		18.	**Don't care** what others think and keep the momentum to reach destination.
		19.	**See the hurdles otherwise** (i.e. opportunities) to learn something. As **Thomas Edison** said, "I have not failed. I have just found 9,999 ways that won't work."
		20.	**Remind** yourself of having some wonderful, unique talents and God-gifts to contribute to the mankind.

		21.	**Write motivational quotes** in notebooks, posters on the walls, etc.
		22.	**Make** yourself a "**PHOENIX**" to make your success from your failure.
		23.	**Keep** a motivational role-model.
		24.	**Celebrate** other's success to be motivated for yours.
		25.	**Listen** to motivational music.
		26.	**Do breathing exercises** like yoga.
		27.	**Love** others and let others love you.

HEALTHY FOOD HABITS

Majority of SSC aspirants often move away from home, and therefore, they have to look after their food and other daily needs on their own. In the pressure of exam's preparation, they often ignore the most basic and important thing, "Healthy Food Habits". Healthy food habits are not only necessary to maintain physical fitness, but to also play a vital role in the overall exam preparation.

Some healthy food habits are given below to keep illness and stress-related health problems at bay.

1. **Follow a balanced diet**

    A balanced diet help in building body immune system and strong physique along with to tackle mental stress. A proper balanced diet must include three full meals, i.e. **heavy breakfast**, **light lunch** and **staple dinner**. These meals provide aspirant all the necessary nutrients required to keep their body fit and mind alert throughout the day.

    *   **Heavy & Healthy Breakfast**

        Heavy and healthy breakfast is very important for the SSC aspirants because early morning is the time when their brain is functioning at its full potential and requires more energy. There is also a maximum gap of 11 hours between two **meals**, ie. previous dinner and breakfast. At this important meal time, having a good breakfast aids the brain's processing power to maintain their stamina for study.

    *   **Take Light & Small Lunch/Dinner**

        SSC aspirants need energy directed towards their brain during their studies. But when they take heavy lunch and dinner at a time that directs blood flow and energy towards digestion process, they feel sleepy and lethargic. Therefore, it is necessary to take light and small lunch and dinner. They should also take **healthy snacks** between breakfast and lunch; and at 5 or 6 O'clock at the evening to refresh.

2. **Water As a Best Friend**

   If SSC aspirants don't take required liquid that may be water, fruit juice, herbal tea or any other combination that suits them, they might get dehydrated. **Dehydration** can make them feel lethargic, irritable and tired. It affects their concentration and peaks to be a hindrance in their study. That is why aspirants must consider water and recommended liquid as their friends or companion. However, they should avoid caffeine and any caffeinated products.

3. **Protein in the Food**

   Aspirants should focus on the foods that are high in proteins as proteins burn slowly, giving a constant source of energy to the body for a longer duration. For this, they can include eggs, nuts, curd, cheese and other low-fat items in their daily food. Food items like poha, idlis, dosa, dhokla are light alternatives that can help them during exam preparation.

4. **Avoid Some Food Items**

   Some food items make aspirants lethargic and fatigued. Carbohydrates are one of such food groups that are digested very quickly and force the consumers to eat more frequently. So, keep away from sugary and processed foods such as **chocolates**, **cookies**, **cakes and candies**. They should also exclude fat rich food items like rice, potatoes, white flour from their diet.

5. **Make Stomach Safe**

   It is important for the aspirants to keep their stomach healthy. To have stomach function normal, they should include **curd** and **buttermilk** in their diet. These food items counter any stomach problems like **acidity**, **constipation** and others.

6. **Avoid Eating Outside**

   Outside food items can't guarantee for quality, health and hygiene followed at the stage of food preparation. So, to avoid any such situation, aspirants are advised to either cook on their own or get their food prepared by a trusted person at home.

HOW TO MANAGE STUDY

Check out the full syllabus and tick the easiest topics

Have a look at the syllabus and identify all the subjects that you need to go through. Note that SSC Services is not like a university exam; the syllabus is more like a guideline and not a boundary that cannot be crossed. Take the syllabus as a guideline and not as a course definition. Classify the syllabus into different subjects and topics and if possible, make a Mind Map of Syllabus of subject/ chapter topic.

It will help to properly plan and distribute study time in a meticulous way. This is important because time at disposal is limited. It can also help in identifying areas of study where an aspirant is comfortable and where he is not. After going through the syllabus and ascertaining the study time available at disposal and identifying areas of strengths and weaknesses vis-a-vis importance of these areas of study from the examination point of view, make a time schedule.

HOW TO MANAGE TIME

SSC is not easy to crack. So, time management is a very crucial part of the preparation. This is because the time is limited and the Syllabus is vast. So the candidates need to make the best possible utilisation of time. Also, if the time managed properly, aspirants will end up wasting time on irrelevant things, while leaving the essential things uncovered. An aspirant should necessarily maintain a time log. This will help them to keep a track of how they spend each hour.

Here are some tips for time management

- Make a schedule and divide your day.
- Keep at least 8 - 10 hours a day for studies (if attending coaching, you'll be able to give only 6 - 8 hours a day).
- While studying for Tier-I, divide the study time into four parts: General Studies, Quant, English & Reasoning. If you are from Mathematics and English background, or are generally good in Aptitude, then you can keep only 4 hours a day for quant, English & Reasoning and devote the rest of the time to General Studies. So, divide your time as per need.
- Devote around 1.5 hrs. for reading newspaper and making current events notes. Don't skip newspapers, nor postpone reading them. You will never find time to complete them later.
- Maintain a habit of reading current affairs magazine.
- Setting deadlines and targets that are small and realistic will help you complete the syllabus within time.
- Get a proper sleep for 6 - 8 hours a day.
- You must spend 1- 2 hours for some **physical activities** like **jogging, cycling, yoga** or **playing a sport** and leisure activities like music, dance, painting, etc.
- Stop studying thoroughly at least 24 hours before the exam as studying now will only leave you anxious. You can go through the Mind Maps of subjects and topics. Just relax yourself for this day.

PLANNING FOR PREPARATION

Planning is important because it tells us how to reach our destination or goal. In the context of the SSC Exam, planning acquires greater significance because one has to cover a comprehensive syllabus in a limited period of time. Good planning really implies maximum results with minimum efforts. Effective planning means that an aspirant works out a mechanism of his own, for checking whether he/she is spending the time effectively or not. Thus, focus on the following tips for success in SSC Examinations.

Master the Basics

Aspirants must keep in mind the following:

"The questions are likely to test the candidate's basic understanding of all relevant issues and ability to analyse and take a view on conflicting socio-economic goals, objectives and demands.

Thus, aspirants don't have to master the topics, all they need is BASIC UNDERSTANDING and the ability to analyse. Basic understanding comes from reading and re-reading. Ability to analyse what they have understood from reading comes from WRITING PRACTICE.

Start From Weak Areas

There is no syllabus in detail or specific for subject or areas for Tier-I point of view. Any question in it can be asked from anywhere, so aspirants must begin their planning and study for subject area in which they are weak. When the weak areas can be overcome, a new confidence will develop that will motivate to cover up other areas/subjects easily and quickly.

Apply Intelligent Meditation in Preparation

It is very important to analyse previous questions asked in SSC Exams and then think over all the aspects and dimensions on which questions can be formed and asked from a particular topic or heading.

Prepare Own Notes & Mind Maps

Writing notes is very helpful in preparing for the examination, particularly when an aspirant studies from different sources. Firstly, while writing notes, the focused aspirant is in a more concentrated manner and many of these points remain in their memory, if they put them on a Mind Map. Secondly, notes help in quick revision.

For writing effective notes, do not start in a hurry, i.e. when aspirants are reading the material for the first time. Without understanding what is read, the candidate is likely to write down too much which may amount to simply reproduction of the material. After understanding the text book for the main points and sub-points, try to write in own words rather than using the same language. While doing this exercise, get sincerely involved and write short notes preferably in points, one liner, short sentence, one or two words, short names or abbreviations. These notes will help in revising the chapters or topics easily in lesser time.

REVISION IS THE KEY TO SUCCESS

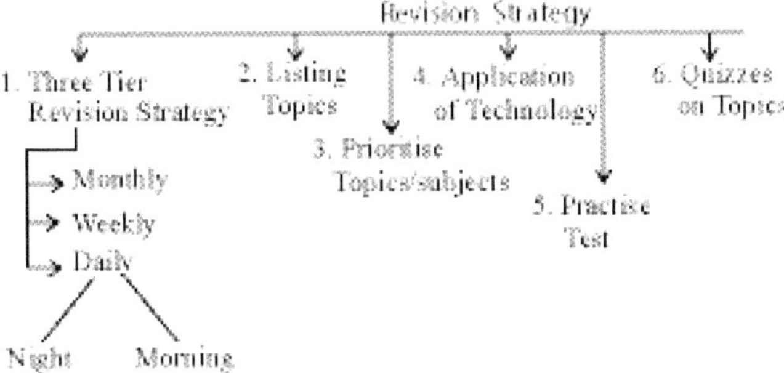

* **Revision** is the most important aspect of preparation for any exam, whether it is academic or competitive. But it plays a greater role in selection when an SSC aspirant follows it, because of the complexity of syllabus and subjects for SSC exam.

  Like study strategy, there is no fixed revision format that will suit each and every aspirant. Aspirants should think over which format can be best and suit them in revision. They can go through others revision techniques before making their own. But revision strategy should be prepared in such a way that will help the aspirants to achieve their study goals in the best possible way.

  Here are some guidelines that will help the aspirants in making best suited revision strategy for SSC exam preparation.

1. Three Tier Revision Strategy

The most suited and successful revision strategy for any exam, particularly SSC exam preparation is

Three Tier Strategy. This format is based on three labels, i.e. day-wise, week-wise and month-wise.

Daily revision is divided into two stages, morning and late-night. In the morning, aspirants should quickly revise all the subjects, chapters and topics they have studied previous day, thereafter, they should start studying new subject/chapter topic for the day. Before going to sleep late in night after study, they must revise all the points they have studied the whole day.

Weekly Revision: It is the second stage of revision which covers all the topics, chapters and subjects, an aspirant has studied in a week, i.e. from Monday to Saturday. It is mostly fixed on Sunday.

Monthly Revision: Just like weekly revision, monthly revision is the third stage of revision of the same topics and chapters, which an aspirant has already revised weekly and daily in a month. This model of revision strategy will help the aspirants to remember what ever they studied in a month.

The next revision can be after three and six months to freshen up aspirants memory of the studies done in this duration. It will help the aspirants in building their confidence in preparation and cracking the exam.

Three Tier Revision Strategy

	Subject	**Chapter**	**Topic**
Daily	Subject name	Chapter name	Topic name
Weekly	—do—	—do—	—do—
Monthly	—do—	—do—	—do—

2. **Listing of Topics for Revision**

   Aspirants study many topics from different subjects and chapters in a day, week and month. But all the topics are not equally relevant and important from exam point of view. So, they must list those topics which are important for revision according to their relevance, complexity and marks allocated for the exam. It will help aspirants to keep a check and complete their revision tasks within the time limit.

3. **Prioritise Subject and Topic**

   Aspirants list many more topics and chapters for revision. But due to lack of time for weekly and monthly revision, they are unable to revise all the listed topics. So, they should prioritise topics for revision according to their importance in the examination and revise accordingly.

4. **Application of Technology in Revision**

   Important points of a topic or chapter should be noted down on Memopad of a mobile phone or tablet to revise during travelling to and from to coaching.

5. **Practice Tests**

   After completing a chapter or topic during preparation, aspirants should test their learning through Practice Test based on that particular topic or chapter. These practice tests are designed on the same examination pattern as followed by SSC to prepare exam. These practice tests will help in evaluating the aspirants preparation. These tests are a mode of revision for the topic or chapter.

6. **Solve the Topic's Quizzes**

   When aspirants finish the topic during preparation, solve the quizzes or questions prepared on that particular topic so that they can assess their preparation and list the topic for revision accordingly.

Solve previous year question papers at regular intervals

As preparation for SSC requires at least 10 months time, so it is easy to lose focus or go off target. To stay on the right path or get on track quickly, the aspirants should keep testing themselves against the previous SSC papers to know the effectiveness of their preparation and identify and overcome their weak points. For this they should grab the previous 5 years solved section-wise Paper Set.

Go for Online Mock Test

After completing syllabus and revision, aspirants can go for a mock test. Conducted in a proper way, a mock test makes aspirants feel the environment and experience of the real exam. It is useful in reviewing their knowledge of the subjects and judging their weak and strong areas of preparation. Through mock test, they can also test their ability of time management. Do not miss the opportunity as and when any institute conducts mock test. They can take mock test online.

B. PLANNING FOR SSC: OBJECTIVE/ MCQS PAPERS

1. Tips and Techniques for General Intelligence/ Reasoning

General Intelligence and Reasoning section plays a very important role in SSC Exams. The chances of Reasoning Questions being attempted wrongly by the candidates are high. Therefore, negative marking in this section is comparatively higher. Generally, candidates find it difficult to score good marks in Reasoning Test, because most of the topics create confusion in their mind and they lack proper knowledge and guidance to perform well.

Exam Pattern of General Intelligence & Reasoning for SSC Exams

Exam	No. of Questions	Total Marks	Marks per Correct Answer	Negative Marking	Paper Mode	Question Type
SSC-CGL	25	50	2	0.5	Online	Objective
SSC- CHSL	25	50	2	0.5	Online	Objective
SSC- CPO	50	50	1	0.25	Online/ Offline	Objective
SSC- Multitasking (MTS)	25	25	1	0.25	Online	Objective
SSC- Stenographers	50	50	1	0.25	Online	Objective
SSC- Junior Engineer	50	50	1	0.25	Online	Objective
SSC-Scientific Assistant	25	25	1	0.25	Online	Objective

Analysis of General Intelligence & Awareness Section in SSC Exams (2017)

Topics	CGL	CHSL	Steno	MTS	CPO	Scientific Assistant
Analogy	3	3	9	3	6	3
Dictionary	1	1	4	1	2	-
Series	2	2	7	2	4	3
Word Formation (can/cannot be formed)	1	1	2	1	2	1
Missing Number (matrix form)	1	1	4	1	2	1
Distance & Direction	1	1	1	1	1	1
Statements & Conclusion	1	1	-	1	-	-
Venn Diagram	1	1	1	1	3	1
Figure Completion	1	1	1	1	2	2
Embedded Figure	1	1	1	1	2	1
Paper Cutting & Folding	1	1	1	1	2	1
Mirror Image	1	1	1	1	2	1
Matrix	1	1	1	1	2	1
Mathematical Operations (Changing of signs)	1	1	1	1	2	1
Counting of figures	1	1	-	1	2	-
Coding-Decoding	2	2	3	2	4	2
Blood relation/ Mathematics Formula/Calendar/ Ranking Order/ Cubes & Dice/ Clocks & Calendar	2	2	2	2	4	1
Syllogism	-	-	2	-	2	1
Arithmetic Reasoning	-	-	1	-	-	1
Classification	3	3	5	3	6	3

Important Topics of General Intelligence & Reasoning for SSC Exams

Analogy

Analogy Reasoning Questions are based on comparisons. The Commission will give some pairs in the exam paper and you have to find out the similar pair from the given pair. There are various types of Logical Reasoning Questions from Analogy.

Example

Q.   Oasis: Sand :: Island: ?

    (a) River   (b) Sea   (c) Water   (d) Waves

Ans. (c)   Here, the first pair is -"**Oasis: Sand**" and the second pair is **"Island: ?"**. And, " :: " sign means first pair and second pair share similar relationship. **'Oasis'** is a mass of water amidst **'Sand'**; similarly **'Island'** is a mass of land amidst **'water'**.

Coding-Decoding

In this segment of common sense reasoning, secret messages or words have to be decoded. They are coded as per a definite pattern/ rule which should be identified first. Then the same is applied to decode another coded word.

Q.   If D = 4 and COVER = 63, then BASIS = ?

Ans.   Clearly, in the given code, A = 1, B = 2, C = 3,... so on

        COVER = 3 + 15 + 22 + 5 + 18 = 63

        $\therefore$ BASIS = 2 + 1 + 19 + 9 + 19 = 50

Ranking and Ordering Test

The position of thing /person, etc. in a definite order is called **'Rank'**. In this type of test, relative position or rank of some person or object is given and candidates are required to find the rank or position of other person or object.

Example

Q. Anita ranks twelfth in a class of forty six. What will her rank be from the last?

    (a) 34th   (b) 35th   (c) 36th   (d) 37th

Solution: (b)

Here, use the following formulae:

1.	**Position of person from upward = [Total no. of persons – position of person from down] + 1**
2.	**Position of person from downward = [Total no. of persons – position of person from up] + 1**
3.	**Position of person from right = [Total no. of persons – position of person from left] + 1**
4.	**Position of person from left = [Total no. of persons – position of person from right] + 1**

Use the appropriate formula from above box to find the

Rank of Anita from the last = [Total No. of students – her rank from first] + 1

$[46\text{-}12] + 1 = 35^{\text{th}}$

Classification/ Odd One

One of the important topics in Reasoning is Odd One / Classification. Here, you can check some of the solved examples.

In each of the following questions, five words are given, out of which four are alike in a certain manner and the fifth one is different.

1.   Choose the odd one
   (a) chicken   (b)   snake
   (c)   tortoise   (d)   swan
   (e)   frog

1.   (a)   chicken

Explanation: Except chicken, all others can live in water.

2   Choose the odd one
   (a)   187   (b)   136
   (c)   141   (d)   238
   (e)   289

2.   **(c) 141**

Explanation: except 141 all are divisible by 17.

Arrangement-Direction

This includes arrangements (Circular, Line, Building, etc.). In arrangement question, you can verify the answer by applying the "condition" given in the question to your arrangement.

Some Basic Rules of Direction Questions

- At the time of sunrise, if a man stands facing the east, his shadow will be towards the west.
- At the time of sunset, the shadow of an object is always in the east.
- If a man stands facing the North, at the time of sunrise, his shadow will be towards his left and at the time of sunset, it will be towards his right.

General Tips to Crack Reasoning Section in SSC Exams

Point 1: "Plan, prepare, and practice"-follow this rule. It is essential to make a plan and follow accordingly.

Point2: As there is no sectional cut off, so try to cover maximum question from this topic.

Point3: During the preparation span, set your target for each topic that is included in this section. You do not have to give your whole day only for this section. Prepare well other topics too.

Point 4: Always remember that the question will be solved by the data given only, don't make unnecessary assumptions or judgment while solving the problem. Use smart and appropriate tricks and methods for solving any problem.

Point 5: Take one topic at a given time, reasoning requires you to think in a certain way and doing 2-3 different types of topics in one go may not be fruitful.

Point 6: Be very careful with words having negative prefixes like **non- , un-.** They can fool the students for facts. So they must read the question very carefully and when they are sure about the question, then they should find its solution.

Point 7: If students are struck with a particular question and can come up to no conclusion, they should try eliminating options as per the information given to get the correct answers. Don't try to answer all the questions because it may lead to negative marking.

Point 8: The understanding of Directions should be accurate i.e. which direction is West, North, East and South.

Point 9: Always remember the sequencing of alphabets i.e., which alphabet comes after/before the particular alphabet and you should also remember their numerical position as per 1 to 26.

Point 10: Students should also try to imagine the object in 3D like dice and paper folding etc. it will help in solving such problems.

Point 11: Time constraint must be kept in mind while attempting this section

Point 12: If students prepared well, this section can fetch you **40-45 marks** easily in SSC,

Point 13: Make your own notes so that you can revise easily

Point 14: Always learn short and simple reasoning tricks to save time

Point 15: It is very important to analyse your preparation. So, students should solve Verbal and Non Verbal Reasoning Questions and give Reasoning Test to find their weak areas.

Point 16: Devote extra time for the weak areas.

Point 17: Students should practice as much as they can by giving mock papers in online and offline mode.

Point 18: Students should analyse their mistakes and try not making mistakes again.

Point 19: Be confident and calm. If students are nervous, they will make unnecessary mistakes.

TIPS AND TECHNIQUES FOR ENGLISH PREPARATION

In this section, Commission tests the Basics of English Language, its vocabulary, grammar, sentence structure, synonyms, antonyms and its correct usage, etc. and the writing ability of the candidates. Each section has its own importance in SSC

Exams and the candidate needs to focus on each one of them to obtain overall top score. English Comprehension/ Language has vast syllabus and paper pattern has a lot of variation. The English Section in the SSC Exams takes less time as compared to the other sections. The candidates can easily attempt the English Section. But the point here is about the accuracy. If they have good accuracy, no one will stop them from scoring well in the SSC English Section.

Exam Pattern of English for SSC Exams

Exam	No. of Qs.	Total Marks	Marks per Correct Answer	Negative Marking	Paper Mode	Question Type
SSC CGL	25	50	2	0.5	Online	Objective
SSC CHSL	25	50	2	0.5	Online	Objective
SSC CPO	50	50	1	0.25	Online/ Offline	Objective
SSC MULTITASKING	50	50	1	0.25	Online	Objective
SSC STENOGRAPHERS	100	100	1	0.25	Online	Objective
SSC JUNIOR ENGINEER	N.A.	N.A	N.A.	N.A.	N.A.	N.A.
Scientific Assistant	25	25	1	0.25	Online	Objective

Analysis of English section In SSC Exams (2017)

Topics	CGL	CHSL	CPO	Stenographer	Multi-Tasking	Scientific Assistant
Sentence Improvement	3	1-2	5	10	2	2
Error Detection	3-4	1-3	5	10	2-3	2
Idiom/Phrases	3	2	5	5	2-3	2
Antonyms/ Synonyms	3-4	3-4	10	10	6	2
One word Substitution	2	2-3	5	-	1	2
Para- Jumbles	2	2	-	5	2-3	2
Close - Test	5	1	5	15	5	5
Spelling Check	2	5	5		2-3	2

Fill in the Blank	-	4-5	5	10	-	2-3
Direct- Indirect Speech	-	1	-	10	-	1
Active- Passive Voice	-	1	-	10	-	1
Comprehension		-	5	15	-	
Total	25	25	50	100	25	25

Important topics of English Section

Spotting Error

In this section, the students have to find grammatical error in the sentence. Four to five questions are expected to come in the Exam from this section. These types of questions require good grammatical sense.

Tips to solve Spotting Error in Exam

(i) Read the whole sentence carefully. There is a greater probability that you will detect the error here itself.

(ii) When reading the whole sentence, carefully check the **subject-verb agreement**.

(iii) If you can still not detect the error or you are still unsure of the correct answer, then you must read each **individual part of the sentence** and closely examine which part consists of an error.

Example 1: Once you graduate (1) / get a job (2) / would be easier (3) / No Errors (4).

Solution: (2): Replace get by "getting".

Example 2: The doctor says that (a)/ the patient will recover (b)/ in few days (c)/ No Error (d).

Solution: (b): Here "in a few days" should be used because it has a positive commutation which is correct in the context.

Fill in the Blanks

In the exam, there will be questions with only single fill in the blank.

Tips to solve this type of question in the exam

(i) Read the statement carefully and choose the word from the options which is suitable for the answer.

(ii) Use the method of elimination by simultaneously checking which of the options best satisfies both the entries.

(iii) You must ensure that the word you have filled in the blank makes the sentence smooth and correct.

Example: She_____ great pleasure and satisfaction from cooking.

   (a) wants   (b) has

   (c) draws   (d) derives

Solution: (c); She draws great pleasure and satisfaction from cooking.

Synonyms and Antonyms

(i)   Learn at least **10 new English words daily**. Note down the Meaning and example of each word you find unfamiliar or difficult to remember. This is the best way to cover Synonyms and Antonyms.

(ii)   Make shortcuts and tricks to help you learn words easy, and try to use them in your daily life.

(iii) Must study all the Synonyms and Antonyms from previous year papers as it is a known you know that SSC usually repeats a lot of questions.

Example: Choose the one which best expresses the meaning of the given word.

Prodigal

   (a) Exclusive   (b) Productive

   (c) Lavish   (d) carefree

Solution: (c); The word *Prodigal* means,*too willing to spend money or waste time, energy or materials; extravagant.* Here, *"Lavish"* expresses the best meaning of the word *"Prodigal"*

Idioms/Phrases & One Word Substitution

Sum up all the one word substitutions and Idioms and phrases from the previous year papers and learn them to score good in English section.

Example 1: Choose the alternative which best expresses the meaning of the given Idiom/Phrase.

A bolt from the blue

   (a) delayed event   (b) an inexplicable event

   (c) an unexpected event   (d) an expected event

Solution: (c) Idiom *'a bolt from the blue'* means, *'an event or a piece of news which is sudden and unexpected; a complete surprise'.*

Example 2: Choose the word which can be substituted for the given word/ sentence.

Stealing of ideas or writings of someone else

   (a) autism   (b) skepticism

   (c) mesmerism   (d) plagiarism

Solution: (d) Plagiarism

Spelling Mistakes

From this topic, you can easily get all the marks in your pocket. You just have to learn some rules for spelling errors that are very important to have an understanding of the usage of spellings in English Grammar.

Example: There are four different words out of which one is correctly spelt. Find the correctly spelt word.

(a) Pursuasive   (b) Persuasive

(c) Persuaseive   (d) Persuasieve

Solution: (b) Persuasive

Sentence Correction

In this topic, you have to find the correct alternatives which may improve the given sentence. Sometimes, there is no correction required then your answer will be 'no improvement'.

Tips to solve 'Sentence Correction' in Exam

(i) Read the original sentence carefully and try to spot grammatical errors by identifying whether something "**sounds**" wrong.

(ii) Always look at every choice.

(iii) Even when the original sentence seems fine, pay attention to the grammar that it tests and look through the choices systematically to see if any option provides a better alternative.

(iv) As you locate each error, **eliminate all the choices** that contain that error.

(v) Do not read each answer choice back into the sentence individually; that wastes time and invites inaccuracy.

(vi) Instead, identify the differences among the choices and eliminate those that offer less effective or grammatically incorrect alternatives.

Example: Choose the correct alternative.

He <u>who will bid the highest</u> will get the product.

(a) who bids the highest   (b) who the highest bids

(c) Who would bid the highest   (d) No Improvement

Solution: (a); He who bids the highest will get the product.

Cloze Test

A passage with 5 blanks is expected to come in **SSC CHSL Exam.** In this test, you are provided with a passage with few blanks and you need to fill these blanks from the given options.

Tips to solve Cloze Test in Exam

(i)   In a passage, almost every sentence is logically related to each other. This logic will give you an idea about the **appropriate word** for the blank space.

(ii)   Sometimes, you can easily spot the correct answer. If not, then **eliminate the improbable options** one by one and get the right answer.

(iii) Find a **logical relation** between all the given options.

READING COMPREHENSION

Step I: Identify the tone of the paragraph. It helps in answering questions quickly.

Step II: Read questions first so that you know what you are looking for.

Step III: Read first and the last paragraph twice and thoroughly.

Important Tips

(i) Read more and more passages. This will improve your speed in reading and understanding English.

(ii) Practice at least 10 comprehension passages daily.

(iii) **The trick here is to read the questions before you read the passage; this way** while reading the passage, you will know exactly what you are looking for. In fact, sometimes, the answers to all the questions which follow the passage lie in the initial paragraphs.

Note: Don't skip the comprehension part. The passages asked in the exam are easy and can be scored off quickly.

IMPORTANT POINTS

- Read newspapers and magazines to improve your reading habits.
- Learn at least 10 new English words and meanings daily.
- Solve previous year papers as there are many questions, which are repeated.
- Read the questions carefully and check what is being asked.
- Use method of elimination in confusing options and then try to get answers.
- Solve at least one mock paper every day.
- Try, solving the mock test yourself section-wise.
- Practice quizzes on the different topics.
- Don't waste much time on one question and move onto the next, if you are not sure about the correct answer.

- After you solve a mock test, review it, in and out. Analyse your errors, time taken, accuracy and approach.

- Try different time-management strategies in different mock tests and adopt the one that suits you the best.

TIPS AND TECHNIQUES FOR QUANTITATIVE APTITUDE

Quantitative Aptitude is one of the indispensable parts of the competitive exams. It is one of the most important and scoring sections in various SSC Exams. If candidates score well in the Quantitative Aptitude for SSC Exams, there are high chances that their overall score will be good, and they may get high profile post. To score well, they should have a good command over the basic concepts and should also be able to make fast calculations using the short tricks and formulae. Candidates must get complete clarity on the fundamental mathematical concepts and then practice with the help of solving questions based on it. This requires more preparation time and concentration, as compared to the other sections of the SSC Exams.

Exam Pattern of SSC Quantitative Aptitude

Exam	No. of Questions	Total Marks	Marks per Correct Answer	Negative Marking	Paper Mode	Question Type
SSC CGL	25	50	2	0.5	Online	Objective
SSC CHSL	25	50	2	0.5	Online	Objective
SSC CPO	50	50	1	0.25	Online/Offline	Objective
SSC Multi-tasking	25	25	1	0.25	Online	Objective
SSC Stenographers	N.A.	N.A.	N.A.	N.A.	N.A.	N.A.
Scientific Assistant	25	50	2	0.5	Online	Objective
SSC Junior Engineer	N.A.	N.A.	N.A.	N.A.	N.A.	N.A.

Analysis of Quantitative Aptitude Section of SSC Exams in 2017

Topic	CGL	CPO	CHSL	MTS	Scientific Assistant
S.I./ C.I.	1-2	3	1-2	2-3	1-2
Mensuration	1	3-5	2-3	4-5	
Trigonometry	2-3	2-3	2-3	-	2
Algebra	2-3	4-6	-	-	2
Time and Work/ Pipes and Cisterns	1-2	1-2	1	5	
Geometry	2	4-6	2-3	1	2-3
Speed and Distance	1	0-2	1	3-4	-
Average	1	1-2	1-2	1-2	1
Percentage	1	1-2	1-2	1-2	2-3
Data Interpretation	0-3	7-10	4	5	5
Profit and loss	1-2	4-5	-	2-3	2
Partnership	-	1	-		
Ratio and Proportion	1-2	4			1-2
Number System	1-2	1-2	1-2		1-2
Mixture and Alligation	1-2	0-1	-		1-2

General Tips to Crack Quantitative Aptitude in SSC Exams

Students should learn shortcuts only after learning and mastering the conventional way of solving quantitative questions. It is also important to be selective about the shortcut tricks. There are plenty of books available in the market that contain shortcut tricks for every topic under the Quant section. Candidates should not learn all the short tricks as it will confuse them.

Learn only the most important shortcuts that will help to arrive at the solution fast. The key is to master both the methods of solving questions conventional method and through shortcut techniques.

How to learn the Shortcut Techniques?

Shortcuts can be personalised also. Every individual can derive their own shortcuts depending on their strengths, weaknesses and understanding of the concepts and practice. Students should come up with shortcut techniques on their own. If and only if they cannot do that, they can refer to the books that contain shortcut techniques.

Likewise, don't waste your time trying to mug up all the formulas to all the questions. Learn only the most important formulas.

Practice Sets

Practice sets help in building concepts. They include topic-wise questions for practice. Each topic contains a variety of questions. Solve the questions from practice sets after learning the concepts. Topic tests sectional tests, and practice sets are created by exam toppers and experts for practice. They include thousands of questions of varying difficulty levels to prepare the students. The tests also provide in-depth analysis of performance, including time taken per topic, accuracy, all-India standing and much more.

Previous Years Question Papers

Once students have covered all the topics, understood all the concepts and practiced sufficiently, it's time to move to the next level solving the Previous Years Question Papers.

Why is it important to solve Previous Years Question Papers?
- The SSC tends to repeat questions from previous years in its question papers.
- Solving previous years question papers gives brief idea of the difficulty levels of the questions asked.
- They help in familiarising with the question patterns.

Revision

Revision is a very important step to retain information learnt and master the concepts. So, candidates must:
- Revise the basics at least twice, before moving on to the competition specific lectures/books
- Revise the practice sets twice.
- Revise important and high-level questions.

Mock Tests
- Take one Mock Test before preparing to assess your level.
- Take Topic Tests during preparation.
- Take complete Mock Tests, post revision stage.

Taking Mock Tests will help candidates measure progress, determine speed and accuracy and identify strong and weak areas. Take as many Mock Tests as possible to enhance Quant preparation.

Basic Points to Remember

1. Maintain a book to write down mistakes you are making and write down questions of higher level. In this way, you won't repeat mistakes again. Make separate notes of formulas of each chapter.
2. Practice questions and take Mock Tests in an Exam like environment to familiarise yourself with it. *Avoid using calculators; minimise the number of rough sheets used and time yourself during practice sessions.*

3. Do not waste too much time on a particular question during the exam. If you find yourself unable to answer a particular question, mark it for review and solve it later, if time permits.

4. If you are good at sections other than the Quant, solve them before Quant in as less time as possible (with great accuracy) and use the saved time for Quant.

5. Minimise the time taken and Maximise the accuracy in the Quant section. Try to solve all the questions in 25 - 30 minutes.

6. Try and answer all the questions. However, you can afford to leave 2-3 time consuming questions unanswered, if you are running out of time

7. Analyse the whole paper first and then attempt the easy questions first.

8. After the easy questions, you can go for the typical questions, in the ascending order of difficulty.

9. In the last 5-10 minutes, check the questions in which you have confusion and solve them accordingly.

10. Don't waste more than 2 minutes on any question. If you are unable to solve any question, just leave it.

11. Focus more on accuracy than the number of questions. This is equally important, along with the number of questions, as there is negative marking in SSC Exams.

12. Take proper rest before the day of the exam and just revise the formulas.

13. If you are not good at remembering short cut tricks for a problem, do not get disheartened. Better prepare to do it in the simple and longer way in a way as fast as the shortcut method.

14. Mental calculation is a must. Get the habit of calculating in your mind, as much as possible. It saves a lot of your time, while you have to attempt as many questions as possible within a given time. Give yourself time to develop this habit because it is all about practice.

15. Do not try to do something you have not done, just before the examination. That last minute effort to master a shortcut for one question, may land you into bigger troubles, concerning the rest of the paper.

16. You need to have a clear idea of concepts and formulas before applying it for a question. Do not try to use guess-work in the paper.

Short Cuts Techniques for Quantitative Aptitude

1. Solve questions by taking 100 as base

Example

Q. What is the profit percentage in selling an article at 20% discount which was earlier sold at 40% profit?

    (a) 20%   (b) 14%   (c) 28%   (d) 12%

Solution: (d) Let's take ₹100 as cost of the article. Man was selling the article for ₹ 140 (₹ 100 cost + ₹ 40 profit), Now, he is selling it at a discount of 20%,Now, 140*20/100 = 28. New selling price = 140-28 = 112

2. Play with options

Example

Q. A man bought 18 oranges for ₹ 100 and sold 12 oranges for ₹ 100 rupees. Calculate profit percentage.

(a) 33.333% (b) 50%

(c) 66.666% (d) Can't be determined

It can be easily seen that man saved 50% of what he sold. He saved 6 oranges, while he sold 12 oranges. Clearly answer is 50%.

Sol. (b)

3. Substitute the values

Example

Q. If $x^2 + 4x + 3 = 0$, then find $x^3 / x^6 + 27x^3 + 27$.

(a) 1 (b) −1 (c) ½ (d) −1/2

Sol. (b) On looking at this equation, we can easily get that $x = -1$ satisfies it. Therefore, $x = -1$ has to be one of its roots. Now, substitute $x = -1$ in the second equation. The value of the expression can be easily found out to be −1.

Let's prove $x^2 + 4x + 3 = 0$

Put the value of $x = -1$ in $x^2 + 4x + 3 = 0$ As per rule, 'BODMAS'

i.e. $-1^2 + 4* -1 + 3 = 0$ That will be $1 - 4 + 3 = 0$; $4 - 4 = 0$

4. Eliminate the Options

Q. A cylinder of radius 2 cm and height 4 cm is to be painted along its curved surface area. If the cost of painting a square cm is ₹2, find the cost of painting the cylinder.

(a) ₹32 Pi (b) ₹27 Pi (c) ₹33 Pi (d) ₹39 Pi

Sol. (a) Use the formula [2 Pi *rh] to find out the surface area of cylinder = 2x Pi × 2 × 4 = 16 Pi sq. cm

Rate of painting is ×2 per Sq. cm

So total cost = 16 Pi × 2 = ₹32 Pi

5. Use L.C.M. to Solve Problems from Unitary Method

Q. A can complete a piece of work in 10 days and B in 8 days. If A and B work on alternate days starting from A, when does the work get completed?

(a) 9 days (b) 5 days (c) 10 days (d) 7 days

Sol. (a) L.C.M. of 10 and 8 is 40. Here, assume that there are 40 units of work to be completed. A will complete 40/10 = 4 units of work per day. B will complete 40/8 = 5 units of work per day. If they work on alternate days, they will complete 9 units of work in 2 days. By the end of the eighth day, A and B will complete 36 units of work. Then will complete the remaining 4 units of work on the ninth day.

6. Use Effective Percentage

The concept of effective percentage can help to reduce your calculation time drastically.

You must have seen offers like 50% + 30% discount. The same kind of questions can be seen in most of the aptitude tests.

This offer means, first you will calculate 50% of the MRP, and then apply a 30% discount on the new value (it is not straight 80%). If a product is worth ₹100, then first apply 50% discount. You will arrive at 50 rupees. Now, apply 30% discount and you will arrive at 35.

An alternate way of doing this is to use effective percentage.

a + b + a*b/100 (a and b are the percentages)
= (-)50 + (-)30 + (-50)(- 30)/100
= -80 + 1500/100
= 65.

It means that 50% off + 30% off actually means flat 65% off on MRP. 65% off on 100 is 35, which is the correct answer we arrived at earlier.

There is a (-) sign at the beginning of percentages because they are discounts We are reducing the amount of 100, not increasing it. Had there been a question of compound interest where the amount gets increased, you would use a (+) sign.

7. How to Calculate Percentages Quickly

Tip-i: One trick that will often help aspirants to quickly calculate these types of percentages is to use the fact that x% of y = y% of x

Example
 36% of 25 = 25% of 36 =9
36x25/100= 25x36/100
9=9

Tip-ii: Learn to approximate percentages using fractions. Sometimes an approximation is good enough, other times it will help you check your answer for reasonableness. This technique requires two fundamental skills:
Proportional Thinking and *Wholes & Parts*
100% = 1 whole
75% = ¾
50% = ½
33.33 % = 1/3
25% = ¼
10% = 1/10

Tip -iii: Usually you need to calculate percentage exactly. Remember 30% means "divided by 100".
So, 30% = 30/100 =.30 =.3
Mentally calculate 16 × .3.

$15 \times 3 = 45$ therefore $16 \times 3 = 48$ so $16 \times .3 = 4.8$ so 30% of 16 is 4.8.

Tip -iv: Breakdown the word '**percent**' as '**per**' means "**for each**" and '**cent**' is the root word for "**100**." Then, '**per cent**' means "**for each 100**."

Example: In the case of a problem like "What is 16% of 475?" you have 16 for the first 100, 16 for the second 100, 16 for the third 100, 16 for the fourth 100 and then 3/4 of 16 or 12 for the 75.

Adding them all, i.e. $16 + 16 + 16 + 16 + 12 = 76$ OR $16 \times 4 + 12 = 76$

This works really well for straight forward percentage problems such as 7% of 300, 9% of 450, 8 × 1/2% of 200, 14% of 425, etc. Thus the aspirants can quickly calculate the answer mentally.

4. TIPS & TECHNIQUES FOR GENERAL AWARENESS

SSC General Awareness is one of the high scoring sections. If you are consistently learning SSC Current Affairs and General Knowledge, then you will surely get good marks in this section.

This is the only section, where you can save your time easily in the exam hall because SSC General Knowledge does not require any short tricks, formulas, logics etc.

Paper Pattern of SSC General Awareness Section

It is very important to know the exam pattern of SSC Exams such as SSC CHSL, CGL etc. The exam pattern shows you the total number of questions with marks for each section. When you have knowledge about paper pattern for SSC General Awareness, then you can boost your preparation easily.

Exam Pattern of General Awareness for SSC Exams

Name of Exam	No. of Questions	Total Marks	Marks Per Correct Answer	Negative Marking	Paper Mode	Question Type
SSC CGL	25	50	2	0.5	Online	Objective
SSC CHSL	25	50	2	0.5	Online	Objective
SSC CPO	50	50	1	0.25	Online/ Offline	Objective
SSC Multitasking	25	25	1	0.25	Online	Objective
SSC Stenographers	50	50	1	0.25	Online	Objective
SSC Junior Engineer	50	50	1	0.25	Online	Objective
Scientific Assistant	25	25	1	0.25	Online	Objective

                                                           Mission SSC

Analysis of No. of Questions Asked in Various SSC Exams in 2017

Topics	CGL	Scientific Assistant	Steno-grapher	Junior Engineer	CHSL	CPO	MTS
History	5-6	4	3-4	5	3-4	6-7	5
Geography	2	3	4-5	3	3-4	5-6	10
Polity	5-6	3	2-3	4-5	2	5-6	5
Economics	2	1	4-5	6	2	4-5	6
Science	7-8	9	18-19	19-20	7-8	18-20	16
Current Affairs	3-4	5	12-15	2-3	3	12-15	4
Miscellaneous	1-2	1-2	7-8	6	2-3	4-5	4
Computers	1-2	1-2	1-2	2-3	2	3-4	1
Total	25	25	50	50	25	50	25

Section Wise Overview of General Awareness for SSC Exams

1. **General Science:** In General Awareness for SSC, around 35-40% questions are asked mainly from Biology, Physics, Chemistry, Daily Science etc. Out of these, around 20-25% questions are from Biology itself.

2. **Current Affairs:** SSC Current Affairs covers around 10% from topics like recent   development in Sports, Awards, Politics, International happenings etc. Few SSC General Awareness Questions from Finance and Banking sector were also asked in previous exams.

3. **Miscellaneous:** This section has around 8-10% weightage of SSC General Awareness Questions in the exam. This section covers topics like National Schemes, Computers, Book Names and Authors, questions from Logical Analysis, Important Days etc.

4. **Static GK:** In this section, SSC General Awareness Questions are asked from static topics like Indian Politics, History and Culture, Economy, Geography etc. This section has around 40-45% weightage in SSC General Knowledge section.

Why scoring is easy in General Awareness Section?

1. **More marks in less time**: Since it is less calculation based, you can complete the GA section quickly. Even if you prepare science and technology, sports and current affairs nicely, you can expect to get at least 20 marks.

2. **Less Chances of Getting Negative Marks**: Again, since there is nothing to solve in General Awareness questions, you will always know whether you know the answer or not. This means there is no chance that you will knowingly mark an answer wrong.

3. **Repeated questions**: The biggest truth with SSC is that it does repeat questions and that too in all sections (Reasoning, Math, English and General Awareness). Have a look at the last 4-5 years question papers of SSC CGL Exams and you will find out that, there are around 2-3 questions in each section which are repeated every time. It is therefore necessary to solve Previous Year Papers.

General Tips

- Do not try to study everything because if you do the same then you will end up cramming and ultimately risk yourself being underprepared.

- Give 1-2 hours daily to get yourself prepared for SSC General Awareness Section.

- Enroll yourself for GK quizzes, which include questions with different difficulty level.

- Practice daily mock test papers with time bound conditions and analyse your preparation.

- Try not to spend more than 12 minutes on GK Section while practicing mock test. Mock Tests are one of the best measures to check the quality and level of your overall preparation.

- Read magazine, newspapers, weekly GK Blog online and watch news channels for SSC General Knowledge.

- Revision plays an important role in this section. Reading once won't give you benefit. You have to memorise those points by revising frequently.

- Practice previous years papers to know the types of questions asked.

- Complete one chapter in one day and solve chapter wise SSC General Awareness questions on the next day.

- Always create notes.

How to effectively read newspapers?

It is often seen that the students are confused on what to read in newspapers (or online media) for a competitive exam. First of all, never read more than one newspaper. With the rise in technology, every newspaper has all the important materials covered which may be asked in the exam.

You must know what you should not read in the newspaper. What is not important? For example,

*World tours of Lady Gaga, Justin Beiber.

*Abhishek Bachchan, Aishwarya Rai photoshoot.

*How many people are killed in a car bomb blast in Pakistan or Afghanistan?

*20 people died in car accident in Ahmedabad.

*Some girl eloped with a neighbour.

*A cop was found taking bribes.

*Arvind Kejriwal watched a movie.

*Anything happening for small-time that does not affect future of the Country or World (i.e. not a national or international issue).

*Personal matters of celebrities like Mulayam Singh said something about Karsevaks.

News items like above should not be touched. They are attractive and easily learned but they only waste time.

Types of General Awareness questions asked in SSC Exams

What is DPT?

What is the SI unit of inductance?

Who introduced Mansabdari system, which was the core foundation of the administrative system of the Mughal Empire?

Limestone is used in?

Which is the best indicator of Economic Development?

Where was the Bill for constitutional amendment initiated?

Who is the Chairman of Film and Television Institute of India (FTII)?

Which is the hardest type of coal?

Directive Principles of State Policy are adopted from which Constitution?

Red soil is found in which state?

Which was the first organic state of India?

Which Indian state has the largest coastline ?

Yogeshwar Dutt is related to which sport?

Where is the Periyar National Park situated?

Where is the Amartya Sen got Noble Prize in which field?

What is total number of Rajya Sabha members?
Which gland of human body secretes insulin ?

Sextant is used to measure?

In space, gravitational force is?

Where is RBI headquarter is located ?

Who constructed Gol Gumbaz Tomb?

Panna National Park is situated in which state?

Which state is also called as "Land of the Midnight Sun"?

What is the Full form of ALU?

What is the minimum age become a Rajya Sabha member?

Who was the first temporary Chairman of the Constituent Assembly?

Which is the biggest gland in the human body?

Some GK Short Tricks

1 .Trick to remember types of Taxes

*   **DIRECT TAXES**
    Trick:— "wepro.co.in"
    We—Wealth tax
    Pro—Property tax
    Co—-Corporate tax
    In—Income tax

*   **INDIRECT TAXES**
    Trick:— "Excuse me"

    Ex——Excise tax
    Cu——-Custom tax
    Se——-Service tax
    M——-Market tax/VAT
    E——-Entertainment tax

2. Trick to remember Mughal Emperors

Trick -"BHAJI SABJI FOR MAASAAB"

    B – Babur
    H –Humayun
    A – Akbar
    JI – Jahangir
    S – Shah Jahan
    A – Aurangzeb
    B – Bahadur Shah
    JI – Jahandar Shah
    For – Farrukhsiyar
    M – Muhammad Shah
    A – Ahmad Shah
    A – Alamgir II
    SA – Shah Alam II
    A – Akbar II
    B -Bahadur Shah Zafar

3. Enzymes secreted by Small Intestine

    Trick —- "SMELL"

    1. S——Sucrase

    2. M——Maltase

    3. E——Erepsin

    4. L——Lactase

    5. L——Lipase

4.   **Himalayan ranges from top to bottom**

    Trick : Kal Zana Padega Desh Se

    K = Karakoram

    Z = Zaskar

    P - Pir Panjal

    D = Dhauladhar

    S = Sivalik

5.   **Countries Through Which Prime Meridian Passes**

    Trick : BSF GAME IN TOTO

    B – Burkina Faso

    S – Spain

    F – France

    G – Ghana

    A – Algeria

    M - Mali

    E - England

    IN TOTO - Niger Toto

Shortcuts can be personalised also. Every individual can device their own shortcuts depending on their strengths and weaknesses and understanding of the concepts and practice.

5.TIPS AND TECHNIQUES FOR DATA ENTRY SPEED TEST (DEST) & COMPUTER PROFICIENCY TEST (CPT)

These are conducted to test the ability to do simple tasks such as to type correctly at a decent speed and knowledge of basic office software tools like the word processor, spreadsheets and slide maker (Microsoft Word, Excel and Power Point).

Important Points

- Both CPT and DEST exams are of qualifying nature.

- Marks obtained will not be counted in merit but if you do not pass exam then you will not get the desired post related to these exams.

- You need not to carry computer/laptop/keyboard as computer will be provided by the commission.

- Exemption for PH candidates is subject to government policy in force at the time.

SSC DEST/CPT Exam Pattern

TEST	TOPICS
CPT	<ul><li>Word Processing</li><li>Spreadsheets</li><li>Generation of Slides</li></ul>
DEST	<ul><li>2000 depressions in 15 minutes for a given passage</li></ul>

Data Entry Speed Test (DEST)/Skill Test

DEST, as the name suggests, is meant to check both speed and accuracy in typing on keyboard.

DEST is applicable for Tax Assistant (CBDT and CBEC) Post

How the DEST is conducted?

In the allocated time of 15 minutes, candidates need to accomplish the task of 2000 key depressions on computer. What this basically means is that they need to type passage/text which requires pressing 2000 keys on the computer keyboard in 15 minutes. *Space, comma, alphabets, numeric characters* – everything gets counted in the 2000 keys. Of course, you also need to be accurate.

Data Entry Skill Test (DEST)

Topic	Details	Tips
Key Depression	<ul><li>Almost similar to word processing in CPT.</li><li>You will be provided with a printed english passage that has to be typed on computer.</li><li>Candidates have to type 2000 characters (key depressions) in 15 minutes, without any formatting (Bold/Underline/Italic etc.)</li></ul>	Practice more and more on your computer by typing an article of approx. 2000 characters in 15 minutes.

Computer Proficiency Test (CPT)

Computer Proficiency Test, or CPT, is a bit more elaborate than DEST.

Computer Proficiency Test is meant for the candidates who have applied for the post of Assistant Section Officer in Central Secretariat Service (CSS).

How is the Computer Proficiency Test conducted?

SSC provides instructions for CPT/DEST. For any exam, the most genuine source of information is its official notification.

Usually, a candidate's ability to work on computers is gauged on three basic computer applications. So there are three modules each for 15 minutes each

Module 1 – Test on Microsoft Word

Module 2 – Test on Microsoft Excel

Module 3 – Test on Microsoft Power Point

Module 1 is similar to DEST. candidates will be given a printed passage and you have to type it within 15 minutes (2000 key depressions). This is not really too difficult for anyone who has some experience of typing on a computer keyboard.

In Module 2, aspirants are given a printed table which has to be created in Excel. They will also be asked to calculate some simple stuff like percentage, absolute increase/decrease, profits etc. using Excel formulas. This can be easily done by anyone who has some basic exposure to Excel. No complicated formulas are asked.

Module 3 tests aspirants on making slides (Microsoft Power Point). They will be given a printed copy of one (or maximum 2) slides. And then they have to make it on then computer in 15 minutes. There will also be instructions to change the font and size of text, use bullets, change header/footer, insert date, change file name etc. All this is basic stuff, assuming they have created a few 'PPT' files

Computer Proficiency Test (CPT)

Topic	Details	Tips
Word Processing	• Aspirants will be provided with a printed English passage that has to be typed on computer. • Candidates have to type 2000 characters (key depressions) in 15 minutes without any formatting (Bold/Underline/Italics etc.)	Practice on computer by typing an article of approx. 2000 characters in 15 minutes. Candidates can count the number of character in Microsoft Word automatically.
Spreadsheets	• They will be provided with a printed sheet that has to be created in Microsoft Excel. • Candidates have to calculate the data by using simple formulas of MS Excel like sum, multiplication, percentages etc.	Practice on computer in MS Excel to get the basic understanding related to spreadsheet creation, calculating the data using inbuilt calculation formulae.

Generation of Slides	<ul><li>They will be provided with a printed sheet showing the print-out of a single slide.</li><li>Candidates have to create the slide similar to that in 15 minutes in Microsoft Power Point.</li></ul>	Acquire basic knowledge of header, footer, date/time insertion, file address and basic understanding of Microsoft Power Point.

Given below is classification of errors. The Commission allows only a certain percentage of mistakes

Full Mistakes: The following errors will be treated as full mistakes:

- Every omission of word/ figure.

- For every substitution of a wrong word /figure.

- For every addition of a word / figure not found in the passage.

Half Mistakes: The following errors will be treated as half mistakes:

- **Spacing Errors:** No space is provided between two words, e.g. '**I think**' or undesired space is provided between the words or letters of a word e.g. I have, '**I have**'.

- For every **spelling error** committed by way of repetition, or addition or transposition or omission or substitution of a letter/letters, e.g. the word 'sleeping' typed as '**seeplings**' etc.

- **Wrong Capitalisation**: Wrong use of capital letter for small letter and vice-versa.

Mistakes Cut-off allowed: Cut-off means that up to this percentage, the mistakes are allowed by candidates for DEST and CPT candidates in Key depression exam:

General	OBC	SC	ST	OH,VH,HH
5%	7%	7%	15%	15%

Cut-off for spreadsheet and slide generation exam (Power Point and Excel sheet) in CPT exam is 120 for General candidates and 100 for all other candidates.

Exemptions of Handicapped Candidates

Orthopaedic Handicapped (OH) candidates who have opted for the post of Tax Assistant in CBDT (Income Tax) are exempted from DEST.

However, OH candidates who have opted for the post of Tax Assistant in CBEC (Excise) are not exempted. Also, candidates belonging to VH and HH category have to give this test. VH candidates are allowed compensatory time of 20 minutes. Also, those VH candidates who had opted for scribes in the written exams will be provided passage reader for DEST.

C.   PLANNING FOR SSC: DESCRIPTIVE EXAM

Exam Pattern

Total marks- 100 marks

Time duration- 1 hour

Paper Mode- Offline (Pen and Paper mode)

Topics- Essay / Passage (250 words)

       Letter / Application (150 words)

Qualifying marks- 33 per cent

Medium- Hindi or English

A. Preparation Tips and Strategy

1. Source of Preparation

Read newspapers and magazines to develop critical-thinking skills. This helps in improving the vocabulary and writing skills. Newspapers which can be followed are The Hindu and The Indian Express.

2. Topics to be covered

The articles you read should cover a wide range of recent **issue and application** based topics. Cover the burning topics from the following areas:

Social issues like unemployment, poverty, education, dowry system and farmers' suicide etc.

i.   **Finance and Economics Issues** like RBI Policy, GST, GDP, demonetisation, and banking frauds, etc.

ii.   **World Politics** like Brexit, North Korea sanctions, Syrian refugee crisis and South China Sea, etc.

iii. **Environmental issues** like Pollution, global warming, climate change and biodiversity, etc.

iv. **Science and Technology** like Mangalyaan, social media and online data security, etc.

v.   **Government Schemes** like Jan Dhan Yojana, Give up LPG Gas Subsidy Scheme, etc.

3. Time Management

Since you have 60 minutes to attempt, you need to devote a fixed amount of time to each question.

4. Good Presentation

An effective presentation is must to have an impact on the reader/examiner. Avoid cutting and overwriting. Make sure to write all points and facts in a very neat handwriting. Make sure your handwriting is legible. Avoid making grammatical mistakes.

5. Improve the Basics

For any competitive descriptive exam, for writing incredible Essays/ Precis/ Letters, you need at least an intermediate understanding of the basic principles of writing. In order to do it, you need to know the basics of grammar and spelling. Every student should know the tricks to write exam-centric content and score maximum marks in the descriptive exam.

6. Try to write everyday

Unfortunately, there are no shortcuts that can transform you into an amazing writer overnight, and even the most talented writers had to learn their craft over a period of time. As an SSC exam aspirant, you need to cultivate writing habits. Write the drafts, read it and do it again; keep writing. Practice will make you perfect. Be in touch with someone who can judge your writing skills. Get feedback and work on it again to make it better.

7. Reading is very important

The best writers are also keen readers and reading on a regular basis is an easy way to start developing writing skills. Expand your reading horizons to the more challenging material than you usually read, and pay attention to sentence structure, word choice, and how the material flows. Read about science, politics, social issues, art subjects, etc. so that you can have sound knowledge of all relevant and important topics. The more you read, the more likely you are to develop an eye for what makes a piece so effective and which mistakes to avoid. Find a writing partner, read each other's work and give feedback. This way you can improve day by day. Talk to your friends in the classroom (or mentors) and ask someone, if they'd be willing to cast an eye over your work – they may spot mistakes that you overlooked.

8. Outlines are very useful

Creating outlines is the first step to write wonderful passage/essay. In SSC Exams, the presentation of the idea is very important. Before you start writing, sketch out an outline of what you plan to write. An outline doesn't have to be complex. A simple framework of which sections should appear in a particular order, along with a few sentences about what each section contains, may be enough. If you start feeling lost, refer back to your outline and complete the essay in an effective way.

9. Edit and Eliminate Unnecessary Words

Editing is a tough skill to learn for beginner compiler, because they place immense value on the time and effort they put into writing in the first place. Develop the discipline it takes to eliminate extra words. Be tough on yourself, and know when to delete or rework something. Your work will be much stronger as a result. First drafts are almost always below the average, and that's okay. Don't get demotivated, just write, down your ideas on the paper first, then go back and start cleaning up. Writing is an iterative process, and even the best writers have to spend a lot of time reworking material, they were probably too embarrassed to show anybody.

Another common mistake among students is writing overly complex sentences in an attempt to "sound" more authoritative and knowledgeable. In many cases, shorter sentences can have a greater impact.

B. How to Write an Essay in SSC?

Essay writing is an important topic in which you are not only tested based on your knowledge and grammar but also on your opinions. The major sources of essay topics are burning issues covered in print media on current affairs ranging from environment, politics, social, economics to Science & Tech.

Structure of Essay

Essay writing should be divided into 3 parts: Introduction, Body, Conclusion.

Introduction and conclusion should be around 50 words each and body should have around 150-200 words.

Introduction

It has direct reference to the topic of the essay. It should catch the attention of the readers. As on its basic, a reader decides whether to read the complete essay or not. Make it catchy, clear and concise. Start with a quote in the introduction, if possible.

Body

The body of the essay can be divided into 2-3 different paragraphs and related ideas can be discussed under these. Use word specific approach and bring in words that are most related to the topic. Bring all the point of views with pros and cons of the topic.

Be balanced with your approach and don't write one sided essay. Do not add too much of the data, but only enough to substantiate what you claim.

Conclusion

It is an important part and contains the crux of all that has been described in the previous passages. Do not end the essay on a negative approach. In this, give an opinion of your own or a suggestion for the future.

For example: Essay written by SSC TOPPER Mr. Narendra Kumar is given in box. Read and try to write in your own language.

TOPIC- Social Media/Cyberspace and Internet: Blessing or curse to human civilization in the long run

Usages of social networking sites like Facebook, Twitter, whatsApp, etc. have dramatically increased recently with the advancement of technology. Although, it has many detrimental effects on the society but its positive side cannot be neglected.

Social networking sites mitigate communication gap not only in the immediate social circle but also with friends and families in remote areas by sharing their news and updates. They provide a rapid and effective way of interaction among people. Furthermore, many social groups exist on such sites which help people to find persons of the same interests and attitudes without confiding them to only geographical boundaries. It has recently been seen that many injustice and social issues were shared in social networking sites and that made a huge impact on authority and that has brought justice to the victims. Social networking sites are a common ground for mass people to share their updates, views and other details. Thus this has created a world without any boundary.

On the other hand, it is often seen that people have become disjointed and fragmented dues to the social networking sites. Most affected are youngsters who would like to spend most of their time on these sites. This has led dire consequences on their physical and psychological health. Moreover, families are greatly affected by this and their social bonding is no more present in contemporary days. People are getting addicted to these websites and thus becoming less social in many cases. Propaganda and fraud relationship have caused many personal and social dilemma.

To sum up, I would like to say that people have become more social and interactive by the use of social networking sites. It gives people a sense of freedom to talk around the world without worrying about the huge cost that incurred previously. However, it has severe negative effects, as most of the people opt to talk using technology than meeting others in person due to their busy lifestyle, it increases the distance in their relationship.

Source: http://www.sscadda.com/2017/03/tier-iii-descriptive-paper-essay-3-by.html

C. Letter Writing Tips

Write a letter in the formal language to present your views. Try to avoid short forms and slangs. You must follow a prescribed format to write a letter or application. While writing a letter, you must keep the following points in your mind: Purpose of writing, To the person (address), Appropriate language, complete message, fluency, what actions are you willing to take and short and accurate information.

1. Format of Formal Letter

Sender's address – on the top left corner of the page

Date – Just below sender's address

Receiver's address

Salutation – (Sir/ Madame) if not sure about gender' just write 'Sir'

Subject – Mention the problem in 6 - 8 words

Body of letter – 3 - 5 paragraphs

1. Introduction
2. Main Contents
3. Conclusion

Thanking you

Yours faithfully/truly

Signature

Note: if it is not mentioned in the question, just write ABC or XYZ. Do not write your name)

2. Format for Informal Letter

Sender's Address- on the top right corner of the page.

Date – Just below sender's address.

Salutation (My dear father/My dear friend)

Good Morning/Hope you are doing well etc.

Body of letter (

)

With best wishes/ With regards

Name of the sender (XYZ)

Important Instructions

- Fill in the Name, Roll No. Ticket No. and Signature in the required boxes.
- You are not allowed to write any of details in the inner pages.
- Boxes are given to write each word. Fill the boxes with each of a single word forming the essay. Only one word is allowed in one box.
- Use the words precisely keeping the word limits in the mind, i.e. 250 words limit is accepted in an essay writing and 150 in the letter writing.

SSC CGL 2016-17 Descriptive Analysis

Question type	Essay	Letter (Informal)	Remarks
Question content	Do's and don't during an earthquake	Letter to your younger brother talking about pros and cons of computer based tests	
Marks	50	50	Total marks: 100
Word limit	250 words	150 words	Try to stick to word limit. 5-10 additional words should not be penalised.
Suggested time to devote	35 minutes	25 minutes	Since the essay has a longer word limit, aspirants should devote a few extra minutes. However, both questions are worth 50 marks, so it is important to give equal weightage to them.
Key success factors	• Legible, handwriting and neat work is more important; for example, cursive writing. • Exceeding word limit by a few words (~5%) shouldn't impact performance. • Better to have a complete answer, instead of adding more points and leaving the answer incomplete.		

Notes:

1. No choice was given to the students.
2. Answer sheet consists of 12 pages and each page consists of 4 columns and 14 rows.
3. It was strictly mentioned that candidates have to follow the word limit. However, they can exceed only 10% of the word limit.
4. They were allowed to write the exam in the black/blue pen. Pens were not provided in the exam hall and they have to bring their own pens. The exam started at 11 AM and finished at 12 PM.

Mathematics- Trending Questions from Past Paper

Number System

1. How many numbers are there from 300 to 650 which are completely divisible by both 5 and 7?

   (SSC CGL 2017)

   (a) 8   (b) 9

   (c) 10   (d) 12

   Ans. (c) LCM of 5 and 7 = 35

   So, the numbers divisible by both 5 and 7 are multilpe of 35. Between 300 and 650. We have 10 multiple of 35. They are : 315, 350, 385, 420, 455, 490, 525, 560, 595, 630.

2. The greatest number that can divide 140, 176, 264 leaving remainders of 4, 6, and 9 respectively is

   (SSC Sub. Ins 2017)

   (a) 85   (b) 34

   (c) 17   (d) 2

   Ans. (c) Required number = H.C.F of $(140-4)$, $(176-6)$ and $(264-9)$ = H.C.F. of 136, 170 and 255.

$$136\overline{)255}(1$$
$$\underline{136}$$
$$119\overline{)136}(1$$
$$\underline{119}$$
$$17\overline{)119}(7$$
$$\underline{119}$$
$$\times$$

$$136\overline{)170}(1$$
$$\underline{136}$$
$$34\overline{)136}(4$$
$$\underline{136}$$
$$\times$$

$\therefore$ Required number = 17

Alternate Method:

Here divisible terms are $140-4=136$, $176-6=170$ and $264-9=255$

Now, difference between these numbers

$170-136=34$

$225-170=85$

H.C.F of difference = 17

Hence required number = 17.

Simplification and Square & Cube Root

3. If the numbers $\sqrt[3]{9}$, $\sqrt[4]{20}$, $\sqrt[6]{25}$ are arranged in ascending order, then the right arrangement is

   (SSC CGL 2017)

   (a) $\sqrt[6]{25} < \sqrt[4]{20} < \sqrt[3]{9}$

   (b) $\sqrt[3]{9} < \sqrt[4]{20} < \sqrt[6]{25}$

   (c) $\sqrt[4]{20} < \sqrt[6]{25} < \sqrt[3]{9}$

   (d) $\sqrt[6]{25} < \sqrt[3]{9} < \sqrt[4]{20}$

Ans. (d) $\sqrt[3]{9}, \sqrt[4]{20}, \sqrt[6]{25}$

LCM of $3, 4, 6 = 24$

$\sqrt[24]{9^8}, \sqrt[24]{20^6}, \sqrt[24]{25^4}$

$\sqrt[24]{25^4} < \sqrt[24]{9^8} < \sqrt[24]{20^6}$

i.e. $\sqrt[6]{25} < \sqrt[3]{9} < \sqrt[4]{20}$

Alternate Method:

$9^{\frac{1}{3}}, 20^{\frac{1}{4}}, 25^{\frac{1}{6}}$

L.C.M of Numbers of Powers $= 12$

$12\sqrt{9^4}, 12\sqrt{20^3}, 12\sqrt{25^2}$

$\sqrt[12]{6561}\ \sqrt[12]{8000}, \sqrt[12]{625}$

$\sqrt[6]{25} < \sqrt[3]{9} < \sqrt[4]{20}$

4. The value of $\dfrac{(2.3)^3 + 0.027}{(2.3)^3 - 0.69 + 0.09}$

(SSC CGL 2017)

(a) 2 (b) 2.27

(c) 2.33 (d) 2.6

Ans.(d) $\dfrac{(2.3)^3 + 0.027}{(2.3)^3 - 0.69 + 0.09}$

$\Rightarrow \dfrac{(2.3 + 0.3)\left[(2.3)^2 - 0.69 + 0.09\right]}{\left[(2.3)^3 - 0.69 + 0.09\right]}$

$\Rightarrow 2.3 + 0.3 = 2.6$

5. If $x = \dfrac{1}{\sqrt{2}+1}$

then $(x + 1)$ equals to

(SSC CGL 2nd Sit. 2017)

(a) 2 (b) $\sqrt{2}-1$

(c) $\sqrt{2}+1$ (d) $\sqrt{2}$

Ans. (d) $x = \dfrac{1}{\sqrt{2}+1} \times \dfrac{\sqrt{2}-1}{\sqrt{2}-1} = \sqrt{2}-1$

Now, $x + 1 = \sqrt{2} - 1 + 1 = \sqrt{2}$

Algebra

6. If $x = 2 + \sqrt{3}$, then what is the value of $\sqrt{2x} + \dfrac{1}{\sqrt{2x}}$?

(SSC CGL 2017)

(a) $2\sqrt{3}$ (b) $3\sqrt{3}$

(c) $(3\sqrt{3}+1)/2$ (d) $2\sqrt{3}+1$

Ans. (c) $\sqrt{2x} + \dfrac{1}{\sqrt{2x}}$

$= \sqrt{2(2+\sqrt{3})} + \dfrac{1}{\sqrt{2(2+\sqrt{3})}}$

$= \sqrt{4 + 2\sqrt{3}} + \dfrac{1}{\sqrt{4 + 2\sqrt{3}}}$

$= \sqrt{(\sqrt{3}+1)^2} + \dfrac{1}{\sqrt{(\sqrt{3}+1)^2}}$

$= \sqrt{3} + 1 + \dfrac{\sqrt{3}-1}{2} = \dfrac{3\sqrt{3}+1}{2}$

7. If $x + \dfrac{1}{x} = 4$, then what is the value of $x^6 + \dfrac{1}{x^6}$? **(SSC CGL 2017)**

   (a) 52   (b) 256
   (c) 1026   (d) 2702

Ans. (d) $x + \dfrac{1}{x} = 4$

then,

$$x^6 + \dfrac{1}{x^6} = ?$$

Let $x + \dfrac{1}{x} = a$

$\because$ $x^6 + \dfrac{1}{x^6} = \left(a^3 - 3a\right)^2 - 2$

$\Rightarrow ((4)^3 - 3 \times 4)^2 - 2$

$\Rightarrow (64 - 12)^2 - 2 = (2704 - 2)$

$= 2702$

---

8. If $y = \dfrac{2 - x - x}{1 + 1 + x}$, then what is the value of $\dfrac{1}{y+1} + \dfrac{2y+1}{y^2 - 1}$?

(SSC CGL 2017)

  (a) $\dfrac{(1+x)(2-x)}{2x-1}$

  (b) $\dfrac{(1-x)(2+x)}{x-1}$

  (c) $\dfrac{(1+x)(2-x)}{1-2x}$

  (d) $\dfrac{(1+x)(1-2x)}{2-x}$

Ans. (c)

Average

9. The average of 5 members of a family is 24 years. If the youngest member is 8 years old, then what was the average age (in years) of the family at the time of the birth of the youngest member?

(SSC CGL 2017)

  (a) 16   (b) 20
  (c) 24   (d) 32

Ans. (b) Required average age

$$= \dfrac{(24 \times 5 - 8 \times 5)}{4}$$

$$\Rightarrow \dfrac{120 - 40}{4} \Rightarrow \dfrac{80}{4} = 20 \text{ years}$$

---

10. The average runs conceded by a bowler in 5 matches is 45 and 15.75 in other 4 matches. What is the average runs conceded by the bowler in 9 matches?

(SSC CGL 2017)

  (a) 15   (b) 32
  (c) 35   (d) 53.5

Ans. (b) Required average runs

$$= \dfrac{(45 \times 5) + (15.75 \times 4)}{9} = \dfrac{288}{9} = 32.$$

Percentage

11. After deducting 60% from a certain number and then deducting 15% from the remainder, 1428 is left. What was the initial number?

  (a) 4200   (b) 3962
  (c) 4150   (d) 4300

Ans. (a) Let initial number be x.

According to question,

$$x \times \frac{40}{100} \times \frac{85}{100} = 1428$$

$$\therefore \quad x = \frac{1428 \times 100 \times 100}{40 \times 85} = 4200.$$

12. 80 litre mixture of milk and water contains 10% milk. How much milk (in litres) must be added to make water percentage in the mixture as 80%?

    (a)   8   (b) 9

    (c)   10   (d) 12

Ans. (c) According to question,

Volume of water

$$= 80 \times \frac{90}{100} = 72 \text{ litres}$$

Volume of milk

$$= 80 \times \frac{10}{100} = 8 \text{ litres}$$

Now,

$$\frac{8+x}{72} = \frac{20}{80}$$

$$\Rightarrow \quad 640 + 80x = 1440$$

$$\therefore \quad x = \frac{(1440 - 640)}{80} = 10 \text{ litres}.$$

13. A person spends 25% of his annual income on house rent. 15% on education of children and 45% on other items. If he saves ₹14,400 annually, then the person's total income is:

    (a)   ₹98,000

    (b)   ₹1,00,000

    (c)   ₹96,000

    (d)   ₹1,20,000

Ans. (c) Total spend of his annual income

$$= (15\% + 25\% + 45\%) = 85\%$$

$\therefore$ Saves $= (100 - 85)\% = 15\%$

$\therefore$ 15% of annual income

$$= 14400$$

$\therefore$ 100% annual income

$$= \frac{14400}{15} \times 100$$

$$= 96,000$$

$\therefore$ Total income $= ₹96,000$

Profit & Loss

14. For an article the profit is 170% of the cost price. If the cost price increases by 20% but the selling price remains same, then what is the new profit percentage?

(SSC CGL 2017)

    (a)   41   (b) 50

    (c)   75   (d) 125

Ans. (d) Let cost price of an article

$$= 100$$

$\therefore$ Profit $= 170$

$\therefore$ S.P. $= 100 + 170 = 270$

Now,

Cost price increased by 20%, then

Cost price $= 120$

S.P. $= 270$

$\therefore$ Profit $= 270 - 120 = 150$

$\therefore$ Profit percentage

$$= \frac{150}{120} \times 100$$

$$= 125\%$$

15. After two successive discount of 20% and 35%, an article is sold for ₹ 50700. What is the marked price (in ₹) of the article?

(SSC CGL 2017)

(a) 92500   (b) 98500
(c) 97500.   (d) 94000

Ans. (c) Let the mark price be x.

after first discount, price

$$= x \times \frac{80}{100}$$

after the second discount, price

$$= x \times \frac{80}{100} \times \frac{65}{100}$$

According to question,

$$x \times \frac{80}{100} \times \frac{65}{100} = 50700$$

$$\therefore \quad x = \frac{50700 \times 100 \times 100}{80 \times 65}$$

$$= 97500.$$

$\therefore$ marked price of article is ₹. 97500.

---

16. By selling 175 pineapples, the gain is equal to the selling price of 50 pineapples. What is the gain percentage? **(SSC CGL 2017)**

(a) 28   (b) 30
(c) 32   (d) 40

Ans.(d) Let S.P. of each pineapple

$= $ Re 1

$\therefore$ Gain $= 50$, SP $= 175$

$\therefore$ CP $= (175 - 50) = 125$

$\therefore$ Required percentage

$$= \frac{50}{125} \times 100$$

$$= 40\%$$

Simple Interest & Compound Interest

17. A person lent certain sum of money at 5% per annum simple interest and in 15 years the interest amounted to ₹ 250 less than the sum lent. What was the sum lent (in ₹)? **(SSC CGL 2017)**

(a) 1000   (b) 1500
(c) 2400   (d) 3000

Ans. (a) Let principal $= x$

Then,

$\therefore$ Simple Interest $= x - 250$

According to question,

$$(x - 250) = \frac{x \times 5 \times 15}{100}$$

$$100x - 25000 = 75x$$

$$25x = 25000$$

$$\therefore \quad x = \frac{25000}{25} = 1000$$

---

18. A certain sum of money triples itself in 5 years at simple interest. In how many years it will be five times?

(SSC CGL 2017)

(a) 5   (b) 8
(c) 10   (d) 15

Ans. (c) Here,

$P = x$

$T = 5$

$A = 3x$

$\therefore$ S.I $= 3x - x = 2x$

$$\therefore \quad 2x = \frac{x \times 5 \times r}{100} \quad \therefore r = 40\%$$

Now,

$P = x$

$A = 5x$

$$\therefore \quad \text{S.I.} = 5x - x = 4x$$
$$T = ?$$
$$\therefore \quad 4x = \frac{x \times 40 \times T}{100}$$
$$\therefore \quad T = \frac{4x \times 100}{x \times 40} = 10 \text{ years.}$$

19. The difference between the compound interest compounding half yearly for 1 year and the simple interest for 1 year on a certain sum of money lent out at 8% per annum is ₹ 64. What is the sum (in ₹)?

(SSC CGL 2017)

(a) 40000   (b) 42000

(c) 44000   (d) 44800

Ans.(a) According to question,

$$64 = \left[P\left(1 + \frac{8}{200}\right)^2 - P \right] - \left[\frac{P \times 8 \times 1}{100} \right]$$
$$64 = \frac{51P}{625} - \frac{2P}{25}$$
$$64 = \frac{51P - 50P}{625}$$
$$\therefore \quad 64 = \frac{P}{625}$$
$$\therefore \quad P = 625 \times 64 = 40{,}000.$$

Ratio, Proportion, Mixture and Partnership

20. ₹ 3200 is divided among A, B and C in the ratio of 3 : 5 : 8 respectively. What is the difference (in ₹) between the share of B and C?

(SSC CGL 2017)

(a) 400   (b) 600

(c) 800   (d) 900

Ans. (b) Share of A $= \dfrac{3200}{16} \times 3 = 600$

Share of B
$$= \frac{3200}{16} \times 5 = 1000$$
Share of C
$$= \frac{3200}{16} \times 8 = 1600$$
$\therefore$ Different between B and C
$$= (1600 - 1000) = 600.$$

21. A, B and C invested amounts in the ratio 3 : 4 : 5 respectively. It the schemes offered compound interest at the rate of 20% per annum, 15% per annum and 10% per annum respectively, then what will be the ratio of their amounts after 1 year?

(SSC CGL 2017)

(a) $3 : 15 : 25$

(b) $6 : 6 : 5$

(c) $36 : 46 : 55$

(d) $12 : 23 : 11$

Ans.(c) Let A, B, and C invested amounts in the ratio $300 : 400 : 500$ respectively.

then,

$\therefore$ Required ratio

$$= \frac{300 \times 120}{100} : \frac{400 \times 115}{100} : \frac{500 \times 110}{100}$$
$$= 36 : 46 : 55.$$

22. If $A : B = 2 : 5$, $B : C = 4 : 3$ and $C : D = 2 : 1$, then what is value of $A : C : D$? **(SSC CGL 2017)**

(a) $6 : 5 : 2$ (b) $7 : 20 : 10$

(c) $8 : 30 : 15$ (d) $16 : 30 : 15$

Ans. (d) $A : B = 2 : 5$

$B : C = 4 : 3$

$$= \left(4 \times \frac{5}{4} : 3 \times \frac{5}{4}\right) = 5 : \frac{15}{4}$$

$C : D = 2 : 1$

$$= \left(2 \times \frac{15}{8} : 1 \times \frac{15}{8}\right) = \frac{15}{4} : \frac{15}{8}$$

$\therefore \quad A : B : C : D = 2 : 5 :$

$$\frac{15}{4} : \frac{15}{8} = 16 : 40 : 30 : 15$$

$\therefore \quad$ Value of $A : C : D = 16 : 30 : 15$

---

23. Raman, Manan, and Kamal are partners and invest in a business such that Raman invests 2/5th of total and Manan invest 3/8th of the total. What is the ratio of profit of Raman, Manan and Kamal respectively?

(a) $16 : 15 : 9$ (b) $16 : 15 : 31$

(c) $2 : 3 : 5$ (d) $15 : 16 : 9$

Ans. (a) Let total investment $= x$

$$\text{Investment by Raman} = \frac{2x}{5}$$

$$\text{Investment by Manan} = \frac{3x}{8}$$

Investment by Kamal

$$= x - \left(\frac{2x}{5} + \frac{3x}{8}\right)$$

$$= \frac{9x}{40}$$

Ratio of invest of Raman, Manan and Kamal

$$= \frac{2x}{5} : \frac{3x}{8} : \frac{9x}{40} = 16 : 15 : 9$$

$\therefore \quad$ Ratio of profit of Raman, Manan and Kamal

$= 16 : 15 : 19$

---

24. A, B and C can complete a work in 20, 24 and 30 days respectively. All three of them starts together but after 4 days A leaves the job and B left the job 6 days before the work was completed. C completed the remaining work alone. In how many days was the total work completed?

(SSC CGL 2017)

(a) 10   (b) 12

(c) 14   (d) 16

Ans. (c) Suppose, the work was finished in x days. Then, A's 4 day's work + B's $(x-6)$ day's work + C's x day's work $= 1$

$$\Rightarrow \quad \frac{4}{20} + \frac{x-6}{24} + \frac{x}{30} = 1$$

$$\Rightarrow \quad \frac{24 + 5(x-6) + 4x}{120} = 1$$

$$\Rightarrow \quad 24 + 5x - 30 + 4x = 120$$

$$\Rightarrow \quad 9x = 126$$

$$\therefore \quad x = \frac{126}{9} = 14 \text{ days}$$

---

25. Raman can do a work in 5 days, Jatin can do the same work in 7 days and Sachin can do the same work in 9 days. If they do the same work together and they are paid ₹ 2860, then what is the share (in ₹) of Raman? **(SSC CGL 2017)**

(a) 1260   (b) 700

(c) 900   (d) 870

Ans. (a) Raman's 1 day's work $= \dfrac{1}{5}$

Jatin's 1 day's work $= \dfrac{1}{7}$

$$\text{Sachin's 1 day's work} = \frac{1}{9}$$

$\therefore$ Ratio of their wages $= 63 : 45 : 35$

$\therefore$ Raman's share $= \dfrac{2860}{143} \times 63$

$= 1260.$

26. A piece of work was finished by A, B, and C together. A and B together finished 60% of the work and B and C together finished 70% of work. Who among the three is the most efficient? **(SSC CGL 2017)**

(a) A (b) B

(c) C (d) A or B

Ans. (c) According to question,

$A + B = 60\%$

$\therefore$ $(A+B) + (B+C) - (A+B+C) = B$

$(60 + 70 - 100) = 30$

$\therefore$ $B = 30\%$

$A = 30\%$ and

$C = 40\%$

Hence, C is most efficient.

Time, Speed & Distance

27. A boat goes 15 km upstream and $10\dfrac{1}{2}$ km downstream in 3 hours 15 minutes. It goes 12 km upstream and 14 km downstream in 3 hours. What is the speed of the boat in still water? **(SSC CGL 2017)**

(a) 4 (b) 6

(c) 10 (d) 14

Ans. (c) Let speed of the boat in still water be x km/h and speed of current be y km/h.

Then,

upstream speed $= (x - y)$ km/h and down stream speed $= (x + y)$ km/h

Now,

$$\frac{15}{(x-y)} + \frac{21}{2(x+y)} = 3\frac{1}{4} \qquad ...(i)$$

$$\frac{12}{(x-y)} + \frac{14}{(x+y)} = 3 \qquad ...(ii)$$

From Equation (i) and (ii)

$x = 10$ km/hr and $y = 4$ km/hr.

28. A train travels 40% faster than a car. Both start from point A at the same time and reach point B, 140 km away at the same time. On the way the train takes 25 minutes for stopping at the stations. What is the speed (in km/hr) of the train?

(SSC CGL 2017)

(a) 67 (b) 134.4

(c) 145.9 (d) 160

Ans. (b) Let speed of car $= x$

$\therefore$ Speed of train

$$= x + \frac{x \times 40}{100} = \frac{7x}{5}$$

According to question,

$$\frac{140}{x} = \frac{140 \times 5}{7x} + \frac{25}{60}$$

$$\frac{140}{x} - \frac{700}{7x} = \frac{25}{60}$$

$$x = \frac{280 \times 60}{25 \times 7} = 96 \text{ km/hr}$$

$\therefore$ Speed of train $= \dfrac{7x}{5} = \dfrac{7 \times 96}{5}$

$= 134.4$ km/hr

29. A train leaves Delhi at 10 a.m. and reaches Jaipur at 4 p.m. on same day. Another train leaves Jaipur at 12 p.m. and reaches Delhi at 5 p.m. on same day. What is the time of day (approximately) when the two trains will meet? **(SSC CGL 2017)**

(a) 1 : 42 p.m. (b) 1 : 27 p.m.

(c) 2 : 04 p.m. (d) 1 : 49 p.m.

Ans.(d) Suppose distance between Delhi and Jaipur is 30 kms.

Then,

Speed of first train

$$= \frac{30}{6} = 5 \text{km/hr}$$

Speed of second train

$$= \frac{30}{5} = 6 \text{km/hr}$$

If trains met after t hours from 10 a.m. then

$$5t + 6 \times (t - 2) = 30$$
$$5t + 6t - 12 = 30$$
$$11t = 42$$

$$t = \frac{42}{11} \text{ hours} = 3 \text{ hours } 49 \text{ minutes}$$

∴ Trains meet 3 hours 49 minutes after 10 a.m. i.e. at 1 : 49 pm.

30. A bus starts running with the initial speed of 21 km/hr and its speed increases every hour by 3 km/hr. How many hours will it take to cover a distance of 252 km?

(SSC CGL 2017)

(a) 3   (b 5

(c) 8   (d) 10

Ans.(c) Since speed of bus increases every hour by 3 km/hr.

∵ Initial speed = 21 km/hr

Total distance = 252 km

According to Arithmatic Progression

$a = 21, d = 3, sn = 252\ n = ?$

$$S_n = \frac{n}{2}\left([2a + (n-1)d]\right)$$

$$252 = \frac{n}{2}(42 + 3n - 3)$$

$$504 = n(3n + 39)$$
$$3n^2 + 39n - 504 = 0$$
$$n^2 + 21n - 8n - 168 = 0$$
$$\Rightarrow\quad n(n + 21) - 8(n + 21) = 0$$
$$\therefore\quad (n - 8)(n + 21)$$
$$\Rightarrow\quad n = 8, n \neq -21$$

∴ So, 8 hours will it take to cover a distance of 252 km.

Mensuration

31. A solid sphere of diameter 17.5 cm is cut into two equal. halves. What will be the increase (in cm^2) in the total surface area? **(SSC CGL 2017)**

(a) 289   (b) 361.5

(c) 481.25   (d) 962.5

Ans. (c) Here,

Radius of sphere

$$= \frac{17.5}{2} \text{ cm} = 8.75 \text{ cm}$$

∴ Total surface Area of sphere $= 4\pi r^2$

$$= 4 \times \frac{22}{7} \times 8.75 \times 8.75$$

$$= 962.5 \text{ cm}^2$$

After cut in two equal halves.

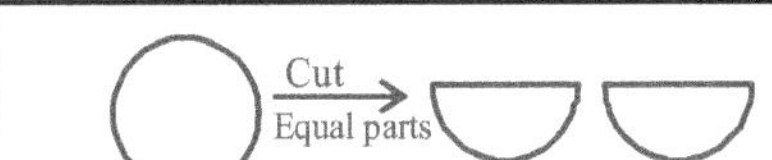

$\therefore$ Total surface of both hemisphere $= 2 \times 3\,\pi r^2$

$\Rightarrow\quad 2 \times 3 \times \dfrac{22}{7} \times 8.75 \times 8.75$

$\Rightarrow\quad 1443.75\,\text{cm}^2$

$\therefore$ Required increased area

$= (1443.75 - 962.5)$

$= 481.25\,\text{cm}^2$

32. If the diameter of a sphere is 14 cm, then what is the surface area (in cm²) of the sphere?

(SSC CGL 2017)

(a) 616 (b) 308

(c) 462 (d) 636

Ans. (a) Diameter of sphere $= 14$ cm

$\therefore$ radius $= \dfrac{14}{2} = 7$ cm

$\therefore$ Surface area of sphere $= 4\,\pi r^2$

$= 4 \times \dfrac{22}{7} \times 7 \times 7 = 616\,\text{cm}^2.$

33. Three solid spheres of radius 3 cm, 4 cm, and 5 cm are melted and recasted into a solid sphere. What will be the percentage decrease in the surface area? **(SSC CGL 2017)**

(a) 12 (b) 14

(c) 16 (d) 28

Ans.(d) Total surface area of three solid spheres

$= 4 \times \dfrac{22}{7} \times (3^2 + 4^2 + 5^2)$

$= 4 \times \dfrac{22}{7} \times 50 = 628.57\,\text{cm}^2$

Now,

Volume of new sphere

$= \dfrac{4}{3} \times \dfrac{22}{7} \times (3^3 + 4^3 + 5^3)$

$\therefore\quad \dfrac{4}{3} \times \dfrac{22}{7} \times R^3 = \dfrac{4}{3} \times \dfrac{22}{7} \times 216$

$R^3 = 216$

$\therefore\quad R = \sqrt[3]{216} = 6$ cm

$\therefore$ Surface Area of new solid sphere

$= 4 \times \dfrac{22}{7} \times (6)^2$

$= 4 \times \dfrac{22}{7} \times 36$

$= 452.5\,\text{cm}^2$

$\therefore$ Required percentage

$= \dfrac{(628.57 - 452.5)}{628.57} \times 100$

$= 28\%.$

34. If the radius of the cylinder is increased by 25%, then by how much percent the height must be reduced, so that the volume of the cylinder remains same?

(a) 36 (b) 56

(c) 64 (d) 46

Ans.(a)

35. The base area of a right pyramid is 57 sq. units and height is 10 units. Then the volume of the pyramid is

(SSC CGL 1 Sit 2017)

(a) 190 c. units

(b) 380 c.units

(c) 540 c.units

(d) 570 c.units

Ans.(a)   Volume of Pyramid

$$= \frac{1}{3} \text{ area of base} \times \text{height}$$

$$= \frac{1}{3} \times 57 \times 10$$

$$= 190 \text{ c. units}$$

Trigonometry

36. A tower is 50 meters high.Its shadow is x metres shorter when the sun's altitude is 45° than when it is 30°. The value of x in metres is

(SSC CGL 1 Sit 2017)

(a) $50\sqrt{3}$

(b) $50\left(\sqrt{3}-1\right)$

(c) $50\left(\sqrt{3}+1\right)$

(d) 50

Ans.(b)   In $\triangle ABC \dfrac{AB}{AC} = \tan 45°$

$$\frac{AB}{50} = 1 \text{ , } AC = 50m$$

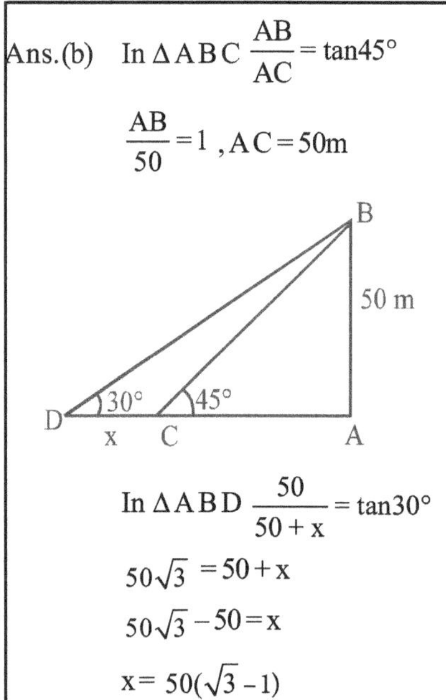

In $\triangle ABD \dfrac{50}{50+x} = \tan 30°$

$$50\sqrt{3} = 50 + x$$

$$50\sqrt{3} - 50 = x$$

$$x = 50(\sqrt{3}-1)$$

37. If A = 30°, B = 60° and C = 135°, then what is the value of $\sin^3 A + \cos^3 B + \tan^3 C - 3\sin A \cos B \tan C$?   **(SSC CGL 2017)**

(a)   0   (b) 1

(c)   8   (d) 9

Ans. (a)   Here,

A = 30°, B = 60° and C = 135°

then,

$\sin^3 A + \cos^3 B + \tan^3 C - 3\sin A \cos B \tan C$

$\sin^3 30° + \cos^3 60° + \tan^3 135° - 3\sin 30° \cos 60° \tan 135°$

$$\left(\frac{1}{2}\right)^3 + \left(\frac{1}{2}\right)^3 + (-1)^3 - 3 \times \frac{1}{2} \times \frac{1}{2} \times (-1)$$

$$\Rightarrow \frac{1}{8} + \frac{1}{8} - 1 + \frac{3}{4}$$

$$\Rightarrow \frac{1+1-8+6}{8} = 0$$

38. What is the simplified value of $1 + \tan A \tan (A/2)$?   **(SSC CGL 2017)**

(a)   sin A/2   (b)   cos A

(c)   sec A   (d)   sin A

Ans. (c) $1 + \tan A . \tan\left(\dfrac{A}{2}\right) = ?$

$$\Rightarrow 1 + \frac{\sin A}{\cos A} \times \frac{\sin(A/2)}{\cos(A/2)}$$

$$\Rightarrow$$

$$1 + \frac{\sin A}{\cos A} \times \frac{2\sin(A/2).\sin(A/2)}{2\sin(A/2).\cos(A/2)}$$

$$\Rightarrow$$

$$1 + \frac{\sin A}{\cos A} \times \frac{2\sin^2(A/2)}{\sin A}$$

$$\Rightarrow 1 + \frac{1-\cos A}{\cos A}$$

$$= 1 + \frac{1}{\cos A} - \frac{\cos A}{\cos A} = \sec A$$

39. What is the least value of $\tan^2\theta + \cot^2\theta + \sin^2\theta + \cos^2\theta + \sec^2\theta + \csc^2\theta$? **(SSC CGL 2017)**

   (a) 1   (b) 3
   (c) 5   (d) 7

Ans. (d) $\tan^2\theta + \cot^2\theta + \sin^2\theta + \cos^2\theta + \sec^2\theta + \csc^2\theta$

   $\Rightarrow$ $\sin^2\theta + \cos^2\theta + \tan^2\theta + 1 + \tan^2\theta + \cot^2\theta + 1 + \cot^2\theta$

   $\Rightarrow$ $1 + 1 + 1 + 2\tan^2\theta + 2\cot^2\theta$

   $\Rightarrow$ $3 + 2(\tan^2\theta + \cot^2\theta)$

   $\Rightarrow$ $3 + 2 \times 2 \Rightarrow 3 + 4 = 7$

Geometry

40. In the given figure, ABC is a triangle. The bisectors of internal $\angle B$ and external $\angle C$ intersect at D. If $\angle BDC = 48°$, then what is the value (in degrees) of $\angle A$?

   (SSC CGL 2017)

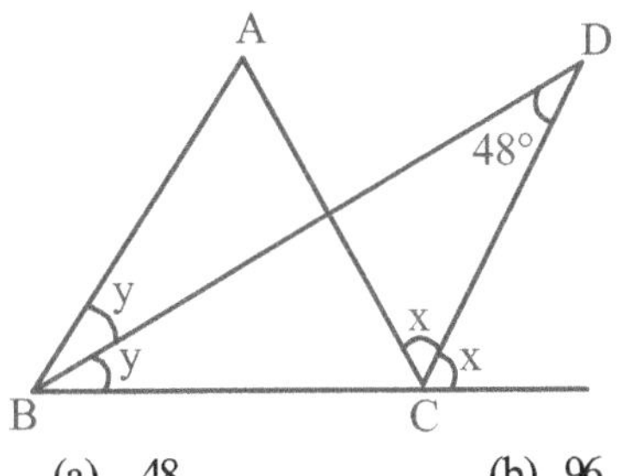

   (a) 48   (b) 96
   (c) 100   (d) 114

Ans. (b)   According to question,

   $\angle A = 2 \times \angle BDC = 2 \times 48° = 96°$

---

41. In the given figure, a smaller circle touches a larger circle at P and passes through its centre O. PR is a chord of length 34 cm, then what is the length (in cm) of PS?

   (SSC CGL 2017)

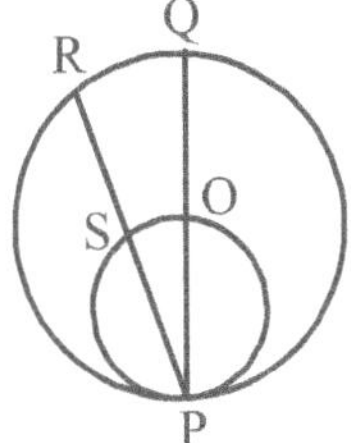

   (a) 9   (b) 17
   (c) 21   (d) 25

Ans. (b) $\angle PSO$ is a right angle (angle of semicircle)

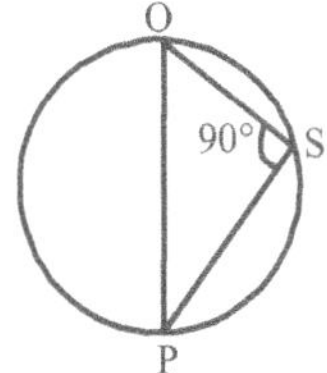

   Again when OS is perpendicular on chord PR and OS passes through the centre of circle PQR, then it must bisect the chord PR at S.

   $\therefore$ PS = RS = 17 cm.

42. In $\triangle ABC$, $\angle BAC = 90°$ and AD is drawn perpendicular to BC. If BD = 7 cm and CD = 28 cm, then what is the length (in cm) of AD?

   (SSC CGL 2017)

   (a) 3.5   (b) 7
   (c) 10.5   (d) 14

Ans. (d) $\triangle ABC$

   $\because$ $\angle BAC = 90°$

   $\because$ $(AD)^2 = BD \times DC$

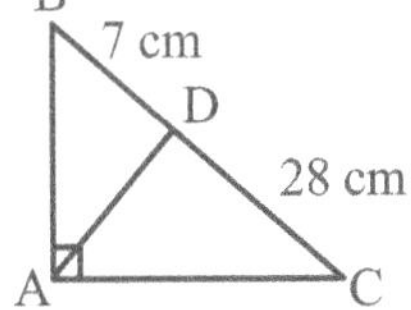

$$AD^2 = 7 \times 28$$

$$\therefore \quad AD = \sqrt{7 \times 28}$$

$$\therefore \quad AD = 14 \text{ cm.}$$

43. In the given figure, $\angle QRN = 40°$, $\angle PQR = 46°$ and MN is a tangent at R. What is the value (in degrees) of x, y and z respectively?

(SSC CGL 2017)

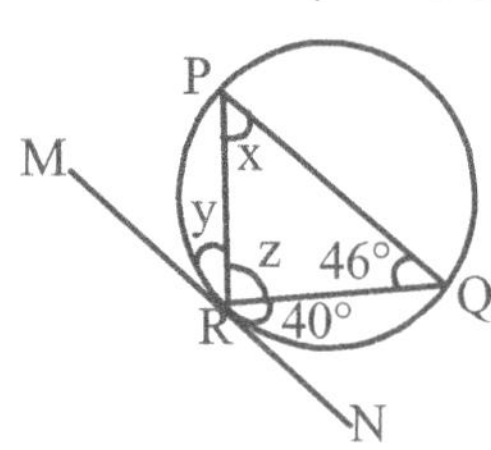

(a) 40, 46, 94   (b) 40, 50, 90
(c) 46, 54, 80   (d) 50, 40, 90

Ans. (a) $\angle MRP = \angle PQR = 46°$

$\therefore \quad \angle y = 46°$

$\angle NRQ = m \angle QPR = 40°$

$\therefore \quad \angle x = 40°$

$\angle x + \angle z + 46° = 180°$

$40° + \angle z + 46° = 180°$

$\therefore \quad \angle z = 94°$

$\therefore$ Value of x, y and z = 40°, 46° and 94°

DIRECTIONS (Qs. 44-47) : The pie chart given below shows the percentage of time taken by different processes in making a car.

(SSC CGL 2017)

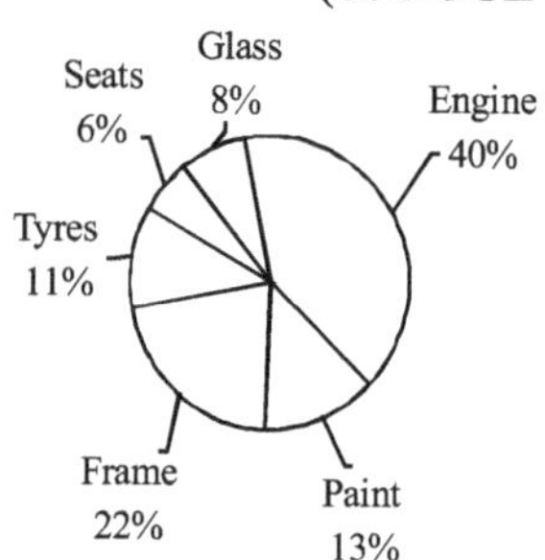

44. If total time taken to make a car is 300 hours, then what is the total time (in hours) taken in paint and frame?

(a) 99   (b) 72
(c) 105   (d) 66

Ans. (c) Total time taken to make a car = 300 hours

$\therefore$ Total time taken in paint and frame

$$= \frac{300}{100} \times 35 = 105 \text{ hours.}$$

Data Interpretation

45. If time taken in seats is 192 hours, then what is the time taken (in hours) in glass?

(a) 256   (b) 352
(c) 416   (d) 278

Ans. (a) Total time taken in glass

$$= \frac{192}{6} \times 8 = 256 \text{ hours.}$$

46. If total time taken in engine and tyres is 127.5 hours, then what is the difference (in hours) in time taken by frame and glass respectively?

(a) 27.5   (b) 12.5
(c) 40   (d) 35

Ans. (d) $\because$ Total time taken in engine and tyres

$$= 127.5 \text{ hours}$$

$\therefore$ Total time taken to make a car

$$= \frac{127.5}{51} \times 100 = 250 \text{ hours.}$$

$$\therefore \quad \text{Required difference}$$
$$= \left(\frac{250 \times 22}{100} - \frac{250 \times 8}{100} \right) \text{hours}$$
$$= (55 - 20) = 35 \text{ hours}$$

47. 15% of total time is spent on quality check and this time is equally taken from all other processes. So What will be the new sectorial angle (in degrees) made by total time of seats and glass?

   (a) 28.6   (b) 32.4
   (c) 35.8   (d) 31.6

Ans. (b)

DIRECTIONS (Qs. 48-50): : The bar graph shows the results of an annual examination in a secondary school in a certain year.

                                                (SSC Sub Ins. 2017)

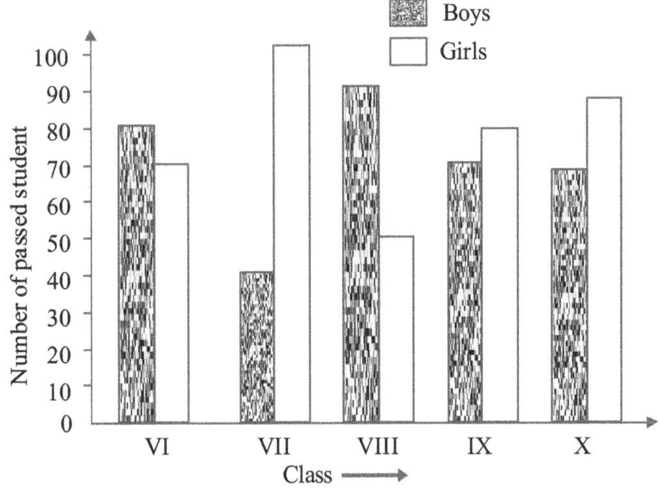

48. The ratio of the total number of boys passed to the total number of gives passed in the three classes VII, VIII and IX is

   (a) 20 : 23   (b) 18 : 21
   (c) 21 : 26   (d) 19 : 25

Ans. (a)

$$\frac{\text{Ratio of boys}}{\text{Ratio of girls}} = \frac{40 + 90 + 70}{100 + 50 + 80}$$
$$= \frac{200}{230} = 20 : 23$$

49. The average number of boys passed per class is

   (a) 75   (b) 78
   (c) 70   (d) 72

Ans. (c)   Average
$$= \frac{80 + 40 + 90 + 70 + 70}{5} = 70$$

50. The class having the highest number of passed student is

   (a) IX   (b) X
   (c) VIII   (d) VII

Ans. (b)   The class X has the highest number of passed students

CHAPTER 8

Reasoning- Trending Questions from Past Paper

Analogy

DIRECTIONS (Qs. 1-4): *In the following questions, select the related term from the given alternatives.*

1. Power : Watt : : ? : ?
   (SSC CGL 2017)
   (a) Pressure : Newton
   (b) Force : Pascal
   (c) Resistance : Mho
   (d) Work : Joule

   Ans.(d) As, Power is measured by Watt.
   Similarly, Work is measured by Joule.

2. Car : Road : : Ship : ?
   (SSC CGL 2017)
   (a) Water
   (b) Air
   (c) Road
   (d) Both Air and Water

   Ans.(a) As the means of transport in 'Road' is 'Car',
   Similarly the means of transport on 'Water' is 'Ship'.

3. Kilometre : Metre : : Tonne : ?
   (SSC CGL 2017)
   (a) Litre   (b) Kilogram
   (c) Hours   (d) Weight

   Ans.(b) As, Metre is a smaller unit of kilometre.
   Similarly, Kilogram is a smaller unit of Tonne.

4. Fire : Burn : : ? : ?
   (SSC CGL 2017)
   (a) Water : Drink
   (b) Wood : Tress
   (c) Ice : Freeze
   (d) Flower : Rose

   Ans.(c) As, Fire will burn
   Similarly, Ice will freeze.

DIRECTIONS (Qs. 5-7): *Choose the related word/letters number from the given alternatives.*

5. Horse : Neigh : : Elephant : ?
   (SSC CHSL 2017)
   (a) Quack   (b) Trumpet
   (c) Mew   (d) Grunt

   Ans.(b) Sound of horse is neigh.
   Similarly,
   Sound of elephant is trumpet.

6. Book : Literature :: ? : ?
   (a) Man : Beast
   (b) Dancer : Musician
   (c) Song : Music
   (d) Species : Science

   Ans.(c) As, Book is a part of literature.
   Similarly, Song is a part of music.

7. Giant : Dwarf :: Genius : ?
   (a) Tiny   (b) Gentle
   (c) Idiot   (d) Wicked

   Ans.(c) As, opposite word of 'giant' is 'dwarf'
   Similarly, opposite word of 'idiot' is 'genius'.

DIRECTIONS (Qs. 8-18) : *In the following question, select the related word from the given alternatives.*

8. Influenza: Virus :: Ringworm: ?
    (SSC Sub. Ins. 2017)
    (a) Bacteria   (b) Fungi
    (c) parasite   (d) Protozoa

Ans.(b) As, Infuenza is caused by virus.
         Similarly, Ring worm is caused by Fungi.

9. Fan: Blades: : ? : ?
    (a) Bonnet : Car
    (b) Room : House
    (c) Arc : Circle
    (d) Book : Chapter

Ans.(d) As, Blade is a part of fan
         Similarly, Chapter is a part of book.

10. Rain : Clouds : : Heat : ?
     (a) Distance   (b) Sun
     (c) Night   (d) Day

Ans.(b) As, Rain is produced by clouds
         Similarly, Heat is produced by Sun.

11. Garden : Plants : : Book : ?
     (a) Words   (b) Pages
     (c) Writing   (d) White

Ans.(b) As, Plants is related to garden.
         Similarly,
         Pages is related to book.

12. Doctor : Patient : : Teacher : ?
     (a) Teach   (b) Student
     (c) School   (d) Old

Ans.(b) As, Patient is cared by doctor
         Similarly, Student is taught by teacher.

13. NPBG : OQCH : : AJOT : ?
     (a) BKPU   (b) BUPK
     (c) BHKP   (d) HBKU

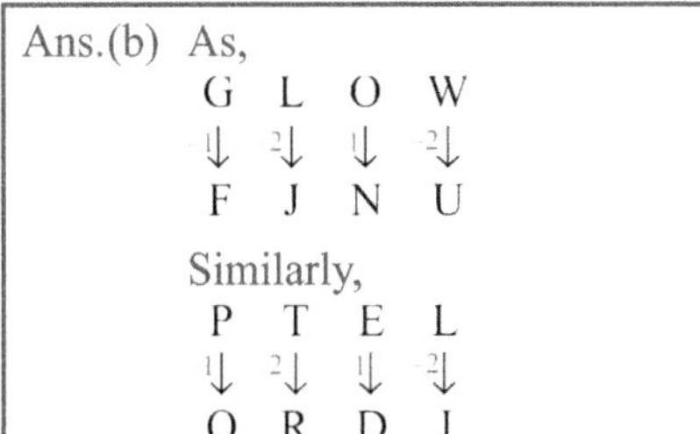

14. GLOW : FJNU : : PTEL : ?
     (a) ORFN   (b) ORDJ
     (c) ORJD   (d) OPNF

15. AGN : IOV : : BLM : ?
     (a) JTU   (b) KTU
     (c) JUV   (d) TUJ

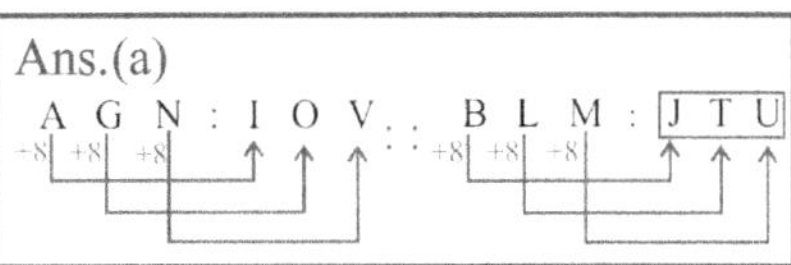

16. KLMN : IJKL : : TUVW : ?
     (a) RSUT   (b) VWXY
     (c) STUV   (d) RSTU

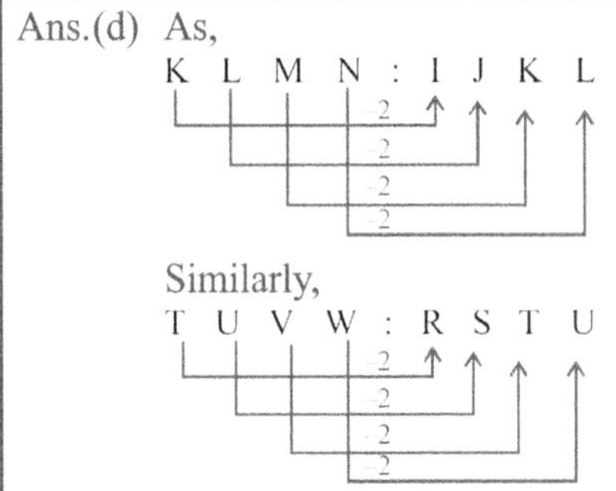

17. GH : 78 : : ? : 1819
    (a) HG   (b) LM
    (c) RS   (d) IJ

Ans.(c) According to alphabetical order :

G H   R S
↓ ↓ Similarly, ↓ ↓
7 8   18 19

18. CAR : RAC : : TYRE : ?
    (a) RUBBER   (b) ERTY
    (c) ERYT   (d) STEEL

Ans. (c) $\dfrac{C\ A\ R}{R\ A\ C}$ ← Reverse Order

Similarly,

$\dfrac{T\ Y\ R\ E}{E\ R\ Y\ T}$ ← Revers Order

DIRECTIONS (Qs. 19-35): *Select the related word/ letters/ number from the given alternatives.*

19. RATE : EATR :: SEAT : ?
    (SSC MTS 2017)
    (a) TSEA   (b) TESA
    (c) TEAS   (d) TSAE

Ans. (c) According to question,

RATE ⟶ EATR

As,

Similarly, SEAT ⟶ TEAS

20. LSFW : NTHX : : PKWE : ?
    (a) RYLF   (b) RLYE
    (c) RLYF   (d) RLGF

Ans.(c) As,

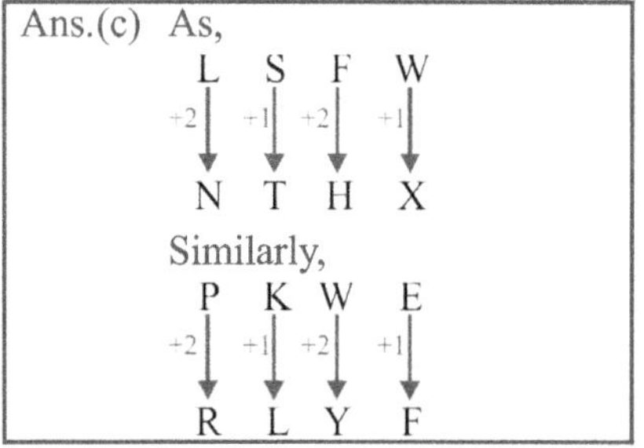

21. LMNO : NQTW :: GHIJ : ?
    (a) ILOR   (b) ILRO
    (c) ILMO   (d) LRMO

Ans. (a) As,

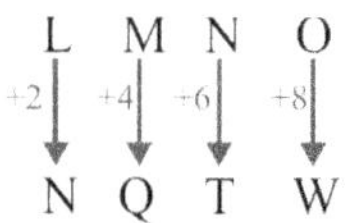

Similarly,

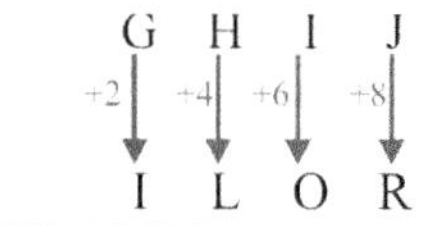

22. CHARGER : DGBQHOS : : CELLULAR : ?
    (a) DDMKVKBQ
    (b) DDNKKVBQ
    (c) DDMKUKCQ
    (d) DDNKUBVQ

Ans.(a) As,

C H A R G E R
+1 −1 +1 −1 +1 −1 +1
↓ ↓ ↓ ↓ ↓ ↓ ↓
D G B Q H D S

Similarly,

C E L L U L A R
+1 −1 +1 −1 +1 −1 +1 −1
↓ ↓ ↓ ↓ ↓ ↓ ↓ ↓
D D M K V K B Q

23. ROME : QNLD : : MORE : ?
    (a) LNQD   (b) LNQC
    (c) LMQD   (d) LMQC

Ans.(a) As,

R O M E
−1 −1 −1 −1
↓ ↓ ↓ ↓
Q N L D

Similarly,

M O R E
−1 −1 −1 −1
↓ ↓ ↓ ↓
L N Q D

24. CHANNEL : XSZMMVO : MUSICAL : ?

    (a) NFHRXZO   (b) NFHQYZP

    (c) NEHRXZP   (d) NFIRXZO

Ans.(a) As,

C	H	A	N	N	E	L
↓	↓	↓	↓	↓	↓	↓
X	S	Z	M	M	V	O

Similarly,

M	U	S	I	C	A	L
↓	↓	↓	↓	↓	↓	↓
N	F	H	R	X	Z	O

25. 101 : 10201 : : 107 : ?
    (a) 10707   (b) 10749
    (c) 11449   (d) 11407

Ans.(c) As, $(101)^2 = 10201$
         Similarly, $(107)^2 = 11449$

26. 5 : 124 : 6 : ?
    (a) 215   (b) 216
    (c) 217   (d) 220

Ans.(a) As, $(5)^3 - 1 = 124$, Similarly, $(6)^3 - 1 = 215$

27. 9143 : 9963 : : 6731 : ?
    (a) 1368   (b) 5666
    (c) 8964   (d) 9694

Ans.(c) As,
$$9143 \Rightarrow 9 + 1 + 4 + 3 = 17$$
$$9963 \Rightarrow 9 + 9 + 6 + 3 = 27$$
Similarly,
$$6731 \Rightarrow 6 + 7 + 3 + 1 = 17$$
$$8964 \Rightarrow 8 + 9 + 6 + 4 = 27$$

28. 3 : 27 : : 4 : ?
    (a) 63   (b) 64
    (c) 65   (d) 15

Ans.(b) As, $(3)^3 = 27$ Similarly, $(4)^3 = 64$.

29. 12 : 60 : : 28 : ?
    (a) 160   (b) 150
    (c) 145   (d) 140

Ans.(d) $12 \times 5 = 60$
         $28 \times 5 = 140$.

30. 21 : 3 :: 574 : ?
    (a) 97   (b) 23
    (c) 82   (d) 113

Ans.(c) As, $\dfrac{21}{3} = 7$
         Similarly, $\dfrac{574}{82} = 7$

31. 11 : 120 :: 13 : ?
    (a) 165   (b) 168
    (c) 170   (d) 169

Ans.(b) As, $(11)^2 - 1 \Rightarrow 121 - 1 = 120$
         Similarly,
         $(13)^2 - 1 \Rightarrow 169 - 1 = 168$

32. 103 : 10609 : : 106 : ?
    (a) 10606   (b) 10306
    (c) 11236   (d) 13636

Ans.(c) As, $(103)^2 = 10609$
         Similarly, $(106)^2 = 11236$

33. 11 : 121 : : 12 : ?
                              (SSC Steno. 2017)
    (a) 144   (b) 169
    (c) 196   (d) 154

Ans.(a) According to pattern,
         $(11)^2 = 121$
         Similarly,
         $(12)^2 = 144$

34. 15 : 256 : : 14 : ?
    (a) 225   (b) 144
    (c) 25   (d) 95

Ans.(a) As, $(15 + 1)^2 = (16)^2 = 256$
         Similarly,
         $(14 + 1)^2 = (15)^2 = 225$.

35. $108 : 11664 : : 107 : ?$
    (a) 11449   (b) 10449
    (c) 10849   (d) 11749

Ans.(a) As,
         $(108)^2 = 11664$
         Similarly,
         $(107)^2 = 11449$.

Classification

DIRECTIONS (Qs. 36-37) : *In the following questions, select the odd term from the given alternatives.*

                            (SSC CGL 2017)
36. (a) Lion   (b) Leopard
    (c) Snake   (d) Tiger

Ans.(c) Except, snake, all others are mammals.

37. (a) Error : Accurate
    (b) Careless : Casual
    (c) Strength : Lethargy
    (d) Gloomy : Cheerful

Ans.(b) Except option (b), All others are opposite word.

DIRECTIONS (Qs. 38-65) : *In the following question, select the odd word from the given alternatives.*

                            (SSC CGL 2017)
38. (a) Chennai   (b) Daman
    (c) Raipur   (d) Shimla

Ans.(b) Except Daman, all others are capital.

39. In the following question, select the odd word from the given alternatives.
    (a) Ludo   (b) Chess
    (c) Polo   (d) Carrom

Ans.(c) Except polo, All others are played by sitting.

40. (a) Sirius
    (b) Proximacentauri
    (c) Deimos
    (d) Alpha centauri

Ans.(c) Except Deimos (It is a satellite), all others are star systems.

41. (a) Cricket   (b) Chess
    (c) Football   (d) Hockey

Ans.(b) Except chess, all others are played at stadium.

42. (a) Newspaper   (b) Journal
    (c) Novel   (d) Magazine

Ans.(c) Only Novel is a type of book.

43. (a) Definite   (b) Specific
    (c) Doubtful   (d) Distinct

Ans.(c) Except Doubt ful, all others are similar word.

44. (a) Sward   (b) Spear
    (c) Gun   (d) Dagger

Ans.(c) Only Gun has bullet.

45. (a) Brown-Colour
    (b) Rice-Grain
    (c) Fan-Air
    (d) Iron-Metal

Ans.(c) According to question,
         Brown is a colour,
         Rice is a type of Grain
         Iron is a metal
     But, fan is not a part of air but it is a electronic device.

46. (a) Cry-Laugh
    (b) Up-Down
    (c) Increase-Decrease
    (d) Walking-Running

Ans. (d)   Except walking-Running, all others are pairs of opposite word.

47. (a) NPR   (b) TVW
    (c) FHJ   (d) KMO

Ans.(b) Except TVW, there is a gap of one letter in a group.

48. (a) B   (b) N
    (c) P   (d) W

Ans.(d) Except 'W' all others are placed at even number position according to alphabet.

49. In the following question, select the odd letters from the given alternatives.
    (a) DGJ   (b) KNQ
    (c) RUX   (d) ILN

Ans.(d) 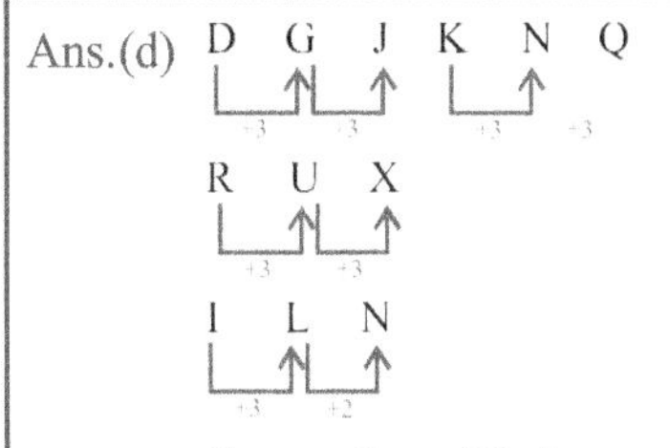

So, option (d) is correct answer.

50. (a) PON   (b) SRQ
    (c) XYZ   (d) VUT

Ans.(c) Except, xyz, all others are opposite alphabetical sequence.

51. (a) HIVW   (b) FGKL
    (c) ACDF   (d) TUOP

Ans.(c) According to question,
$$H \xrightarrow{+1} I, V \xrightarrow{+1} W$$
$$F \xrightarrow{+1} G, K \xrightarrow{+1} L$$
$$T \xrightarrow{+1} U, O \xrightarrow{+1} P$$
But, $A \xrightarrow{+2} C, D \xrightarrow{+2} F$
So, ACDF does not follow this pattern.

52. (a) BEHK   (b) JMPS
    (c) PSVY   (d) EHKM

Ans.(d) According to question,
$$B \xrightarrow{+3} E \xrightarrow{+3} H \xrightarrow{+3} K$$
$$J \xrightarrow{+3} M \xrightarrow{+3} P \xrightarrow{+3} S$$
$$P \xrightarrow{+3} S \xrightarrow{+3} V \xrightarrow{+3} Y$$
But, $E \xrightarrow{+3} H \xrightarrow{+3} K \xrightarrow{+2} M$

53. (a) AD   (b) PT
    (c) EH   (d) JM

Ans.(b) Here,
$$A \xrightarrow{+3} D$$
$$E \xrightarrow{+3} H$$
$$J \xrightarrow{+3} M$$
But $P \xrightarrow{+4} T$

54. (a) KM   (b) PR
    (c) TV   (d) EH

Ans. (d) According to question,
$$K \xrightarrow{+2} M$$
$$P \xrightarrow{+2} R$$
$$T \xrightarrow{+2} V$$
But $E \xrightarrow{+3} H$

55. (a) RQP   (b) LKJ
    (c) HGF   (d) ECB

Ans. (d)   According to question,

$$R \xrightarrow{-1} Q \xrightarrow{-1} P$$

$$L \xrightarrow{-1} K \xrightarrow{-1} J$$

$$H \xrightarrow{-1} G \xrightarrow{-1} F$$

But $E \xrightarrow{-2} C \xrightarrow{-1} B$

56. (a) 69   (b) 59
       (c) 61   (d) 53

Ans.(a)   Except 69, all others are prime numbers.

57. (a) 11 – 120   (b) 17 – 290
       (c) 21 – 442   (d) 12 – 145

Ans.(a) $(11)^2 - 1 = 120$
          $(17)^2 + 1 = 290$
          $(21)^2 + 1 = 442$
          $(12)^2 + 1 = 145$
          So, (11–120) is an odd number pair.

58. (a) 313   (b) 426
       (c) 925   (d) 1034

Ans.(a)   Except 313, all others are composite number.

59. (a) 1919   (b) 5656
       (c) 6761   (d) 7760

Ans.(b) $1919 \Rightarrow 1 + 9 + 1 + 9 = 20$
          $5656 \Rightarrow 5 + 6 + 5 + 6 = 22$
          $6761 \Rightarrow 6 + 7 + 6 + 1 = 20$
          $7760 \Rightarrow 7 + 7 + 6 + 0 = 20$
          Except 5656, Sum of all digit of number is equal to 20.

60. (a) 2890   (b) 3375
       (c) 1728   (d) 1331

Ans.(a)   Except 2890, All are cube of a number.
          $(15)^3 = 3375, (12)^3 = 1728,$
          $(11)^3 = 1331.$

61. (a) 23   (b) 17
       (c) 13   (d) 63

Ans.(d)   Except 63, all others are prime number.

62. (a) 12 - 48   (b) 7 - 28
       (c) 5 - 20   (d) 11 - 55

Ans.(d)   Here,
          $$\frac{48}{12} = 4, \frac{28}{7} = 4, \frac{20}{5} = 4$$
          But $\frac{55}{11} = 5$
          So, (11 – 55) is odd one out.

63. (a) 12 - 28   (b) 20 - 36
       (c) 42 - 58   (d) 72 - 90

Ans.(d)   Here,
          $28 - 12 = 16$
          $36 - 20 = 16$
          $58 - 42 = 16$
          But, $90 - 72 = 18$
          So, (90 – 72) is odd one out.

64. (a) 7 - 50   (b) 11 - 122
       (c) 15 - 226   (d) 13 - 168

Ans.(d)   According to question,
          $(7)^2 + 1 = 50$
          $(11)^2 + 1 = 122$
          $(15)^2 + 1 = 226$
          But $(13)^2 + 1 \neq 168 = 170$

65. (a) 7 - 56   (b) 10 - 110
       (c) 9 - 90   (d) 8 - 96

Ans.(d)   According to question,
          The pattern is :
          $n \times (n - 1)$
          $8 \times 7 = 56$
          $11 \times 10 = 110$
          $10 \times 9 = 90$
          But, $9 \times 8 \neq 96 = 72$

Series

66. A series is given with one term missing. Select the correct alternative from the given ones that will complete the series.
BCF, CDG, DEH,?

(SSC CGL 2017)

(a) EFI   (b) EFG
(c) DFI   (d) EGI

Ans.(a) 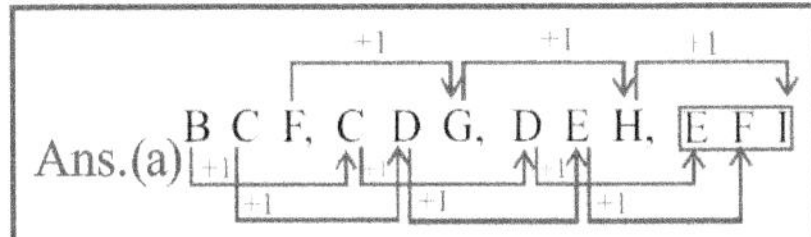

DIRECTIONS (Qs. 67-68) : *A series is given with one term missing. Select the correct alternative from the given ones that will complete the series.*

67. Q, P, O, N, ?   **(SSC CGL 2017)**

(a) M   (b) L
(c) O   (d) J

Ans. (a) 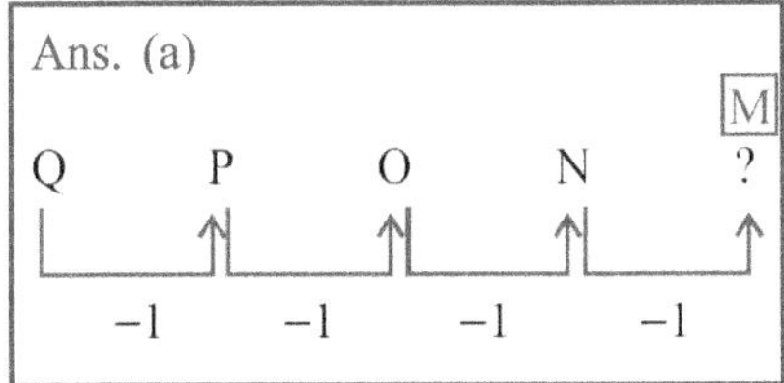

68. AG, LR, WC, HN,?

(SSC CGL 2017)

(a) QY   (b) RX
(c) SY   (d) TZ

Ans. (c) The pattern is :
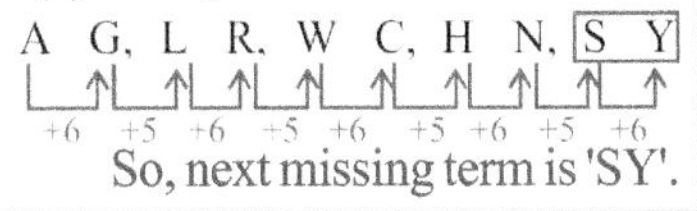
So, next missing term is 'SY'.

DIRECTIONS (Qs. 69-73) : *A series is given with one term missing. Select the correct alternative from the given ones that will complete the series.*

69 BT, DR, FP, ?

(a) HO   (b) HN
(c) NH   (d) OH

Ans.(b) 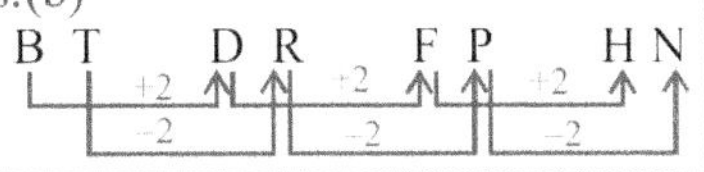

70. Double, Triple, Quadruple, ?

(a) Quintuple   (b) Nonuple
(c) Sextuple   (d) Octuple

Ans.(a) The next term is quintuple because quintuple means five times.

71. AC, EG, ?, MO

(a) IK   (b) IJ
(c) IL   (d) IM

Ans.(a) The common difference between first and second letter is one letter according to alphabetical sequence. So, answer will be IK.

72. ?, WX, AB, FG

(a) TU   (b) XW
(c) PQ   (d) UV

Ans.(a)
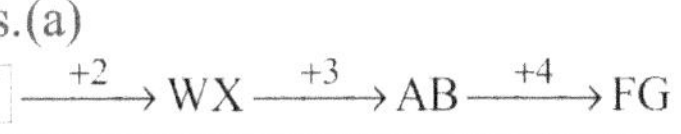

73. BKS, DJT, FLU, HHV, ?

(a) IGU   (b) IGX
(c) JGW   (d) IJX

Ans.(c) The pattern is as follows :
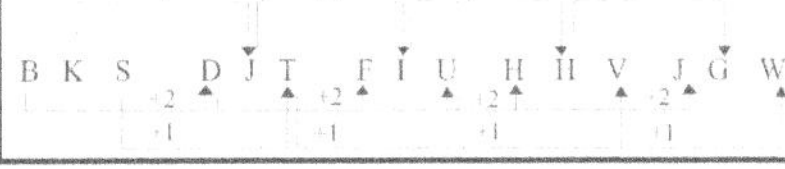

DIRECTIONS (Qs. 74-75) : *A series is given with one term missing. Select the correct alternative from the given ones that will complete the series.*

74. A, B, D, G,? **(SSC Sub. Ins. 2017)**

(a) K   (b) J
(c) L   (d) I

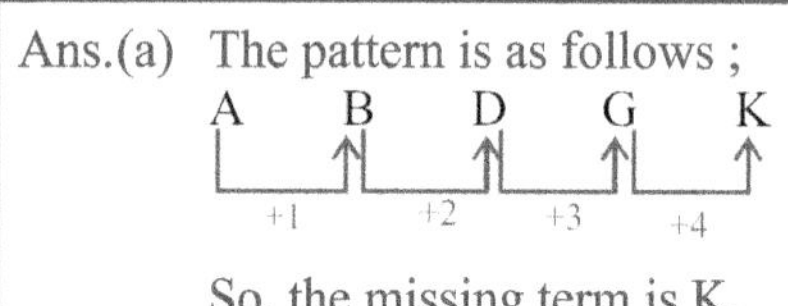

So, the missing term is K.

75. VWR, TUP, RSN,?

    (a) PLQ   (b) PQL
    (c) LPQ   (d) PRM

Ans.(b) The pattern is as follows :

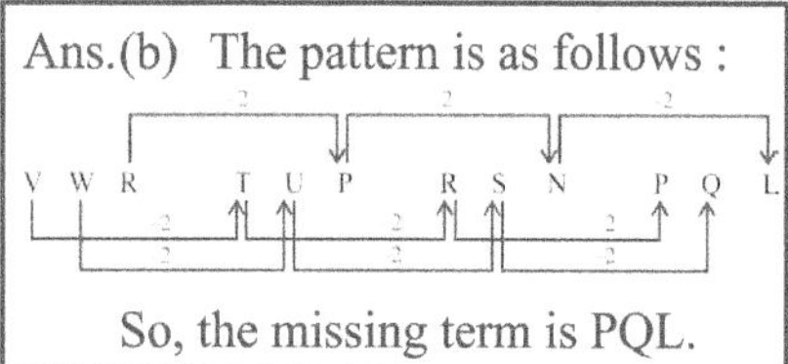

So, the missing term is PQL.

DIRECTIONS (Qs. 76-78) : *A series is given with one term missing. Select the correct the correct alternative system from the given ones that will complete the series.*

                        (SSC Sten. 2017)

76. ADCB, FIHG, KNML, ?

    (a) PSRQ   (b) PSQR
    (c) QTRS   (d) QSTR

Ans.(a) The pattern is :

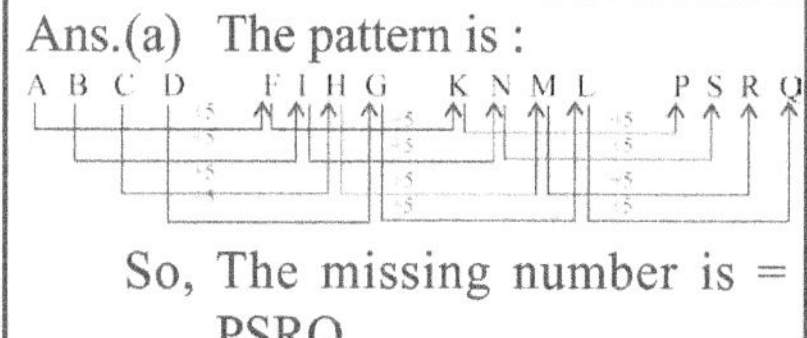

So, The missing number is = PSRQ.

77. BDG, HJM, NPS, ?

    (a) TVY   (a) TVW
    (c) UVX   (d) UWZ

Ans.(a) The pattern is :

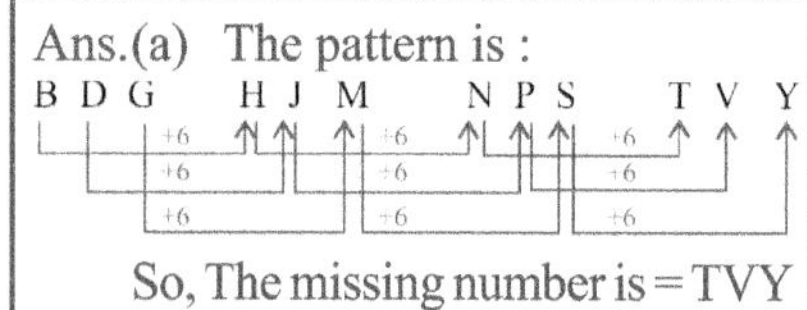

So, The missing number is = TVY

78. GF, KJ, ON, ?

    (a) RS   (b) SR
    (c) ST   (d) TS

Ans.(b) The pattern is :

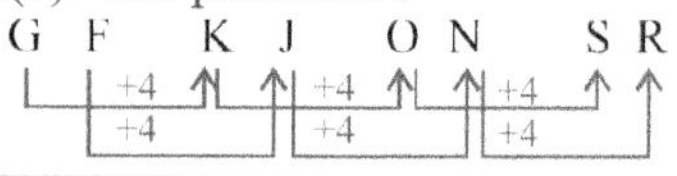

79. In the following question, select the missing number from the given series.

2, 5, 12, 27, ?   **(SSC CGL 2017)**

    (a) 53   (b) 56
    (c) 57   (d) 58

Ans.(d)

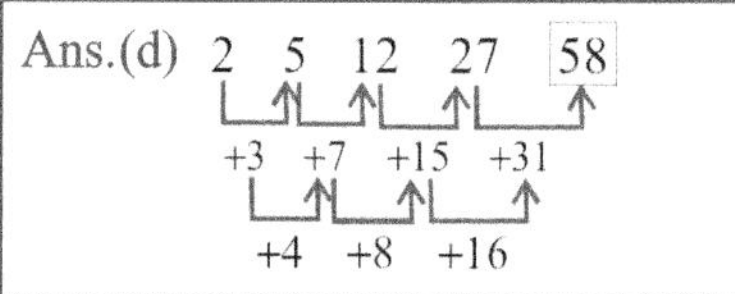

DIRECTIONS (Qs. 80-81) : *In the following question, select the missing number from the given series.*

80. 6, 9, 15, 24, 39, 63, ?

                     (SSC CGL 2017)

    (a) 97   (b) 115
    (c) 102   (d) 124

Ans.(c) The pattern is as follow : first number + second number = next number.

$$6 + 9 = 15$$
$$9 + 15 = 24$$
$$15 + 24 = 39$$
$$24 + 39 = 63$$

So, next number is $(39 + 63) = 102$

81. 13, 16, 11, 18, 9, 20, ?

    (a) 3   (b) 5
    (c) 6   (d) 7

Ans. (d) The pattern is :

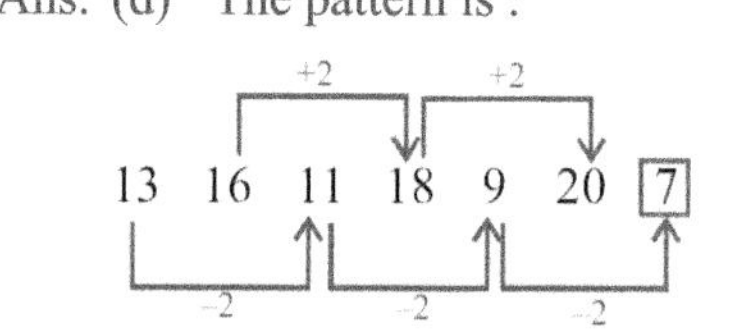

So, next missing number is 7.

DIRECTIONS (Qs. 82-89) : *In the following question, select the missing number from the given series.*

82. 3, 8, 5, 27, 8, 64, 12, 125, 17, ?
    (a) 216   (b) 361
    (c) 625   (d) 441

Ans.(a) 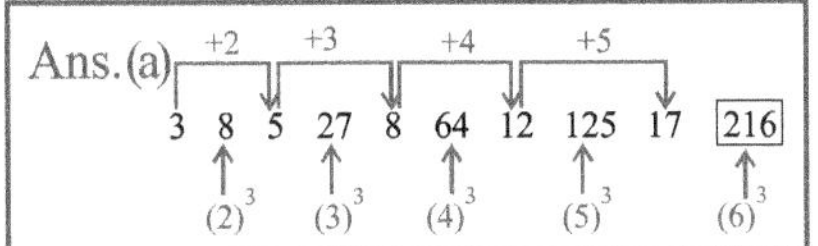

83. 30, 60, 360, 3600, ?
    (a) 48500   (b) 50500
    (c) 50400   (d) 40800

Ans.(c)

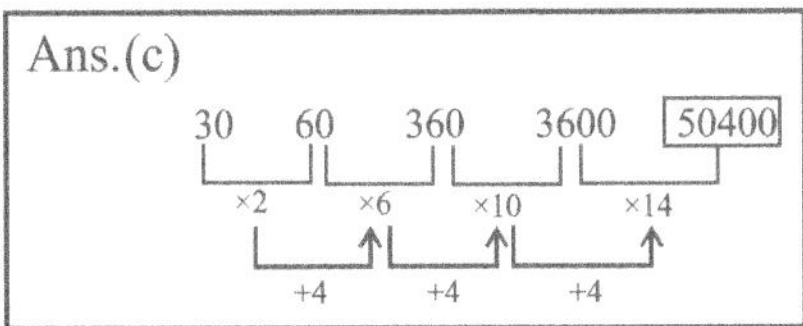

84. 5, 7, 11, 17, 25, ?
    (a) 35   (b) 32
    (c) 34   (d) 33

Ans.(a) The pattern is as follows :

$$5 \quad 7 \quad 11 \quad 17 \quad 25 \quad \boxed{35}$$

$$+2 \quad +4 \quad +6 \quad +8 \quad +10$$

So, the next number is = 35.

85. 3, 10, 31, 94, ?
    (a) 197   (b) 127
    (c) 283   (d) 317

Ans.(c) The pattern is as follows :
$$3 \times 3 + 1 = 10$$
$$10 \times 3 + 1 = 31$$
$$31 \times 3 + 1 = 94$$
$$94 \times 3 + 1 = 283$$
So, the missing number is 283.

86. 3, 4, 12, 48, 576, ?
    (a) 27648   (b) 13824
    (c) 23040   (d) 28166

Ans.(a) The pattern is as follows :
$$4 \times 3 = 12$$
$$12 \times 4 = 48$$
$$48 \times 12 = 576$$
$$576 \times 48 = 27648$$
So, the missing number is 27648.

87. 2, 3, 7, 16, 32, ?
    (a) 57   (b) 76
    (c) 62   (d) 67

Ans.(a) The pattern is :

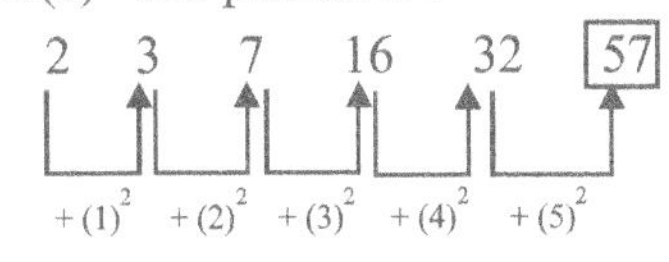

So, The missing number is = 57.

88. 8, 11, 14, 17, 20, ?
    (a) 21   (b) 22
    (c) 23   (d) 27

Ans.(c) The pattern is :

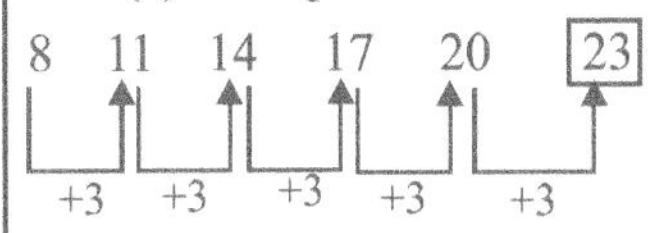

So, The missing number is = 23.

89. 18, 14, 10, 6, ?
    (a) 2   (b) 3
    (c) 4   (d) 5

Ans.(a) The pattern is :

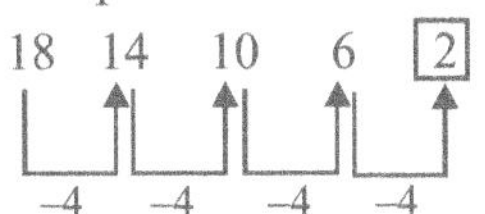

So, The missing number is = 2

Alphabet Test

90. In the following question, from the given alternative words, select the word which cannot be formed using the letters of the given word.

(SSC CGL 2017)

Suspensefulness
(a) Sense   (b) Fuels
(c) Useful   (d) Fullness

Ans.(d) Fullness as a lettter is not there in word suspense fulness.

91. In the following question, from the given alternative words, select the word which cannot be formed using the letters of the given word.
(SSC CGL 2017)
Herringbone
(a) Biner   (b) None
(c) Bane   (d) Hinge

Ans.(c) Bane cannot be formed using Herringbone

92. In the following question, from the given alternative words, select the word which cannot be formed using the letters of the given word.
UNIFORMITY   **(SSC CGL 2017)**
(a) ANNUITY   (b) FORUM
(c) MINT   (d) UNIFORM

Ans.(a) ANNUITY is the word which cannot be formed from letters of 'UNIFORMITY' as, A is not in it.

93. In the following question, from the given alternative words, select the word which cannot be formed using the letters of the given word.
(SSC CGL 2017)
Biological
(a) Logic   (b) Globe
(c) Bail   (d) Bill

Ans.(b) 'E' is not appearing in the word 'Biological'. Hence Globe cannot formed from the given word.

94. Out of the four words given, choose the word which cannot be formed

using the letters of the following word.
TRANSLATION
(SSC MTS 2017)
(a) RATIO   (b) NATION
(c) TRANSMIT (d) TRANSIT

Ans.(c) Transmit cannot be formed as there is no 'M' in the word 'TRANSLATION'.

95. In the following question, select the word which cannot be formed using the letters of the given word.
Instructor   **(SSC Sub. Ins. 2017)**
(a) Rust   (b) Tort
(c) Stop   (d) Stint

Ans.(c) Stop cannot be formed as there is no 'P' in the word 'Instructor'.

DIRECTIONS (Qs. 96-98) : *In the following question, Select the word which cannot be formed using the letters of the given word.*

96. **Encourage (SSC Sub. Ins. 2017)**
(a) Courage   (b) Court
(c) Race   (d) Encore

Ans.(b) Court cannot be formed as there is no 'T' in the word 'Encourage'.

97. FUNDAMENTALY
(SSC Steno. 2017)
(a) SUNDAY   (b) MEANT
(c) FUNNY   (d) TUNED

Ans.(a) Sunday cannot be formed as there is no 'S' in the word ' FUNDAMENTALY'.

98. DISTRIBUTION
(a) BUTTON   (b) DISTURB
(c) BRITAIN   (d) BURNT

Ans.(c) Britain cannot be formed as there is no 'A' in the word ' DISTRIBUTION'.

99. Arrange the given words in the sequence in which they occur in the dictionary. **(SSC CGL 2017)**
    (1) Ropped   (2) Roster
    (3) Roasted   (4) Road
    (5) Roller
    (a) 3 5 4 1 2   (b) 4 5 3 1 2
    (c) 3 4 5 1 2   (d) 4 3 5 1 2

Ans.(d) Meaningful order of the words in ascending order:
4. Road
↓
3. Roasted
↓
5. Roller
↓
1. Ropped
↓
2. Roster

100. Arrange the given words in the sequence in which they occur in the dictionary. **(SSC CGL 2017)**
    1. Pragmatic   2. Protect
    3. Pastel   4. Postal
    5. Pebble
    (a) 43521   (b) 35412
    (c) 34512   (d) 43512

Ans.(b) Arranging the words according to dictionary.
Pastel → Pebble → Postal → Pragmatic → Protect.
So answer is 35412.

101. Arrange the given words in the sequence in which they occur in the dictionary. **(SSC CGL 2017)**
    (1) Ball   (2) Balanced
    (3) Balls   (4) Balance
    (5) Balancing
    (a) 24135   (b) 42135
    (c) 42513   (d) 54213

Ans.(c) Arrangement of words according to Dictionary :
4. Balance
↓
2. Balanced
↓
5. Balancing
↓
1. Ball
↓
3. Balls
So, answer is 42513.

102. Arrange the given words in the sequence in which they occur in the dictionary. **(SSC CGL 2017)**
    1. Storm   2. Strap
    3. Strangle   4. Stamped
    5. Satire
    (a) 51432   (b) 51342
    (c) 54132   (d) 53412

Ans.(c)

103. Arrange the given words in the sequence in which they occur in the dictionary. **(SSC CHSL 2017)**
    (i) Treadmill   (ii) Treason
    (iii) Treacherous (iv) Tread
    (a) (ii), (iii), (iv), (i)   (b) (iii), (iv), (ii), (i)
    (c) (iii), (iv), (i), (ii)   (d) (i), (ii), (iii), (iv)

Ans.(c) According to dictionary order,
Treacherous→Tread→Treadmill→Treason.
(1) (2) (3) (4)

104. Which one of the given responses would be a meaningful order of the following? **SSC MTS 2017)**
    1. Cutting   2. Dish
    3. Vegetable   4. Market
    5. Cooking.
    (a) 1, 2, 4, 5, 3   (b) 5, 3, 2, 1, 4
    (c) 3, 2, 5, 1, 4   (d) 4, 3, 1, 5, 2

Ans.(d) Meaningful order of words :

4. Market
↓
3. Vegetable
↓
1. Cutting
↓
5. Cooking
↓
2. Dish

Ans.(b) Arrangement of words according to the Dictionary.

1. Den
↓
4. Desk
↓
5. Doom
↓
2. Dragon
↓
3. Drop

DIRECTIONS (Qs. 105-106): *Arrange the given words in the sequence in which they occur in the dictionary.*

(SSC CGL 2017)

105. 1. Ale   2. Align
    3. Amend   4. Anatomy
    5. Alpine
(a) 51342   (b) 35412
(c) 12354   (d) 12534

Ans.(d) Arrangement of words according to the Dictionary.

1. Ale
↓
2. Aligen
↓
5. Alpine
↓
3. Amend
↓
4. Anatomy

106. 1. Den   2. Dragon
    3. Drop   4. Desk
    5. Doom
(a) 54312   (b) 14523
(c) 31245   (d) 13245

DIRECTIONS (Q. 107) : *Which word will appear fouth when arranged in order of dictionary?*

(SSC Steno. 2017)

107. 1. Dictation   2. Dictionary
    3. Dimple   4. Dinner
    5. Deputy
(a) Dinner   (b) Dimple
(c) Dictation   (d) Dictionary

Ans.(b) According to dictionary, Dimple will appear fourth position.

DIRECTIONS (Q. 108) : *Arrange the given words in the sequence in which they occur in the dictionary.*

(SSC Steno. 2017)

108. 1. Slowly   2. Slam
    3. Slump   4. Sledge
    5. State
(a) 25431   (b) 52413
(c) 25413   (d) 52431

Ans.(c) Arrangement of the words as per dictionary

2. slam
↓
5. slate
↓
4. sledge
↓
1. slowly
↓
3. slump

Coding-Decoding

109. In a certain code language, "BAD" is written as "7" and "SAP" is written as "9". How is "BAN" written in that code language?

(SSC CGL 2017)

(a) 8   (b) 3
(c) 4   (d) 6

Ans.(a) As,
    BAD = 2 + 1 + 4 ⇒ 7
    SAP = 19 + 1 + 16 = 36 ⇒ 3 + 6 = 9
    Similarly,
    BAN = 2 + 1 + 14 = 17 ⇒ 1 + 7 = 8

110. In a certain code language "NIGHT" is written as "ODDGM" and "DARK" is written as "GOYC". How is "GREEN" written in that code language?

(SSC CGL 2017)

(a) IABPF   (b) MCBNB
(c) OGHVL   (d) FPBAI

Ans.(a) As,

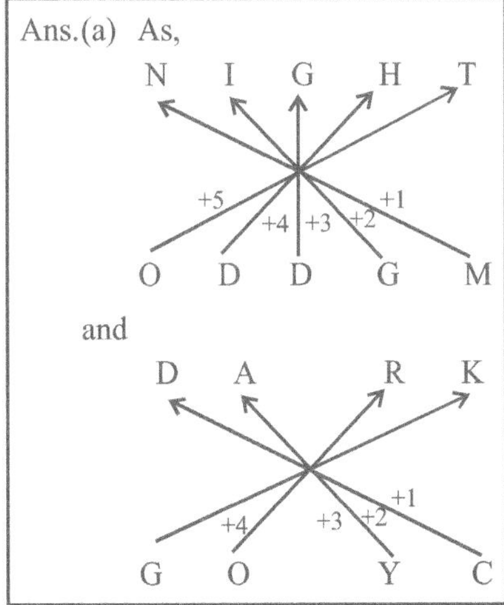

and

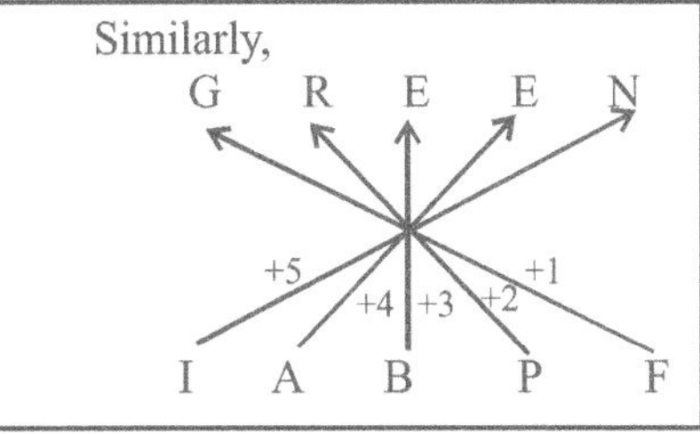

111. In a certain code language, **"TIRED"** is written as **"56"** and **"BRAIN"** is written as **"44"**. How is **'LAZY"** written in that code language?   **(SSC CGL 2017)**

(a) 64   (b) 61
(c) 58   (d) 43

Ans.(a) As,
    TIRED = 20 + 9 + 18 + 5 + 4 = 56
    BRAIN = 2 + 18 + 1 + 9 + 14 = 44
    Similarly,
    LAZY = 12 + 1 + 26 + 25 = 64.

112. In a certain code language **"who are you"** is written as **"432"**, **"they is you"** is written as **"485"** and **"they are dangerous"** is written as **"295"**. How is **"dangerous"** written in that code language?

(SSC CGL 2017)

(a) 2   (b) 4
(c) 5   (d) 9

Ans. (d)

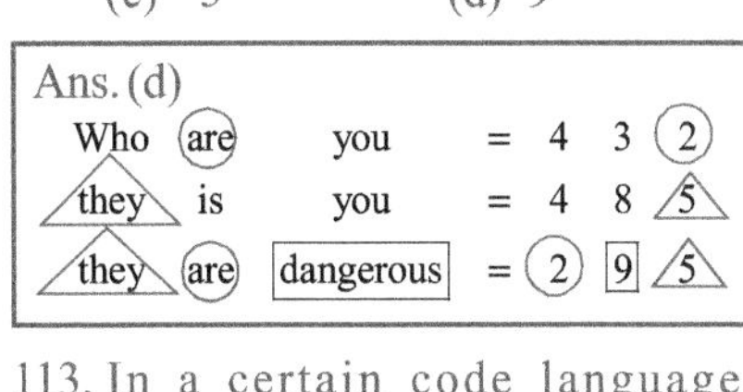

113. In a certain code language, "RIVER" is written as "12351" and "RED" is written as "156". How is "DRIVER" written in that code language? **(SSC CHSL 2017)**

(a) 612311   (b) 612531
(c) 621351   (d) 612351

Ans.(d) As,

R	I	V	E	R		R	E	D
↓	↓	↓	↓	↓		↓	↓	↓
1	2	3	5	1		1	5	6

114. If 'LONDON is coded as MPOEPO. What code is needed for 'DELHI'?

(SSC MTS 2017)

(a) DEHLI   (b) HLDEI
(c) EFIMJ   (d) EFMIJ

Ans.(d) As,

L O N D O N
+1↓ +1↓ +1↓ +1↓ +1↓ +1↓
M P O E P O

Similarly,

D E L H I
+1↓ +1↓ +1↓ +1↓ +1↓
E F M I J

115. In a certain code language, **"SUN** is written as **"54"** and **"PUT"** is written as **"57"**. How is **"CAT"** Written in that code language?

(SSC Sub. Ins. 2017)

(a) 28   (b) 24
(c) 52   (d) 36

Ans.(b)   A = 1, B = 2,.......... Z = 26
As,
SUN ⇒ (19 + 21 + 14) = 54
PUT ⇒ (16 + 21 + 20) = 57
Similarly,
CAT ⇒ (3 + 1 + 20) = 24

116. In a certain code language, "POTTER" is written as "ONSUFS". "WALKER" written in that code language?

(SSC Steno. 2017)

(a) VZKLFS   (b) VZLKFS
(c) VZKLFT   (d) WALLFS

Ans.(a) As,

P O T T E R
−1↓ −1↓ −1↓ +1↓ +1↓ +1↓
O N S U F S

Similarly,

W A L K E R
−1↓ −1↓ −1↓ +1↓ +1↓ +1↓
V Z K L F S

117. In a certain code language, "TOMB" is written as "MOVE" and "TACKLE" is written as "MFDGPR". How is "TABLET" written in that code language?

(SSC Steno. 2017)

(a) MFEPRT   (b) MFDVER
(c) MERPTS   (d) MFEPRM

Ans.(d)

T	O	M	B		T	A	C	K	L	E
↓	↓	↓	↓	,	↓	↓	↓	↓	↓	↓

MOVEMFDGPR

Therefore,
TABLET
↓ ↓ ↓ ↓ ↓ ↓
MFEPRM

118. A word is represented by only one set of numbers as given in any one of the alternatives. The sets of numbers given in the alternatives are represented by two classes of alphabets as shown in the given two matrices. The columns and rows of **Matrix – I** are numbered from 0 to 4 and that of **Matrix – II** are numbered from 5 to 9. A letter from these matrices can be represented first by its row and next by its column for example 'K' can be represented by 01, 34 etc and **'P'** can be represented by 65, 99 etc. Similarly, you have to identify in set for the word **"BLAND"**.   **(SSC CGL 2017)**

Matrix – I

	0	1	2	3	4
0	A	K	B	L	C
1	B	A	C	K	L
2	L	C	K	B	A
3	C	B	L	A	K
4	K	L	A	C	B

Matrix– II

	5	6	7	8	9
5	N	O	P	S	D
6	P	D	S	N	O
7	O	P	N	D	S
8	D	S	O	P	N
9	S	N	D	O	P

(a) 10, 14, 00, 68, 79
(b) 31, 41, 33, 96, 86
(c) 44, 20, 42, 88, 59
(d) 23, 32, 24, 55, 66

> Ans.(d) By matching code :
> 23, 32, 24, 55, 66 letters resemble to BLAND in the MATRIX.

119. A word is represented by only one set of numbers as given in any one of the alternatives. The numbers of sets given in the alternatives are represented by two classes of alphabets as shown in the given two matrices. The columns and rows of Matrix – I are numbered from 0 to 4 and that of Matrix numbered from 5 to 9. A letter from these matrices can be represented by its row and next by its, column for example. 'C' can be represented by 10, 34 etc., and 'D' can be represented by 85, 98 etc. Similarly, you have to identify the set for the word "STEAL".

(SSC CGL 2017)

Matrix – I

	0	1	2	3	4
0	T	S	C	E	K
1	C	K	E	T	S
2	K	E	S	C	T
3	S	T	K	E	C
4	E	C	T	S	K

Matrix – II

	5	6	7	8	9
5	P	D	A	I	L
6	L	I	D	A	P
7	I	A	L	P	A
8	D	P	I	L	A
9	A	L	P	D	I

(a) 01, 13, 04, 76, 66
(b) 14, 31, 40, 95, 59
(c) 22, 42, 21, 69, 67
(d) 43, 24, 33, 57, 58

> Ans.(b) 14, 31, 40, 95, 59 are the codes matches from two Matrices for STEAL.

120. A word is represented by only one set of numbers as given in any one of the alternatives. The sets of numbers given in the alternatives are represented by two classes of alphabets as shown in the given two matrices. The columns and rows of Matrix – I are numbered from 0 to 4 and that of Matrix – II are numbered from 5 to 9. A letter from these matrices can be represented first by its row and next by its column, for example, 'E' can be represented by 02, 11, etc. and 'G' can be represented by 65, 56 etc. Similarly, you have to identify the set for the word 'EAGER;'.

(SSC CHSL 2017)

Matrix – I

	0	1	2	3	4
0	S	T	E	D	B
1	A	E	O	F	A
2	E	T	P	A	N
3	D	G	A	S	M
4	G	A	Q	W	I

Matrix – II

	5	6	7	8	9
5	F	G	M	R	C
6	G	N	R	K	L
7	A	R	Y	J	F
8	R	B	W	G	Y
9	S	V	Q	H	T

(a)   02, 10, 65, 11, 68
(b)   02, 10, 65, 87, 85
(c)   02, 10, 65, 11, 85
(d)   02, 10, 65, 59, 85

Ans.(c)

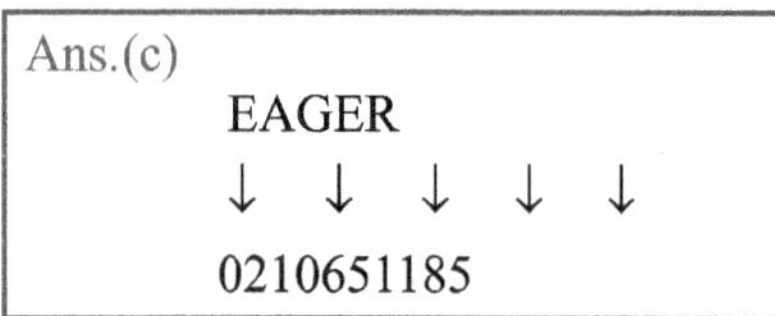

EAGER

↓   ↓   ↓   ↓   ↓

0210651185

Blood Relations

121. If 'P 3 Q' means 'P is daughter of Q', 'P 5 Q' means 'P is father of Q', 'P 7 Q' means 'P is mother of Q' and 'P 9 Q' means ' P is sister of Q', then how is J related to K in J 3 L 9 N 3 0 5 K?   **(SSC CGL 2017)**

(a)   Mother   (b)   Wife
(c)   Niece   (d)   Daughter

Ans.(c)   J 3 L ⇒ J is daughter of L
L 9 N ⇒ L is sister of N
N 3 O ⇒ N is daughter of O
O 5 K ⇒ O is father of K.
Hence J is niece of K.

122. P and Q are brothers, P is the father of S, R is the only son of Q and is married to U. How is U related to S?   **(SSC CGL 2017)**

(a)   Sister – in – law
(b)   Mother – in – law
(c)   Sister
(d)   Mother

Ans.(a)

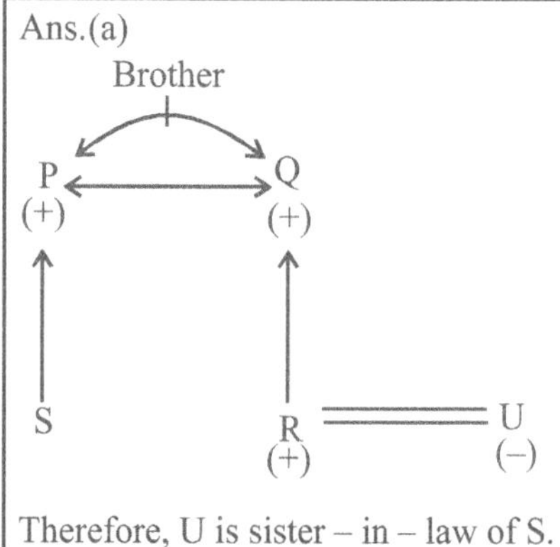

Therefore, U is sister – in – law of S.

123. Punit said to lady, "The sister of your father's wife is my aunt". How is the lady related to Punit?   **(SSC CGL 2017)**

(a)   Daughter
(b)   Grand Daughter
(c)   Niece
(d)   Cousin sister

Ans.(d)   The lady is the cousin sister of Punit.

124. Pointing to a lady, Diwakar said, "Her mother's only grandson is my son". How is that lady related to Diwakar?   **(SSC CGL 2017)**

(a)   Aunty   (b)   Sister
(c)   Mother   (d)   Wife

Ans.(d)   According to blood relation analysis: A lady related to Diwakar as a sister.

125. Introducing a boy Ankit said, "He is the son of daughter of my

grandfather's son". How is that boy related to Ankit?

(SSC CHSL 2017)

(a) Cousin
(b) Brother
(c) Father – in – law
(d) Nephew

Ans.(d) Nephew.

126. Pointing to a lady, Rohit said "She is the sister of the daughter of my father's wife's son". How is the lady related to Rohit?

(SSC Steno. 2017)

(a) Daughter
(b) Sister
(c) Niece
(d) Daughter or Niece

Ans.(d)

Directions and Distance

127. Neeraj is facing north, then he turns 45 degree right and goes 25 m, then turns in south – east direction to move 25 m and from there 25 m to east. In which direction/place is he from his original place?

(SSC CHSL 2017)

(a) North
(b) East
(c) West
(d) South

Ans.(b)

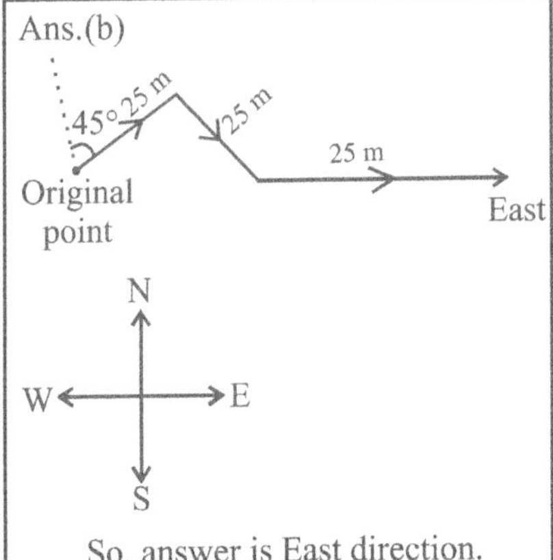

So, answer is East direction.

128. 'Z' started walking straight towards South. He walked a distance of 15 metres and then took a left turn and walked a distance of 30 metres. Then he took a right turn and walked a distance of 15 metres again. Z is facing which direction?

(SSC MTS 2017)

(a) North
(b) West
(c) South
(d) East

Ans.(c)

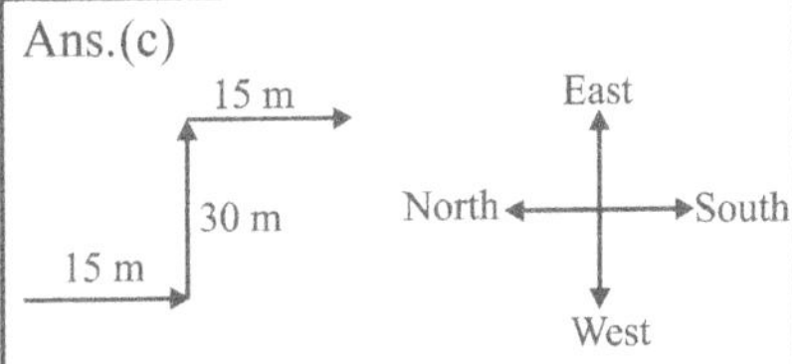

So, After walked; Z is facing south direction.

129. Sunita walks 45 metres towards south. Then turns right and walk another 45 metres. Then turn right and walks for 20 metres to reach point L. She then again turns to her right and walks for 45 metres. How far (in metres) is she from point L?

(SSC Sub. Ins. 2017)

(a) 50
(b) 45
(c) 25
(d) 60

Ans.(b) According to the given information the direction diagram is as follows :

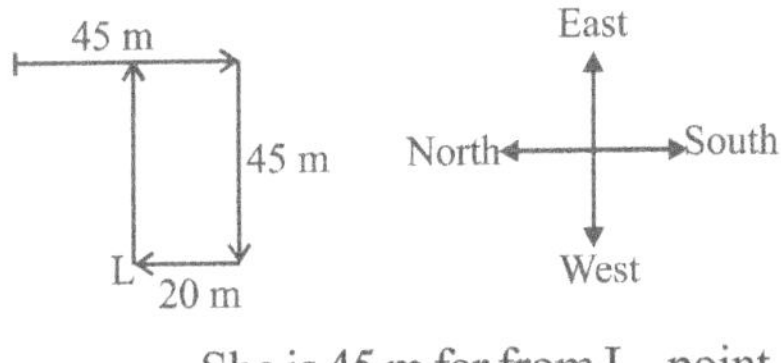

She is 45 m far from L - point

Time Sequence Number and Ranking Test

130. There are 45 trees in a row. The lemon tree is 20th from right end.

What is the rank of lemon tree from left end? **(SSC CGL 2017)**

(a) 26
(b) 24
(c) 25
(d) 27

Ans.(a) Required rank of lemon tree
$= (45 + 1) - 20 = 26.$

131. Priyank ranks 6th from the bottom and 28th from the top in a class. How many students are there in the class? **(SSC Sub. Ins. 2017)**

(a) 31
(b) 32
(c) 33
(d) 34

Ans.(c) Priyank is 6th from the bottom 28th from top.

So, total number of students
$= 6 + 28 - 1 = 33$

132. In a row of people Manu is 7th from bottom end of row. Shrey is 10 ranks above Manu. If shrey is 8th from top, then how many people are there in this row?

(SSC Sub. Ins. 2017)

(a) 25
(b) 26
(c) 24
(d) 23

Ans.(c) Manu's rank from bottom end $= 7^{th}$

Shrey's rank from bottom end $= (7 + 10) = 17^{th}$

Shrey's rank from top end $= 8^{th}$

133. In a class, there are 40 students. Some of them passed the examination and others failed. Raman's rank among the student who have passed is 13th from top and 17th from bottom. How many students have failed?

(SSC Steno. 2017)

(a) 11
(b) 10
(c) 9
(d) Cannot be determined

Ans.(a) Total number of students who have failed
$= (40 + 1) - (13 + 17)$
$\Rightarrow (41 - 30) = 11$

Number Puzzle

134. In the following question, select the number which can be placed at the sign of question non marking the given alternatives.

(SSC CGL 2017)

	3			4			2	
2	31	1	2	145	6	1	?	7
	5			3			5	

(a) 43
(b) 49
(c) 59
(d) 71

Ans.(d) As,
$3 \times 1 \times 5 \times 2 + 1 = 31$ and
$4 \times 6 \times 3 \times 2 + 1 = 145$
Similarly,
$2 \times 7 \times 5 \times 1 + 1 = 71$

135. In the following question, select the number which can be placed the sign of question mark (?) from the given alternatives.

(SSC CGL 2017)

7	6	3
2	5	1
8	9	4
115	273	?

(a) 14
(b) 15
(c) 16
(d) 18

Ans.(b) Here,
$7 \times 2 \times 8 + 3 = 115$
$6 \times 5 \times 9 + 3 = 273$
$\therefore \quad 3 \times 1 \times 4 + 3 = 15$
So, answer is 15.

136. In the following question, select the number which can be at the sign of

question mark (?) from the given alternatives.   **(SSC CGL 2017)**

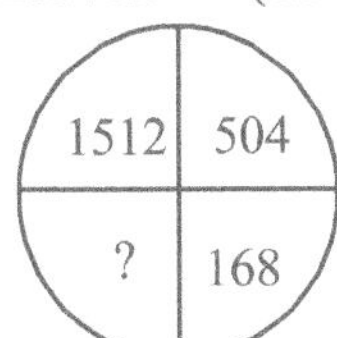

(a) 53
(b) 56
(c) 59
(d) 66

Ans.(b) The pattern is :

1512 ÷ 3 = 504

504 ÷ 3 = 168

168 ÷ 3 = 56.

So, answer is 56.

137. In the following question, select the number which can be placed at the sign of question mark (?) from the given alternatives.

(SSC CGL 2017)

3	10	6	186
9	5	3	138
5	7	1	36
3	2	5	?

(a) 35
(b) 42
(c) 45
(d) 95

Ans.(a) The pattern is :

As,

$3 \times 10 \times 6 + 6 = 186$

$9 \times 5 \times 3 + 3 = 138$

$5 \times 7 \times 1 + 1 = 36$

Similarly,

$3 \times 2 \times 5 + 5 = 35.$

138. In the following question, select the missing number from the given series.   **(SSC CHSL 2017)**

49	169	484
81	144	625
16	25	?

(a) 37
(b) 47
(c) 48
(d) 25

Ans.   (b)

$\sqrt{49} = 7 \qquad \sqrt{169} = 13 \qquad \sqrt{484} = 22$

$\sqrt{81} = \dfrac{+9}{16} \qquad \sqrt{144} = \dfrac{+12}{25} \qquad \sqrt{625} = \dfrac{+25}{47}$

So, Answer is 47.

139. Find the missing number from the given responses **(SSC MTS 2017)**

7	3	10
3	4	7
2	7	?
42	84	140

(a) 2
(b) 17
(c) 9
(d) 34

Ans. (a) The pattern is as follows :

$(7 \times 3 \times 2) = 42$

$(3 \times 4 \times 7) = 84$

$(10 \times 7 \times x) = 140$

$\Rightarrow \quad \therefore \ x = \dfrac{140}{70} = 2$

$\therefore$ The missing number is = 2.

140. In the following question, select the number which can be placed at the sign of question mark (?) from the given alternatives.

(SSC Sub. Ins. 2017)

7	3	2
6	11	5
5	1	8
72	?	50

(a) 38
(b) 40
(c) 42
(d) 44

Ans.(d) The pattern is as follows :

$(7 \times 6) + (6 \times 5) = 42 + 30 = 72$

$(3 \times 11) + (11 \times 1) = 33 + 11 = 44$

$(2 \times 5) + (5 \times 8) = 10 + 40 = 50$

141. In the following question, select the number which can be placed at the sign of question mark (?) from the given alternatives.

(SSC Sub. Ins. 2017)

1	7	2
8	6	4
9	2	5
4	7	?

(a) 9   (b) 10
(c) 11   (d) 12

Ans.(c) The pattern is as follows :
$$(1 + 8 + 9 + 4) = 22$$
$$(7 + 6 + 2 + 7) = 22$$
$$(2 + 4 + 5 + ?) = 22$$
$$? + 11 = 22$$
$$? = 22 - 11 = 11$$

142. In the following question, select the number which can be placed at the sign of question mark (?) from the given alternatives.

(SSC Sten. 2017)

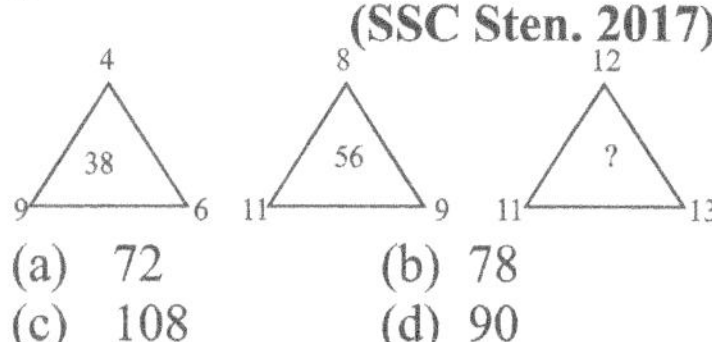

(a) 72   (b) 78
(c) 108   (d) 90

Ans. (a) As, $(4 + 6 + 9) \times 2 = 38$
$$(8 + 9 + 11) \times 2 = 56$$
Similarly,
$$(12 + 13 + 11) \times 2 = 72$$

Venn Diagram

143. In the given figure, how many pens are blue? **(SSC CGL 2017)**

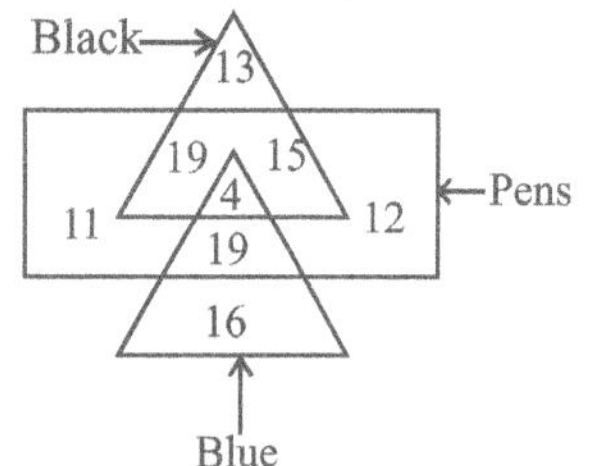

(a) 23   (b) 19
(c) 12   (d) 15

Ans.(a) Total number of pens are blue $= 19 + 4 = 23$.

144. In the given figure, how many people study 2 subjects?

(SSC CGL 2017)

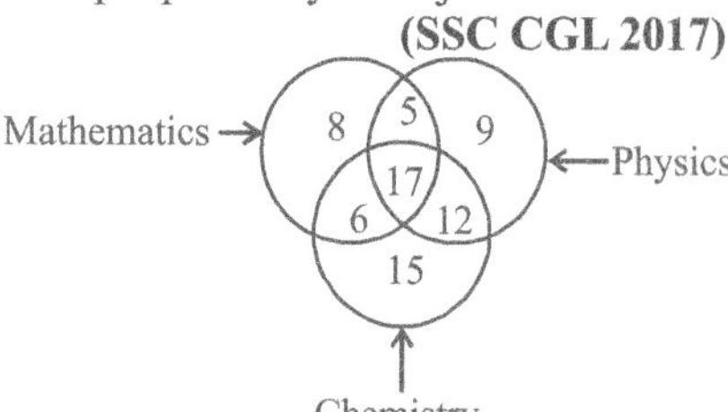

(a) 11   (b) 23
(c) 12   (d) 40

Ans.(b) Total number of peoples, who study only 2 subjects
$$\Rightarrow 5 + 12 + 6 = 23$$

145. Identify the diagram that best represents the relationship among the given classes. Music Instrument, Piano, Guiter **(SSC CGL 2017)**

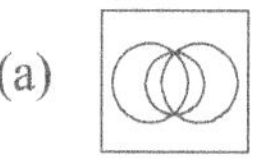

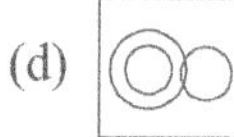

(a)   (b)

(c)   (d)

Ans.(b)

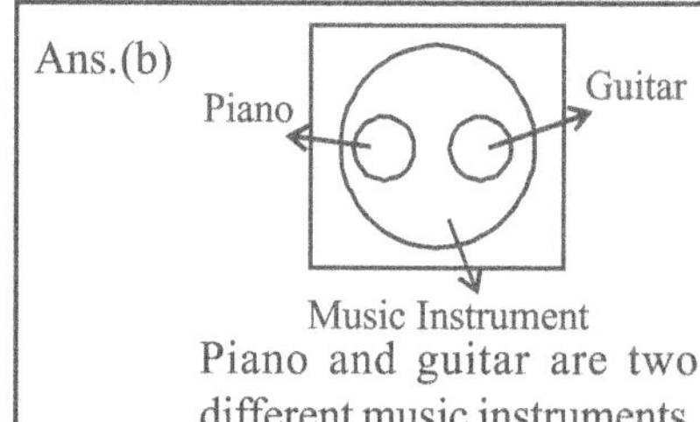

Piano and guitar are two different music instruments.

146. In the given figure, how many are musical toys? **(SSC CGL 2017)**

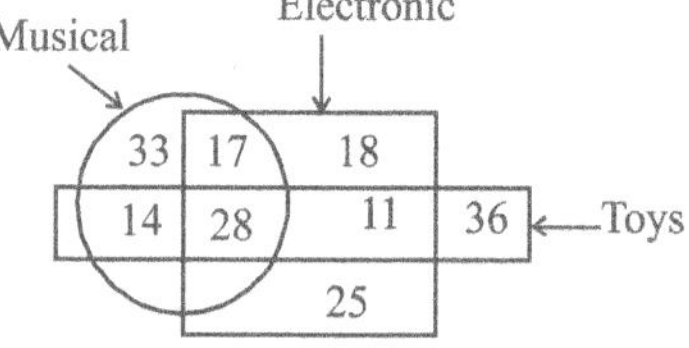

(a) 53   (b) 61
(c) 42   (d) 45

> **Ans.(c)** Total number of musical toys
> = 14 + 28 = 42.

147. Identify the diagram that best represents the relationship among the given classes.
(SSC CHSL 2017)

Earth, Saturn, Planet, Star

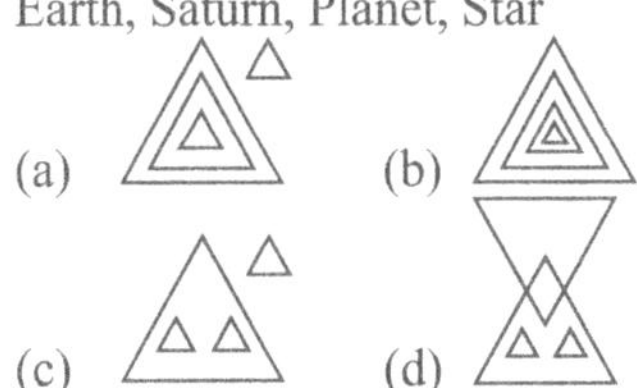

(a)   (b)

(c)   (d)

> **Ans.(c)**
>
> 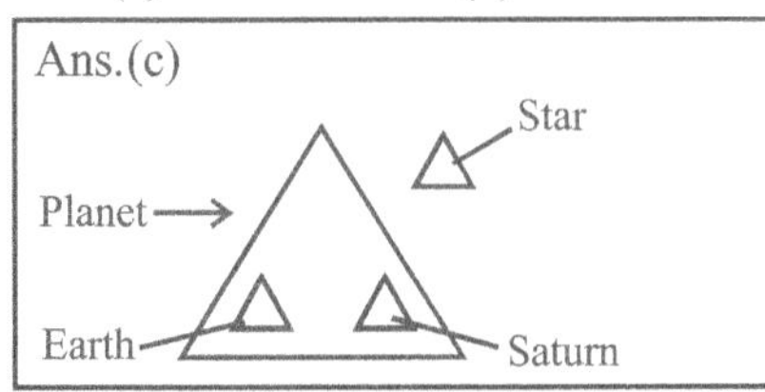
>

148. Choose the correct Venn diagram which best illustrates the relationship among Hockey, Cricket, Games.
(SSC MTS 2017)

(a)   (b)

(c)   (d)

> **Ans.(b)** Both hockey and cricket are games but different from each other.

149. In the given figure, which letter represents carnivorous plants which are not green?
(SSC Sub.ins. 2017)

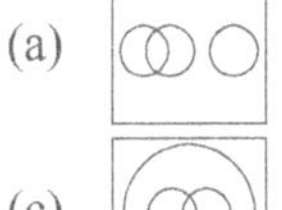
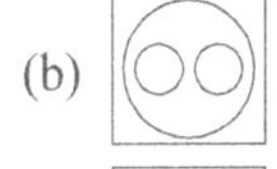

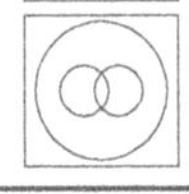
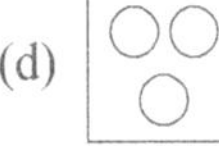
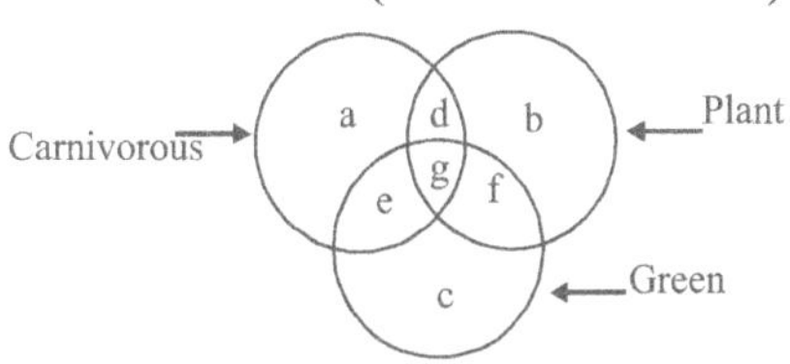

(a) d   (b) g
(c) e   (d) f

> **Ans.(a)** According to figure, 'd' letter represents carnivorous plants which are not green.

150. In the given figure, how many yellow birds are there?
(SSC Sub.ins. 2017)

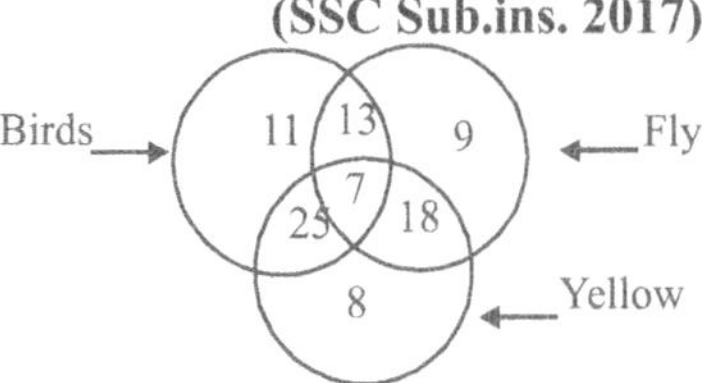

(a) 25   (b) 32
(c) 18   (d) 20

> **Ans.(b)** According to question,
> Total number of yellow birds
> = (25 + 7) = 32.

Mathematical Operation and Arithmetical Reasoning

151. In the following question, correct the equation by interchanging two signs. **(SSC CGL 2017)**

$9 \times 3 + 8 \div 4 - 7 = 28$

(a) $\times$ and $-$ (b) $+$ and $-$
(c) $\div$ and $+$ (d) $\times$ and $\div$

> **Ans.(c)** Option (a),
> $9 - 3 + 8 \div 4 \times 7 = 28$
> $20 \div 28$
> option (b),
> $9 \times 3 - 8 \div 4 + 7 = 28$
> $32 \div 28$
> option (c),
> $9 \div 3 + 8 \times 4 - 7 = 28$
> $28 = 28$
> $\therefore$ option (c) is correct.

152. If $4 * 5 \% 3 = 8000$ and $2 * 3 \% 2 = 36$, then $4 * 3 \% 3 = ?$
(SSC CGL 2017)

(a)   432   (b)   1728
(c)   36   (d)   144

Ans.(b)   As,

$$4 * 5 \% 3 = 8000$$
$$\Rightarrow (4 \times 5)^3 = 8000$$

and

$$2 * 5 \% 2 = 36$$
$$\Rightarrow (2 \times 3)^2 = 36$$

Similarly,

$$4 * 3 \% 3 = ?$$
$$(4 \times 3)^3 = 1728$$

153. In the following question, correct the equation by interchanging two signs. **(SSC CGL 2017)**

$$4 \times 3 - 6 \div 2 + 7 = 8$$

(a) $-$ and $+$ (b) $\times$ and $-$
(c) $\div$ and $\times$ (d) $\times$ and $+$

Ans.(a)   option (a),

$$4 \times 3 + 6 \div 2 - 7 = 8$$
$$15 - 7 = 8$$

So, option (a) is correct.

154. In the following question, by using which mathematical operator will the expression become correct?

18 ? 6 ? 9 ? 27   **(SSC CGL 2017)**

(a) $\times, \div$ and $=$ (b) $\div, \times$ and $=$
(c) $\times, +$ and $=$ (d) $+, -$ and $=$

Ans.(b)   From option (b).

$$18 \div 6 \times 9 = 27$$
$$\frac{18}{6} \times 9 = 27$$

So, option (b) is correct.

155. If "P" denotes "multiplied by", "R" denotes "subtracted from", "S" denotes "added to " and "Q" denotes "divided by", "then which of the following equation is true?

(SSC CGL 2017)

(a)   18 R 60 Q 15 S 2 = 8
(b) 15 S 16 Q 2 P 4 = 47
(c)   3 P 5 R 18 Q 3 = 6
(d) 15 S 28 Q 4 P 2 = 27

Ans.(b)   The expression is :

$$15 \text{ S } 16 \text{ Q } 2 \text{ P } 4 = 47$$
$$15 + 16 \div 2 \times 4 = 47$$
$$47 = 47$$

So, option (2) is true.

156. If "+" means "minus", "×" means "divided by", " ÷ " means "plus" and "–" means "multiplied by", then

$$126 \times 14 + 7 - 3 \div 2 = ?$$

(SSC CHSL 2017)

(a) $- 10$ (b) $- 12$
(c) $- 17$ (d) $- 41$

Ans.(a)   If,

$+ = -$	$\times = \div$
$\div = +$	$- = \times$

then,

$$126 \div 14 - 7 \times 3 + 2 = - 10$$

157. Some equations are solved on the basis of certain system. Find out the correct answer for the unsolved equation on that basis.

(SSC MTS 2017)

If $12 \times 9 = 810$ and $15 \times 9 = 513$ then $13 \times 8 = ?$

(a)   104   (b)   410
(c)   411   (d)   401

Ans.(b)   According to question;

As, $12 \times 9 = 108 \Rightarrow 810$
$15 \times 9 = 135 \Rightarrow 513$

Similarly,

$$13 \times 8 = 104 \Rightarrow 410.$$

158. If P denotes '÷', Q denotes '×', R denotes '+' and S denotes '–', then 18Q12P4R5S6 is equal to:

(SSC MTS 2017)

(a)   65   (b)   36
(c)   53   (d)   34

Ans.(c) If
P = ÷
Q = ×
R = +
S = –
Then, 18 Q 12 P 4 R 5 S 6 = ?
$\Rightarrow$ 18 × 12 ÷ 4 + 5 – 6
$\Rightarrow$ 18 × 3 + 5 – 6
$\Rightarrow$ 59 – 6 = 53.

159. In the following question, by using which mathematical operators will the expression become correct?
14 ? 2 ? 4 ? 6 ? 4
(SSC Sub. Ins. 2017)

(a) ×, ÷, > and × (b) ÷, ×, > and ×
(c) ÷, +, = and × (d) ÷, +, > and ×

Ans.(b) From option, (b)
14 ÷ 2 × 4 > 6 × 4
28 > 24
$\therefore$ Option (b) is correct.

160. In the following question, correct the equation by inter-changing two signs. **(SSC Sub. Ins. 2017)**
43 + 9 – 6 ÷ 3 × 8 = 50
(a) ÷ and × (b) + and ÷
(c) – and + (d) – and ×

Ans.(c) From option (c)
43 – 9 + 6 ÷ 3 × 8 = 50
$\Rightarrow$ 43 – 9 + 2 × 8
$\Rightarrow$ 43 – 9 + 16
$\Rightarrow$ 50 = 50
So, option (c) is correct.

161. If 85 × 5 – 3 = 20 and 18 × 2 –1 = 10, then 100 × 20 – 5 =?
(SSC Steno. 2017)
(a) 15 (b) 20
(c) 10 (d) 13

Ans.(c) As,
85 × 5 – 3 = 20 $\Rightarrow$ 85 ÷ 5 + 3 = 20
18 × 2 – 1 = 10 $\Rightarrow$ 18 ÷ 2 + 1 = 10
Similarly,
100 × 20 – 5 = 10 $\Rightarrow$ 100 ÷ 20 + 5 = 10

162. By interchanging which two signs the equation will be correct?
25 + 18 ÷ 2 – 4 = 20
(SSC Steno. 2017)
(a) + and ÷
(b) ÷ and –
(c) + and –
(d) None of these

Ans.(c) Option (c)
25 + 18 ÷ 2 – 4 = 20 (By interchanging + and –)
25 – 18 ÷ 2 + 4 = 20
25 – 9 + 4 = 20
So, option (c) is correct.

Statement & Arguments and Statement & Conclusions

163. In each of the following question below are given some statements followed by some conclusions. Taking the given statements to be true even if they seem to be at variance from commonly known facts, read all the conclusions and then decide which of the given conclusion logically follows the given statements.**(SSC CGL 2017)**
Statements :
I. Some pens are pencils.
II. All pencils are erasers.
Conclusions :
I. Some pens are erasers.
II. No pens are erasers.
III. Some erasers are pencils.

(a) Only conclusion (II) follows.
(b) Only conclusion (I) and (II) follow.
(c) Only conclusion (I) and (III) follow.
(d) No conclusion follows.

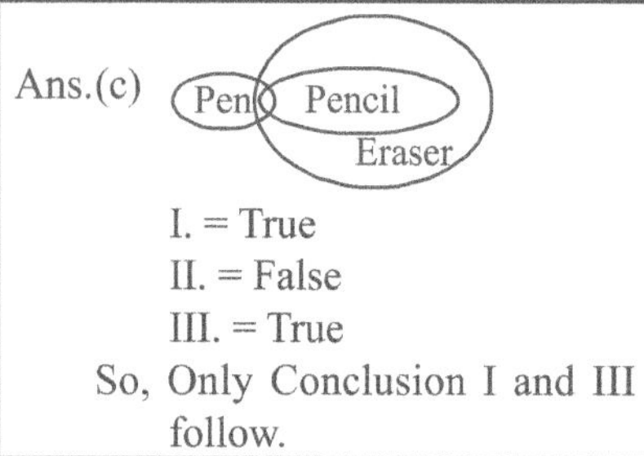

Ans.(c)

I. = True
II. = False
III. = True

So, Only Conclusion I and III follow.

164. In the following question below are given some statements followed by some conclusions. Taking the given statements to be true even if they seem to be at variance from commonly known facts, read all the conclusions and then decide which of the given conclusion logically follows the given statements.

(SSC CGL 2017)

Statements :
I. Some pens are pencils.
II. All pencils are erasers.

Conclusions :
I. Some pencils are not pens.
II. Some erasers are not pens.
(a) Only conclusion (I) follows.
(b) Only conclusion (II) follows.
(c) Neither conclusion (I) nor conclusion (II) follows.
(d) Both conclusions follow.

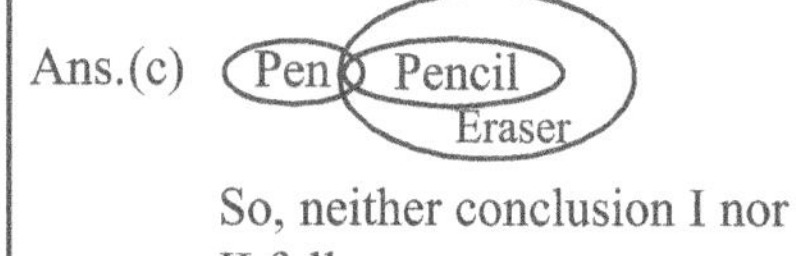

Ans.(c)

So, neither conclusion I nor II follows.

165. In each of the following question below are given some statements followed by some conclusions.

Taking the given statements to be true even if they seem to be at variance from commonly known facts, read all the conclusions and then decide which of the given conclusion logically follows the given statements.

(SSC CGL 2017)

Statements :
I. All cups are vegetable.
II. All vegetable are pens.

Conclusions :
I. some pens are vegetable.
II. Some pens are cups.
(a) Only conclusion (I) follows
(b) Only conclusion (II) follows
(c) Both conclusion follow.
(d) Neither conclusion
(I) nor conclusion
(II) follows

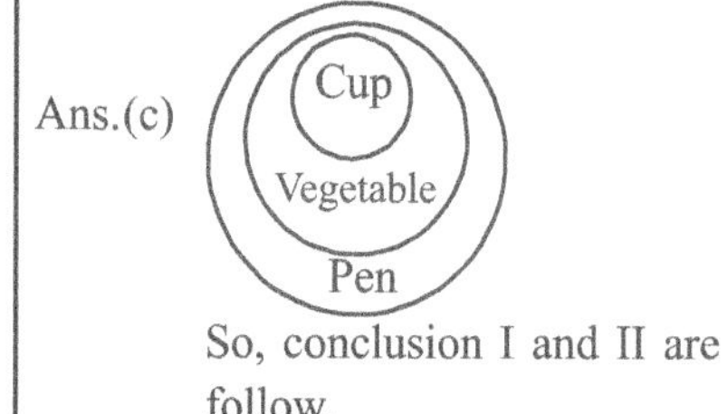

Ans.(c)

So, conclusion I and II are follow.

166. In each of the following question below are given some statements followed by some conclusions. Taking the given statements to be true even if they seem to be at variance from commonly known facts, read all the conclusions and then decide which of the given conclusion logically follows the given statements.

(SSC Sub. Ins. 2017)

Statements :
I. All women are hardworking.
II. All intelligent are advocate.
III. Some intelligent are women.

Conclusions :

I. Some advocates are women.

II. Some hardworking are women.

III. Some women are advocate.

IV. Some hardworking are intelligent.

(a) Only conclusion (II), (III) and (IV) follow

(b) Only conclusion (I), (II), and (III) follow

(c) Only conclusion (I), (III), and (IV) follow

(d) All conclusions follow

Ans.(d)

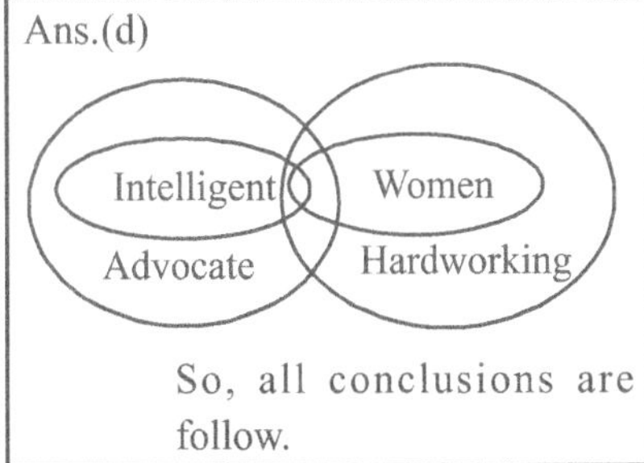

So, all conclusions are follow.

167. In each of the following question below are given some statements followed by some conclusions. Taking the given statements to be true even if they seem to be at variance from commonly known facts, read all the conclusions and then decide which of the given conclusion logically follows the given statements.

(SSC Sub. Ins. 2017)

Statements :

I. Some pins are cups.

II. No cup is book.

Conclusions :

I. Some pins are books.

II. Some pins are not books.

(a) Only conclusion (I) follows

(b) Only conclusion (II) follows

(c) Both conclusion follow

(d) Neither conclusion (I) nor conclusion (II) follows

Ans.(b)
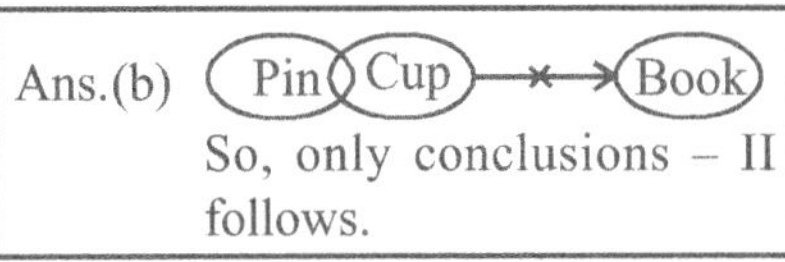

So, only conclusions – II follows.

Completion of Figures & Embedded Figures

168. Which answer figure will complete the pattern in the question figure?

(SSC CGL. 2017)

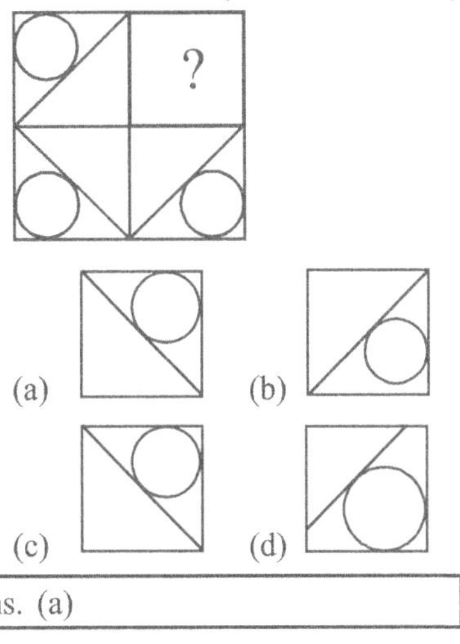

Ans. (a)

169. Which answer figure will complete the pattern in the question figure?

(SSC CGL. 2017)

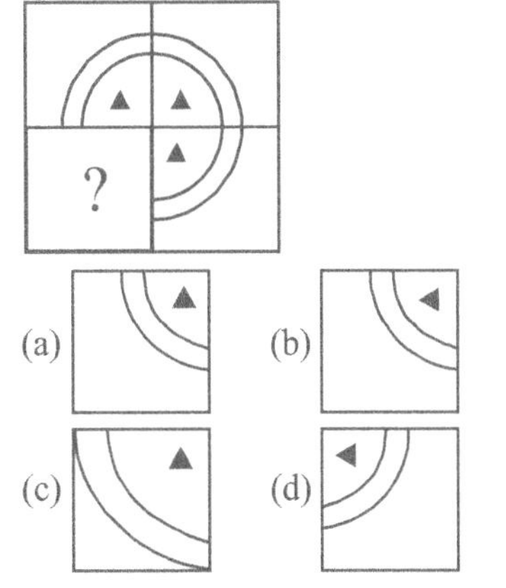

Ans. (a)

170. Which answer figure will complete the pattern in the question figure?

(SSC CGL. 2017)

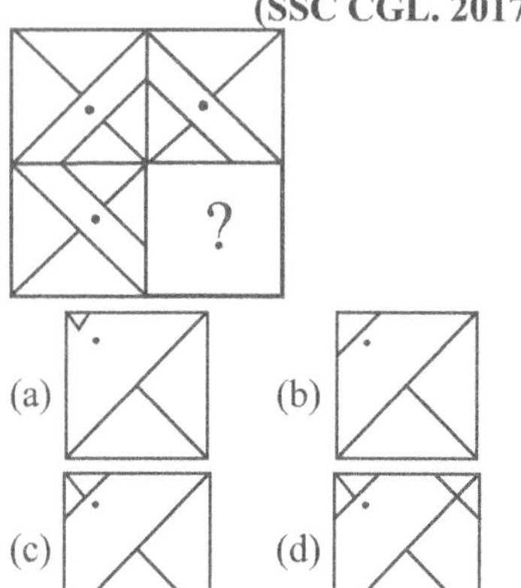

Ans.(c)

171. Which answer figure will come the pattern in the question figure?

(SSC CGL. 2017)

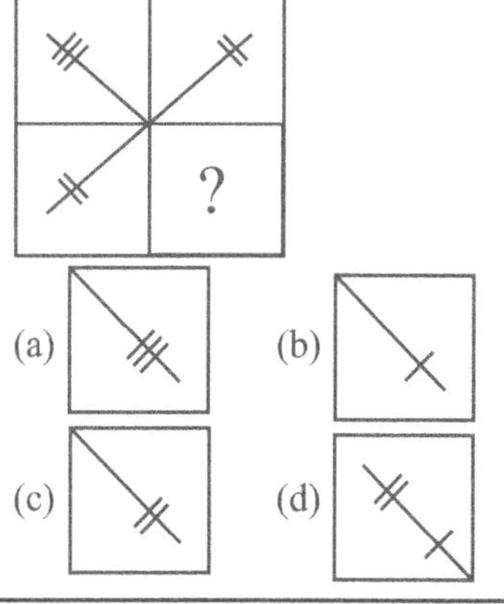

Ans.(a)

172. Which answer figure will complete the pattern in the question figure?

(SSC Sub. ins 2017)

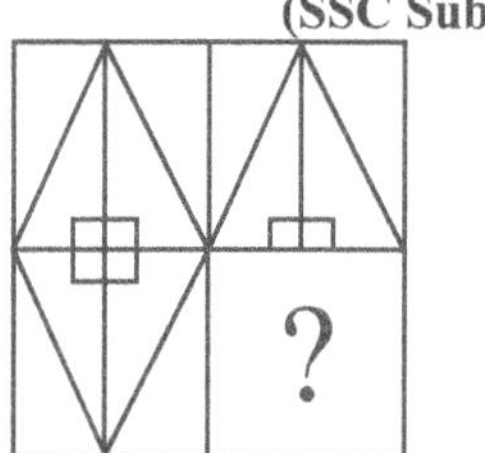

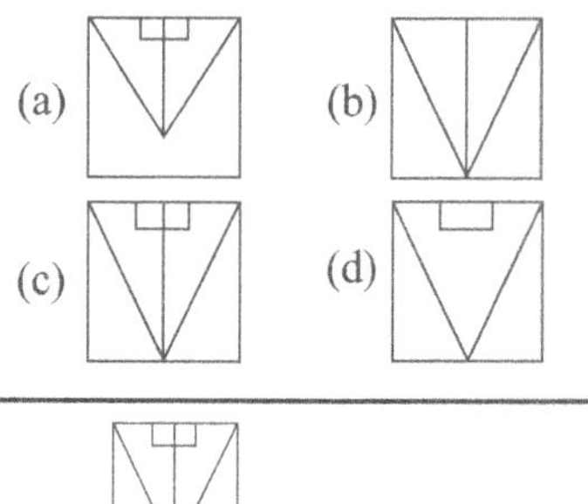

Ans.(c)

173. From the given answer figures, select the one in which the question figure is hidden/embedded.

(SSC CGL. 2017)

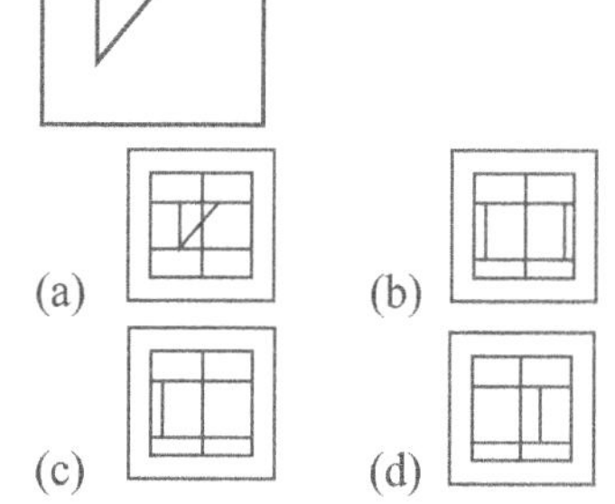

Ans.(a)

174. From the given answer figures, select the one in which the question figure is hidden/embedded.

(SSC CGL. 2017)

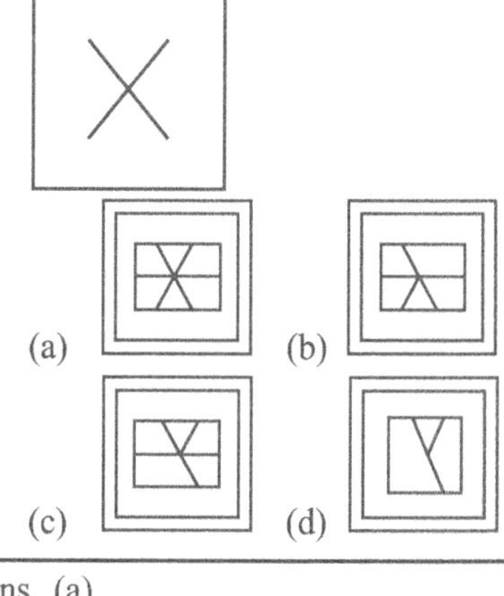

Ans. (a)

175. From given answer figures, select the one in which question figure is hidden/embedded.

(SSC CGL. 2017)

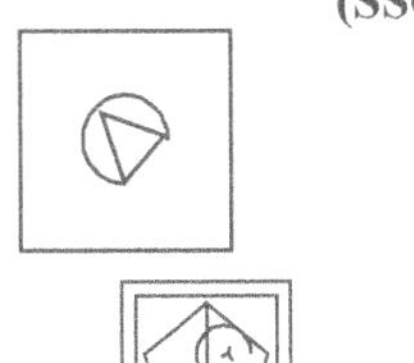

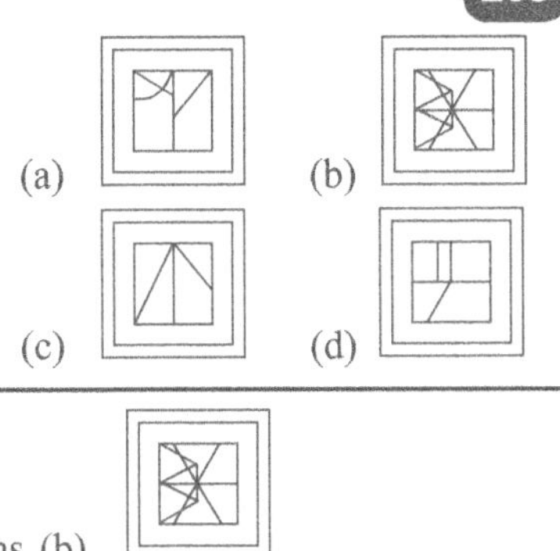

(a)   (b)

(c)   (d)

Ans.(b)

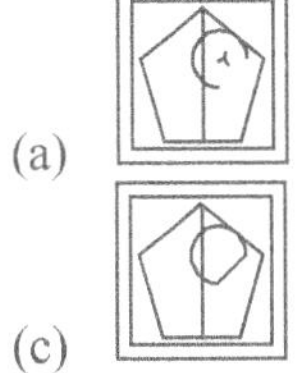
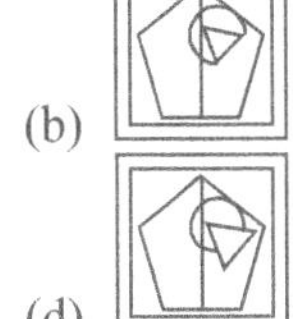

(a)   (b)

(c)   (d)

176. From the given answer figures, select the one in which the question figure is hidden/embedded.

(SSC Sub. ins 2017)

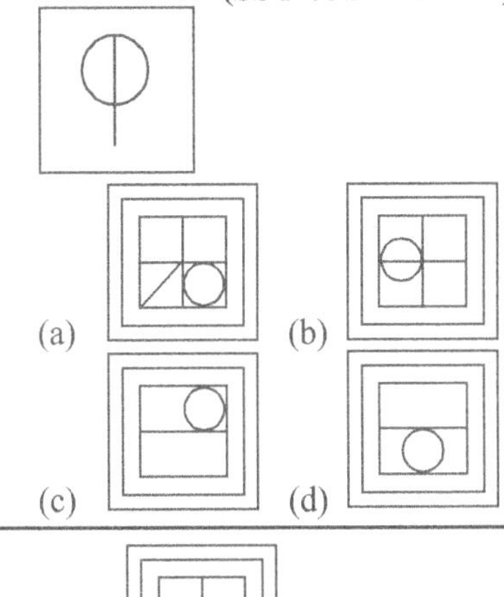

(a)   (b)

(c)   (d)

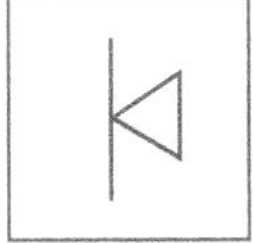

Ans.(b)

177. From the given answer figures, select the one in which the question figure is hidden/embedded.

(SSC Sub. ins 2017)

178. From the given answer figures, select the one in which the question figure is hidden/embedded.

(SSC Sten. 2017)

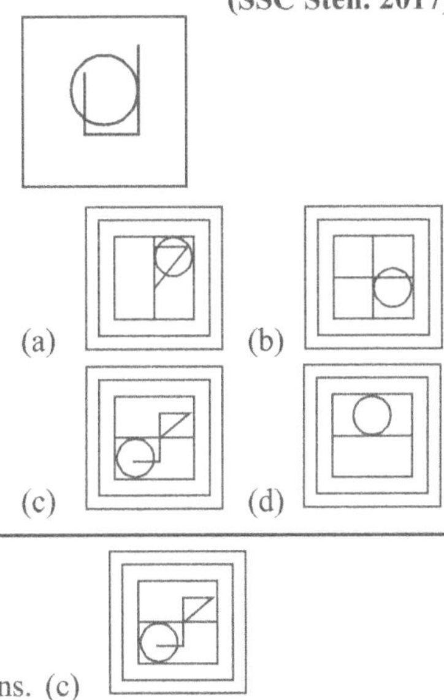

(a)   (b)

(c)   (d)

Ans. (c)

Counting of Figures/Figure Formation & Analysis, Grouping of Figures

179. How many triangles are there in the given figure?   **(SSC CGL 2017)**

(a)   32

(b)   34

(c)   37

(d)   40

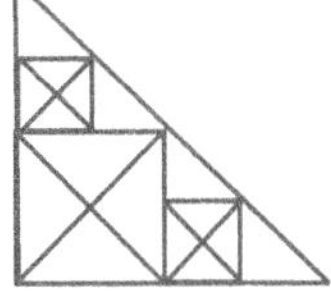

Ans. (c)   Total number of triangles = 37.

180. How many triangles are there in the given figure? 0   **(SSC CGL 2017)**

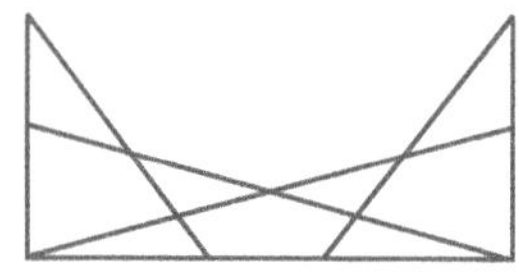

(a)   14   (b)   15

(c)   17   (d)   18

Ans. (c)

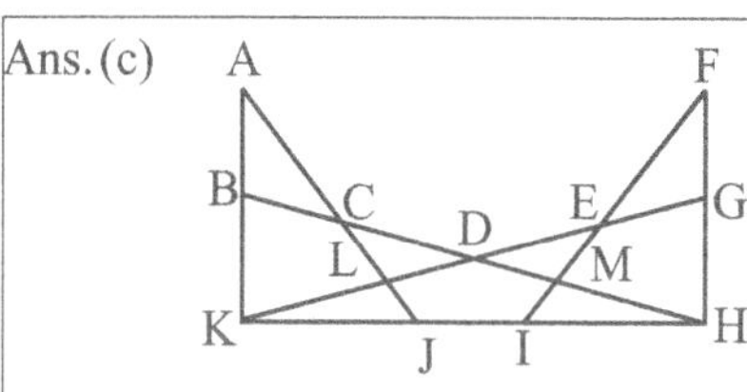

The Triangles are :

ABC, AKL, AKJ, BDK, BHK, KLM, KIM, KHG, FGE, FHM, FHI, CDL, DEM, MIH, GDH, CHJ and KEI.

So, total triangles are 17.

---

181. How many triangles are there in the figure?   **(SSC CGL 2017)**

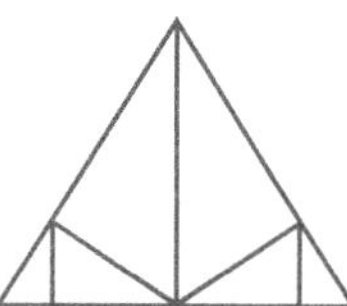

(a)   10   (b)   11

(c)   12   (d)   13

Ans. (b)

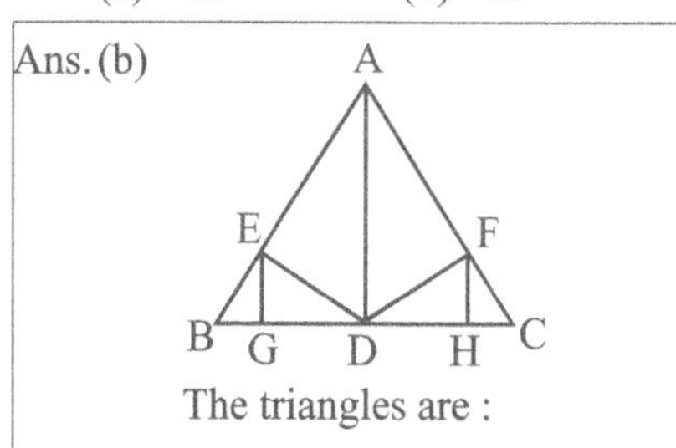

The triangles are :

ABC, △ABD, △ADC, △AED, △AFD, △BEG, △BED, △GED, △DFC, △FHC and △DFH.

△   Total number of triangles = 11.

---

182. How many triangles are there in the given figure?   **(SSC MTS 2017)**

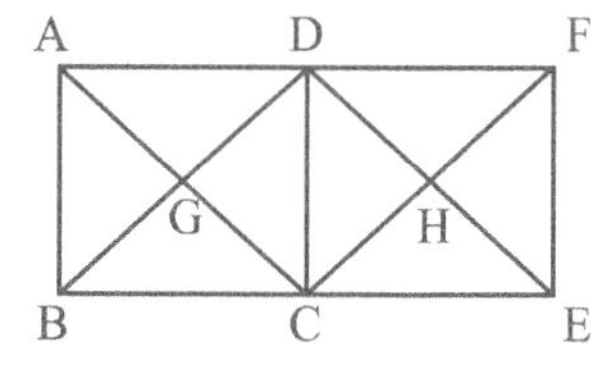

(a)   16   (b)   18

(c)   8   (d)   12

Ans. (b)   According to figure,

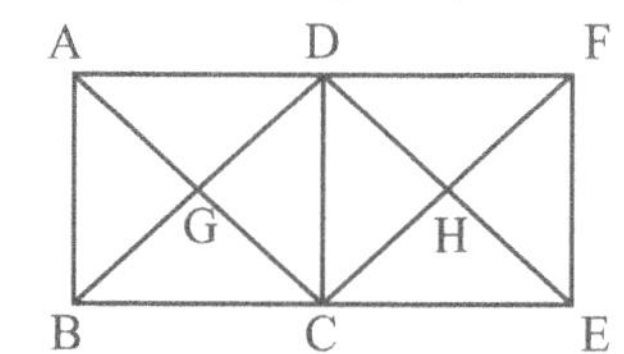

The triangles are :

△AGD; △AGB; △ADB; △ACF; △ABC; △ADC

△BGC; △BDC; △BDE; △DGC; △DHF; △DHC

△DCF; △DFC; △DFE; △CHE; △CFE; △FHE

Thus, there are 18 triangles.

---

183. How many quadrilaterals are there in the given figure?

(SSC Sub. Ins. 2017)

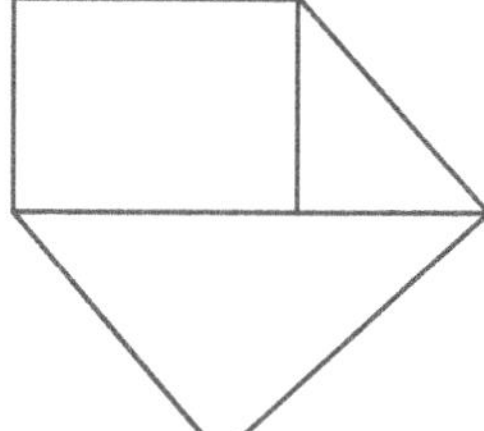

(a) 2   (b) 3
(c) 4   (d) 5

Ans. (a)

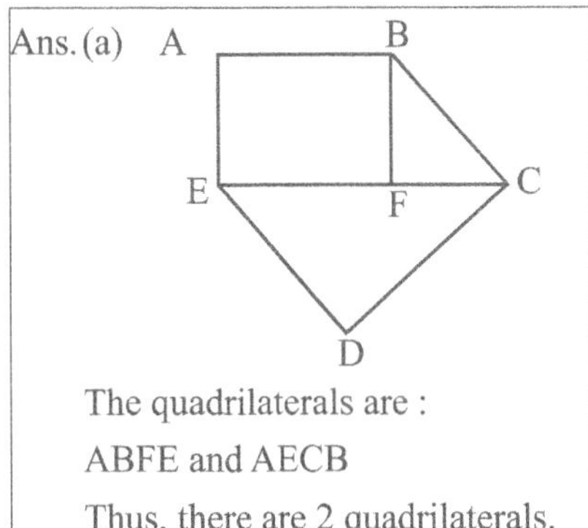

The quadrilaterals are :

ABFE and AECB

Thus, there are 2 quadrilaterals.

184. How many triangles are there in the given figure ?

(SSC Sub. Ins. 2017)

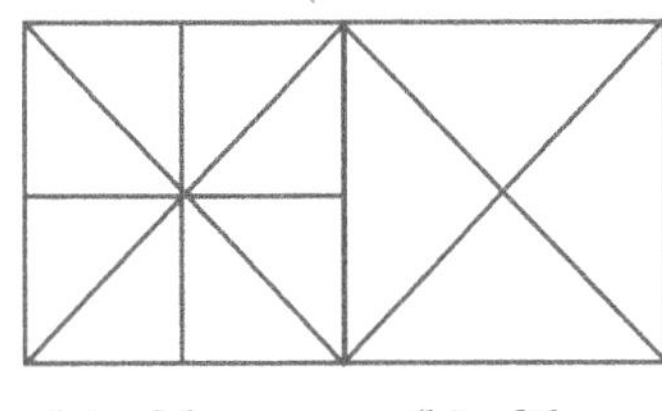

(a) 24   (b) 26
(c) 28   (d) 30

Ans. (b)

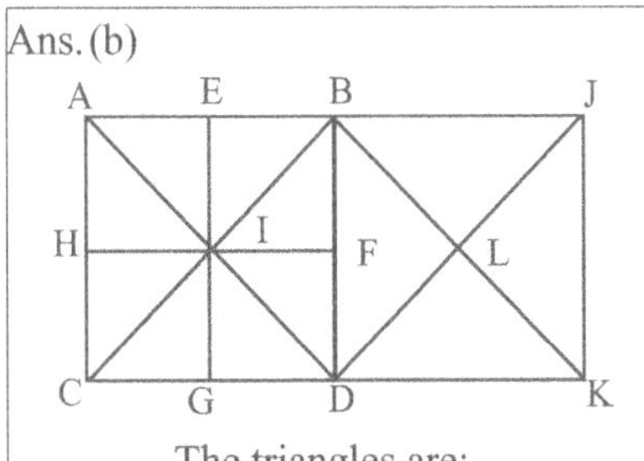

The triangles are:

△AIH ; △AIE; △EIB; △BFI;

△IHC; △IGC; △IGD; △DFI;
△IAB; △IBD; △ICD; △IAC;

△BAC; △ACD; △BDC; △BDA;

△BLD; △LDK; △KLJ; △JLB;

△JBK; △BDK; △DBJ; △DKJ

△ADJ; △CBK.

Thus, there are 26 triangles.

Paper Cutting & Folding

185. A piece of paper folded and punched as shown below in the question figures. From the given answer figure, indicate how it will appear when opened.

(SSC CGL 2017)

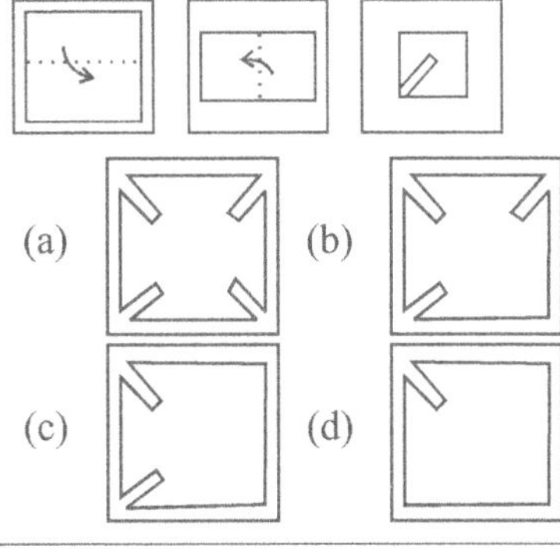

Ans. (a)

186. A piece of paper is folded and punched as shown below in the question figures. From the given answer figures, indicate how it will appear when opened?

(SSC CGL 2017)

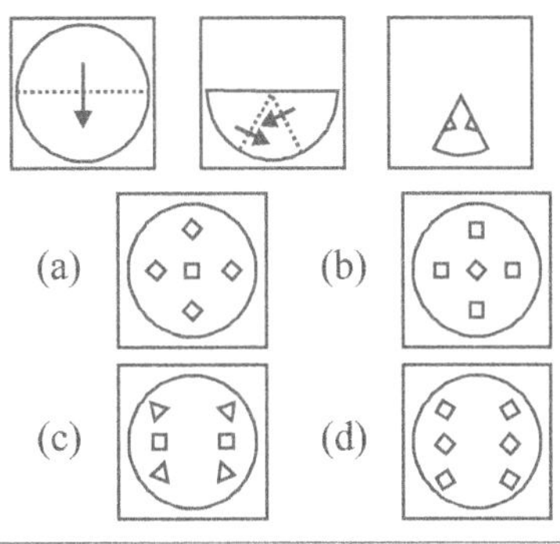

Ans. (d)

187. A piece paper is folded and punched as shown below the question figures. From the given answer figures, indicate how it will appear when opened? **(SSC CGL 2017)**

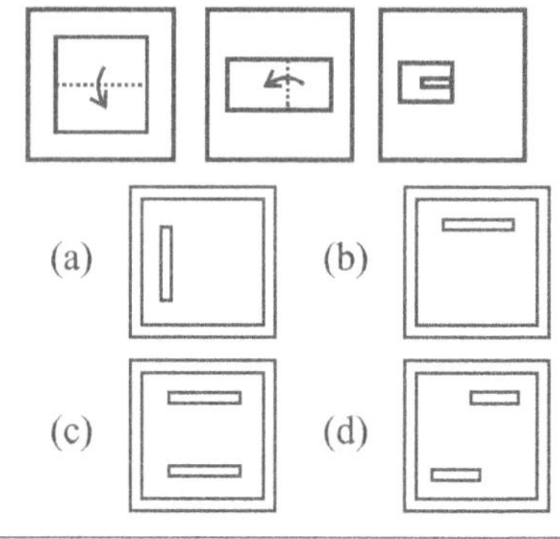

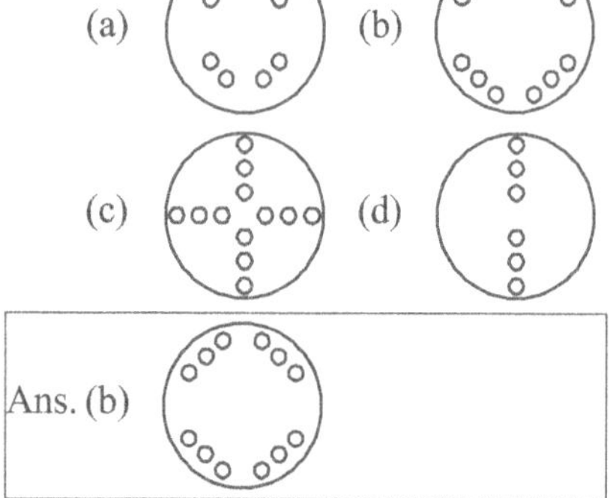

Ans. (c)

Ans. (b)

188. A piece of paper is folded and punched own below in the question figures. From the given answer figures, indicates how it will appear when opened. **(SSC CHSL 2017)**

190. A piece of paper is folded and punched as shown below in the question figures. From the given answer figures, indicate how it will appear when opened?

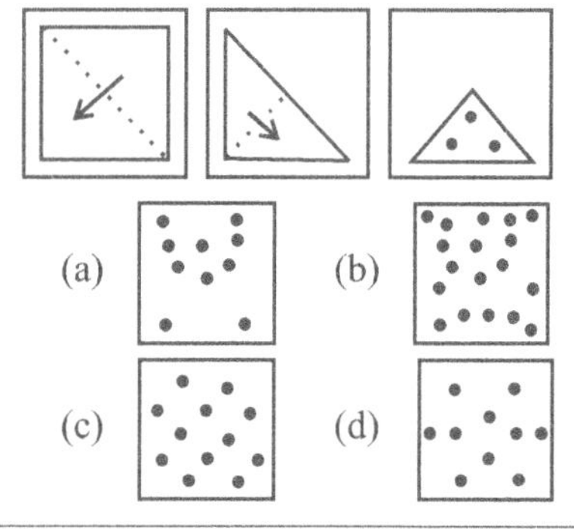

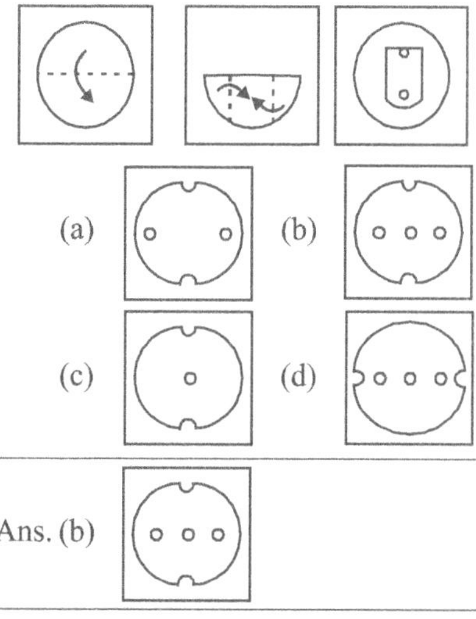

Ans. (c)   Required answer =

Ans. (b)

189. A piece of paper is folded and cut as shown below in the question figures. From the given answer figures, indicate how it will appear when opened.

Mirror & Water Image

191. If a mirror is placed on the line AB, then which of the answer figures is the right image of the given figure?

Question Figure

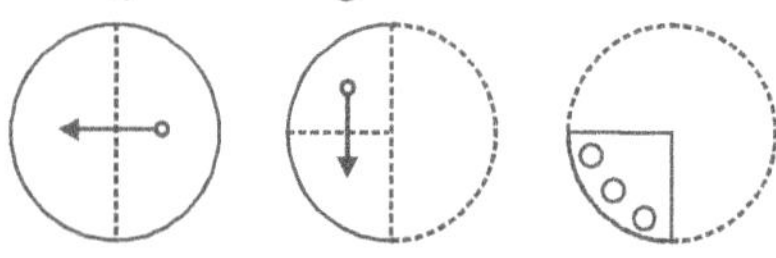

Answer Figures

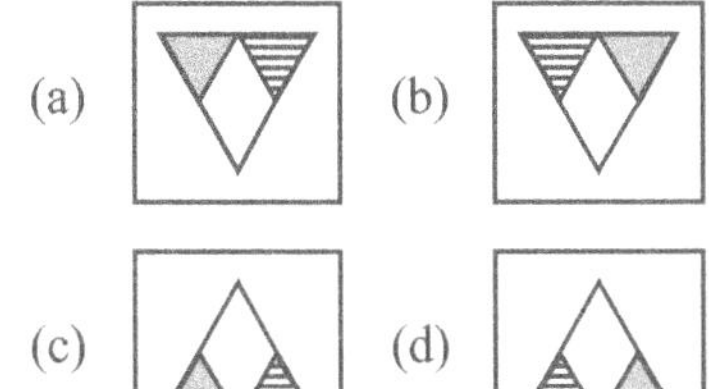

(a)   (b)

(c)   (d)

Ans. (c)

192. If a mirror is on the line AB, then which of the answer figures the right image of the given figure?

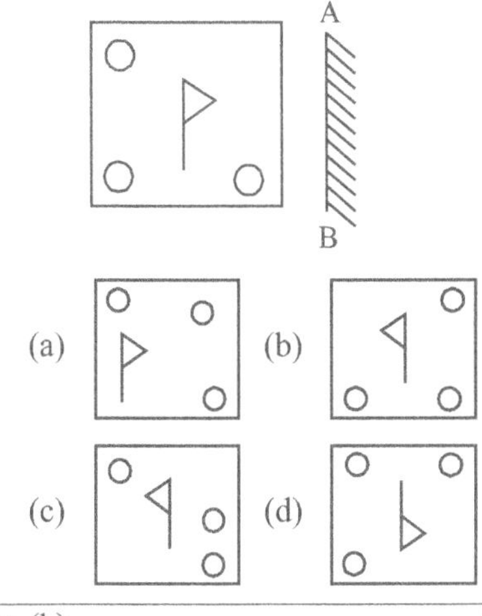

(a)   (b)

(c)   (d)

Ans. (b)

193. If a mirror is placed on the line AB, then which of the answer figure is the right image of the given figure?

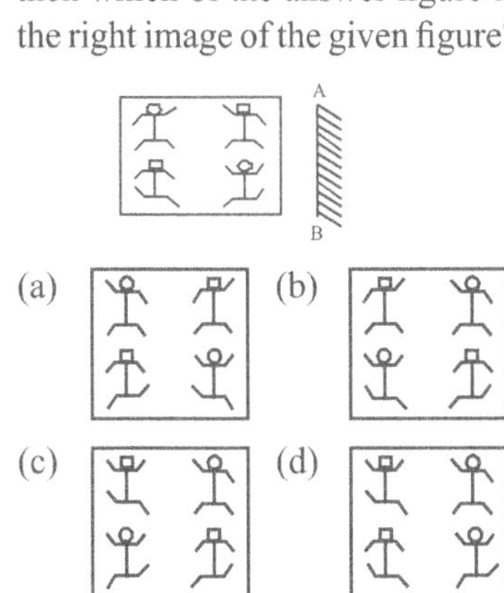

(a)   (b)

(c)   (d)

Ans. (b)

194. If a mirror placed on the line AB, then which of the answer is the right image of the given figure?

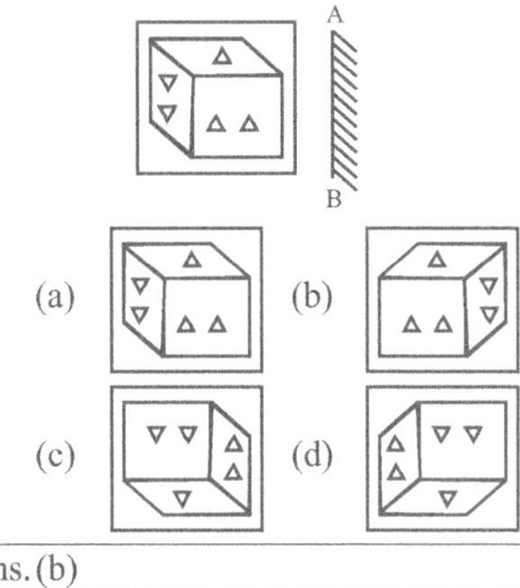

(a)   (b)

(c)   (d)

Ans. (b)

195. If a mirror is placed on the line MN, then which of the answer figure is the right image of the given figure?

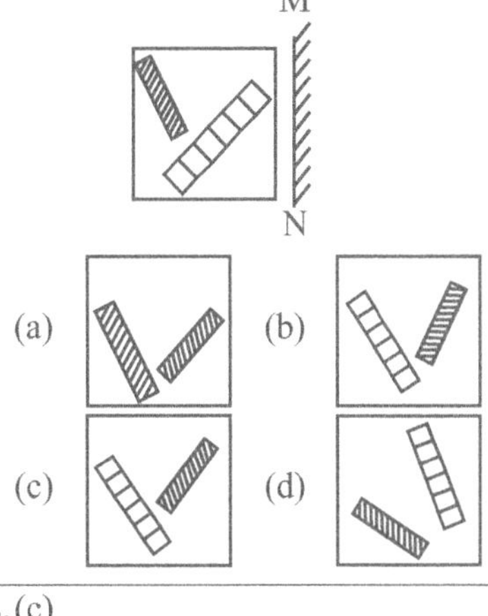

(a)   (b)

(c)   (d)

Ans. (c)

196. If a mirror is placed on the line AB, then which of the answer figures is the right image of the given figure?

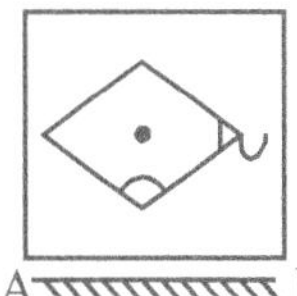

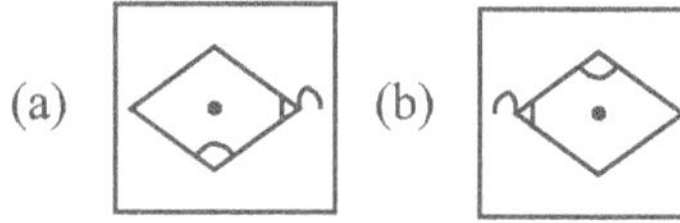

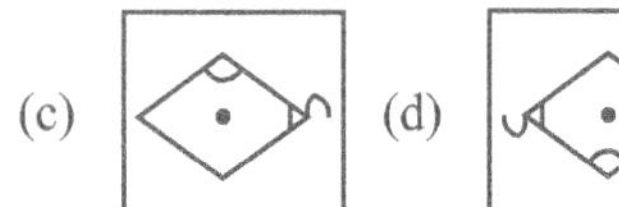

Ans.(c)

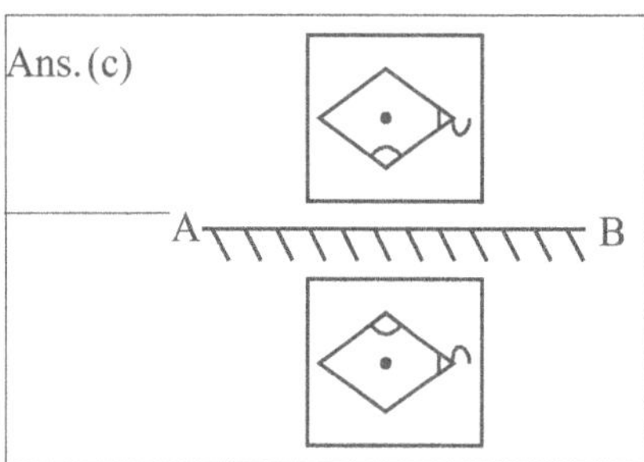

VISUAL REASONING, NON-VERBAL SERIES & CLASSIFICATION

197. Three positions of a cube are shown below. What will come opposite to face containing (I) ?

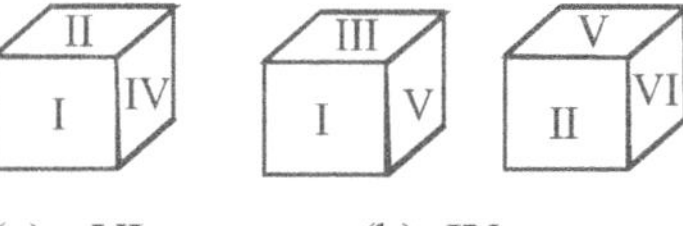

(a) VI   (b) IV
(c) II   (d) V

Ans.(a) Therefore, the number II, IV, III and V are on the adjacent faces of number I.
Therefore, the number IV liles opposite I.

198. Three positions of a cube are shown below. What will come opposite to face containing '$'?

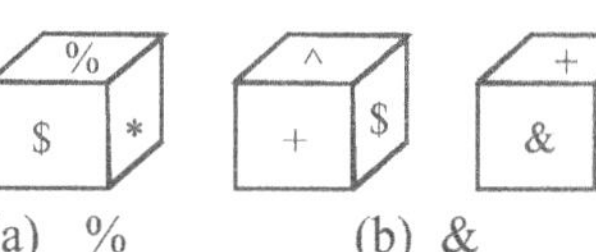

(a) %   (b) &
(c) ^   (d) +

Ans.(b) By looking, the dice position, we can say that %, *, ^ and + are adjacent faces of $.
therefore,
∴ & will come opposite of $.

199. Three positions of a cube are shown below. What will come opposite to face containing '4'?

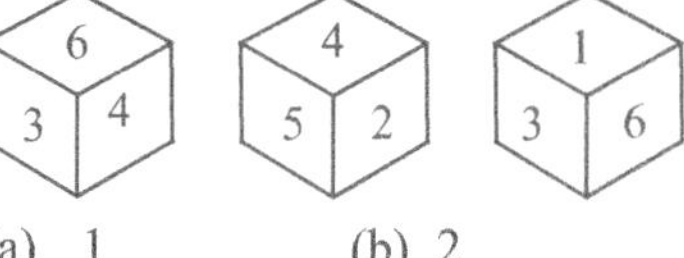

(a) 1   (b) 2
(c) 4   (d) 5

Ans.(a) As the numbers 2, 3, 5 and 6 are adjacent to 4.
Hence, the number on the face opposite to 4 is 1.

200. Three creation of a cube are shown below. what will opposite to face containing '5'?

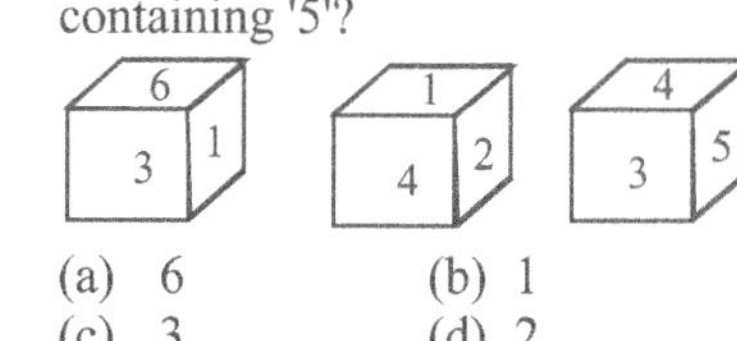

(a) 6   (b) 1
(c) 3   (d) 2

Ans.(b) The numbers 2, 3, 4 and 6 are on the adjacent faces of the number 1.
So, the number 5 lies opposite 1.

CHAPTER 9

English-Trending Questions from Past Paper

Synonyms

DIRECTIONS (Qs. 1-23) : *In the following questions, out of the four alternatives, select the word similar in meaning to the word given.*

(SSC CGL 2017 set-1)

1. Opulent
   - (a) Fake
   - (b) Gloomy
   - (c) Rich
   - (d) Selfish

   Ans.(c) 'Opulent' means wealthy and rich.

2. Morose
   - (a) Flatter
   - (b) Gloomy
   - (c) Friendly
   - (d) Savvy

   Ans.(b) 'Morose' means gloomily or sullenly ill-humored.

3. Frivolous
   - (a) Captious
   - (b) Wise
   - (c) Puerile
   - (d) Spiritual

   Ans.(c) Frivolous means not having serious purpose or value.

4. Petrify
   - (a) Adorn
   - (b) Calm
   - (c) Curious
   - (d) Harden

   Ans.(d) Petrify means to make someone so frightened that they are unable to move.

5. Mellifluous
   - (a) Shiver
   - (b) Frank
   - (c) Immoral
   - (d) Dulcet

   Ans.(d) Mellifluous means pleasingly smooth and musical to hear.

6. Dodge
   - (a) Soften
   - (b) Order
   - (c) Avoid
   - (d) Chaotic

   Ans.(c) Dodge means a sudden quick movement to avoid something.

7. **Eloquent**
   - (a) Fluent
   - (b) Ignorant
   - (c) Rude
   - (d) Significant

   Ans.(a) 'Eloquent' means fluent or persuasive in speaking or writing.

8. **Nefarious**
   - (a) Iniquitous
   - (b) Purposeful
   - (c) Suspicious
   - (d) Virtuous

   Ans.(a) 'Nefarious' means morally bad in principles or practice.

9. Select the synonym of
   To subsume   **(SSC CHSL 2017)**
   - (a) To bate
   - (b) To obviate
   - (c) To preclude
   - (d) To incorporate

   Ans.(d) 'Subsume' means to include something in a particular group. The word 'incorporate' also has similar meaning. So option (d) is the correct answer.

10. Select the synonym of

    To lash   (SSC CHSL 2017)
    (a) To endear   (b) To fondle
    (c) To chastise (d) To snuggle

Ans.(c) To lash means to hit something with great force. The word 'chastise' refers to punishing somebody physically. It is a synonym of the word 'lash'. So option (c) is the right answer.

11. Amateur
    (a) Timid   (b) Beginner
    (c) Weary   (d) Dispirited

Ans.(b) Amateur means a person who is unqualified or insufficiently skillful i.e. a starter or a beginner.

12. Gumption
    (a) Acumen   (b) Starry
    (c) Futile   (d) Fallow

Ans.(a) Gumption means the ability to decide what is the best thing to do in a particular situation. Acumen means skill in making correct decisions and judgments in a particular subject.

13. Laconic
    (a) Shrewd   (b) Whim
    (c) Climax   (d) Concise

Ans.(d) Laconic means using very few words. Concise means giving a lot of information clearly and in a few words.

14. Veledictory
    (a) Hesitant   (b) Terminal
    (c) Ridicule   (d) Deception

Ans.(b) Valedictory means serving as a farewell (end). Terminal means forming or situated at the end or extremity of something.

15. Denouement
    (a) Climax   (b) Systematic
    (c) Improper   (d) Glorious

Ans.(a) Denouement means the outcome of a situation, when something is decided or made clear. Climax means the most intense, exciting, or important point of something; the culmination.

16. Distinct
    (a) Obscure   (b) Similar
    (c) Clear   (d) Vague

Ans.(c) Distinct means recognizably different in nature from something else of a similar type. Its synonym is clear meaning easy to perceive, understand, or interpret.

17. Condemn
    (a) Approve   (b) Laud
    (c) Belittle   (d) Commend

Ans.(c) Condemn means to say in a strong and definite way that someone or something is bad or wrong. Belittle means to make a person or an action seem as if he, she or it is not important.

18. Dingy
    (a) Pure   (b) Sterile
    (c) Immaculate   (d) Drab

Ans.(d) Dingy means gloomy and drab.

19. Clever
    (a) Clear   (b) Cunning
    (c) Foolish   (d) Intelligent

Ans.(d) Clever means quick to understand, learn, and devise or apply ideas; intelligent.

20. Constant
    (a) Changing   (b) Flowing
    (c) Moving   (d) Fixed

Ans.(d) Constant means a situation that does not change. The word similar to meaning of constant is fixed.

21. Exactly
    (a) Different   (b) Precisely
    (c) Similar   (d) Same

Ans. (d) Same and exactly have the same meaning.

22. Answer
    (a) Response   (b) Speak
    (c) Question   (d) React

Ans. (a) Answer and response are synonyms and similar in meaning.

23. Pain
    (a) Comfort   (b) Vibration
    (c) Ache   (d) Throb

Ans. (c) Pain and ache are synonyms and similar in meaning.

Antonyms

DIRECTIONS (Qs. 24-28): *In the following questions, choose the word opposite in meaning to the given word.*

(SSC Steno. 2016)

24. Inflammable
    (a) Combustible
    (b) Non-flammable
    (c) Flammable
    (d) Excitable

Ans.(b) The opposite of inflammable is non-flammable.

25. Hasty
    (a) Harsh   (b) Unhurried
    (c) Rapid   (d) Cautious

Ans.(d) Hasty means without much thought whereas, cautious means careful, watchful.

26. Attachment
    (a) Attraction   (b) Rejection
    (c) Detachment (d) Aversion

Ans.(c) The opposite of attachment is detachment.

27. Uniform
    (a) Variable   (b) Common
    (c) Unfamiliar (d) A measure

Ans.(a) Uniform means consistent which is the opposite of variable.

28. Obscure
    (a) Hidden   (b) Obvious
    (c) Concealed (d) Zealous

Ans.(b) Obscure means easily understandable whereas obvious means understandable.

DIRECTIONS (Qs. 29-30) : *In the following questions, out of the four alternatives, select the word opposite in meaning to the word given.*

(SSC CGL 2017)

29. Irk
    (a) Attract   (b) Discourage
    (c) Irritate   (d) Please

Ans.(d) 'Irk' means to irritate some one, hence, its opposite will be to please.

30. Grotesque
    (a) Free   (b) Odd
    (c) Plain   (d) Queer

Ans.(c) Grotesque means distorted and unnatural in shape or size, hence, its antonym will be 'plain'.

DIRECTIONS (Qs. 31-32): *In the following questions, out of the four alternatives, select the word opposite in meaning to the word given.*

(SSC CGL 2017)

31. Gregarious

    (a) Affable   (b) Genial

    (c) Introvert   (d) Urbane

Ans.(c) 'Gregarious means' sociable, while 'introvert' means solitary.

32. Tremulous

    (a) Feeble   (b) Frugal

    (c) Stable   (d) Vital

Ans.(c) 'Tremulous' means shaking or quivering slightly while 'stable' means firmly fixed.

DIRECTIONS (Qs. 33-34): *In the following questions, out of the four alternatives, select the word opposite in meaning to the word given.*

(SSC CGL 2017)

33. Meretricious

    (a) Brazen   (b) Natural

    (c) Exemplary   (d) Gaudy

Ans.(b) Meretricious means superficial, hence, natural will be its antonyms.

34. Nebulous

    (a) Definite   (b) Inchoate

    (c) Dismal   (d) Sullen

Ans.(a) Nebulous means indefinite, hence, its opposite will be definite.

DIRECTIONS (Qs. 35-36): *In the following questions, out of the four alternatives, select the word opposite in meaning to the word given.*

(SSC CGL 2017)

35. Ensconce

    (a) Establish   (b) Impudence

    (c) Request   (d) Unveil

Ans.(d) 'Ensconce' means to conceal, hence unveil is the correct opposite word.

36. Lugubrious

    (a) Clumsy   (b) Lucid

    (c) Optimistic   (d) Sinister

Ans.(c) 'Lugubrious' means looking sad and dismal, while optimistic means cheerful and positive hence, it is the correct antonym.

37. Select the antonym of

    Amenable   **(SSC CHSL 2017)**

    (a) Responsive

    (b) Pliable

    (c) Docile

    (d) Unsusceptible

Ans.(d) 'Amenable' means 'easy to control' or some one who can be easily influenced. Options (a), (b) and (c) are synonyms of the word, hence are incorrect. Option (d) means opposite of the word 'amenable', hence, it is the right answer.

38. Select the antonym of

    To muster   **(SSC CHSL 2017)**

    (a) To convocate

    (b) To rally

    (c) To estrange

    (d) To aggregate

Ans.(c) 'To muster' means to gather or aggregate things whereas 'to estrange' means to isolate or alienate.

DIRECTIONS (Qs. 39-43): *In the following questions, out of four alternatives, select the word opposite in meaning to the word given.*

39. Bucolic **(SSC Sub. Insp. 2017)**
    (a) Rustic   (b) Dull
    (c) Tranquil (d) Fierce

Ans.(d)	Bucolic means relating to the pleasant aspects of the countryside and country life while fierce means having or displaying a violent or ferocious aggressiveness.

40. Compendium
    (a) Expansion (b) Reference
    (c) Precis   (d) Outline

Ans.(a)	Compendium means a collection of concise but detailed information about a particular subject while expansion means the action of becoming larger or more extensive.

41. Chastise
    (a) Praise   (b) Resist
    (c) Prefer   (d) Repel

Ans.(a)	Chastise means to criticize someone severely while praise means express warm approval or admiration of.

42. Daunt
    (a) Rejoice   (b) Encourage
    (c) Decrease (d) Discard

Ans.(b)	Daunt means to make someone feel slightly frightened or worried about their ability to achieve while encourage means to give support.

43. Oblivious
    (a) Hideous
    (b) Victorious
    (c) Conscious
    (d) Advantageous

Ans.(c)	Oblivious means not aware of or concerned about what is happening around one while conscious means aware of and responding to one's surroundings.

DIRECTIONS (Qs. 44-51): *In the following question, out of the four given alternatives, select the word opposite in meaning to the word given.*

(SSC Steno. 2017)

44. Confine
    (a) Permit   (b) Restrain
    (c) Restrict (d) Imprison

44. (a)	Confine means keep or restrict someone or something within certain limits. Thus, its opposite is permit. which means officially allow (someone) to do something.

45. Defeat
    (a) Beat   (b) Attainment
    (c) Collapse (d) Loss

Ans.(b)	Defeat means to win against someone in a fight, war, or competition. The opposite is attainment which means to accomplish something.

46. Fervent
    (a) Passionate (b) Cold
    (c) Zealous   (d) Blazing

Ans.(b)	Fervent means having or displaying a passionate intensity. Cold is its opposite meaning lacking affection or warmth of feeling; unemotional.

47. Imitation
    (a) Copy   (b) Echo
    (c) Genuine (d) Follow

Ans.(c)	Imitation means a thing intended to simulate or copy something else. Its opposite is genuine.

48. Immense
    (a) Big   (b) Tiny
    (c) Huge   (d) Grand

Ans.(b) Immense means extremely large or great. Its opposite is tiny.

49. Scatter   **(SSC MTS 2017)**
    (a) Store   (b) Pile
    (c) Hoard   (d) Collect

Ans.(d) Scatter means to disperse hence, collect is its antonym.

50. Peak
    (a) Inferior   (b) Deep
    (c) Mount   (d) Bottom

Ans.(d) Peak means the point of highest activity, quality, or achievement. Its opposite is bottom.

51. despair
    (a) Hope   (b) Sorrow
    (d) Repair   (d) Empty

Ans.(a) Despair means the complete loss or absence of hope. Its opposite is hope.

Fill in the Blanks & Cloze Test

DIRECTIONS (Qs. 52-53): *In the following questions, the sentence given with blank to be filled in with an approperiate word. Select the correct alternative out of the four and indicate it by selecting the appropriate option.*

(SSC CGL 2017)

52. Don't toilet __________ the corridor.
    (a) around   (b) off
    (c) of   (d) at

Ans.(a)

53. I will scold him when __________.
    (a) he will come
    (b) he comes
    (c) he would come
    (d) he had come

Ans.(b)

DIRECTIONS (Qs. 54-58): *In the following passage some of the words have been left out. Read the passage carefully and select the correct answer for the given blank out of the four alternatives.*

Democracy should __54__ dignity of the individual. It should also aim at the __55__ good of the greatest __56__. The opposition party should __57__ the wrong plans, policies and decisions of the government in power. The government should cater to the __58__ needs of the people to make its position solid.   **(SSC CGL 2017)**

54. (a) built   (b) ensure
    (c) keep   (d) support

Ans.(b)

55. (a) greatest   (b) smallest
    (c) largest   (d) heaviest

Ans.(a)

56. (a) people   (b) digit
    (c) number   (d) individual

Ans.(c)

57. (a) rely on   (b) against
    (c) support   (d) oppose

Ans.(d)

58. (a) genuine   (b) mere
    (c) emotional   (d) luxurious

Ans.(a)

DIRECTIONS (Qs. 59-60): *In the following questions, the sentence given with blank to be filled in with an appropriate word. Select the correct alternative out of the four and indicate it by selecting the appropriate option.*

(SSC CGL 2017)

59. Keith has __________ with a failure in English examination thrice.
    (a) caught   (b) gone
    (c) got   (d) met

Ans.(d)

60. The manager was _________ an explanation of his conduct.
    (a) called for   (b) called off
    (c) called to   (d) called up

Ans.(a)

DIRECTIONS (Qs. 61-65): *In the following question, the sentence given with blank to be filled in with an appropriate word. Select the correct alternative out of the four and indicate it by selecting the appropriate option.*

Corruption is a __61__ which has been spread in the mind of wrong people of the society, community and __62__. It is the mistreatment of public resources just for getting some __63__ advantage to fulfil little wish. It is concerned with the unnecessary and wrong use of both power and __64__ by anyone whether the government or non government organisation. It affects the growth and development organisation. If affect the growth and development of the nation in all aspects like socially, __65__ and politically. **(SSC CGL 2017)**

61. (a) havoc   (b) poison
    (c) pollutant   (d) grassroot

Ans.(b)

62. (a) country   (b) world
    (c) universe   (d) company

Ans.(a)

63. (a) fruitful   (b) wishful
    (c) favourite   (d) unfair

Ans.(b)

64. (a) position   (b) growth
    (c) status   (d) symbol

Ans.(a)

65. (a) emotionally
    (b) scientifically
    (c) manually
    (d) economically

Ans.(d)

66. In the following question, the sentence given with blank is to be filled in with an appropriate word. Select the correct alternative out of the four and indicate it by selecting the appropriate option.

Arun's financial __________ has helped him earn a fortune on the stock market. **(SSC CHSL 2017)**
    (a) dexterity   (b) readiness
    (c) expertise   (d) knack

Ans.(c) 'Expertise' refers to expert knowledge or skill in a particular subject or activity. 'Financial expertise' is the correct usage in the given context. So option (c) is the correct answer.

67. In the following question, sentence given with blank is to be filled in with an appropriate word. Select the correct alternative out of the four and indicate it by selecting the appropriate option.

Fuel suppliers will __________ the national oil shortage by raising prices to increase their bottom lines. **(SSC CHSL 2017)**
    (a) use   (b) misuse
    (c) ventuse   (d) exploit

Ans.(d) 'Exploit' means to treat someone unfairly to get benefit for yourself. In the given context, it is the most appropriate usage of the word. So, option (d) is the correct answer.

DIRECTIONS (Qs. 68-72): *In the following passage, some of the words have been left out. Read the passage carefully and select the correct answer for the given blank out of the four alternatives.*

The scenario __68__ dramatically today. We have the __69__ of powerfull Internet monopolies that are much bigger __70__ the telcos.

Not surprisingly, these companies now see the _____71_____ of monopoly. They would like to combine with telcos to create monopolies for their platforms, ensuring that they control the future of the Internet and freeze their competition _____72_____.   **(SSC CHSL 2017)**

68. (a) change   (b) had changed
    (c) has changed (d) changing

Ans. (c) Since, the sentence refers to something that has happened in present tense. So, the its verb form should be in present perfect tense. Only option (c) is in the appropriate tense. So, it is the right answer.

69. (a) emerging   (b) emerge
    (c) emergence (d) emergency

Ans. (c) The 'of' after the blank indicates that there should be a noun in the blank. In the given context 'emergence of powerful internet monopolies' makes the most appropriate sense. So (c) is the correct answer.

70. (a) then   (b) than
    (c) to   (d) of

Ans. (b) There is comparative form 'bigger' before the blank. It should be followed by 'than' to make the sentence correct. So, option (b) is the correct answer.

71. (a) virtues
    (b) respectability
    (c) trust
    (d) innocence

Ans. (a) In the given context, 'Virtues of monopoly' is the correct usage. So, option (a) is the right answer.

72. (a) off   (b) about
    (c) in   (d) out

Ans. (d) The phrase 'freeze out' means to prevent someone from taking part in something. In the given context, its use is appropriate. So, option (d) is the right answer.

DIRECTIONS (Qs. 73-77): *In the following question, the sentence given with blank to be filled in with an appropriate word. Select the correct alternative out of the four and indicate it by selecting the appropriate option.*

(SSC Sub. Insp. 2017)

73. Suman has _______ for the final round of the competition.
    (a) Superior   (b) decided
    (c) declared   (d) qualified

Ans. (d) Qualified is the most appropriate word.

74. Her supporters began to _____ and she was left alone.
    (a) fall over   (b) fall away
    (c) fall off   (d) fall on

Ans. (b) 'Fall away' is the most appropriate option.

75. No_____ than fifteen boys failed in a class of forty.
    (a) little   (b) less
    (c) few   (d) fewer

Ans. (d) 'fewer' is the most appropriate word.

76. Sania was compensated _____ the loss of her belongings at the airport.
    (a) for   (b) of
    (c) against   (d) over

Ans. (a) 'for' is the most appropriate word.

77. Suraj is acquainted _____ Kapil.
    (a) of   (b) with
    (c) from   (d) to

Ans. (b) 'With' is the most appropriate option.

DIRECTIONS (Qs. 78-82): *In the following passage some of the words have been left out. Read the passage carefully and select the correct answer for the given blank out of the four alternatives.*

Youth is the _____ gift of the god, says an old "upanishad". Let us _____ in it. It is the great formative _____ of our life, brief but powerful. We are then able to _____ the world with feelings pure and with _____ unworldly.

(SSC Sub. Insp. 2017)

78. Youth is the _____ gift of the god, says an old "unpanishad'.
    (a) inexpensive (b) best
    (c) useless (d) small

Ans. (b) 'best' is the most appropriate word.

79. Let us _____ in it. It is the great formative.
    (a) rejoice (b) live
    (c) dance (d) sleep

Ans. (a) 'Rejoice' is the most appropriate word.

80. _____ of our life, brief but powerful.
    (a) lesson (b) resource
    (c) period (d) idea

Ans. (c) 'period' is the most appropriate word.

81. We are then able to _____ the world with feelings pure
    (a) challenge (b) roam
    (c) target (d) face

Ans. (d) 'face' is the most appropriate word.

82. and with _____ unwordly.
    (a) ambitions (b) Passively
    (c) religiously (d) resources

Ans. (a) 'ambitions' is the most appropriate word.

DIRECTIONS (Qs. 83-92): *In the following passage some of the words have been left out. Read the passage carefully and select the correct answer for the given blank out of the four altirnatives.*

You can spend hours looking for_____, days waiting for that Eureka_____, moving things around on screen, starting at blank pieces of paper,_____down half-formed ideas, all to_____no avail. Sometimes coming up with just one creative idea can feel_____. You feel this way because creativity is a process, a_____that has to be learned and honed._____you're a marketer, designer, entrepreneur or any thing in between, creative thinking is a valuable skill to _____. It can help us find_____, tailored solutions to problems and create memorable and effective_____. **(SSC Steno. 2017)**

83. You can spend hours looking for_____.
    (a) dedication (b) inspiration
    (c) solutions (d) ideas

Ans. (b) 'inspiration' is the most appropriate option.

84. Days waiting for that Eureka _____.
    (a) moment (b) movement
    (c) type (d) day

Ans. (a) 'moment' is the most appropriate option.

85. _____ down half-formed ideas
    (a) idea (b) pencil
    (c) jotted (d) writes

Ans. (c) 'jotted' is the most appropriate option.

86. _____ no avail.
    (a) absolutely (b) silence
    (c) full (d) rightly

| Ans. (a) | 'absolutely' is the most appropriate option. |

87. Creative idea can feel________.
   (a) impossible (b) lazy
   (c) cold   (d) hot

| Ans. (a) | 'impossible' is the most appropriate option. |

88. A________that has to be learned and honed.
   (a) talent   (b) hobby
   (c) skill   (d) sense

| Ans. (c) | 'skill' is the most appropriate option. |

89. ________you're a marketer
   (a) and   (b) but
   (c) still   (d) Whether

| Ans. (d) | 'whether' is the most appropriate option. |

90. Creative thinking is a valuable skill to ________.
   (a) possess   (b) have
   (c) should   (d) get

| Ans. (a) | 'possess' is the most appropriate option. |

91. It can help us find________.
   (a) senseless (b) unique
   (c) ugly   (d) worst

| Ans. (b) | 'unique' is the most appropriate option. |

92. Create memorable and effective ________.
   (a) memories
   (b) commucications
   (c) borders
   (d) relations

| Ans. (b) | 'communications' is the most appropriate option. |

DIRECTIONS (Qs. 93-102): *In the following passage some of the words have been left out. Read the passage carefully and select the correct answer for the given blank out of the four alternatives.*

(SSC Steno. 2017)

Art movement is described as a ____93____ or way of doing art of art that spans over a ___94____ of time that is subtly or ___95____ different than another movement of art. The style or method "moves" or changes to a different way if you will. These styles are used to ___96____ art practiced by a group of ___97___within the same time period and/or region. Some art____98____that have been influenced by another art movement show obvious____99____ while others seem to defy their cousins because of ___100____. It is interesting to study the differences between art ___101___and also to study the different ____102____of art.

93. Art movement is deseribed as a ________.
   (a) type   (b) style
   (c) like   (d) practice

| Ans. (b) | 'style' is the most appropriate option. |

94. Art that spans over a ________of time.
   (a) tide   (b) wait
   (c) period   (d) during

| Ans. (c) | 'period' is the most appropriate option. |

95. ________different than another movement of art.
   (a) distinctly (b) easy
   (c) newly   (d) otherwise

| Ans. (a) | 'distinctly' is the most appropriate option. |

96. These styles are used to ______art practiced.
   (a) Visualise (b) Describe
   (c) Imgine   (d) Ignore

Ans.(b) 'describe' is the most appropriate option.

97. Group of _______within the same period and/or region.
    (a) businessmen
    (b) actors
    (c) ventors
    (d) artists

Ans.(d) 'artists' is the most appropriate option.

98. Some art _______that have been influenced.
    (a) movements (b) pictures
    (c) books   (d) scenes

Ans.(a) 'Movements' is the most appropriate option.

99. Art movement show obvious _______while others.
    (a) alike   (b) same
    (c) eagerness (d) similarities

Ans.(d) 'Similarities' is the most appropriate option.

100. Defy their cousins because of _______.
    (a) limitations (b) benefits
    (c) distance   (d) time

Ans.(a) 'limitations' is the most appropriate option.

101. Study the differences between art _______.
    (a) movements (b) flow
    (c) revolution (d) adequate

Ans.(a) 'movements' is the most appropriate option.

102. Study the different _______of art.
    (a) length   (b) timezone
    (c) periods   (d) duration

Ans.(c) 'periods' is the most appropriate option.

DIRECTIONS (Qs. 103-107): *In the following question, the sentence given with blank to be filled in with an appropriate word. Select the correct alternative out of the four and indicate it by selecting the appropriate option.*

(SSC Steno. 2017)

103. Each item was sold _______ a pound
    (a) at   (b) for
    (c) in   (d) of

Ans.(b) 'For' is the most appropriate word.

104. Be just _______fear nothing.
    (a) but   (b) while
    (c) and   (d) until

Ans.(c) 'And' is the most appropriate word.

105. He came two hours _______us.
    (a) before   (b) ago
    (c) above   (d) ahead

Ans.(a) 'Before' is the most appropriate word.

106. Sunaina said,"She is sick _______ the whole business."
    (a) by   (b) of
    (c) for   (d) with

Ans.(b) 'of' is the most appropriate word.

107. He was quite _______when he heard what had happened.
    (a) laughing   (b) amused
    (c) lovable   (d) beautiful

Ans.(b) 'amused' is the most appropriate word.

DIRECTIONS (Qs. 108-117): *Sentence given with blank to be filled in with appropiate word(s). Four alternatives are suggested for each question. Choose the most appropriate alternative out of the four.*

(SSC MTS 2017)

108. As soon as this workshop is over, I am going to ________ every duty and go on a holiday.
    (a) sidetrack   (b) abandon
    (c) overthrow   (d) close down

Ans.(b) As soon as this workshop is over, I am going to abandon every duty and go on a holiday.

109. She ______ great pleasure and satisfaction from cooking.
    (a) wants   (b) has
    (c) draws   (d) derives

Ans.(c) She draws great pleasure and satisfaction from cooking.

110. Poetry is a ________ form of expression in which the particularity of the word and the image to evoke feeling, assumes great importance.
    (a) Suppressed (b) patronized
    (c) compressed (d) digressed

Ans.(c) Poetry is a compressed form of expression in which the particularity of the word and the image to evoke feeling, assumes great importance.

111. He was so filled with contempt for the prisoner that he gave him a ________ look.
    (a) humiliated (b) derisive
    (c) pitying   (d) hurtful

Ans.(a) He was so filled with contempt for the prisoner that he gave him a **humiliated** look.

112. Next summer we're going ________ a trip to Canada.
    (a) to   (b) for
    (c) on   (d) over

Ans.(c) Next summer, we are going on a trip to Canada.

113. Romeo and Juliet's ________ affairs is probably the most loved of all times.
    (a) secret   (b) covert
    (c) candid   (d) clandestine

Ans.(b) Romeo and Juliet's **covert** affair is probably the most loved of all times.

114. The ________ towards the school was very steep.
    (a) ascend   (b) ascent
    (c) assent   (d) accent

Ans.(b) The **ascent** towards the school was very steep. [Ascend means go up or climb. Ascent means a climb or walk to the summit of a mountain or hill. Assent means the expression of approval or agreement. Accent means pronunciation.]

115. Some interesting matters ________ in our discussion yesterday.
    (a) came up   (b) got up
    (c) came in   (d) came about

Ans.(a) Some interesting matters came up in our discussion yesterday.

116. He loaded the ________ of cotton on the truck.
    (a) baskets   (b) bales
    (c) bunches   (d) bundles

Ans.(b) He loaded the bales of cotton on the truck. [Bales mean large quantity of something tied together tightly]

117. Anything is ________ which is not against the nature of things.
    (a) practicable (b) parable
    (c) probable   (d) possible

Ans.(d)	Anything is **possible** which is not against the nature of things. [Parable means a simple story used to illustrate a moral or spiritual lesson; Practicable means capable of being put into practice or of being done or accomplished. Probable means likely to happen.

Spotting Errors

DIRECTIONS (Qs. 118-119): *In the following questions, some part of the sentence may have errors. Find out which part of the sentence has an error and select the appropriate option. If a sentence is free from error, select 'No Error'.*

(SSC CGL 2017, Set-1)

118. The two men were (1)/quarrelling with one another (2)/ claiming the same watch as their own. (3)/ No Error (4).
    - (a) 1
    - (b) 2
    - (c) 3
    - (d) 4

Ans.(b)	For two – each other and for more than two - one another. Here in this sentence the subject is "The two men" reciprocal pronoun one another should be replaced by each other.

119. Everybody knows (1)/that Bhutan is the most peaceful (2)/of all other countries of the world. (3)/No Error (4).
    - (a) 1
    - (b) 2
    - (c) 3
    - (d) 4

Ans.(c)	Any other/all other should not be used with the superlative degree as they are the part of comparative degree. Structure : The + Superlative degree + singular noun Or, The + superlative degree + of all + plural noun. The correct uses should be of all countries in part (3).

DIRECTIONS (Qs. 120-121): *In the following questions, some part of the sentence may have errors. Find out which parts of the sentence has an error and select the appropriate option. If a sentence is free from error, select 'No Error'.*

(SSC CGL 2017, Set-2)

120. No sooner did I come out of my home to go to market (1)/when it started raining heavily (2)/which drenched me completely. (3)/No Error (4)
    - (a) 1
    - (b) 2
    - (c) 3
    - (d) 4

Ans.(b)	If the second event occurs immediately after the first, we can express that using the structure no sooner ...... than/hardly or scarcely .... when./ As soon as. Here in part (2) when should be replaced by than.

121. Unless you don't obey (1)/ your elders you (2)/ will not suceed in your life. (3)/ No error (4).
    - (a) 1
    - (b) 2
    - (c) 3
    - (d) 4

Ans.(a)	Do not use other negative word in the clause starting with conjunctions until and unless. The correct uses should be Unless you obey in part (1).

DIRECTIONS (Qs. 122-123): *In the following questions, some part of the sentence may have errors. Find out which part of the sentence has an error and select the appropriate option. If a sentence is free from error, select 'No error'.*

(SSC CGL 2017, Set-3)

122. If you had (1)/ told me earlier (2)/ I will help you. (3) / No Error (4)
    - (a) 1
    - (b) 2
    - (c) 3
    - (d) 4

Ans.(c)　Replace "will help you" by "would have helped you" in part (3)

123. Her mother is (1)/ angry and (2) / indifferent to me. (3)/No Error (d)
- (a)　1
- (b)　2
- (c)　3
- (d)　4

Ans.(b)　Every verb used in a sentence should be followed by separate prepositions. Word angry is followed by preposition with.

DIRECTIONS (Qs. 124-133): *In the following questions, some part of the sentence may have errors. Find out which part of the sentence has an error and select the appropriate option. If a sentence is free from error, select 'No Error'.*

(SSC Stenographer 2017)

124. Hema doesn't has (1)/ to give (2)/ the dissertation to me (3)/No Error (4)
- (a)　1
- (b)　2
- (c)　3
- (d)　4

Ans.(a)　Replace 'doesn't has' by 'doesn't have'.

125. My mother (1)/ is having (2)/ grey hairs (3)/ No Error (4)
- (a)　1
- (b)　2
- (c)　3
- (d)　4

Ans.(c)　Replace hairs by hair. [Hair, as a noun, is generally a non-countable noun, and therefore has no plural.]

126. Oh dear, (1)/ do have some relief (2)/ on my nerves (3)/ No Errors (4)
- (a)　1
- (b)　2
- (c)　3
- (d)　4

Ans.(b)　Replace 'do have some relief' by 'have some relief'.

127. Once you graduate (1)/ get a job (2)/ would be easier (3)/ No Errors (4)
- (a)　1
- (b)　2
- (c)　3
- (d)　4

Ans.(b)　Replace get by 'getting'.

128. He has been (1)/ working here (2)/ for quite some time (3)/ No Error (4)
- (a)　1
- (b)　2
- (c)　3
- (d)　4

Ans.(d)　No improvement.

129. I decided (1)/ to climbed to the (2)/ top of the hill (3)/ No Error (4)
- (a)　1
- (b)　2
- (c)　3
- (d)　4

Ans.(b)　Replace 'climbed' by 'climb'.

130. Reading (1)/ provides nutrition (2)/ with the mind (3)/ No Error (4)
- (a)　1
- (b)　2
- (c)　3
- (d)　4

Ans.(c)　Replace 'with' by 'to'.

131. Despite of minimal use of technology (1)/ they are able to manage (2)/ everything in a simple manner (3)/ No error (4)
- (a)　1
- (b)　2
- (c)　3
- (d)　4

Ans.(a)　Replace 'despite of' by 'despite'.

132. Sri Lanka is an island country (1)/ into the Indian Ocean (2)/, south of India. (3)/ No error (4)
- (a)　1
- (b)　2
- (c)　3
- (d)　4

Ans.(b)　Replace ' into' by 'in'.

133. I'm content with what I make (1)/ and I am found simple joys in seeing a smile on customer's face (2)/ when they smell the jasmine flowers. (3)/ No error (4)
- (a)　1
- (b)　2
- (c)　3
- (d)　4

Ans.(b)	Replace 'and I am found simple joys in seeing a smile on customer's face' by 'and I have found simple joys in seeing a smile on customer's face'.

DIRECTIONS (Qs. 134-143): *Some part of the sentences have errors and some are correct. Find out which part of a sentence has an error and blacken the circle corresponding to the appropriate correct option. If a sentence is free from error, blacken the circle corresponding to "No Error".*

(SSC MTS 2017)

134. Could you please maintain silence for a while?
    (a) please maintain silence
    (b) for a while?
    (c) Could you
    (d) No error

Ans. (b)	Could you please maintain silence for a while? is not a question, to which an answer is expected. A request disguised as a question does not require a question mark. Such formulations can usually be reduced to the imperative. Replace the question mark with full stop.

135. She hopes to become an engineer after she will complete her education.
    (a) an engineer after she
    (b) will complete her education.
    (c) She hopes to become
    (d) No error

Ans. (b)	Replace 'she will complete' by 'she has completed'.

136. Kindly please direct the tourists to the museum.
    (a) Kindlly please
    (b) direct the tourists
    (c) to the museum
    (d) No error

Ans. (a)	Both the adverbs are used in polite requests, and one of the meanings of kindly is please. Although, it is technically possible, one or the other is redundant, and no, they should not be used in proximity to each other. Remove either of the two from the sentence to make it correct grammatically.

137. If you stand with me in hour of need, I will never forget you.
    (a) No error
    (b) I will never forget you.
    (c) If you stand
    (d) with me in hour of need,

Ans. (d)	Replace ' with me in hour of need' by 'by me in hour of need'.

138. At last he married with a poor girl.
    (a) At last
    (b) he married
    (c) No error
    (d) with a poor girl.

Ans.(d)	The correct sentence should be- At last he married to a poor girl.

139. Our team played a football match.
    (a) played
    (b) Our team
    (c) a football match.
    (d) No error

Ans.(d)	No error.

140. It is better to stay at home than go to market when it is raining.
    (a) when it is raining
    (b) No error

(c) It is better to stay at home

(d) than go to market

Ans.(d) Replace ' than go to market' by ' than going to market'.

141. All the girls students are advised to attend the meeting positively.

(a) attend the meeting positively

(b) No error

(c) All the girls students

(d) are advised to

Ans.(c) Write 'girl students' instead of 'girls student'.

142. The thief had hardly put the cash in his pocket then the owner woke up.

(a) No error

(b) The thief had hardly

(c) then the owner woke up.

(d) put the cash in his pocket

Ans.(c) Replace 'then' by 'when'.

143. Bengal tigers are now almost extincted.

(a) Bengal tigers

(b) Are now

(c) Almost extincted

(d) No error

Ans.(c) Replace 'almost extincted' by 'almost extinct'. [Extincted is grammatically wrong word.]

DIRECTIONS (Qs. 144-145): *In the following question, some part of the sentence may have errors. Find out which part of the sentence has an error and select the appropriate option. If a sentence is free from error, select 'No Error'.*

144. Soon as he (A)/saw the policeman, (B)/he ran away, (C)/No error (D). **(SSC CHSL 2017)**

(a) A (b) B

(c) C (d) D

Ans.(a) There is incorrect use of idiom 'as soon as' in this part. The sentence should begin with "As soon as he ...".

145. You must not (A)/look down into (B)/ parents' advice. (C)/ No error(D) **(SSC CHSL 2017)**

(a) A (b) B

(c) C (d) D

Ans.(b) In part of 'B' of the sentence there is incorrect use of the phrase. The correct phrase should be 'look down on' which means to undervalue or disregard something.

Sentence Improvement

DIRECTIONS (Qs. 146-147): *Improve the bracketed part of the sentence.*

(SSC CGL 2017, Set-1)

146. She did not like to have coffee (nor I did).

(a) neither I liked it

(b) nor did I

(c) nor I like it

(d) No improvement

Ans.(b)

147. Taj Mahal is (a worth seeing monument) in Agra.

(a) a monument to see its worth

(b) a monument worth seeing

(c) one of worth seeing monuments

(d) No improvement

Ans.(b)

DIRECTIONS (Qs. 148-149): *Improve the bracketed part of the sentence.*

(SSC CGL 2017, Set-1)

148. I had (a few) eggs in the fridge, so we need to go to the market to buy them.

(a) a little

(b) few

(c) little

(d) No improvment

Ans.(b)

149. My brother is indifferent (about) whatever I say.
    (a) in
    (b) of
    (c) to
    (d) No improvement

Ans.(c)

DIRECTIONS (Qs. 150-151): *Improve the bracketed part of the sentences.*

(SSC CGL 2017)

150. By rescuing the child from fire, the local resident (added another feather to his cap.)
    (a) mode a significant achievement
    (b) was gifted with precious thing
    (c) was crowned and rewarded
    (d) No improvement

Ans.(a)

151. The government plans to (take up) the construction project soon.
    (a) Take on
    (b) Take off
    (c) Take in
    (d) No improvement

Ans.(d)

DIRECTIONS (Qs. 152-153): *Improve the bracketed part of the sentence.*

(SSC CGL 2017)

152. He has painted that picture so often that he can do it with his **(eyes closed).**
    (a) arms full
    (b) eyes opened
    (c) mind blank
    (d) No improvement

Ans.(a)

153. If you talk to her nicely, she will probably **(allow you)** her notes.
    (a) allow that you have
    (b) let you have
    (c) let you to have
    (d) No improvement

Ans.(b)

DIRECTIONS (Qs. 154-158): *Improve the bracketed part of the sentence.*

(SSC Sub. Insp. 2017)

154. Neha was too clever to (see through Rohan's tricks).
    (a) see at Rohan's tricks
    (b) see into Rohan's tricks.
    (c) see Rohan's tricks.
    (d) No improvement

Ans.(d) No improvement

155. He has been working **(off and on)** for several years on this theory.
    (a) regularly
    (b) on or off
    (c) on and off
    (d) No improvement

Ans.(c) Replace' off and on' by 'on and off'.

156. I am definitely late, the bus (will have left) the bus stop by the time I reach there.
    (a) would have left
    (b) will be leaving
    (c) will leave
    (d) No improvement

Ans.(a) Replace 'will have left' by 'would have left'.

157. (Having had) in the USA Ebassy for a long time, Mr. Gupta has met many prominent personalities.
    (a) He has been
    (b) Having been
    (c) Had he been
    (d) No improvement

Ans (b) Replace 'Having had' by 'Having been'.

158. The guest stood quietly for (few) moments.
    (a) a few moments
    (b) the few moments
    (c) few time
    (d) No improvement

Ans.(a) Replace' few' by 'a few'.

DIRECTIONS (Qs. 159-170): *In the following question, out of the four alternatives, select the alternative which will improve the bracketed part of the sentence. In case no improvement is needed, select "no improvement".*

(SSC Stenographer 2017)

159. **(The bundle of coins were the only source)** of information for them.
    (a) The bundles of coins were the only source
    (b) The bundles of coins were the only sources
    (c) The bundle of coin was the only source
    (d) No Improvement

Ans. (a)	The bundles of coins were the only source of information for them. [bundles should be plural]

160. No sooner **(do the phone ring)** that he was out of home.
    (a) did the phone rang
    (b) did the phone rings
    (c) did the phone ring
    (d) No improvement

Ans. (c)	No sooner did the phone ring that he was out of home.

161. Two more employees (will be hiring) by the company.
    (a) be hiring
    (b) will be hired
    (c) will hire
    (d) No Improvement

Ans. (b)	Two more employees will be hired by the company. [The sentence is in passive voice, thus be +ed will be used].

162. This **(modern furnitures will be sold)** in the main market.
    (a) modern furniture will be sold
    (b) modern furnitures will be selling
    (c) modern furniture will be selling
    (d) No Improvement

Ans. (a)	This modern furniture will be sold in the main market. [Furniture is always used in singular form.]

163. My boss (have being given) me a lot of work.
    (a) was being given
    (b) is being given
    (c) have been giving
    (d) No Improvement

Ans. (c)	My boss have being giving me a lot of work. [the sentence is in Present Perfect Progressive tense, and hence have been+ V+ing is used].

164. I (wander about) the stars up in the sky.
    (a) wander for
    (b) wonder about
    (c) wander in
    (d) No improvement

Ans. (b)	I wonder about the stars up in the sky.

165. Go to the right and (keep a sharp left turn) you will reach the place.
    (a) take a sharp left turn
    (b) do a sharp left turn
    (c) make a sharp left turn
    (d) No Improvement

Ans. (a)	Go to the right and take a sharp left turn, you will reach the place.

166. Heena (keep a eye) on his son.
    (a) kept a eye
    (b) keep an eye
    (c) keeps an eye
    (d) No Improvement

Ans. (c)	Heena keeps an eye on his son.

167. (why is) your working going on?
    (a) How is
    (b) What is
    (c) When is
    (d) No Improvement

Ans.(a) How is your working going on? [A 'why' question tries to find a reason & a 'how' question tries to find a description.]

168. **(Pack your bags)** and come with me.
    (a) keep your bag
    (b) Have your bag
    (c) unpack your bag
    (d) No Improvement

Ans.(d) No Improvement.

169. I perfer black coffee (over) cappuccino. **(SSC CHSL 2017)**
    (a) rather than
    (b) to
    (c) instead of
    (d) no improvement

Ans.(b) 'I prefer black coffee to cappuccino' is the correct usage of preposition 'to' here. So option (b) is the correct answer.

170. The priest agreed (to answer on) questions on theology.
    (a) to answer
    (b) for answering
    (c) to answer for
    (d) no improvement

Ans.(a) The bracketed part, 'to answer on', is incorrect usage. The correct usage is 'to answer'. So, option (a) is the right answer.

One Word Substitution

DIRECTIONS (Qs.171-172): *In the following questions, out of the four alternatives, select the alternative which is the best substitute of the phrase.*

(SSC CGL 2017, Set–1)

171. That which cannot be corrected
    (a) Impregnable
    (b) Immolation
    (c) Incorrigible
    (d) Ineligible

Ans.(c) An incorrigible person or incorrigible behaviour is bad and impossible to change or improve.

172. A person who is blamed for the wrong doings of others
    (a) Bursar   (b) Captor
    (c) Phlegmatic (d) Scapegoat

Ans.(d) A scapegoat is a person or animal which takes on the sins of others.

DIRECTIONS (Qs. 173-174): *In the following questions, out of the four alternatives, select the alternative which is the best substitute of the phrase.*

(SSC CGL 2017, Set–2)

173. A funeral poem
    (a) Elegy
    (b) Pandemonium
    (c) Parody
    (d) Sonnet

Ans.(a) 'Elegy' is typically a lament for the dead.

174. One who walks in sleep
    (a) Drover
    (b) Fastidious
    (c) Numismatist
    (d) Somnambulist

Ans. (d) 'Somnambulist' is a person who walks about in their sleep.

DIRECTIONS (Qs. 175-179): *In the following questions, out of the four alternatives, select the alternative which is the best substitute of the phrase.*

(SSC CGL 2017, Set–3)

175. A man devoid of kind feeling and sympathy.
  (a) Callous   (b) Credulous
  (c) Gullible   (d) Bohemian

Ans. (a) A callous person or action is very cruel and shows no concern for other people or their feelings.

176. One who eats two much
  (a) Impostor
  (b) Glutton
  (c) Hypochondriac
  (d) Intestate

Ans. (b) A glutton person eats and drinks excessively or voraciously.

DIRECTIONS (Qs. 177-179): *In the following questions, out of the four alternatives, select the alternative which is the best substitute of the phrase.*

(SSC CGL 2017, Set–4)

177. Easily duped or fooled
  (a) Bigot   (b) Gullible
  (c) Ridicule   (d) Venerable

Ans. (b) A gullible person can be easily persuaded to believe something.

178. Atonement for one's sins
  (a) Elite   (b) Ignoramus
  (c) Incendiary (d) Repentance

Ans. (d) 'Repentance' is the activity of reviewing one's action and feeling regret for past wrongs.

179. In the following questions, out of the four alternative, select the alternative which is the best substitute of the phrase.

A person famous and respected within a particular sphere.

(SSC CHSL 2017)

  (a) eminent   (b) obscure
  (c) despotic   (d) imperative

Ans. (a) A person famous and respected within a particular sphere is known as 'eminent'.

DIRECTIONS (Qs. 180-184): *Out of the four alternatives, choose the one which can most appropriately substitute the given word(s) or sentence.*

(SSC MTS 2017)

180. The centre of attraction.
  (a) cynosure   (b) focus
  (c) custodian   (d) point

Ans. (a) Cynosure means centre of attraction.

181. The murder of one's father.
  (a) Patricide   (b) homicide
  (c) fratricide   (d) regicide

Ans. (a) Patricide is the act of killing one's father. Homicide (act of one human killing another); Fratricide (the killing of one's brother or sister.); Regicide (the action of killing a king.).

182. Overturn in water.
  (a) drown   (b) swim
  (c) wreck   (d) capsize

Ans. (d) Capsize means be overturned in the water.

183. One whose wife is dead.
  (a) widower   (b) spinster
  (c) bachelor   (d) widow

| Ans.(a) | Widower is a man whose wife is dead. Spinster means an unmarried woman and especially one past the common age for marrying. Widow is a woman whose man is dead. Bachelor is an unmarried man/woman. |

184. That cannot be explained.

   (a) intolerable (b) inexplicit
   (c) irrevocable (d) inexplicable

| Ans.(d) | Inexplicable is what cannot be explained. Intolerable means unable to be endured. Inexplicit means not definitely or clearly expressed or explained. Irrevocable means not able to be changed, reversed, or recovered. |

DIRECTIONS (Qs. 185-189): *In the following question, out of the four alternatives, select the alternative which is the best substitute of the phrase.*

(SSC Sub. Insp. 2017)

185. Government by a few people

   (a) aristocracy (b) oligarchy
   (c) dictatorship (d) bureaucracy

| Ans.(b) | An oligarchy is a government ruled by a small group of powerful people. |

186. The state of living unmarried

   (a) celibacy (b) neogamist
   (c) chaperon (d) implorer

| Ans.(a) | Celibacy is the state of abstaining from marriage and sexual relations. Neogamist is a newlywed; implorer means to beg; chaperon is a person who accompanies and looks after another person or group of people. |

187. An event which happens once in five years.

   (a) septennial
   (b) quinquennial
   (c) interregnum
   (d) pun

| Ans.(b) | Quinquennial is an event occurring or being done every five years. [Septennial is recurring in seven years. Interregnum means the time during which a throne is vacant between two successive reigns or regimes. Pun is a joke exploiting the different possible meanings of a word or the fact that there are words which sound alike but have different meanings.] |

188. A person who looks after horses at an inn

   (a) matron (b) chandler
   (c) ostler (d) effeminate

| Ans.(c) | Ostler is a man employed to look after the horses of people staying at an inn. [Matron is a woman in charge of domestic and medical arrangements at a boarding school or other institution. Chandler is a dealer in supplies and equipment for ships and boats. Effeminate means unmanly.] |

189. To struggle helplessly

   (a) implorer (b) yokel
   (c) flounder (d) chum

| Ans.(c) | Flounder is to struggle with stumbling or plunging movements. [Implorer means to beg, yokel means an uneducated and unsophisticated person from the countryside. Chum means a close friend.] |

Spelling Test

DIRECTIONS (Qs. 190-204): *In the following questions, four words are given out of which one word is incorrectly spelt. Select the incorrectly spelt word.*

(SSC CGL 2017, Set-1)

190. (a) Conceive   (b) Leisure
     (c) Neice   (d) Reign

Ans.(c)

191. (a) Dictionory (b) Irrelevant
     (c) Perishable (d) Tangible

Ans.(a)

DIRECTIONS (Qs. 192-193): *In the following questions, four words are given out of which one word in incorrectly spelt. Select the incorrectly spelt words.*

(SSC CGL 2017, Set-2)

192. (a) Gaurantee (b) Itinerary
     (c) Magnificent (d) Writing

Ans.(a)

193. (a) Etiquete   (b) Exquisite
     (c) Restaurant (d) Scavenger

Ans.(a)

DIRECTIONS (Qs. 194-195): *In the following questions, four words are given out of which one word is incorrectly spelt. Find the incorrectly spelt word.*

(SSC CGL 2017, Set-3)

194. (a) Forfeit   (b) Gorilla
     (c) Blissfull   (d) Corrupt

Ans.(c)

195. (a) Afforestation
     (b) Translusent
     (c) Foreigner
     (d) Achievement

Ans.(b)

DIRECTIONS (Qs. 196-197): *In the following questions, four words are given out of which one word is incorrectly spelt. Select the incorrectly spelt word.*

(SSC CGL 2017, Set-4)

196. (a) Usable   (b) Defense
     (c) Inventor   (d) Annaul

Ans.(d)

197. (a) Changeable (b) Inedible
     (c) Tracable   (d) Valuable

Ans.(c)

198. Select the word with the correct spelling.   **(SSC CHSL 2017)**
     (a) brooches   (b) linoleam
     (c) limekilne   (d) cherubick

Ans.(a)

199. Select the word with the correct spelling.   **(SSC CHSL 2017)**
     (a) lammented (b) scabbard
     (c) ordenance (d) synaptick

Ans.(b) 'Scabbard' is the only correctly spelt word.
Correct spellings of other words are as follows:
Lammented → Lamented
Ordenance → Ordinance
Synaptick → Synaptic

DIRECTIONS (Qs. 200-204): *In the following question, four words are given out of which one word is incorrectly spelt. Select the incorrectly spelt word.*

(SSC Sub. Inspec. 2017)

200. (a) adherent   (b) aironaut
     (c) adversary (d) admissible

Ans.(b) Aironaut is incorrect spelling. The correct spelling is aeronaut.

201. (a) passenger (b) quarralled
     (c) remittance (d) attendence

Ans.(d) Attendence is the incorrectly spelt word. The correct spelling is attendance.

202. (a) beautisian   (b) bilingual
     (b) barbarian   (d) balloon

Ans.(a) Beautisian is the incorrectly spelt word. The correct spelling is beautician.

203. (a) embarrassment
     (b) exasperation
     (c) emanicipation
     (d) fermentation

Ans.(c) Emanicipation is the incorrectly spelt word. The correct spelling is emancipation.

204. (a) gorgeous   (b) granduer
     (c) gratuitous   (d) glutton

Ans.(b) Granduer is the incorrectly spelt word. The correct spelling is grandeur.

DIRECTIONS (Qs. 205-210): *Four words are given, out of which only one word is correctly spelt. Find the correctly spelt word.*

(SSC MTS 2017)

205. (a) hiar   (b) hier
     (c) heir   (d) heirr

Ans.(c) Heir is the correctly spelt word.

206. (a) milenium   (b) millennium
     (c) milennium   (d) millenium

Ans.(b) Millennium is the correctly spelt word.

207. (a) hygene   (b) higene
     (c) hygiene   (d) higiene

Ans.(c) Hygiene is the correctly spelt word.

208. (a) government
     (b) governnment
     (c) guvernment
     (d) goverrment

Ans.(a) Government is the correctly spelt word.

209. (a) skeem   (b) scheme
     (c) skeme   (d) sceme

Ans.(b) Scheme is the correctly spelt word.

210. (a) sillabus   (b) cyllabus
     (c) syllabus   (d) sylabus

Ans.(c) Syllabus is the correctly spelt word.

Parajumbles

DIRECTIONS (Qs. 211-212): *The questions below consist of a set of labelled sentences. Out of the four options given, select the most logical order of the sentences to form a coherent paragraph.*

(SSC CGL 2017, Set-1)

211. P - It had been umpteen years since we had seen each other.

Q - One dull dark in autumn, I was travelling on horseback through a dreary stretch of countryside.

R - This was the house of Roderick Usher, who had been my childhood pal.

S - At night fall, I came in sight of the house of Usher.

     (a) PQSR   (b) PSQR
     (c) QSRP   (d) QRSP

Ans.(c)

212. P-According to various estimates between 1942 and 1944 there were approximately 400 victims of this practice daily in Warsaw alone, with numbers on some days reaching several thousands.

Q - A common German practice in occupied Poland was to roundup random civilians on the streets of Polish cities.

R - For example, on 19th September 1942 close to 3000 men and women were transported by train to Germany - they had been caught in the massive round - ups all over Warsaw the previous two days.

S - The term, "lapanka" carried a sardonic connotation from the word's earlier use for the children's game known in English as "tag".

(a) SQRP   (b) SRPQ
(c) QSPR   (d) QPRS

Ans.(c)

DIRECTIONS (Qs. 213): *The questions below consist of a set of labelled sentences. These sentences, when properly sequenced form a coherent paragraph. Select the most logical order of sentences from among the options.*

(SSC CGL 2017, Set-2)

213. P – But he did not know how to find one at that hour.

Q – It was his first visit to the city and he didn't know where to go.

R – Mohanlal's train was late and it reached Kolkata a little after midnight.

S – He thought he would go to a choultry where he would not have to pay rent.

(a) PSQR   (b) QRSP
(c) RQSP   (d) RSQP

Ans.(c)

DIRECTIONS (Qs. 214-215): *The questions below consists of a set of labelled sentences. Out of the four options given, select the most logical order of the sentences to form a coherent paragraph.*

(SSC CGL 2017)

214. P – The aim must be to ensure that our country does not experience either paucity or a-surfeit of trained manpower in any specific segment of our economy.

Q – When we set about the task of higher education, we should be absolutely clear in our perception of the goals of education in the specific context of our nation's development.

R – No doubt, one of the important aims of education would be to create the required range and nature of trained manpower assessed to be needed by different sectors of national growth.

S – The entire educational apparatus must be geared progressively to fulfill the requirements of different phases of our growth in every sector primary, secondary and tertiary.

(a) SQPR   (b) QRSP
(c) SRQP   (d) PSQR

Ans.(b)

215. P – Bureaucratic cultures can smother those who want to respond to shifting conditions.

Q – Arrogant managers can overevaluate their current performance and competitive position listen poorly and learn slowly.

R – And the lack of leadership leaves no force inside these organizations to break out of the morass.

S – Inwardly focused employees can have difficulty seeing the very forces that present threats and opportunities.

(a) PRQS   (b) SPQR
(c) RQPS   (d) QSPR

Ans.(d)

Idioms/Pharases

DIRECTIONS (Qs. 216-217): *In the following questions, out of the four alternatives, select the alternative which best expresses the meaning of the idiom/phrase.*

(SSC CGL 2017)

216. To keep the wolf from door
   (a) Avoid starvation
   (b) Crack the deal
   (c) Entry Prohibited
   (d) Have a pleasant tour

Ans.(a) "To keep the wolf" from door means to word off starvation or financial ruin.

217. Teething problems
   (a) Oral problems
   (b) Problems at the start of a new project
   (c) Problems for quite a long time in adjusting in the new place
   (d) Problem of having good dentist.

Ans.(b) If a project or new product has teething problems, it has problems in its early stages or when it first becomes available.

DIRECTIONS (Qs. 218-219): *In the following questions, out of the four alternatives, select the alternatives, select the alternative which best expresses the meaning of the idiom/phrase.*

(SSC CGL 2017)

218. The alpha and the omega
   (a) Happy and sad
   (b) The beginning and the end
   (c) The love and the hatred
   (d) Truth and dare

Ans.(b) Alpha and omega are the first and last letters of the greek alphabet. It means from beginning to end.

219. Throw up the sponge
   (a) To attack
   (b) To laugh at someone
   (c) To surrender
   (d) To talk loudly

Ans.(c) Throw up the sponge means to admit defeat.

DIRECTIONS (Qs. 220-221): *In the following questions, out of the four alternatives, select the alternative which best expresses the meaning of the idiom/Phrase.*

(SSC CGL 2017)

220. Spick and Span
   (a) High and low
   (b) Dark and light
   (c) Neat and clean
   (d) Happy and sad

Ans.(c) Spick and span means spotlessly clean.

221. To draw the longbow
   (a) To nullify
   (b) To exaggerate
   (c) To underrate
   (d) To demarcate

Ans.(b) The idiom "to draw the long bow" means to exaggerate.

DIRECTIONS (Qs. 222-225): *In the following questions, out of the four alternatives, select the alternative which best expresses the meaning of the idiom/phrase.*

(SSC CGL 2017)

222. Ended in a fiasco
   (a) A complete failure
   (b) A successful event
   (c) Changed one completely
   (d) Twisted around

> **Ans.(a)** Ended in a fiasco means to end with a failure.

223. Sow wild oats
    - (a) To make someone fool
    - (b) To make space to red
    - (c) To take revenge
    - (d) To waste time by doing foolish things

> **Ans.(d)** Sow wild oats means to do wild and foolish things.

224. In the following question, out of the four alternatives, select the alternative which best expresses the meaning of the idiom/phrase:

    An outline representing or bounding the shape or form of something.

    (SSC CHSL 2017)

    - (a) tracery
    - (b) contour
    - (c) doodle
    - (d) pattern

> **Ans.(b)** An outline representing or bounding the shape or form of something is called 'contour'.

225. In the following question, out of the four alternatives, select the alternative which best expresses the meaning of the idiom/phrase.

    Head over heels

    (SSC CHSL 2017)

    - (a) to think with instead of heart
    - (b) to run away from an unpleasant situation
    - (c) to take a nasty fall
    - (d) to be madly in love

> **Ans.(d)** 'Head over heels' means to be madly in love.

DIRECTIONS (Qs. 226-229): *In the following questions, out of the four alternatives, select the alternative which best expresses the meaning of the idiom/phrase.*

(SSC Sub. Insp. 2017)

226. Get into a soup
    - (a) To make things difficult
    - (b) To be worrisome
    - (c) To be familiar of
    - (d) To get an advantage

> **Ans.(a)** 'Get into a soup' mean be in, or get yourself or somebody into, trouble or difficulties.

227. Haul over the coals
    - (a) Talk irrelevantly
    - (b) Laugh heartily
    - (c) To scold
    - (d) Without hope

> **Ans.(c)** 'Haul over the coals' means to scold, reprimand, or reprove someone severely for an error or mistake.

228. To carry the day
    - (a) To run away
    - (b) To die while in service
    - (c) To take an unimportant task
    - (d) To succeed

> **Ans.(d)** 'To carry the day' mean to be victorious or successful.

229. Go over
    - (a) Continue
    - (b) Review
    - (c) Harmonize
    - (d) Terminate

> **Ans.(b)** 'Go over' means to examine or look at something in a careful or detailed way.

DIRECTIONS (Qs. 230-232): *In the following questions, out of the four given alternatives, select the alternative which best expresses the meaning of the Idiom/Phrase.*

230. Apple of ons's eye
    - (a) the person with sweet tastes
    - (b) the person with wide pupils
    - (c) the person who likes apple
    - (d) the person who someone loves or cherishes the most

Ans. (d) Apple of one's eye means something or someone that one cherishes above all others.

231. Ball is in your court

(a) Make the right decision

(b) The judgement in is your favour

(c) You should catch the ball

(d) It is upto you to decide something

Ans. (d) Ball is in your court means -One needs to take some action to keep something going.

232. Back to Square One

(a) to go back to the beginning

(b) going forward

(c) yor are holding a grudge

(d) to go back to a square

Ans. (a) Back to square one means back to where one started, with no progress having been made.

DIRECTIONS (Qs. 233-235): *In the following questions, four alternatives are given for the Idiom/Phrase underlined in the sentence. Choose the alternative which best expresses the meaning of the Idiom/Phrase.*

(SSC MTS 2017)

233. John was **as good as his word** and came on time for the meeting.

(a) convincing

(b) punctual

(c) able to fulfill his promise

(d) a promising young man

Ans. (c) 'As good as word' means obedient to one's promise; dependable in keeping one's promises.

234. He came to work looking very **off colour.**

(a) tired   (b) unhappy

(c) worried   (d) ill

Ans. (d) 'Off colour' means slightly unwell.

235. I was asked to **take a hike** for a comment I made.

(a) be quiet   (b) think

(c) leave   (d) take a break

Ans. (c) 'Take a hike' means leave or go away (used as an expression of irritation or annoyance).

Speeches/Voices

236. In the following question, a sentence has been given in Active/ Passive voice. Out of the four alternatives suggested, select the one which best expresses the same sentence in Passive/Active voice.

(SSC CGL 2017, Set-1)

An elephant may be helped even by a ant.

(a) An ant can even help a elephant.

(b) An ant may even help a elephant.

(c) Even an ant may help an elephant.

(c) Even an ant ought to help an elephant.

Ans. (c) Change passive voice into active voice.

237. In the following question, a sentence has been given in Direct/ Indirect speech. Out of the four alternatives suggested, select the one which best expresses the same sentence in Direct/Indirect Speech.

(SSC CGL 2017, Set-1)

"Please don't cry" he said.

(a) He begged that I should not cry.

(b) He begged me not to cry.

(c) He said to please him and not cry.

(d) He told me to not to cry

Ans. (b)	Change 'said' into 'begged' use conjunction 'that' change reported speech into statement speech.

238. In the following question, a sentence has been given in Active/Passive voice. Out of the four alternatives suggested, select the one which best expresses the same sentence in Passive/Active voice.

(SSC CGL 2017, Set-2)

Ram was singing a beautiful song for his mother.

(a) A beautiful song was being sung by Ram for his mother.

(b) A beautiful song was sang Ram for his mother.

(c) A beautiful song was sung by Ram for his mother.

(d) A beautiful song was sung for his mother by Ram.

Ans. (a)	'A beautiful song' is used as subject in passive voice

239. In the following question, a sentence has been given in Direct/Indirect speech. Out of the four alternatives suggested, select the one which best expresses the same sentence in Indirect/Direct Speech.

(SSC CGL 2017, Set-2)

Priya advised me not to go the school the next day.

(a) "Don't go to school next day" Priya said to me.

(b) "Don't go to school tomorrow" Priya said to me.

(c) Priya said, "Will you not go to school tomorrow?"

(d) Priya told me that, "Don't go to school tomorrow."

Ans. (b)	The given sentence is in reported speech, change it into direct speech.

240. In the following question, a sentence has been given in Active/Passive voice. Out of four alternatives suggested, select the one which best expresses the same sentence in Passive/Active voice.

(SSC CGL 2017, Set-3)

She teaches us English.

(a) English is being taught to us by her.

(b) We are taught English by her.

(c) English have been taught to us by her.

(d) We had been taught English by her.

Ans. (b)	Use subjective case 'we' in passive sentence. Use 'her' in the objective case.

241. In the following question, a sentence has been given in Direct/Indirect speech. Out of the four alternatives suggested, select the one which best expresses the same sentence in Indirect/Direct speech.

(SSC CGL 2017, Set-3)

Nisha said to Swati, " Will you help me in my project just now"?

(a) Nisha told Swati whether she will help her in her project just now.

(b) Nisha asked Swati if she would help her in her project just then.

(c) Nisha questioned to Swati that will you help me in my project just now.

(d) Nisha asked to Swati that will she help her in her work just now.

Ans.(b) Change 'said to' into 'asked;' use 'whether', write reported speech in statement form, change 'now' into then, change pronoun 'me' into 'her'

242. In the following question, a sentence has been given in Active/Passive voice. Out of the four alternatives suggested, select the one which best expresses the same sentence in passive/Active voice.

(SSC CGL 2017, Set-4)

He saw him conducting the seminar on personality development.

(a) He was seen by me the conduct the seminar on personality development.

(b) He was seen conducting the seminar on personality development.

(c) He saw the seminar on personality development being conducted by him.

(d) He saw the seminar on personality development to be conducted by him.

Ans.(c) Make 'conducting' as 'being conducted in passive voice.

243. In the following question, a sentence has been given in Direct/Indirect speech. Out of the four alternatives suggested, select the one, which best express the same sentence in Indirect/Direct speech. Gokul said to Sumit, "Why did not you attend the meeting yesterday?"

(SSC CHSL 2017)

(a) Gokul asked Sumit why he did not attend the meeting the day before.

(b) Gokul asked Sumit why he had not attended that meeting yesterday.

(c) Gokul asked Sumit why he had not attended the meeting the day before.

(d) Gokul asked Sumit why he did not attend that meeting yesterday.

Ans.(c) Since, the given sentence is in past tense, it will be changed to past perfect tense in indirect speech; Gokul asked Sumit why he had not attended the meeting the day before.

DIRECTIONS (Qs. 244-250): *A sentence has been given in Active/Passive voice. Out of the four given alternatives, select the one which best expresses the same sentence in passive/Active Voice.*

(SSC Steno 2017)

244. We saw you and him.

(a) You and he were seen by us.

(b) He and you were seen by us.

(c) You were seen by us with him.

(d) Both of you were seen by us.

Ans.(a) You and he were seen by us.

245. Tom painted the entire house.

(a) The entire house was painted by Tom.

(b) The entire house is painted by Tom.

(c) The entire house were painted by Tom.

(d) The house is painted by Tom.

Ans.(a) The entire house was painted by Tom.

246. The science class viewed the comet.

(a) The class viewed the comet.

(b) The comet was viewed by the science class.

(c) The comet is been viewed by the science class.

(d) The comet is viewed by the science class.

Ans.(b) The comet was viewed by the science class.

247. The kangaroo carried her baby in her pouch.
    (a) The baby was carried by the kangaro in her pouch.
    (b) The kangaroo carried the baby in pouch
    (c) The baby is carried by kangaroo in her pouch.
    (d) The baby is being carried up by kangaroo in her pouch.

Ans.(a) The baby was carried by the kangaroo in her pouch.

248. Grandma is knitting the sweater.
    (a) The sweater is being knit by grandma.
    (b) The sweater was being knit by grandma.
    (c) Grandma knit the sweater.
    (d) Grandma knitted the sweater.

Ans.(a) The sweater is being knit by grandma.

249. Who teaches you English?
    (a) Do you know who teaches you English?
    (b) English is taught by who?
    (c) By whom are you taught English?
    (d) Who taught you English?

Ans.(c) By whom are you taught English?

250. Mohita was weaving the basket.
    (a) The basket was woven by Mohita
    (b) The basket is woven by Mohita
    (c) The basket is being woven by Mohita
    (d) The basket was being woven by Mohita

Ans.(d) The basket was being woven by Mohita.

DIRECTIONS (Qs. 251-255): *A sentence has been given in Direct/ Indirect Speech. Out of the four given alternatives, select the one which best expresses the same sentence in Indirect/ Direct Speech.*

(SSC Steno 2017)

251. "What time does the train arrive?" she asked.
    (a) She enquired at what time the train arrived
    (b) She asked about train
    (c) When will the train arrive she asked
    (d) She said when does the train arrive

Ans.(a) The given statement is in direct speech. Its indirect form is - She enquired at what time the train arrived.

252. He said,"I must work hard."
    (a) He told him to work hard
    (b) He was going to work hard.
    (c) He said that he had to work hard.
    (d) He said I must be working hard.

Ans.(c) The given statement is in direct speech. Its indirect form is - He said that he had to work hard.

253. He said,"My sister is writing letter to my uncle."
    (a) He said that his sister was writing letter to his uncle.
    (b) He said that her sister is writing a letter to uncle.
    (c) He told that his sister is writing letter to his uncle.
    (d) He said to me that his sister is writing a letter

Ans.(a) The given statement is in direct speech. Its indirect form is - He said that his sister was writing letter to his uncle.

254. He said to me,"I have told you not to touch any electrical switches with wet hand."

   (a)   He reprimanded me that he had told me not to touch any electrical switches with wet hand.

   (b)   He asked me not to touch any electrical switches with wet hand.

   (c)   He told me not to touch any electrical switches with wet hand.

   (d)   He reminded me that he had told me not to touch any electrical switches with wet hand.

Ans.(d) The given statement is in direct speech. Its indirect form is - He reminded me that he had told me not to touch any electrical switches with wet hand.

255. He said,"Let us wait for him at the restaurant."

   (a)   He ordered that they should wait for him at the restaurant.

   (b)   He said that they should wait for him at the restaurant

   (c)   He proposed that they should wait for him at the restaurant.

   (d)   They should wait for him at the restaurant he ordered.

Ans.(c) The given statement is in direct speech. Its indirect form is - He proposed that they should wait for him at the restaurant.

Reading Comprehension

DIRECTIONS (Qs. 256-260): *Read the following passage and answer the questions that follow :*

A passage is given with five questions following it. Read the passage carefully and select the best answer to each question out of the given four alternatives.

Antarctica is a mostly unpopulated continent. It is the coldest, driest and most remote place in the world. And it is the world's only continent that does not have a native population. No single country owns the Antarctic. However a number of countries, including Argentina, Australia, Chile, New Zealand, France and the United Kingdom, have already laid claim to the Antartic and others will probably follow. In some areas of the continent, two countries claim the same land.

The Antarctic Treaty was signed in 1959 and creates the rules for the exploration of the Antarctic. The treaty forbids military activity in the Antarctic, as well as mining. Many countries, however, think that there are valuable materials and minerals locked up under the frozen Antarctic. ice. In addition, the treaty bans nuclear testing as well as dumping nuclear waste. The Antarctic. Treaty was made to protect the continent and avoid further disputes. By 2048, the treaty must be renewed. New rules and regulations could be imposed by then.

Currently, almost all of the 70 bases in the Antarctic are used for research and scientific activity. The snow–covered continent is perfect for tracking satellites and space research because it offers clear blue, cloudless skies. Climatologists are studying the development of the ozone layer with growing concern. It was here that a hole in the layer was discovered for the first time. More than 4000 scientists operate the research stations in the Antarctic summer, while only about a thousand populate the continent during the harsh and severe winters.

Environmentalists fear that exploiting Antarctica for military and economic reasons will damage the environment. At present, there is no economic activity in Antarctica, except for cruise ships that travel around the continent. This could change, if a new treaty allows mining in the Antarctic. As mineral resources are dwindling in other areas, nations could turn to Antarctica to find and exploit valuable raw materials.

Some geologists say that there are over 200 billion barrels of oil under the Antarctic ice. At the moment getting at these reserves would be very expensive. In addition, economic experts claim that there are large amounts of coal, nickel and copper under the Antarctic ice.

(SSC Sub. Ins. 2017)

256. Which country's name is not being mentioned in the passage?
    (a) Argentina
    (b) Chile
    (c) New Zealand
    (d) Austria

> **Ans.(d)** Austria is not mentioned in the passage.

257. When was the Antarctic Treaty signed?
    (a) 1959   (b) 1958
    (c) 1960   (d) 1969

> **Ans.(a)** The Antarctic Treaty was signed in 1959 for creating the rules for exploration of Antarctica.

258. Why was Antarctic Treaty signed?
    (a) to protect the continent
    (b) to ban dumping of nuclear waste
    (c) to create rules for its exploration
    (d) All of these.

> **Ans.(d)** the Antarctic Treaty bans nuclear testing and dumping of nuclear waste and creates rules for exploration of Antarctica. Its main aim is to protect the continent.

259. Why did environmentalists have fear of exploting Antarctica for military and economic reasons.
    (a) unfavourable weather conditions
    (b) high involvement of cost
    (c) damage to environment
    (d) None of these

> **Ans.(c)** Environmentalists fear that exploiting Antarctica for military and economic reasons will damage the environment.

260. According to the passage, the reserves of which mineral is not found under the Antarctic ice?
    (a) coal   (b) iron
    (c) nickel   (d) copper

> **Ans.(b)** Economic experts claim that there are large amounts of coal, nickel and copper under the Antarctic ice.

DIRECTIONS (261-265): *Read the given passage carefully and select the best answer to each question out of the four given alternatives.*

For most people, music is an important part of daily life. Some rely on music to get them through the morning commute, while others turn up a favorite playlist to stay pumped during a workout. Many folks even have the stereo on when they'fre cooking a meal, taking a shower, or folding the laundry. Music is often linked to mood. A certain song can make us feel happy, sad, energetic, or relaxed. Because music can have such an impact on a person's mindset and well-being, it should come as no surprise that music therapy has been studied for use in managing numerous medical conditions. All forms of music may have therapeutic effects, although music from ons's own culture may be most effective. In Chinese medical theory, the five internal organs and meridian systems are believed to have corresponding musical tones, which are used to encourage healing.

(SSC Stenographer 2017)

261. Music is often linked to_______
_______.
   (a) anger   (b) mood
   (c) anxiety   (d) happiness

Ans.(b) Music is often linked to mood. A certain song can make us feel happy, sad, energetic, or relaxed.

262. How is music an important part of life?
   (a) It makes us feel different emotions
   (b) It makes us sad
   (c) It helps in our daily activities
   (d) It helps us in remembering things

Ans.(a) Music helps one feel different emotions. Based on the mood, a certain song can make us feel happy, sad, energetic, or relaxed.

263. Which of the statements is true?
   (a) All forms of music may heal wounds
   (b) All forms of music may have good effect
   (c) All forms of music may be sooting
   (d) All forms of music may have therapeutic effects

Ans.(d) All forms of music may have therapeutic effects, although music from one's own culture may be most effective.

264. How can music be used as a therapy?
   (a) It can help us to manage our day to day activities
   (b) It can help us in managing numerous medical conditions
   (c) It can help us manage our life
   (d) It can help us manage our careers

Ans.(b) Because music can have such an impact on a person's mindset and well-being, it should come as no surprise that music therapy has been studied for use in managing numerous medical conditions.

265. In Chinese medical theory, the five internal organs and meridian systems_________.
   (a) are believed to have musical chords
   (b) are believed to have no musical tones
   (c) are believed to have same musical tones
   (d) are believed to have corresponding musical tones

Ans.(d) In Chinese medical theory, the five internal organs and meridian systems are believed to have corresponding musical tones, which are used to encourage healing.

DIRECTIONS (266-270): *Read the given passage carefully and select the best answer to each question out of the four given alternatives.*

Approximately half of India's 1.2 billion people are under the age of 26, and by

2020 we are forecasted to be the youngest country in the world, with a median age of 29 years. With this tremendous forecast, it becomes imperative to ensure an environment which promotes positive well-being. Unfortunately, India has the highest suicide rate in the world among the youth standing at 35.5 per 100,000 people for 2012. The reason for such high numbers can be attributed to lack of economic, social, and emotional resourses. More specifically, academic pressure, workplace stress, social pressures, modernisation of urban centers, relationship concerns, and the breakdown of support systems. Some researchers have attributed the rise of youth suicide to urbanisation and the breakdown of the traditional large family support system. The clash of values within families is an important factor. As young Indians become more progressive, their traditionalist households become less supportive of their choices pertaining to financial independence, marriage age, premarital sex, rehabilitation and taking care of the elderly.

(SSC Stenographer 2017)

266. Approximately half of India's 1.2 billion people are under the age of__________.
    (a) 30   (b) 26
    (c) 22   (d) 18

Ans.(b)   Approximately half of India's 1.2 billion people are under the age of 26.

267. What are the reasons for high number of suicide rates among the youth in India.?
    (a) lack of monetary help by the government
    (b) lack of healthy foods
    (c) lack of economical, social and emotional resources
    (d) lack of good roads and transports

Ans.(c)   The reason for such high numbers can be attributed to lack of economic, social, and emotional resources.

268. By which year India will become the youngest country in the world?
    (a) 2017   (b) 2030
    (c) 2019   (d) 2020

Ans.(d)   By 2020, India is forecasted to be the youngest country in the world, with a median age of 29 years.

269. The__________within families is an important factor.
    (a) clash of values
    (b) clash of resources
    (c) clash of power
    (d) clash of thinking

Ans.(a)   The clash of values within families is an important factor. As young Indians become more progressive, their traditionalist households become less supportive of their choices pertaining to financial independence, marriage age, premarital sex, rehabilitation and taking care of the elderly.

270. How can we prevent youth from committing suicide?
    (a) by making families progressive
    (b) by creating an environment that which promotes good behaviour
    (c) by creating an environment that which promotes positive well being
    (d) by creating career opportunities

Ans.(c)   Youth can be prevented from committing suicide by creating an environment that which promotes positive well being.

CHAPTER 10

General Awareness Trending Questions from Past Paper

History

1. Who was the son of Chandragupta Maurya? **(SSC CGL 2017)**
   - (a) Bindusara
   - (b) Chandragupta II
   - (c) Ashoka
   - (d) Binbsara

   Ans.(a) Bindusara was the son of Chandragupta and the father of Ashoka, Susima, Vitashoka.

2. Which dynasty came to power in India after the Tughlaq dynasty? **(SSC CGL 2017)**
   - (a) The Guptas
   - (b) The Khiljis
   - (c) The Mughals
   - (d) The Sayyids

   Ans.(d) The Sayyids(1414-1451) came to power after the Tughlaq dynasty(1321-1414).

3. Who has built the Vijay Stambha (Tower of Victory) in Chittorgarh? **(SSC CGL 2017)**
   - (a) Maharana Pratap
   - (b) Rana Kumbha
   - (c) Rana Sanga
   - (d) Kunwar Durjan Singh

   Ans.(b) The tower was constructed by the Mewar king, Rana Kumbha, in 1448 to commemorate his victory over the combined armies of Malwa and Gujarat led by Mahmud Khilji.

4. Who raised the slogan "Swaraj is my birthright and I shall have it"? **(SSC CGL 2017)**
   - (a) Mahatma gandhi
   - (b) Subhash Chandra Bose
   - (c) Bal Gangadhar Tilak
   - (d) Lal Lajpat Rai

   Ans. (c) The slogan 'Swaraj is my birthright and I shall have it' was given by Lokmanya Bal Gangadhar Tilak.

5. Which one is the correct chronological order of the following events? **(SSC CGL 2017)**
   - (I) Quit India Movement
   - (II) Shimla Conference
   - (III) Poona Pact
   - (IV) Cabinet Mission
   - (a) II, IV, I, III
   - (b) III, IV, II, I
   - (c) III, I, II, IV
   - (d) IV, II, III, I

   Ans. (c)

Events	Date
Poona Pact	24,September 1932
Quit India Movement	08, August 1942
Shimla conference	June, 1945
Cabinet Mission	23, March 1946

6. In 1917, which movement was launched by Mahatma Gandhi from Champaran? **(SSC CGL 2017)**
   - (a) Satyagraha
   - (b) Non co-operation movement
   - (c) Quit India movement
   - (d) Swadeshi movement

Ans. (a) The Champaran Satyagraha of 1917 was Mahatma Gandhi's first Satyagraha.

7. Who amongst the following was the successor of Sikh Guru Har Krishna? **(SSC CGL 2017)**
   - (a) Guru Angad Dev
   - (b) Guru Tegh Bahadur
   - (c) Guru Hargobind
   - (d) Guru Amar Das

Ans.(b) The sequence of Sikh gurus are Guru Nanak, Guru Angad, Guru Amar Das, Guru Ram Das, Guru Arjan, Guru Hargobind, Guru Har Rai, Guru Har Krishan, Guru Tegh Bahadur, Guru Gobind Singh.

8. Lord Cornwallis is known for __. **(SSC CGL 2017)**
   - (a) permanent revenue settlement of Bengal
   - (b) attacking the caste system
   - (c) land revenue settlement of United States
   - (d) ryotwari settlement of Madras

Ans.(a) The Permanent Settlement (also Permanent Settlement of Bengal) was introduced by Lord Cornwallis in 1793.

9. Which of the following sultans adopted Persian customs and manners in court.**(SSC MTS 2017)**
   - (a) Iltutmish
   - (b) Jalaluddin Khilji
   - (c) Balban
   - (d) Alauddin Khilji

Ans.(c) Ghiyas Ud din Balban was the ninth Sultan of Mamluk dynasty of Delhi and He adopted Persian custom and manners in court.

10. Who convened the 'Congress of Vienna', 1815? **(SSC MTS 2017)**
    - (a) Bismarck
    - (b) Mussolini
    - (c) Metternich
    - (d) Napoleon Bonaparte

Ans.(c) Klemens Von Metternick Connened the 'Congress of Vienna' 1815.

11. Buland Darwaza is located in which fort? **(SSC MTS 2017)**
    - (a) Red Fort at Agra
    - (b) Red Fort at Delhi
    - (c) Fateh Pur Sikri
    - (d) Hawa Mahal

Ans.(c) Buland Darwaza or the "Gate of Magnificence", was built in 1601 A. D. by Akbar to commemorate his victory over Gujarat. It is the main entrance to the place at Fatehpur Sikri.

12. Stories of Buddha's birth and his previous lives are contained in : **(SSC MTS 2017)**
    - (a) Tripitakas
    - (b) Jataka tales
    - (c) Panchatantra tales
    - (d) Triratnas

Ans.(b) The Jataka tales are a volumnous body of literature native to India concerning the previous births of Gautam Buddha, in both Human and Animal form.

13. Which of the following is considered as a port town of Indus Valley Civilization?

(SSC Stenographer 2017)

(a) Harappa   (b) Lothal
(c) Ropar   (d) Banawali

Ans.(b)   Lothal is a port town of Indus Valley Civilization where trade once flowes hed with other ancient civilizations.

14. Krishnadevaraya was the ruler of which dynasty?

(SSC Stenographer 2017)

(a) Chola   (b) Bahmani
(c) Pallava   (d) Vijayanagara

Ans.(d)   Krishnadevaraya was the ruler of Vijayanagra dynasty. Who reigned from 1509–1529.

15. The details of coronation ceremony are narrated in which of the following scripture?

(SSC Stenographer 2017)

(a) Kenopanishad
(b) Vishnu Puran
(c) Aitareya Brahmana
(d) Atharv Veda

Ans.(c)   Aitareya Brahmana of the Rig veda has the details of the coronation ceremony]

16. Which among the following is correctly matched?

(SSC Stenographer 2017)

(i)   Shamse Siraj Asif - Tarikh-e-Firozshahi
(ii) Ziyauddin Barni - Tarikh-e-Muhammadi
(iii) Amir Khusarau -Tabakat-e-Nasiri
(iv) Ibn Batuta-Fatawa-e-jahandari

(a) (i)   (b) (ii)
(c) (iii)   (d) (iv)

Ans.(a)   Shamse Siraj Atif–Tarikn-e-Firozshahi.

17. Which planet is considered as the Dwarf planet?   **(SSC CGL 2017)**

(a) Earth   (b) Jupiter
(c) Pluto   (d) Saturn

Ans.(c)   The International Astronomical Union recognized Pluto's special place in our solar system by designating dwarf planet.

18. Sandstone is which type of rock?

(SSC CGL 2017)

(a) Calcareous Rock
(b) Igneous Rock
(c) Metamorphic Rock
(d) Sedimentary Rock

Ans.(d)   Sand stone is a type of Sedimentary rocks. Sedimentary rocks are made when other rocks are broken into fragments and those fragments are cemented together to form a new rock.

19. Which Indian state is the largest in terms of the total area covered?

(SSC CGL 2017)

(a) Maharashta
(b) Madhya Pradesh
(c) Rajasthan
(d) Tamil Nadu

Ans.(c)   Rajasthan is the largest state of India in terms of area (342239 km^2).

20. Which Indian state has the longest Coastline?   **(SSC CGL 2017)**

(a) Kerala
(b) Gujarat
(c) Andhra Pradesh
(d) Tamil Nadu

> **Ans.(b)** Gujarat has the longest coast-line (1214.7 km) among the states of Indian.

21. What is the name of the tropical cyclones in the China Sea?
(SSC CGL 2017)
    (a) Hurricanes   (b) Tornado
    (c) Twister   (d) Typhoon

> **Ans.(d)** In the northwestern Pacific, powerful Cyclonic storms are called typhoons.

22. Which among the following country is not a part of Scandinavia?
(SSC CGL 2017)
    (a) Norway   (b) Finland
    (c) Sweden   (d) Denmark

> **Ans.(b)** The term Scandinavia always includes the three kingdoms of Denmark, Norway, and Sweden. Therefore Finland is not a part of it.

23. 49th Parallel is the boundary line between which two countries?
(SSC CGL 2017)
    (a) USA and Canada
    (b) North and South Vietnam
    (c) Germany and France
    (d) Brazil and Chile

> **Ans.(a)** 49th Parallel. It is the boundary line between the United States of America and Canada

24. How does La – Nina affect the Pacific Ocean? **(SSC CGL 2017)**
    (a) Decreases salinity of ocean
    (b) Cools downs the temperature of water
    (c) Maintains stable temperature of water
    (d) Increases salinity of ocean

> **Ans.(b)** La Niña is a phenomenon that describes cooler than normal ocean surface temperatures in the Eastern and Central Pacific Ocean; regions close to the equator off the west coast of South America.

25. The longest day of the year in the Northern Hemisphere occur on __________.**(SSC CHSL 2017)**
    (a) 20th May   (b) 21st June
    (c) 20th July   (d) 21st August
Ans.(b)

26. Match the following.

Mountain		**Continent**
1.	Mount Etna	a. Asia
2.	Mount K2	b. Africa
3.	Mount Kilimanjaro	c. Europe

(SSC Sub inspector 2017)
    (a) 1 - a, 2 - b, 3 - c
    (b) 1 - b, 2 - a, 3 - c
    (c) 1 - c, 2 - a, 3 - b
    (d) 1 - a, 2 - c, 3 - b

> **Ans (c)**
>
> | **Mountain** | **Continent** |
> |---|---|
> | (1) Mount Etna | Europe |
> | (2) Mount K2 | Asia |
> | (3) Mount Kilimanjaro | Africa |

27. Suez Canel connects which of the following water bodies?
(SSC Sub inspector 2017)
    (a) Mediterranean Sea and Black sea
    (b) Mediterranean Sea and Red sea
    (c) pacific Ocean and Atlantic Ocean
    (d) Mediterranean Sea and Arctic Ocean

Ans.(b) The Suez canal is an artificial sea–level waterway in Egypt, connecting the Mediterranean sea to the Red Sea through the Isthmus of Suez.

28. Which of the following Indian state does not share International land border?**(SSC Sub Inspector 2017)**
    (a) Jammu and Kashmir
    (b) Uttar Pradesh
    (c) Bihar
    (d) Madhya Pradesh

Ans.(d) Madhya Pradesh is one of the Indian states which does not share International land border.

29. The highest plateau of India is the:
    (SSC MTS 2017)
    (a) Chota Nagpur
    (b) Malwa
    (c) Ladakh
    (d) Deccan

Ans.(c) Ladakh Plateau is the highest plateau in India with much of it being over 3000 m (9800 ft.). It extends from the Himalayan to the Kunlun Ranges and includes the upper Indus River Valley.

30. Through which states does the river Chambal flow? **(SSC MTS 2017)**
    (a) MP, Gujrat, UP
    (b) UP, MP, Rajasthan
    (c) Gujrat, MP, UP, Bihar
    (d) Rajasthan, MP, Bihar

Ans.(b) The chambal flows within the Semi-arid Zone of north-western India at the border of Madhya Pradesh, Rajasthan and Uttar Pradesh States.

31. Which one of the following is a land locked country? **(SSC MTS 2017)**
    (a) Russia   (b) Austria
    (c) India   (d) China

Ans.(b) Austria is a land locked country in Europe.

32. An area reserved for the protection of the wildlife is called:
    (SSC MTS 2017)
    (a) Sanctuary
    (b) National Park
    (c) Zoological Park
    (d) Reserved Forest

Ans.(a) Sanctuary is an area which is reserved for the protection of the wildlife.

33. Which among the following is the oldest mountain series in India?
    (SSC Stenographer 2017)
    (a) Satpura   (b) Nilgiri
    (c) Himalaya   (d) Aravali

Ans.(d) Aravali is the oldest mountain series in India and is the source area of many rivers.

34. Indravati, Pranhita and Sabari are important tributaries of which of these rivers?
    (SSC Stenographer 2017)
    (a) Ganga   (b) Godavari
    (c) Cauvery   (d) Krishna

Ans.(b) Godavari is India's second longest river after Ganga, its important tributaries are Indravati, Pranhita and Sabari.

35. Which type of forest is appropriate for Sandalwood trees
    (SSC Stenographer 2017)
    (a) Evergreen
    (b) Tundra
    (c) Desert
    (d) Tropical Deciduous

Ans.(d) Tropical Deciduous forest is appropriate for sandalwood trees as it lose its leaves seasonally

36. Which one of the following bio-reserves of India is not included in the world of bioreserve?
    (SSC Stenographer 2017)
    (a) Manas
    (b) Nanda Devi
    (c) Gulf of Mannar
    (d) Nilgiri

Ans.(a) Manas Bio–Reserve located in Assam is not included in the world network of bioreseve.

Polity

37. What is the minimum age required to become vice – president of India?
    (SSC CGL 2017)
    (a) 30 years   (b) 35 years
    (c) 40 years   (d) 37 years

Ans.(b) As per article 66, the candidate contesting for election of Vice-President of India, He must have completed age of 35 years.

38. Which of the following "writ" of the High Court or the Supreme Court is issued to restrain a person from holding a public office which he is not entitled to? **(SSC CGL 2017)**
    (a) Centiorari
    (b) Mandamus
    (c) Prohibition
    (d) Quo Warranto

Ans.(d) Quo Warranto is a writ issued with a view to restrain a person from holding a public office to which he is not entitled.

39. NITI Aayog has been formed to replace which of the following institution? **(SSC CGL 2017)**
    (a) Planning Commission
    (b) IRDA
    (c) Department of Telecommuni-cations (DoT)
    (d) Department of Information Technology

Ans.(a) National Institution for Transforming India (NITI) Aayog was established by the NDA government to replace the Planning Commission in January 2015.

40. Whose recommendation is man-datory to impeach the President of India from his office before the completion of his/her term?
    (SSC CGL 2017)
    (a) The Prime Minister
    (b) The Speaker of the Sabha
    (c) The Chief Justice of India
    (d) The two houses of the parliament

Ans.(d) According to the article 61 of Indian constitution, the recommendation of the two houses of the parliament is mandatory to impeach the President of India from his office before the completion of his/her term.

41. How many types of Writ are there in the Indian Constitution?
    (SSC CGL 2017)
    (a) 5   (b) 4
    (c) 3   (d) 2

Ans.(a) There are five types of writs in the Indian Constitution - Habeas Corpus, Certiorari, Quo-Warranto, Mandamus and Prohibition. Thus, Supreme Court under Article 32(2) and High Courts under Article 226 are empowered to issue writs for the enforcement of Fundamental Rights.

42. Who administers the oath of the President of India?

    (SSC CGL 2017)

    (a) Governor General of India
    (b) Chief Justice of India
    (c) Prime Minister of India
    (d) Vice President of India

> Ans.(b) According to article 60 of the Indian constitution, Chief justice of India or, in his absence, the senior most Judge of the Supreme Court available, administers the oath of the President of India.

43. Who among the following gave monistic theory of sovereignty?

    (SSC CGL 2017)

    (a) Austin   (b) Darwin
    (c) Aristotle (d) Marx

> Ans.(a) In the 19th century the theory of sovereignty as a legal concept was perfected by Austin, an English Jurist.

44. Fundamental duties are mentioned in which of the following part of India Constitution?

    (SSC CGL 2017)

    (a) Part II   (b) Part III
    (c) Part V   (d) Part IV A

> Ans.(d) Fundamental Duties have been enumerated in Article 51-A in part-IV A of our Constitution.

45. What is the minimum age for becoming a Governor of state in India?   **(SSC CGL 2017)**

    (a) 30 years   (b) 25 years
    (c) 35 years   (d) 45 years

> Ans.(c) As per the 157 of the Constitution of India, No person shall be eligible for appointment as Governor unless he is a citizen of India and has completed the age of 35 years.

46. The number of parliamentary seats (Lok Sabha) of Punjab is _________.**(SSC CHSL 2017)**

    (a) 2   (b) 13
    (c) 20   (d) 25

Ans. (b)

47. _________ is a form of government in which the rulers are elected by the people.   **(SSC Sub. Ins. 2017)**

    (a) Autocratic
    (b) Monarchic
    (c) Democratic
    (d) Authoritarian

> Ans.(c) The Democratic form of government is an institutional configuration that allows for popular participation through the electoral process.

48. Members of Rajya Sabha are elected for how many years?

    (SSC Sub. Ins. 2017)

    (a) Two years   (b) Three years
    (c) Five years   (d) Six years

> Ans.(d) Rajya Sabha is a permanent house and is not subject to dissolution. However, one-third members of the Rajya Sabha retire after every six years.

49. Under which pardoning power of the President, duration of sentence is reduced without changing its character?   **(SSC Sub. Ins. 2017)**

    (a) Commutation
    (b) Remission
    (c) Respite
    (d) Reprieve

Ans.(b) Article 72 gives the pardoning power to the president in which duration of sentence is reduced without changing its character.

50. In pocket Veto, the president of India can keep a bill for how much duration? **(SSC Sub. Ins. 2017)**
   (a) 1 month
   (b) 6 month
   (c) 12 month
   (d) Indefinite period

Ans.(d) Pocket veto empowers the president to simply keep the bill pending for an indefinite period. The president neither ratifies nor rejects nor returns the bill.

51. The President's seat can be left vacant for how much duration? **(SSC Sub. Ins. 2017)**
   (a) 6 Months   (b) 3 Months
   (c) 9 Months   (d) 12 Months

Ans.(a) The president's seat can be left vacant for atmost 6 months, after that fresh elections has to be conducted.

52. Which constitutional Amendment Act of India reduced voting age from 21 years to 18 years? **(SSC Sub. Ins. 2017)**
   (a) 42nd Amendment Act
   (b) 61st Amendment Act
   (c) 74th Amendment Act
   (d) 83rd Amendment Act

Ans.(b) 61st constitutional amendment Act of India, 1989, lowered the voting age of elections to the LOK Sabha and to the legislative Assemblies of state from 21 years to 18 years.

53. Who amongst the following is the Vice-Chairman of the newly formed NITI AAYOG? **(SSC MTS 2017)**
   (a) Arvind Panagariya
   (b) A.B. Bhattacharya
   (c) K.G. Vaidya
   (d) B. V. Kamath

Ans.(a) Arvind Panagariya, is the Vice Chairman of the newly formed NITI AAYOG.

54. Does the President of India have veto power **(SSC MTS 2017)**
   (a) No
   (b) The constitution is silent on this
   (c) Only for Money bills
   (d) Yes

Ans.(d) Yes. In India, the president has three veto power i.e. absolute, suspension & Pocket.

55. The consumer is compared to a king under? **(SSC MTS 2017)**
   (a) Communism
   (b) Mixed Economy
   (c) Capitalism
   (d) Socialism

Ans.(b) In Mixed Economy, forces of demand and supply operates in the market. Therefore, consumer is compared to the King.

56. Which of the following is an example of direct democracy? **(SSC MTS 2017)**
   (a) Village Panchayat
   (b) Gram Sabha
   (c) District Panchayat
   (d) Nagar Panchayat

Ans.(a) Village Panchayat is an example of direct democracy.

57. The words socialist and secular were inserted in the Preamble to the Constitution by:
    (SSC MTS 2017)
    (a) The 16th Amendment
    (b) The 42nd Amendment
    (c) The 44th Amendment
    (d) The 7th Amendment

Ans.(b) The words socialist and secular were added to preamble to the constitution by the 42nd Amendment.

58. Which of the following elicits the Public opinion on a Bill?
    (SSC MTS 2017)
    (a) Referendum (b) Recall
    (c) Plebiscite (d) Initiative

Ans.(c) Plebiscite elicits the Public opinion on a Bill.

59. Fraternity means:**(SSC MTS 2017)**
    (a) Unity and Integrity
    (b) Elimination of Economic Justice
    (c) Fatherly treatment
    (d) Spirit of brotherhood

Ans.(d) Fraternity means spirit of brotherhood.

60. The planning commission is replaced by NITI Aayog. What is the full form of NITI?
    (SSC Stenographer 2017)
    (a) National Institute of Team India
    (b) National Institution of Transforming India
    (c) New India and Team India
    (d) No option is correct

Ans.(b) NITI full form is National Institution for Transforming India and it replaced the planning commission.

61 What is the main purpose of inclusion of Directive Principles in the Constitution of India?
    (SSC Stenographer 2017)
    (a) to establish socio-economic democracy
    (b) to establish social democracy
    (c) to establish Gandhian democracy
    (d) to establish political democracy

Ans.(a) The main purpose of inclusion of Directive Principles in the constitution of India is to establish socio-economic democracy.

62. The Panchayati Raj is based on which of the principle?
    (SSC Stenographer 2017)
    (a) centralisation of power
    (b) unification of power
    (c) decentralisation of power
    (d) bifurcation of law

Ans.(c) Panchayati Raj is based on the Principle of decentralisation of power.

63. Who presides over the joint session of Lok Subha and Rajya Sabha?
    (SSC Stenographer 2017)
    (a) President of India
    (b) Vice President of India
    (c) Speaker of Lok Sabha
    (d) Prime Minister of India

Ans.(c) Speaker of Lok Sabha is empowered to preside over the joint session of Lok Sabha and Rajya Sabha.

64. By which Constitutional Amendment Bill was the voting age reduced from 21 years to 18 years in India?
    (SSC Stenographer 2017)
    (a) 48th   (b) 59th
    (c) 61st   (d) 78th

Ans.(c)	The Sixty first Amendment of the constitution of India, 1989, lowered the voting age of elections to the Lok, Sabha and to the Legislative assemblies of states from 21 years to 18 years.

65. Who among the following elects the Vice President of India?

(SSC Stenographer 2017)

(a) By the members of Parliament
(b) By the members of Rajya Sabha
(c) By the elected members of Lok Sabha
(d) Members of Parliament and State Legislative Assemblies

Ans.(a)	The Vice President of India is elected by the members of Parliament in both the Lok Sabha and Rajya Sabha.

66. Whose absence from the Democracy makes its functioning impossible?

(SSC Stenographer 2017)

(a) Home Ministry
(b) Prime Minister
(c) Political Parties
(d) Panchayati Raj System

Ans.(c)	Political Parties absence from the Democracy makes its functioning impossible.

Economics

67. At which rate, Reserve Bank of India borrows money from commercial banks?

(SSC CGL 2017)

(a) Bank Rate
(b) Repo Rate
(c) Reverse Repo Rate
(d) Statutory Liquidity Rate

Ans.(c)	The RBI borrows from the commercial banks as per the monetary demand & supply and to control the liquidity in the market. It borrows at an interest rate called the Reverse Repo Rate.

68. Movement along the supply curve is known as __________.

(SSC CGL 2017)

(a) Contraction of supply
(b) Expansion of supply
(c) Increase in supply
(d) Expansion and contraction of supply

Ans.(d)	The movement in supply curve can be of two types- extension and contraction. Extension in a supply curve is caused when there is increase in the price or quantity supplied of the commodity while contraction is caused due to decrease in the price or quantity supplied of the commodity.

69. Which one of the following is a component of Food Security System? **(SSC CGL 2017)**

(a) Buffer stock
(b) Minimum support price
(c) Fair price shops
(d) Mid day meals

Ans.(a)	There are three major components of food security; Availability (Buffer stock), Access and utilization/ consumption.

70. What is the accepted average Calorie requirement for rural area in India? **(SSC CGL 2017)**

(a) 2100   (b) 2200
(c) 2300   (d) 2400

Ans.(d)	The accepted average calorie requirement in India is 2400 calories per person per day in rural areas and 2100 calories per person per day in rural area.

71. Who gave the 'General Equilibrium Theory'? **(SSC CGL 2017)**
    - (a) J.M. Keynes
    - (b) Leon Walras
    - (c) David Ricardo
    - (d) Adam Smith

Ans.(b) Leon Walras developed general equilibrium theory to solve a much-debated problem in economics.

72. Which of the following is not true about a Demand Draft? **(SSC CGL 2017)**
    - (a) It is a negotiable instrument.
    - (b) It is a banker's cheque.
    - (c) It may be dishonoured for lack of funds.
    - (d) It is issued by a bank.

Ans.(c) The Demand Draft is a pre-paid Negotiable Instrument, wherein the drawee bank undertakes to make payment in full when the instrument is presented by the payee for payment. So it may not be dishonored for lack of funds.

73. 7 workers work in a printing press. Each gets paid ₹450 per day. The 8th worker demands ₹500 per day. If this worker is hired then all other workers must be paid ₹500. The marginal resource (labour) cost of the 8th worker is _______. **(SSC CHSL 2017)**
    - (a) ₹50
    - (b) ₹ 850
    - (c) ₹400
    - (d) ₹100

Ans. (b)

74. Which of the following is a basic characteristic of 'Oligopoly'? **(SSC Sub. Ins. 2017)**
    - (a) Many sellers, many buyers
    - (b) Few sellers, few buyers
    - (c) Few sellers, many buyers
    - (d) Many sellers, few buyers

Ans.(c) Oligopoly is a market structure in which a small number of firms has the large majority of market share.

75. The law of demand states that when: **(SSC MTS 2017)**
    - (a) income and price rises demand rises
    - (b) price rises demand rises
    - (c) price falls demand rises
    - (d) income rises demand rises

Ans.(c) In microeconomics, the law of demand states that, "Other things being equal, as the price of a good increases its demand decreases and vice versa."

76. In an inflationary situation, which of the following statements is false for a country? **(SSC MTS 2017)**
    - (a) Cost of living rises
    - (b) Profits rise faster than wages
    - (c) Value of money falls
    - (d) Country's export's become more competitive

Ans.(d) In an inflationary Situation, country's export's declines as the goods which were cheaply available earlier now becomes expensive.

77. Which one of the following statement is True regarding rate of interest: **(SSC MTS 2017)**
    - (a) Rate of interest may be zero
    - (b) Rate of interest increases with economic growth
    - (c) Rate of interest can not be zero
    - (d) Rate of interest cannot be determined

Ans.(a) Rate of Interest may be zero is true regarding rate of interest.

78. What is GST? **(SSC Steno. 2017)**
    (a) A direct tax
    (b) An indirect tax
    (c) A corporat tax
    (d) A municipal tax

Ans.(b) Goods and Services Tax is an indirect tax which was introduced in India on 1 July 2017 and was applicaple throughout India, which replaced multiple cascading taxes levied by the central and state governments.

79. Which of the following is the not a small-scale industry in India?
    (SSC Steno. 2017)
    (a) Sugar Industry
    (b) Cotton Industry
    (c) Petroleum Industry
    (d) Handloom Industry

Ans.(c) The Petroleum Industry is not a small scale Industry. Small scale Enterprise is one in which the investment in plant and macniroy is between ₹ 25 Lakhs to ₹ 10 crores.

80. Which of the following is known as market clearing price?
    (SSC Steno. 2017)
    (a) Equilibrium price
    (b) Disequilibrium price
    (c) Ceteris paribus
    (d) No option is correct

Ans.(a) Equilibrium Price is the market price where the quanti by of goods supplied is equal to the quantity of goods demanded. It is also known as market clearing Price.

81. Snakes, turtle, lizards and crocodiles falls under which category of animals? **(SSC CGL 2017)**
    (a) Pisces   (b) Amphibian
    (c) Reptilian   (d) Aves

Ans.(c) Lizards, snakes, crocodiles and tortoises belong to the reptile group.

82. What is the SI unit of Force?
    (SSC CGL 2017)
    (a) Pascal   (b) Boyle
    (c) Newton   (d) Watt

Ans.(c) The SI unit of force is the newton, symbol N.

83. Which one of the following is a bad Thermal Conductor?
    (SSC CGL 2017)
    (a) Aluminium (b) Copper
    (c) Glass   (d) Silver

Ans.(c) Substances become bad conductors of heat when they contain a large number of free electrons. Glass, asbestos, wood, cork, cotton wool and air are some examples of Bad conductor.

84. Who proposed five kingdom classification? **(SSC CGL 2017)**
    (a) Ernst Mayr
    (b) R.H. Whittaker
    (c) M.W. Beijerinck
    (d) D.I. Ivanovsky

Ans.(b) Whittaker proposed an elaborate five kingdom classification-Monera, Protista, Fungi, Plantae and Animalia.

85. Which of the following device is best suited for measuring the temperature inside metallurgical furnaces? **(SSC CGL 2017)**
    (a) Pyrometer
    (b) Thermocouple
    (c) Thermometer
    (d) Thermistor

> **Ans.(a)** A thermocouple is a device used extensively for measuring temperature. It is best suited for measuring the temperature inside metallurgical furnace.

86. Cattle quickly swallow grass and store it in their __________.
    (SSC CGL 2017)
    (a) rumen
    (b) esophagus
    (c) small intestine
    (d) salivary glands

> **Ans.(a)** Cows are known as "ruminants" because the largest pouch of the stomach is called the rumen. Cattles store grass in it after swallow.

87. Which of the following carries oxygen to various parts of human body? **(SSC CGL 2017)**
    (a) Red blood cells
    (b) White blood cells
    (c) Plasma
    (d) Nerves

> **Ans.(a)** Red blood cells (Hemoglobin) transports oxygen to all the parts of the body and ultimately to all the cells.

88. Which of the following function is performed by the kidneys in the human body? **(SSC CGL 2017)**
    (a) Excretion
    (b) Respiration
    (c) Digestion
    (d) Transportation

> **Ans.(a)** The primary function of the kidney is to remove nitrogenous wastes (mainly urea) from the body.

89. The bending of light when it passes around a corner or a slit is due to __________. **(SSC CGL 2017)**
    (a) reflection
    (b) refraction
    (c) diffraction
    (d) total internal reflection

> **Ans.(c)** Light does travel around corners a little. This effect is called diffraction.

90. Bishnoi movement was started against which of the following? **(SSC CGL 2017)**
    (a) Cutting of Trees
    (b) Inequality of Women
    (c) Killing of Animals
    (d) Increasing Pollution

> **Ans.(a)** The Bishnois are considered as the first environmentalists of India. It was started in 1485AD by Saint Guru Jambheshwar in the Thar Desert of Rajasthan, India. It was started against of cutting of trees.

91. Cinnamon is obtained from which part of the plant? **(SSC CGL 2017)**
    (a) Stem   (b) Bark
    (c) Roots   (d) Fruits

> **Ans.(b)** Cinnamon is obtained from barks of the plants.

92. Insulin is a kind of __________
    (SSC CGL 2017)
    (a) hormone   (b) Protein
    (c) enzyme   (d) vitamin

> **Ans.(a)** The body manufactures insulin in the pancreas, and the hormone is secreted by its beta cells, primarily in response to glucose.

93. Which among the following carries impure blood to human heart?
(SSC CGL 2017)
(a) Aorta
(b) Pulmonary vein
(c) Pulmonary arteries
(d) Vena Cava

Ans.(c) The only Pulmonary arteries carry impure blood to human heart.

94. Why does water tank appear shallower when viewed from the top?
(SSC CGL 2017)
(a) Due to reflection
(b) Due to refraction
(c) Due to diffraction
(d) Due to total internal reflection

Ans.(b) The light travels straight as long as it is in the water, but if it emerges obliquely from the water into the air it is bent downward toward the surface. This bending is known as refraction, and this is the main cause that water tank appear shallower when viewed from the top.

95. Which colour is formed when Red and Green are mixed?
(SSC CGL 2017)
(a) Light blue   (b) Yellow
(c) White   (d) Grey

Ans.(b) In light, yellow is a secondary color, and is made by combining Red and Green.

96. What is an endothermic reaction?
(SSC CGL 2017)
(a) Reaction in which heat is released
(b) Reaction in which heat is absorbed
(c) Reaction in which neither heat is released nor absorbed
(d) None of these

Ans.(b) An endothermic reaction is any chemical reaction that absorbs heat from its environment.

97. Which of the following is an ore of Aluminium?   **(SSC CGL 2017)**
(a) Galena   (b) Cryollite
(c) Cinnabar   (d) Epsom Salt

Ans.(b) Besides Bauxite, Cryollite (Na3Alf6) is also the ore of Aluminium.

98. Which of the following gas was released during Bhopal gas tragedy?   **(SSC CGL 2017)**
(a) Methyl isocyanate
(b) Sodium isothiocyanate
(c) Nitrogen isothiocynate
(d) Potassium isothiocynate

Ans.(a) Bhopal gas tragedy occurred on the night of 2–3 December 1984 at the Union Carbide India Limited (UCIL) pesticide plant. Over 500,000 people were exposed to methyl isocyanate (MIC) gas and other chemicals.

99. Which drug is used as an Anti–Anxiety drug? **(SSC CHSL 2017)**
(a) Warfarin   (b) Diazepam
(c) Latanoprost (d) Hydralazine

Ans. (b)

100. Which of the following is false with reference to a photo-voltaic cell?
(SSC CHSL 2017)
(a) It is another name as solar cell
(b) It can be used as infra-red detectors
(c) It can store light energy in the form of electrical energy
(d) It converts electric energy into light energy

Ans. (d)

101. Methane an air pollutant is produced
________. **(SSC CHSL 2017)**
 (a) by action of ultraviolet light on nitrogenous compounds.
 (b) as a by-product of manufacturing ammoniacal fertilizers
 (c) by burning of coal in insufficient air
 (d) by digestion of food by animals

Ans. (d)

102. Rate of work done is ________
. **(SSC CHSL 2017)**
 (a) Energy (b) Power
 (c) Momentum (d) Impulse

Ans. (b)

103. What is the unit of the physical quantity, "Young's modulus"?
(SSC CHSL 2017)
 (a) newton (b) erg
 (c) joule (d) pascal

Ans. (d)

104. Where is bile stored?
(SSC Sub. Ins. 2017)
 (a) Liver (b) Kidney
 (c) Gall bladder (d) Spleen

Ans.(c) Bile is stored in Gall bladder after being secreted from Liver.

105. Which of the following is not a connective tissue?
(SSC Sub. Ins. 2017)
 (a) Adipose Tissue
 (b) Compact Bone
 (c) Cardiac Muscle
 (d) Areolar Tissue

Ans.(c) Others are connective Tissue but Cardic muscle is an involuntary, striated muscle that is found in the walls of the heart.

106. Normally how many times the human heart beats in a minute?
(SSC Sub. Ins. 2017)
 (a) 82 (b) 75
 (c) 72 (d) 85

Ans.(c) Normally, human heart beats 72 times a minute.

107. Muscle fatigue occurs due to accumulation of ________.
(SSC Sub. Ins. 2017)
 (a) ATP
 (b) ADP
 (c) Lactic Acid
 (d) Carbonic Acid

Ans.(c) Muscle fatigue occurs due to accumulation of Lactic acid which is an organic compound formed when there is anaerobic energy production at high rates.

108. The inexhaustible source of energy of stars is due to ________.
(SSC Sub. Ins. 2017)
 (a) Conversion of hydrogen to helium
 (b) Conversion of helium to hydrogen
 (c) Decay of radioactive elements.
 (d) Excess of oxygne

Ans.(a) The inexhaustible source of energy of stars is due to conversion of hydrogen to helium.

109. Which of the following waves has the highest frequency?
(SSC Sub. Ins. 2017)
 (a) Radio (b) Infrared
 (c) Microwaves (d) Gamma-rays

Ans.(d) Gamma Rays are penetrating electromagnetic rays which has the highest frequency.

110. Which of the following gas is used in bulb? **(SSC Sub. Ins. 2017)**
 (a) Hydrogen
 (b) Carbon-dioxide
 (d) Carbon-mono-oxide
 (d) Argon

Ans.(d) Argon is a gas used to fill incandescent light bulbs.

111. Chlorine gas is a major component of which of the following?

(SSC Sub. Ins. 2017)

(a) Water
(b) Tear gas
(c) Liquified petroleum Gas
(d) Gobar gas

Ans.(b) Tear gas Known as La chrymator has chlorine gas one of its major component that cause severe eye, respiratory and skin irritation, pain, bleeding and even blindness.

112. What is Brine solution?

(SSC Sub. Ins. 2017)

(a) Excess salt + water
(b) Silver
(c) Excess Ethanol + water
(d) Excess Starch + water

Ans.(a) Brine is a solution of excess salt and water. The high salt content in Brine prevents the growth of Bacteria and thus helps to preserve the food for a long time.

113. Which of the following primarily causes lead pollution?

(SSC Sub. Ins. 2017)

(a) CFL Lamp
(b) Automobile Battery
(c) polymer
(d) Diesel Engine

Ans.(b) Automobile Battery primarily causes lead pollution which is harmful for environment.

114. What was the main aim of Montreal protocol? **(SSC Sub. Ins. 2017)**

(a) Protection of Ozone layer
(b) Bio- diversity Conservation
(c) Global Warming
(d) Climate Change

Ans.(a) Montreal protocol is an international treaty signed on 14 September 1987 to protect the ozone layer.

115. Supersonic jets cause thinning of which layer?**(SSC Sub. Ins. 2017)**

(a) O2 layer   (b) O3 layer
(c) CO2 layer   (d) SO2 layer

Ans.(b) Super sonic jets cause thinning of O_3. layer which protects earth from harmful sun radiation.

116. Biogas is formed through:

(SSC MTS 2017)

(a) Fermentation
(b) Reduction
(c) Aerobic respiration
(d) Oxidation

Ans.(a) Biogas is formed through Fermentation in which anaerobic digestion takes place inside a closed system.

117. Slow and uniform cooling of hot iron in its metallurgy is known as:

(SSC MTS 2017)

(a) chilling   (b) annealing
(c) quenching   (d) tempering

Ans.(c) Quenching is a process of cooling a material at a rapid rate. In ferrous alloys, this will often produce a harder metal, while non-ferrous alloys will usually become softer than normal.

118. In the context of alternative sources of energy, ethanol as a viable bio - fuel can be obtained from:

(SSC MTS 2017)

(a) Potato   (b) Wheat
(c) Sugarcane   (d) Rice

Ans.(c) Ethanol which is a viable bio-fuel can be obtained from Sugarcane.

119. Distant objects can be seen with the help of? **(SSC MTS 2017)**
  (a) spectroscope (b) telescope
  (c) microscope (d) cronometer

> **Ans.(b)** Distant objects can be seen with help of Telescope. It is an optical instrument that aids in the observation of remote objects by collecting electromagnetic radiation. (such as visible light).

120. The largest part of our brain is: **(SSC MTS 2017)**
  (a) Hypothalamous
  (b) Medulla oblongata
  (c) Cerebellum
  (d) Cerebrum

> **Ans.(d)** The cerebrum is the largest part of the human brain, making up about two – third of the brain's mass.

121. Insulin activates in __________. **(SSC Steno. 2017)**
  (a) Pancreas   (b) Parathyroid
  (c) Thymus   (d) Pituitary

> **Ans.(a)** Pancreas is a vital part of digestive system and a critical controller of Insulin.

122. Which among the following is not related to vitamin B complex group? **(SSC Steno. 2017)**
  (a) Rivoflavin
  (b) Thaimin
  (c) Ascorbic acid
  (d) Folic acid

> **Ans.(c)** Ascorbic Acid is not related to vitamin B complex group. Vitamin B complex group contains 8 water soluble. Vitamins–Vitamin B1, B2, B3, B6, B12, folate, biotin and pant othenic acid.

123. Viruses are usually made of which of the following? **(SSC Steno. 2017)**
  (a) Protein + Carbohydrates
  (b) Protein + Nucleic acid
  (c) Protein + Ascorbic Acid
  (d) Protein + Lipid

> **Ans.(b)** A virus is made up of a core of genet material either DNA or RNA, small which are made up of protein and nucleic Acid.

124. "Shrubs" are woody plants generally smaller and more compact than trees. Which of the following is not a shrub tree? **(SSC Steno. 2017)**
  (a) Sunflower
  (b) Rose-of-Sharon
  (c) Butterfly Bush
  (d) Barberry

> **Ans.(a)** Sunflower is a Large plant and is not a shrub.

125. A medical procedure, during which a small sample of tissue is removed from a part of the body, is __________. **(SSC Steno. 2017)**
  (a) MRI
  (b) CT Scan
  (c) Biopsy
  (d) All options are correct.

> **Ans.(c)** Biopsy, is a medical procedure during (SF) which a small sample of tissue is removed from a part of the body.

126. Which among the following is cryogenic engines are used? **(SSC Steno. 2017)**
  (a) In rocket technology
  (b) To run the navy ships
  (c) In frost free referigerators
  (d) All options are correct.

Ans.(a) A Cryogenic rocket engine is a rocket engine that uses cryogenic fuel or oxidizer, its fuel are gases liquefied and stored at very low temperature

127. During photosynthesis light energy is converted into which of the following? **(SSC Steno. 2017)**
    (a) Mechanical energy
    (b) Chemical energy
    (c) Heat energy
    (d) Radiation energy

Ans.(b) During photosynthesis light energy is connected into chemical energy. The light energy is intercepted by chlorophyll, then some of the light energy is converted to chemical energy. During the process; a phosphate is added to a molecule to cause the formation of ATP.

128. What is the reason of surface tension in a liquid?
    (SSC Steno. 2017)
    (a) Electrical force between molecules
    (b) Cohesive force between molecules
    (c) Adhesive force between molecules
    (d) Gravitational force between molecules

Ans.(b) Cohesive force between molecules is the reason of surface tension of liquid. Cohesine force is the action or property of like molecules sticking together.

129. In which process there is gain of electron? **(SSC Steno. 2017)**
    (a) Decomposition
    (b) Reduction
    (c) Oxidation
    (d) Modification

Ans.(b) Reduction is the process of adding oxygen to form an oxide. In this there is gain of electrons.

Computers

130. Which of the following stores data permanently in a computer?
    (SSC CGL 2017)
    (a) ALU
    (b) Cache Memory
    (c) RAM
    (d) ROM

Ans.(d) ROM stores data permanently in a computer which can be read only.

131. What is the full form of 'LAN'?
    (SSC CGL 2017)
    (a) Line Area Network
    (b) Linear Area Network
    (c) Local Area Network
    (d) Land Area Network

Ans.(c) A LAN (Local area network) is a group of computers and network devices connected together, usually within the same building.

132. FORTRAN is not used for ______.
    (SSC CGL 2017)
    (I) Drawing pictures
    (II) Carrying out mathematics computations
    (a) Only (I)
    (b) Only (II)
    (c) Both (I) and (II)
    (d) Neither (I) nor (II)

Ans.(a) FORTRAN (Formula Translation) is a third-generation (3GL) programming language that was designed for use by engineers, mathematicians, and other users and creators of scientific algorithms.

133. What is the full form of JPEG?
(SSC CGL 2017)
(a) Joint Photographic Experts Group
(b) Joint Protocol Experts Graphics.
(c) Joint Programming Experts Graphics
(d) Joint Project Experts Group

Ans.(d) JPEG or JPG: Joint Photographic Experts Group (graphics file compression standard).

134. Vacuum Tubes were used by ______ Generation of Computers.
(SSC CHSL 2017)
(a) First
(b) Second
(c) Third
(d) Fourth

Ans.(a)

135. Dot-Matrix is an example of which of the following?
(SSC Sub. Ins. 2017)
(a) A software
(b) Scanner
(c) Printer
(d) Keyboard

Ans.(c) Dot matrix printer is a type of computer. Which uses a print head that moves back and froth.

136. Which of the following pair is INCORRECT?
(SSC Sub. Ins. 2017)
(a) 10 MB - 10240 KB
(b) 1 GB-10240 MB
(c) 1 TB - 1024 GB
(d) 1 KB - 1024 Bytes

Ans.(b) 1 GB – 1024 MB

137. A ________ is a program that interprets and displays Web Pages?
(SSC MTS. 2017)
(a) Server
(b) Browser
(c) Website
(d) Link

Ans.(b) A web Browser, is a program that interprets and displays web pages and enables you to view and interact with a web page.

138. A Computer that keeps copies of responses and recent requests is known as ________.
(SSC MTS. 2017)
(a) Mail Server
(b) Proxy Server
(c) Server
(d) Web Server

Ans.(b) A computer that keeps copies of responses and recent requests is known as Proxy Server.

139. Which of the following is an input device?
(SSC Steno. 2017)
(a) Printer
(b) Headphone
(c) Monitor
(d) Scanner

Ans.(d) An input device is used to provide data and control signals to an information processing system such as computer. Scanner is an input device.

140. Which of the following is not a computer language?
(SSC Steno. 2017)
(a) Fortran
(b) Pascal
(c) Cobol
(d) English

Ans.(d) English is not a computer language.

General Knowledge

141. Which of the following venue hosted its first ever test match on 9th November, 2016 which was played between India and England?
(SSC CGL 2017)
(a) JSCA International Stadium complex, Ranchi
(b) Saurashtra Cricket Association Stadium, Rajkot
(c) Himachal Pradesh Cricket Association Stadium, Dharamshala
(d) Holkar Cricket Stadium, Indore

Ans.(b) Saurashtra Cricket Association Stadium, Rajkot, hosted it's ever test match on 9th Nov. 2016, which played between India and England.

142. Match the following :

(SSC CGL 2017)

Artist	Art form
1.	Gori Shankar Devilal	a. Flute
2.	Hari Prasad Chaurosia	b. Painting
3.	M. F. Hussain	c. Kathak
4.	Zakir Hussain	d. Tabla

(a)   1 - a, 2- d, 3- b, 4 - c
(b)   1 - b, 2- c, 3- a, 4 - d
(c)   1 - c, 2- a, 3- b, 4 - d
(d)   1 - c, 2- b, 3- a, 4 - d

Ans. (c)

Artist	Art form
1.	Gori Shankar Devilal	Kathak
2.	Hari Prasad Chaurosia	Flute
3.	M. F. Hussain	Painting
4.	Zakir Hussain	Tabla

143. Who is the only Indian cricketer to have received the Polly Umrigar award 3 times? **(SSC CGL 2017)**
(a)   Sachin Tendulkar
(b)   Virender Sehwag
(c)   Virat Kohli
(d)   Ravichandran Ashwin

Ans.(c)   Virat Kohli has received Polly Umrigar Award, first Indian cricketer to get it on three occasions.

144. Who is the author of the book titled "The Sellout"? **(SSC CGL 2017)**
(a)   Paul Beatty
(b)   Arvind Adiga
(c)   Elenor Catton
(d)   Howard Jacobson

Ans. (a)   The Sellout is a 2015 novel by Paul Beatty published by Farrar, Straus and Giroux, and in the UK by One world Publications in 2016.

145. Which country was designated as the major defence partner of USA in December, 2016?
(SSC CGL 2017)
(a)   Canada
(b)   Israel
(c)   India
(d)   United Kingdom

Ans. (c)   India was designated as a major defence partner of the United States in December, 2016.

146. With which country India did its seventh edition of bilateral EKU-VERIN Exercise 2016 at Kadhdhoo? **(SSC CGL 2017)**
(a)   Nepal   (b)   Pakistan
(c)   Maldives   (d)   Bhutan

Ans. (c)   Seventh edition of Exercise EKUVERIN was held from 15 to 28 Dec 2016 at Kadhdhoo, Laamu Atoll, Maldives.

147. 'Vikalp' is a scheme launched by Indian Railway to help wait – listed passengers. Which of the following is NOT true about this scheme?
(SSC CGL 2017)
(a)   Confirmed berths in alternate trains.
(b)   No – extra charges will be taken from passengers.
(c)   Wait – listed passengers can avail opportunity of travelling in Rajdhani/Shatabdi/Special trains even when booking made is in other mail/express trains.
(d)   Vikalp scheme will be initially available for e – tickets only.

Ans. (a)   Opting for VIKALP does not mean that confirmed berth will be provided to passengers in alternate train. It is subject to train and berth availability.

148. Who discovered the Cholera causing germ? **(SSC CGL 2017)**
  (a) Filippo Pacini
  (b) Robert Koch
  (c) M. Laveran
  (d) Felix Hoffman

Ans. (a)	Italian scientist, **Filippo Pacini**, discovered the Cholera causing germ.

149. Match the following: **(SSC CGL 2017)**

Player		Sport
1.	Mithali Raj	a. Hockey
2.	Poonam Rani	b. 3000 m Steeplechases
3.	Lalita Babar	c. Cricket

  (a) 1 – c, 2 – b, 3 – a
  (b) 1 – a, 2 – b, 3 – c
  (c) 1 – a, 2 – c, 3 – b
  (d) 1 – c, 2 – a, 3 – b

Ans. (d)	
Player	Sport
Mithali Raj	Cricket
Poonam Rani	Hockey
Lalita Babar	300 Steeplechases

150. 'Hunar Haat' an exhibition to exhibit and promote the arts and artisans from minority community was launched at which of the following events? **(SSC CGL 2017)**
  (a) Pushkar Fair, 2016
  (b) IITF, New Delhi, 2016
  (c) Suraj Kund Craft Mela, 2017
  (d) Kumbh Mela, 2015

Ans. (b)	The Union Ministry of Minority Affairs had inaugurated Hunar Haat (Skill Haat) at India International Trade Fair (2016) at Pragati Maidan in New Delhi.

151. How many players are there in a team of Volleyball? **(SSC CGL 2017)**
  (a) 2   (b) 4
  (c) 6   (d) 5

Ans. (c)	The game of volleyball is played with two teams, each composed of six players. Members of each team attempt to score by landing a ball over a dividing net onto the opponent team's court.

152. Silk worms feed on **(SSC CGL 2017)**
  (A) Basil Leaves
  (B) Curry Leaves
  (C) Rose Leaves
  (D) Mulberry Leaves
  (a) 1-B, 2-C, 3-A
  (b) 1-C, 2-A, 3-B
  (c) 1-A, 2-C, 3-B
  (d) 1-B, 2-A, 3-C

Ans. (d)	The leaves of soyabean, mulberry and tea had the strongest attractivity, but the silkworm larva gathered around Mulberry leaves and eats when hungry.

153. Who among the following has been recently awarded with 'Indian of the year' award? **(SSC CGL 2017)**
  (a) Sunita Rani
  (b) Dhiraj Singh
  (c) Preety Shenoy
  (d) Abhishek kumar

Ans. (c)	Writer Preeti Shenoy, one of India's top five highest selling women authors, was honoured with the Indian of the Year award on 30th June, 2017.

154. Who is the author of the book titled 'Selection Day'?**(SSC CGL 2017)**
    (a) Aravind Adiga
    (b) Anil Menon
    (c) Krishna Sobti
    (d) Arunava Sinha

> **Ans. (a)** "Selection Day" a novel by Aravind Adiga, is about cricket and corruption.

155. Which of the following country is not a member of BRICS association? **(SSC CGL 2017)**
    (a) Brazil   (b) Russia
    (c) Iceland   (d) China

> **Ans. (c)** Members of BRICS association are Brazil, Russia, India, China and South Africa. Iceland is not the member of this association.

156. With which of its neighbouring country India has Kalapani territorial dispute?
    (SSC CGL 2017)
    (a) Nepal   (b) Bangladesh
    (c) Pakistan   (d) Sri Lanka

> **Ans. (a)** The Kalapani disputed area is located in the Greater Himalayas along the border of India, China and Nepal. Nepal claims that the river to the west of Kalapani is the main Kali, hence the area belongs to Nepal.

157. What is the name of the scheme for the Employees state Insurance Corporation (ESIC) beneficiaries launched in Delhi region?
    (SSC CGL 2017)
    (a) Sakushal Humesha
    (b) Kahin bhi kabhi bhi
    (c) Jeevan Arogya
    (d) Shramik Kalyan

> **Ans. (b)** The Employees' State Insurance Corporation (ESIC) launched 'Kahin Bhi-Kabhi Bhi' medical service for its insured in the Delhi region under which the beneficiaries can visit day-care units for minor ailments.

158. Match the following
    (SSC CGL 2017)

1.	Joseph Thomson	a. Optical Fiber
2.	Alexander randming	b. Radium
3.	Kapany	c. Electron
4.	Marie Curie	d. Penicillin

    (a) 1 - c, 2 - d, 3 - a, 4 - b
    (b) 1 - a, 2 - d, 3 - c, 4 - b
    (c) 1 - c, 2 - a, 3 - d, 4 - b
    (d) 1 - a, 2 - d, 3 - b, 4 - c

> **Ans. (a)**
>
> | Name | Discovery |
> |---|---|
> | Joseph Thomson | Electron |
> | Alexander randming | Penicillin |
> | Kapany | Optical Fiber |
> | Marie Curie | Radium |

159. Term 'Gambit' is associated with which of the following sport?
    (SSC CGL 2017)
    (a) Basketball   (b) Chess
    (c) Boxing   (d) Golf

> **Ans. (b)** 'Gambit' is used in the game of Chess. It is a chess opening in which a player, more often White, sacrifices material, usually a pawn, with the hope of achieving a resulting advantageous position.

160. Madhuri Dixit is association with which Indian Dance form?

(SSC CGL 2017)

(a) Bharatnatyam

(b) Kuchipudi

(c) Kathak

(d) Kathakali

> **Ans. (c)** Madhuri Dixit from her school time is a Kathak dancer.

161. Who among the following is a Sanjay Chopra Award recipient for 2016? **(SSC CGL 2017)**

(a) Abhinash Mishra

(b) Arjun Singh

(c) Aromal SM

(d) Srawanand Saha

> **Ans. (b)** A 16-year-old Arjun Singh, who fought a tiger in Uttarakhand to save his mother, was honoured with Sanjay Chopra award for 2016.

162. 'My story' is an autobiography of which famous cricketer?

(SSC CGL 2017)

(a) Kumar Sangakara

(b) Kevin Peterson

(c) Brendon Mccullum

(d) Micheal Clarke

> **Ans. (d)** My story is an autobiography which was written by MICHAEL Clarke.

163. Which country has approved more than 500 new settler homes in East Jerusalem? **(SSC CGL 2017)**

(a) USA (b) UAE

(c) Israel (d) UnitedKingdom

> **Ans. (c)** Israel has approved the construction of 566 settler homes in East Jerusalem in January, 2017.

164. Which of the following country is not a member of SAARC?

(SSC CGL 2017)

(a) Nepal (b) Maldives

(c) China (d) Afghanistan

> **Ans. (c)** SAARC member states include Afghanistan, Bangladesh, Bhutan,India, Nepal, the Maldives , Pakistan and Sri Lanka. China is not the member of this organization.

165. Ghumura is a folk dance of______.

(SSC CHSL 2017)

(a) Odisha

(b) Andhra Pradesh

(c) Jammu & Kashmir

(d) Maharashtra

Ans. (a)

166. Nitin Thimmaiah is related to which sport? **(SSC Sub-Ins. 2017)**

(a) Table Tennis (b) Boxing

(c) Cricket (d) Hockey

> **Ans.(d)** Nitin Thinmaiah is an Indian field hockey player who plays as a forward.

167. Match the following.

	Temple	Religion
1.	Dilwara Temple	a. Bahai
2.	Golden Temple	b. Hinduism
3.	Lotus Temple	c. Sikhism
4.	Sun Temple	d. Jainism

(SSC Sub-Ins. 2017)

(a) 1 - d, 2 - c, 3 - a, 4 - b
(b) 1 - c, 2 - d, 3 - a, 4 - b
(c) 1 - b, 2 - a, 3 - d, 4 - c
(d) 1 - d, 2 - a, 3 - b, 4 - c

Ans. (a)	Temple	Relegion
	Dilwara Temple	Jainism
	Golden Temple	Sikhism
	Lotus Temple	Bahai
	Sun Temple	Hinduism

168. Which chief Minister has been awarded with the 'Transformative Chief Minister Award' on May 8, 2017? **(SSC Sub-Ins. 2017)**
(a) Yogi Adityanath, Uttar Pradesh
(b) Chandrababu Naidu, Andhra Pradesh
(c) Arvind Kejriwal, Delhi
(d) Vasundhara Raje Scindia, Rajasthan

Ans.(b) Chandrababu Naidu, Chief Minister of Andhra Pradesh has been awarded with the 'Transformative Chief Minister Award' on May 8, 2017.

169. Who wrote the book named 'Exile'?
(SSC Sub-Ins. 2017)
(a) Barkha Dutt
(b) Valmik Thapar
(c) Tasleema Nasreen
(d) Ranbir Singh Sindhu

Ans.(c) Tasleema Nasreen , wrote the book named Exile.

170. Pakistan has leased Gwadar port to state-run firm of which country for 40 years? **(SSC Sub-Ins. 2017)**
(a) Iran (b) China
(c) Afghanistan (c) India

Ans.(b) Pakistan has leased Gwadar port to state run firm of china for 40 years.

171. Which neighbouring country of India is not among the founding members of SAARC?
(SSC Sub-Ins. 2017)
(a) Nepal (b) Bangladesh
(c) Afghanistan (d) Bhutan

Ans.(c) The SAARC is the regional intergovernmental organization and geopolitical Union of nations in South Asia. Afghanistan is not among the founding members of SAARC.

172. Amrita Shergil was a famous ____.
(SSC MTS. 2017)
(a) singer (b) dancer
(c) actress (d) painter

Ans.(d) Amrita Shergil was famous Hungarian–Indian Painter. She has been called "one of the grealest avant-grade women artists of the early 20th century.

173. Hepatitis is a disease of the :
(SSC MTS. 2017)
(a) Kidney (b) Liver
(c) Heart (d) Eyes

Ans.(b) HEPATITIS is a viral liver disease that can mild to severe illness.

174. Katherine Espin who won the crown of 2016 Miss Earth belongs to which country? **(SSC MTS. 2017)**
    (a) Columbia   (b) Philippines
    (c) Ecuador   (d) Venezuela

Ans.(c) Katherine Elizabeth Espin is an Ecuadorian model and beauty queen who was appointed as Miss Earth ecuador 2016.

175. India signed the 'Paris Agreement' on 'Climatic change' in April 2016 at: **(SSC MTS. 2017)**
    (a) New Delhi   (b) Geneva
    (c) New-York   (d) Paris

Ans.(c) India signed the 'Paris Agreement' on 'Climate change' from April 22, 2016 to April 21, 2017 at the UN Headquarters in New York.

176. Nek Chand Saini name is associated with which of the following gardens: **(SSC MTS. 2017)**
    (a) Shalimar Bagh, Srinagar
    (b) Rock garden, Chandigarh
    (c) Vrindavan Garden, Mysore
    (d) Hanging Garden, Mumbai

Ans.(b) Nek Chand Saini, was a self taught Indian Artist, known for building the Rock, garden of Chandigarh.

177. Which country will host the under - 17 FIFA World Cup in 2017? **(SSC MTS. 2017)**
    (a) Germany   (b) Brazil
    (c) India   (d) Spain

Ans.(c) India has qualified to host the under – 17 FIFA World Cup in 2017.

178. Himalayan Forest Research Centre is located at : **(SSC MTS. 2017)**
    (a) Dehradun   (b) Bhutan
    (c) Srinagar   (d) Shimla

Ans.(d) Himalayan Forest Research Centre is located at Shimla in Himachal Pradesh. It works under the Indian Council of Forestry Research and Education.

179. A hinged door is an example of : **(SSC MTS. 2017)**
    (a) First order lever
    (b) Third order lever
    (c) Cantilever
    (d) Second order lever

Ans.(d) A hinged door is an example of second class levers.

180. The objective of Sangam Yojana of the government is : **(SSC MTS. 2017)**
    (a) To ensure welfare of handicaps and disables
    (b) To unite various Hindu groups
    (c) To make Ganga water pollution free
    (d) To make Sangam region of Allahabad more attractive for tourists

Ans.(a) The objective of Sangam Yojana of the Government is to ensure welfare of handicaps and disables.

181. Who among the following not an Olympics medal winner? **(SSC MTS. 2017)**
    (a) K. Malleshwari
    (b) Abhinav Bindra
    (c) Jwala Gutta
    (d) Mary Kom

Ans.(c) Jwala Guatta is a left-handed Badminton Player has won medals at all major international badminton tournaments and multi-sport events, except for Olympics.

182. A pressure cooker reduces cooking time because : **(SSC MTS. 2017)**
   (a) the boiling point of the water inside is elevated
   (b) it absorbs more heat from its flame
   (c) the higher pressure tenderises the food
   (d) the heat is more evenly distributed

Ans.(a) Inside a pressure cooker, once the water is bling and the steam is trapped, the pressure from the trapped stream increases and this pushes on the liquid which increases its boiling temperature.

183. What is the constituent of tear gas? **(SSC Steno. 2017)**
   (a) Ethane (b) Methane
   (c) Chloropicrin (d) Ether

Ans.(c) Chloropicrin is the constituent of tear gas, it is a chemical weapon that causes severe eye, respiratory, and skin irritation.

184. Which of the following gas is present in bio-gas? **(SSC Steno. 2017)**
   (a) Ethane (b) Methane
   (c) Oxygen (d) Nitrogen

Ans.(b) Biogas is a mixture of different gases produced by the breakdown of organic matter in the absence of oxygen.

185. Which of the following diseases is NOT caused by the smog? **(SSC Steno. 2017)**
   (a) Asthma
   (b) Throat Cancer
   (c) Emphysema
   (d) Breathing problem

Ans.(b) Throat Cancer is not produced by Smog. Smog is a type of air pollutant which consists of smoke and fog.

186. What is the full form of "PMSBY":? **(SSC Steno. 2017)**
   (a) Pradhan Mantri Suraksha Bima Yojana
   (b) Pradhan Mantri Sukanya Bima Yojana
   (c) Pradhan Mantri Swachchh Bharat Yojana
   (d) None of the is correct.

Ans.(a) "PMSBY" full form is Pradhan Mantri Suraksha Bima Yojana. This Yojana is a government–backed inscurance scheme in India.

187. Which of the following schemes was replaced by APY in 2015? **(SSC Steno. 2017)**
   (a) Antyodaya Yojana
   (b) Swavablamban Yojana
   (c) National Pension System
   (d) Swabhiman Yojana

Ans.(b) Swabhiman Yojana.

188. Who invented Mercury Thermometer? **(SSC Steno. 2017)**
    (a) Galieo
    (b) Michael Faraday
    (c) J.J. Thompson
    (d) Fahrenheit

Ans.(d) Fahrenheit invented Mercury Thermometer in Amsterdam (1714).

189. The word "Smash" is associated with which game?
    (SSC Steno. 2017)
    (a) Volleyball   (b) Hockey
    (c) Lawn Tennis (d) Cricket

Ans.(c) Smash is associated with Lawn Tennis. It is a shot that is hit above the hitter's head with a serve–like motion.

190. England was defeated by which of the following countries in T-20 world cup 2016 final?
    (SSC Steno. 2017)
    (a) India   (b) West Indies
    (c) Australia   (d) Pakistan

Ans.(b) West Indies defeated England in T-20 World Cup 2016 Final.